The Internet of Things (IoT) and Its Application in Monitoring

The Internet of Things (IoT) and Its Application in Monitoring

Guest Editors

Cristina Stolojescu-Crisan
Fabrizio Marozzo

MDPI

Basel • Beijing • Wuhan • Barcelona • Belgrade • Novi Sad • Cluj • Manchester

Guest Editors
Cristina Stolojescu-Crisan
Communications Department
Politehnica University of Timisoara
Timisoara
Romania

Fabrizio Marozzo
Department of Informatics, Modeling, Electronics and Systems Engineering (DIMES)
University of Calabria
Rende
Italy

Editorial Office
MDPI AG
Grosspeteranlage 5
4052 Basel, Switzerland

This is a reprint of the Special Issue, published open access by the journal *Applied Sciences* (ISSN 2076-3417), freely accessible at: https://www.mdpi.com/journal/applsci/special_issues/I2U02E5V90.

For citation purposes, cite each article independently as indicated on the article page online and as indicated below:

Lastname, A.A.; Lastname, B.B. Article Title. *Journal Name* **Year**, *Volume Number*, Page Range.

ISBN 978-3-7258-8101-7 (Hbk)
ISBN 978-3-7258-8102-4 (PDF)
https://doi.org/10.3390/books978-3-7258-8102-4

Contents

About the Editors

Cristina Stolojescu-Crisan

Cristina Stolojescu-Crisan is a Lecturer with the Department of Communications, part of the Faculty of Electronics, Telecommunications and Information Technologies, at the University Politehnica Timisoara, Romania. Her research interest includes energy management, IoT, smart cities, cyber security, and communication systems.

Fabrizio Marozzo

Fabrizio Marozzo is an Associate Professor of Computer Engineering with the Department of Informatics, Modeling, Electronics and Systems Engineering at the University of Calabria, Italy. His research activity concerns big data analytics, machine learning, generative artificial intelligence, large language models, and distributed cloud-edge computing systems. He has also worked extensively on social media analysis, scalable data-intensive applications, and explainable AI.

Preface

The Internet of Things (IoT) has emerged as one of the most transformative technological paradigms of recent decades, reshaping the way data is collected, analyzed, and acted upon across nearly every sector of modern life. This Reprint brings together a curated collection of contributions that examine the rapidly advancing role of IoT in monitoring applications, with the aim of capturing both the current state of the field and the directions in which it is evolving.

The scope of this Reprint is deliberately broad, reflecting the pervasive nature of IoT-enabled monitoring. The contributions address applications ranging from smart home automation and personalized healthcare to traffic management, environmental monitoring, and waste management. Alongside these application-focused works, the Reprint also engages with the cybersecurity dimension of large-scale IoT deployments, considering the vulnerabilities introduced by unsecured devices and the data privacy concerns inherent in interconnected environments.

The motivation for assembling this Reprint stems from the recognition that IoT-enabled monitoring is no longer a future prospect but a present reality, with measurable impact on operational efficiency, sustainability, convenience, and data-driven decision making. As deployments scale and use cases multiply, there is a clear need for consolidated resources that bring together rigorous research, practical experimentation, and forward-looking analysis. This Reprint responds to that need by gathering high-impact advances and innovative solutions in a single volume.

This Reprint is addressed to a diverse readership. Researchers and graduate students will find substantive technical contributions and pointers to open problems. Practitioners and engineers working in IoT system design, deployment, and security will benefit from applied insights and case studies. Policymakers and decision makers concerned with the responsible adoption of IoT technologies in critical infrastructure, urban environments, and healthcare will find context for the opportunities and risks involved.

We hope that this Reprint serves both as a reference for the current state of IoT in monitoring and as a stimulus for further inquiry, collaboration, and innovation in this rapidly evolving field.

Cristina Stolojescu-Crisan and Fabrizio Marozzo
Guest Editors

applied sciences

MDPI

Editorial

The Internet of Things (IoT) and Its Application in Monitoring

Cristina Stolojescu-Crisan [1] and Fabrizio Marozzo [2,*]

[1] Communications Department, Politehnica University of Timisoara, 300223 Timisoara, Romania; cristina.stolojescu-crisan@upt.ro
[2] Department of Informatics, Modeling, Electronics and Systems Engineering (DIMES), University of Calabria, 87036 Rende, Italy
* Correspondence: fabrizio.marozzo@unical.it

1. Introduction

The Internet of Things (IoT) has become one of the enabling paradigms of contemporary digital transformation, supporting pervasive sensing, real-time data acquisition, intelligent automation, and continuous monitoring across a broad range of domains. Advances in embedded systems, wireless networking, cloud and edge computing, artificial intelligence, and data analytics have made it possible to deploy increasingly sophisticated monitoring infrastructures in smart homes [1], industrial plants [2], healthcare facilities [3], critical infrastructures [4], transportation systems [5], and environmental scenarios [6]. In parallel, the evolution toward edge–cloud integration has created new opportunities to process monitoring data more efficiently and in a location nearer to where it is produced, thereby improving responsiveness, scalability, and resilience in distributed applications [7]. As a result, IoT-based monitoring is no longer limited to data collection; it is becoming a key component of intelligent decision support and adaptive control.

At the same time, the rapid expansion of IoT monitoring systems has highlighted several open challenges. Heterogeneous devices, dynamic operating conditions, privacy constraints, cybersecurity threats, communication limitations, and energy constraints make it difficult to design systems that are simultaneously accurate, scalable, trustworthy, and sustainable [8]. Moreover, many application contexts require not only robust sensing infrastructures, but also advanced methods for personalization, anomaly detection, fault diagnosis, predictive analysis, and digital representation of physical assets [9]. These needs are particularly visible in complex environments such as healthcare, industrial production, critical infrastructures, and smart energy systems, where monitoring must support timely and reliable interventions.

This Special Issue, entitled "The Internet of Things (IoT) and Its Application in Monitoring", was conceived as a means of collecting research that addresses these challenges from different perspectives. The nine papers published in the Special Issue provide a representative snapshot of recent developments in IoT-based monitoring, including architectural overviews, digital-twin-enhanced monitoring, federated learning for heterogeneous devices, cybersecurity requirements in industrial environments, machine-learning-based failure detection, resilience assessment of cyber–physical systems, optimization of monitored healthcare processes, and low-power environmental sensing platforms. Taken together, these contributions help clarify the current state of the art and indicate several promising research directions for the next generation of monitoring systems.

2. Overview of the Published Papers

The first contribution in the Special Issue is the paper by Witczak and Szymoniak, providing a broad review of monitoring and control systems based on the Internet of Things [10]. The article offers a useful entry point into the field by discussing architectures, communication aspects, representative applications, and current technological challenges. As a survey contribution, it helps contextualize many of the issues addressed more specifically by the other papers collected in this issue.

Several papers focus on intelligent monitoring architectures that combine IoT sensing with advanced computational models. Stogia et al. present a scalable and user-friendly framework integrating IoT and digital twins for home energy management systems, showing how digital representations of residential environments can support more adaptive and efficient energy monitoring and control [11]. Jang and Choi address another important challenge in IoT environments, namely data and device heterogeneity, by proposing FedSeq, a personalized federated learning approach based on sequential layer expansion in representation learning [12]. Their work is especially relevant in settings where monitoring data remain distributed across clients and privacy-preserving model training is required. Along similar cyber–physical integration lines, Nieves et al. propose an artificial-intelligence-based digital twin approach for improving rejection rates and mechanical properties in an investment casting plant, demonstrating how data-driven digital replicas can strengthen process monitoring and quality control in manufacturing [13]. These studies collectively show how the combination of IoT infrastructures with digital twins, artificial intelligence, and distributed learning is redefining the capabilities of modern monitoring systems.

Another group of papers addresses the reliability, safety, and resilience of monitored systems. Kasprzyczak et al. examine cybersecurity requirements for industrial machine control systems, highlighting the need to interpret industrial security levels and standards in light of the increasing connectivity brought by the industrial Internet of Things [14]. Ferreno-Gonzalez et al. investigate the detection of pipe ruptures in shipboard firefighting systems using machine learning and deep learning techniques, illustrating how sensor data can be exploited to detect anomalies and localize failures in safety-critical maritime environments [15]. Aghazadeh Ardebili et al. focus on IoT-driven resilience monitoring in a cyber–physical system, using a smart energy system as a case study to show how resilience indicators can be monitored in real time under cyber–physical disturbances [16]. Together, these papers make clear that monitoring is not merely an observational activity; it is increasingly tied to risk reduction, security assurance, fault management, and resilient operation.

This Special Issue also includes contributions centered on application-specific optimization and sustainable deployment. Nucci et al. study the optimized scheduling of IoT devices in healthcare facilities, formulating the allocation of patient monitoring resources as a multi-objective optimization problem that must balance economic costs and quality of care [17]. Their paper underscores the importance of operational intelligence in healthcare monitoring, where scarce sensing resources must be allocated carefully and ethically. Finally, Trînc et al. present a cost-effective TinyML-ready design and field deployment of a solar-powered environmental monitoring data collector using LTE-M communication [18]. This work is particularly significant because it addresses practical constraints that are central to real-world IoT deployments, including autonomy, communication reliability, low-power operation, and edge intelligence in outdoor sensing scenarios. These last two papers highlight the dual necessity of application awareness and engineering pragmatism in building useful monitoring solutions.

https://doi.org/10.3390/app16104998

3. Discussion

Although the nine papers cover different domains and technical approaches, several common themes emerge from the Special Issue. First, the issue confirms that IoT-based monitoring is evolving from simple sensing and reporting toward more integrated forms of intelligence. Monitoring systems are increasingly expected to support prediction, diagnosis, personalization, optimization, and adaptive control, often through the integration of digital twins, machine learning, and distributed analytics [11–13]. This transition creates new possibilities, but also raises questions about model robustness, interoperability, data governance, and lifecycle management.

Second, the Special Issue highlights an important gap between conceptual advances and deployment-ready solutions. While research has produced many promising algorithms and architectures, operational settings such as industry, healthcare, transportation, and environmental monitoring still present significant barriers related to cybersecurity, resource constraints, fault tolerance, maintainability, and long-term autonomy [14–18]. In this respect, the papers in the Special Issue contribute not only new methods, but also practical evidence on how IoT monitoring solutions behave under realistic constraints. This is particularly valuable in a field where real-world deployment issues often determine the actual impact of a proposed approach.

Third, the collected papers make it evident that heterogeneity remains one of the defining characteristics and challenges of IoT monitoring. Heterogeneity appears at multiple levels, including sensors, protocols, users, environments, computational resources, and application objectives. Personalized federated learning, modular digital-twin frameworks, and solar-powered sensing platforms are all responses to this challenge, each addressing it from a different angle [11,12,18]. The Special Issue therefore helps bridge an important knowledge gap by showing that scalable and trustworthy monitoring cannot rely on one-size-fits-all solutions; rather, it requires adaptive frameworks that can operate across diverse conditions.

4. Future Research Directions

The papers published in this Special Issue suggest several priorities for future research. A first direction concerns the tighter integration of IoT monitoring with edge intelligence and edge–cloud continuum architectures. As monitoring deployments become more distributed and data-intensive, researchers will need to design solutions that can make decisions dynamically regarding where sensing, filtering, inference, aggregation, and storage should take place, while respecting latency, privacy, energy, and reliability constraints [7]. This will require not only new systems architectures, but also orchestration strategies capable of adapting to changing conditions.

A second direction involves trustworthiness and security. Future monitoring platforms must be secure by design, especially in industrial, healthcare and critical infrastructure settings. Cybersecurity requirements, resilience metrics, secure personalization, and explainable fault diagnosis should be integral parts of IoT monitoring research rather than secondary additions [12,14,16]. Closely related to this is the need for stronger privacy-preserving methods and governance frameworks for monitored data, especially when sensitive personal or operational information is involved.

A third priority concerns sustainability and long-term deployment. Solar-powered sensing nodes, low-power communication technologies, TinyML, and lightweight analytics are likely to become increasingly important as monitoring expands into remote, large-scale, or resource-constrained environments [18]. Future studies should therefore address not only accuracy and functionality, but also maintainability, lifecycle costs, carbon-aware operation, and the robustness of deployments over time. Finally, more domain-oriented

https://doi.org/10.3390/app16104998

benchmarking efforts are needed to compare approaches fairly across application areas and to support reproducibility and technology transfer.

5. Conclusions

The nine papers collected in this Special Issue provide a broad and timely overview of current research on IoT and its application in monitoring. They show a field that is simultaneously expanding in scope and deepening in technical maturity, moving beyond data acquisition toward intelligent, secure, adaptive, and sustainable monitoring ecosystems. The Special Issue covers foundational reviews, advanced digital-twin-based approaches, personalized federated learning, cybersecurity and resilience studies, healthcare optimization, anomaly detection, and low-power field deployments, thereby offering a multifaceted view of the state of the art.

Overall, this Special Issue helps address key gaps in the literature by combining conceptual, methodological, and application-driven contributions. It shows that the future of IoT monitoring will depend on the ability to integrate sensing, intelligence, security, and sustainability into coherent and trustworthy systems. We hope that the papers included here will stimulate further research on the design, evaluation, and deployment of monitoring solutions that are not only technically effective but also robust, scalable, and beneficial in real-world contexts.

Conflicts of Interest: The authors declare no conflicts of interest.

References

1. Alaa, M.; Zaidan, A.A.; Zaidan, B.B.; Talal, M.; Kiah, M.L.M. A review of smart home applications based on Internet of Things. *J. Netw. Comput. Appl.* **2017**, *97*, 48–65. [CrossRef]
2. Gungor, V.C.; Hancke, G.P. Industrial Wireless Sensor Networks: Challenges, Design Principles, and Technical Approaches. *IEEE Trans. Ind. Electron.* **2009**, *56*, 4258–4265. [CrossRef]
3. Li, C.; Wang, J.; Wang, S.; Zhang, Y. A review of IoT applications in healthcare. *Neurocomputing* **2024**, *565*, 127017. [CrossRef]
4. Fausto, A.; Gaggero, G.B.; Patrone, F.; Girdinio, P.; Marchese, M. Toward the Integration of Cyber and Physical Security Monitoring Systems for Critical Infrastructures. *Sensors* **2021**, *21*, 6970. [CrossRef] [PubMed]
5. Belcastro, L.; Marozzo, F.; Orsino, A.; Talia, D.; Trunfio, P. Edge-Cloud Continuum Solutions for Urban Mobility Prediction and Planning. *IEEE Access* **2023**, *11*, 38864–38874. [CrossRef]
6. Ullo, S.L.; Sinha, G.R. Advances in Smart Environment Monitoring Systems Using IoT and Sensors. *Sensors* **2020**, *20*, 3113. [CrossRef] [PubMed]
7. Belcastro, L.; Marozzo, F.; Orsino, A.; Talia, D.; Trunfio, P. Navigating the edge-cloud continuum: A state-of-practice survey. *IEEE Access* **2026**, *14*, 40622–40647. [CrossRef]
8. Alaba, F.A.; Othman, M.; Hashem, I.A.T.; Alotaibi, F. Internet of Things security: A survey. *J. Netw. Comput. Appl.* **2017**, *88*, 10–28. [CrossRef]
9. van Dinter, R.; Tekinerdogan, B.; Catal, C. Predictive maintenance using digital twins: A systematic literature review. *Inf. Softw. Technol.* **2022**, *151*, 107008. [CrossRef]
10. Witczak, D.; Szymoniak, S. Review of Monitoring and Control Systems Based on Internet of Things. *Appl. Sci.* **2024**, *14*, 8943. [CrossRef]
11. Stogia, M.; Naserentin, V.; Dimara, A.; Eleftheriou, O.; Tzitzios, I.; Papaioannou, C.; Pantusheva, M.; Papaioannou, A.; Spaias, G.; Anagnostopoulos, C.N.; et al. A Scalable and User-Friendly Framework Integrating IoT and Digital Twins for Home Energy Management Systems. *Appl. Sci.* **2024**, *14*, 1834. [CrossRef]
12. Jang, J.W.; Choi, B.J. FedSeq: Personalized Federated Learning via Sequential Layer Expansion in Representation Learning. *Appl. Sci.* **2024**, *14*, 2024. [CrossRef]
13. Nieves, J.; Garcia, D.; Angulo-Pines, J.; Santos, F.; Rodriguez, P.P. An Artificial Intelligence-Based Digital Twin Approach for Rejection Rate and Mechanical Property Improvement in an Investment Casting Plant. *Appl. Sci.* **2025**, *15*, 2013. [CrossRef]
14. Kasprzyczak, L.; Manowska, A.; Dźwiarek, M. Cybersecurity Requirements for Industrial Machine Control Systems. *Appl. Sci.* **2025**, *15*, 1267. [CrossRef]
15. Ferreno-Gonzalez, S.; Diaz-Casas, V.; Miguez-Gonzalez, M.; San-Gabino, C.G. Detection of Pipe Ruptures in Shipboard Firefighting Systems Using Machine Learning and Deep Learning Techniques. *Appl. Sci.* **2025**, *15*, 1181. [CrossRef]

https://doi.org/10.3390/app16104998

16. Aghazadeh Ardebili, A.; Martella, C.; Longo, A.; Rucco, C.; Izzi, F.; Ficarella, A. IoT-Driven Resilience Monitoring: Case Study of a Cyber-Physical System. *Appl. Sci.* **2025**, *15*, 2092. [CrossRef]
17. Nucci, F.; Papadia, G.; Fedeli, E. Optimized Scheduling of IoT Devices in Healthcare Facilities: Balancing Cost and Quality of Care. *Appl. Sci.* **2025**, *15*, 4456. [CrossRef]
18. Trînc, E.C.; Niţă, V.; Stolojescu-Crisan, C.; Ancuţi, C.; Mihai, R.M.; Sultănoiu, C.P. Cost-Effective TinyML-Ready Design and Field Deployment of a Solar-Powered Environmental Monitoring Data Collector Using LTE-M Communication. *Appl. Sci.* **2026**, *16*, 3237. [CrossRef]

https://doi.org/10.3390/app16104998

applied sciences

MDPI

Article

Cost-Effective TinyML-Ready Design and Field Deployment of a Solar-Powered Environmental Monitoring Data Collector Using LTE-M Communication

Emanuel-Crăciun Trînc [1,*], Valentin Niţă [1], Cristina Stolojescu-Crisan [1], Cosmin Ancuţi [1], Răzvan Marius Mihai [2] and Cristian Paţachia Sultănoiu [2]

[1] Communications Department, Polytechnic University of Timișoara, 300006 Timișoara, Romania; valentin.nita@upt.ro (V.N.); cristina.stolojescu-crisan@upt.ro (C.S.-C.); cosmin.ancuti@upt.ro (C.A.)

[2] Orange Romania S.A., 010665 Bucharest, Romania; razvan.mihai@orange.com (R.M.M.); cristian.patachia@orange.com (C.P.S.)

* Correspondence: emanuel.trinc@yahoo.com

Abstract

Environmental monitoring is essential for smart agriculture, renewable energy assessment, and climate-aware farm management. However, deploying autonomous sensing platforms in rural environments remains challenging because of energy constraints, communication reliability, and real-time processing requirements. This paper presents a modular, solar-powered environmental monitoring platform integrating LTE-M communication and TinyML-enabled edge sensing. The proposed system adopts a dual-microcontroller architecture that combines an Arduino Nano 33 BLE for real-time sensor acquisition and edge processing with an Arduino MKR NB 1500 dedicated to low-power wide-area communication. The platform integrates temperature, humidity, atmospheric pressure, rainfall, wind, and light sensors within a scalable framework. Two monitoring stations were deployed in rural regions of Romania to evaluate communication robustness, sensing stability, and energy autonomy. Field results demonstrated reliable LTE-M connectivity (4306 received signal strength indicator [RSSI] samples; mean −75.51 dBm) and strong agreement with a regional weather station, with mean deviations of −0.71 °C (temperature), 4.98% (humidity), and a stable pressure offset of −9.58 hPa attributable to altitude differences. Despite a total system cost of €315, the platform achieved measurement performance comparable to that of professional meteorological stations while maintaining long-term solar-powered operation. The proposed architecture provides a scalable and cost-effective solution for distributed smart agriculture and environmental monitoring applications.

Keywords: NB-IoT; LTE-M; Cat-M1; TinyML; environmental monitoring; IoT weather station; smart agriculture; renewable energy sensing; solar-powered IoT; edge computing

1. Introduction

Data-driven agriculture is essential for improving crop productivity, resource efficiency, and climate resilience [1–3]. Continuous monitoring of environmental parameters, such as temperature, humidity, rainfall, solar radiation, wind speed, and wind direction, enables farmers to optimize irrigation schedules, detect crop stress conditions, improve yield prediction, and reduce operational costs. Environmental sensing also supports the evaluation of renewable energy resources and smart city environmental monitoring, where accurate meteorological data assist solar and wind energy planning, microclimate modeling, and urban climate management.

Traditional environmental monitoring stations are typically expensive and difficult to deploy across large agricultural or rural regions. Installation, calibration, and maintenance costs limit scalability, particularly in distributed farming environments, where localized sensing is required. Many commercial weather-monitoring systems have acquisition costs that exceed several thousand euros (€5000+), restricting their widespread adoption in data-driven agriculture and highlighting the need for affordable monitoring platforms with comparable sensing capabilities and modular extensibility.

Recent advancements in Internet of Things (IoT) technologies have enabled the development of low-cost, distributed environmental monitoring platforms [4,5] capable of real-time data collection. Among the available IoT communication technologies, narrowband Internet of Things (NB-IoT), such as LTE-M, has emerged as a promising solution for low-power, long-range communication in rural environments. NB-IoT and LTE-M have emerged as promising low-power wide-area network (LPWAN) technologies for rural IoT deployments owing to their extended coverage and low energy consumption [6,7]. These technologies provide improved coverage, enhanced scalability, and reduced energy consumption compared to traditional cellular communication systems, making them particularly suitable for remote environmental monitoring applications.

Meanwhile, the emergence of Tiny Machine Learning (TinyML) has enabled intelligent data processing directly on microcontroller-based embedded systems [8,9]. Edge-based processing allows for local data filtering, anomaly detection, adaptive sampling, and event-driven sensing, thereby reducing communication overhead and improving system responsiveness. Such capabilities are particularly valuable in agricultural monitoring scenarios, where continuous sensing generates large volumes of data that may not require constant cloud transmission.

Despite recent progress in IoT environmental monitoring systems, several challenges remain. These include ensuring long-term autonomous operation through renewable energy harvesting, integrating heterogeneous sensor modules within a unified architecture, achieving reliable communication in rural environments with variable signal coverage, and enabling intelligent edge-based processing while maintaining low power consumption. Energy harvesting using solar power has been widely adopted to extend the operational lifetime of wireless environmental sensor networks [10,11]. However, many existing monitoring platforms focus on single-domain applications and lack flexibility for multi-domain sensing and modular expansion.

To address these challenges, in this study, we propose a modular, solar-powered environmental monitoring platform that integrates LTE-M/NB-IoT communication and TinyML-enabled real-time sensing. The system adopts a dual-microcontroller architecture that separates high-frequency sensor acquisition and edge intelligence from long-range wireless communication tasks.

Specifically, the Arduino Nano 33 BLE (Arduino/Qualcomm Italy) is responsible for real-time sensor interfacing, interrupt-driven acquisition of mechanical sensing components, and future TinyML-based inference tasks. Its higher computational capability (64 MHz CPU), extended SRAM, and larger flash memory enable local preprocessing, adaptive sampling strategies, and edge analytics. In contrast, the Arduino MKR NB 1500 is dedicated to LTE-M communication and cloud data transmission, ensuring reliable low-power wide-area connectivity in rural environments.

This functional separation improves system scalability, enhances energy efficiency by isolating communication bursts from sensing logic, and increases robustness by reducing the cross-dependencies between the computation and transmission subsystems. The

https://doi.org/10.3390/app16073237

dual-microcontroller architecture, along with the primary hardware characteristics and communication roles of each module, is illustrated in Figure 1.

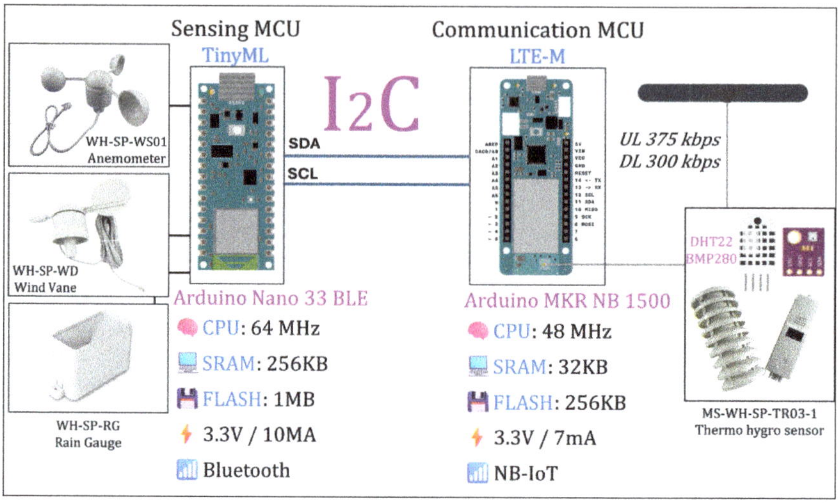

Figure 1. Dual-microcontroller architecture of the proposed environmental monitoring platform. The Arduino Nano 33 BLE performs real-time sensor acquisition (Misol mechanical units) and TinyML-based edge processing, while the Arduino MKR NB 1500 provides LTE-M/NB-IoT communication for reliable long-range cloud connectivity (also driving thermo hygro sensors installed inside Misol MS-WH-SP-TR03-1 (Jiaxing Misol Import & Export Co., Ltd., Jiaxing, China)).

In addition to architectural modularity, the proposed system was designed with a strong emphasis on real-world deployability and long-term autonomy. The integration of solar energy harvesting, $LiFePO_4$ battery storage, heterogeneous environmental sensing modules, and LTE-M communication enables fully autonomous operation in geographically dispersed agricultural areas. Accurate solar radiation forecasting using machine learning has become an active research area owing to its relevance in renewable energy planning [12]. Particular attention was given to communication robustness under varying cellular coverage conditions, sensing stability under environmental exposure, and energy-aware system operation.

To validate the proposed architecture under practical operating conditions, field deployments were conducted in two geographically distinct regions (Figure 2) characterized by different cellular coverage profiles and environmental conditions. The deployments were intentionally selected to evaluate communication reliability and energy autonomy in heterogeneous rural scenarios. One monitoring station was installed in Sânandrei, Timiș County, representing a suburban environment with stable LTE-M network coverage, whereas the second station was deployed in Rogoz de Beliu, Arad County, representing a remote rural environment with limited cellular signal availability.

The main contributions of this paper are summarized as follows:

- Proposal and implementation of a dual-microcontroller, solar-powered environmental monitoring architecture integrating LTE-M/NB-IoT communication and TinyML-enabled edge intelligence.
- Development of a low-energy sensing platform enabling long-term autonomous deployment in rural agricultural environments.
- Integration of heterogeneous environmental sensors within a unified real-time sensing and edge-processing framework.

https://doi.org/10.3390/app16073237

- Experimental field validation in geographically distinct deployment regions with different cellular coverage characteristics.
- Performance evaluation in terms of communication reliability, sensing stability, and energy autonomy.

Figure 2. Field deployment of the proposed solar-powered environmental monitoring platform in Sânandrei (**left**), Timiș County, and Rogoz de Beliu (**right**), Arad County. The installation illustrates the real-world integration of the sensing platform within an agricultural environment characterized by stable LTE-M network coverage.

The remainder of this paper is organized as follows: Section 2 reviews related work on Internet of Things (IoT)-based environmental monitoring systems and smart agriculture sensing platforms. Section 3 presents the system architecture and hardware design. Section 4 presents the experimental deployment results and performance evaluation. Section 5 discusses the limitations, and Sections 6–8 conclude this paper and outline future research directions.

2. Related Work

2.1. IoT-Based Weather Stations and Environmental Data Collectors

Low-cost IoT weather stations have been increasingly studied for environmental monitoring and climate-aware agriculture. Recent systematic reviews highlight the growing adoption of affordable hardware platforms, modular sensor integration, and scalable communication protocols for resource-constrained agricultural environments [13,14]. These platforms aim to provide continuous environmental monitoring while reducing deployment costs compared to traditional meteorological systems.

https://doi.org/10.3390/app16073237

Several implementations have focused on low-cost microcontroller-based weather-monitoring systems. For instance, Khan et al. [15] proposed a weather-monitoring platform based on ESPRESSIF ESP32-S3-WROOM-1 microcontrollers (Pune, Maharashtra) and ESP-NOW communication, capable of measuring temperature, humidity, rainfall, wind speed, and light intensity. Their work emphasizes affordability and low-power communication for distributed sensing environments. Similarly, Jasso-Reyes et al. [16] presented a modular IoT meteorological station architecture, demonstrating the feasibility of integrating multiple environmental sensors into portable and scalable monitoring platforms.

Broader research efforts have examined the role of IoT sensing in smart agriculture ecosystems. Eyasin et al. [17] introduced IoT-based multi-sensor crop monitoring solutions aimed at improving crop productivity through continuous environmental data acquisition and analysis. Furthermore, Zhurakovskyi et al. [18] proposed a machine-learning-based environmental monitoring framework capable of performing real-time data analysis and environmental forecasting, highlighting the growing integration of predictive analytics into environmental sensing systems.

From a communication perspective, Low-Power Wide-Area Network (LPWAN) technologies such as NB-IoT and LTE-M have gained increasing attention for agricultural and rural IoT deployments. Zhao et al. [19] investigated NB-IoT and 5G dual-channel communication architectures for autonomous agricultural machinery, demonstrating the potential of cellular LPWAN technologies for large-scale field operations. Additionally, real-world experimental evaluations of NB-IoT energy consumption [20,21] provide detailed insights into power profiles, transmission states, and device-level energy trade-offs. More recently, Trabelsi et al. [22] analyzed NB-IoT performance characteristics and delay-sensitive traffic scheduling, emphasizing the importance of communication optimization in cellular IoT systems.

Despite these advancements, several limitations remain in existing IoT weather-monitoring systems. Many low-cost platforms rely on single microcontroller architectures, in which sensing, processing, and communication tasks share computational resources. This architectural design may limit scalability when integrating advanced edge intelligence while maintaining reliable long-range communication. Although several studies investigate cost-effective hardware, energy-efficient sensing, and cloud-based analytics, fewer works explicitly address the integration of TinyML-capable edge processing with cellular LPWAN technologies such as NB-IoT or LTE-M within modular, solar-powered environmental monitoring platforms.

The proposed system differentiates itself by combining:

- A dual-microcontroller architecture separating real-time sensing and edge intelligence from communication tasks;
- LTE-M/NB-IoT connectivity validated under real rural deployment conditions;
- Solar-powered autonomous operation;
- TinyML-ready hardware resources for future adaptive communication and sensing strategies.

By addressing sensing reliability, communication robustness, and architectural modularity simultaneously, the proposed platform contributes toward scalable and intelligent environmental monitoring systems suitable for precision agriculture and renewable energy assessment.

2.2. NB-IoT Communication for Environmental Monitoring Systems

Narrowband Internet of Things (NB-IoT) is a low-power wide-area network (LPWAN) technology standardized by the 3rd Generation Partnership Project (3GPP) to support massive machine-type communications in Internet of Things (IoT) applications. NB-IoT

https://doi.org/10.3390/app16073237

operates within licensed cellular frequency bands and provides extended coverage, high connection density, and improved energy efficiency compared to traditional short-range wireless communication technologies.

NB-IoT has attracted increasing attention in agricultural and environmental monitoring applications owing to its capability to support reliable long-range communication in rural and geographically distributed environments. Zhao et al. [19] demonstrated the integration of NB-IoT and 5G communication channels in an IoT-based platform for autonomous agricultural machinery, highlighting the suitability of NB-IoT for large-scale agricultural sensing and monitoring systems requiring reliable connectivity and cloud-based data processing.

Energy efficiency is a critical factor in autonomous environmental monitoring deployments. Several studies have analyzed the power consumption characteristics of NB-IoT communication modules under real-world deployment conditions. Lukic et al. [20] performed an in-depth real-world evaluation of NB-IoT module energy consumption and demonstrated that optimized transmission scheduling and power management techniques significantly improve device lifetime in battery-powered IoT sensing platforms. Similarly, Michelinakis et al. [21] conducted empirical measurements of NB-IoT device energy consumption and provided detailed insights into communication energy profiles, highlighting the importance of optimizing data transmission intervals for long-term autonomous sensing systems.

Compared to alternative LPWAN technologies, such as LoRa and Sigfox, NB-IoT benefits from operating within existing cellular infrastructure, thereby enabling improved security, quality of service, and network scalability. These characteristics render NB-IoT particularly suitable for mission-critical environmental sensing applications that require reliable bidirectional communication and centralized cloud integration.

Despite these advantages, the integration of NB-IoT communication within modular and low-cost environmental monitoring platforms remains an active research area. Several existing sensing systems rely on single microcontroller architectures and prioritize communication reliability over distributed intelligent processing capabilities. Furthermore, although previous studies have extensively analyzed NB-IoT communication performance and energy consumption, few studies have investigated its integration with TinyML-based edge processing within solar-powered and modular sensing architectures designed for long-term field deployments.

This study was motivated by these limitations and proposes an environmental monitoring platform that integrates NB-IoT communication with TinyML-enabled edge processing using a dual-microcontroller architecture. The proposed system evaluates NB-IoT communication reliability under heterogeneous signal coverage conditions and supports real-time intelligent sensing in distributed agricultural monitoring environments.

3. Materials and Methods

3.1. General Architecture of the Environmental Data Collector

The proposed environmental data collector is designed as a modular, solar-powered IoT monitoring platform capable of supporting real-time environmental sensing, edge processing, and long-range wireless communication. The system integrates heterogeneous sensing modules, embedded computation, cellular communication, and autonomous energy management into a unified architecture suitable for remote agricultural and environmental deployments. The design philosophy emphasizes scalability, energy efficiency, and functional decoupling between sensing, processing, and transmission tasks in order to ensure long-term reliable operation under outdoor conditions.

https://doi.org/10.3390/app16073237

Figure 3 illustrates the overall system-level architecture and its physical decomposition. From an integration perspective, the platform can be structured into three tightly coupled yet functionally distinct layers: (i) a mechanical sensing layer mounted on a supporting pillar, (ii) an embedded processing and communication layer enclosed within a weatherproof housing, and (iii) an autonomous power management layer based on photovoltaic energy harvesting and battery storage.

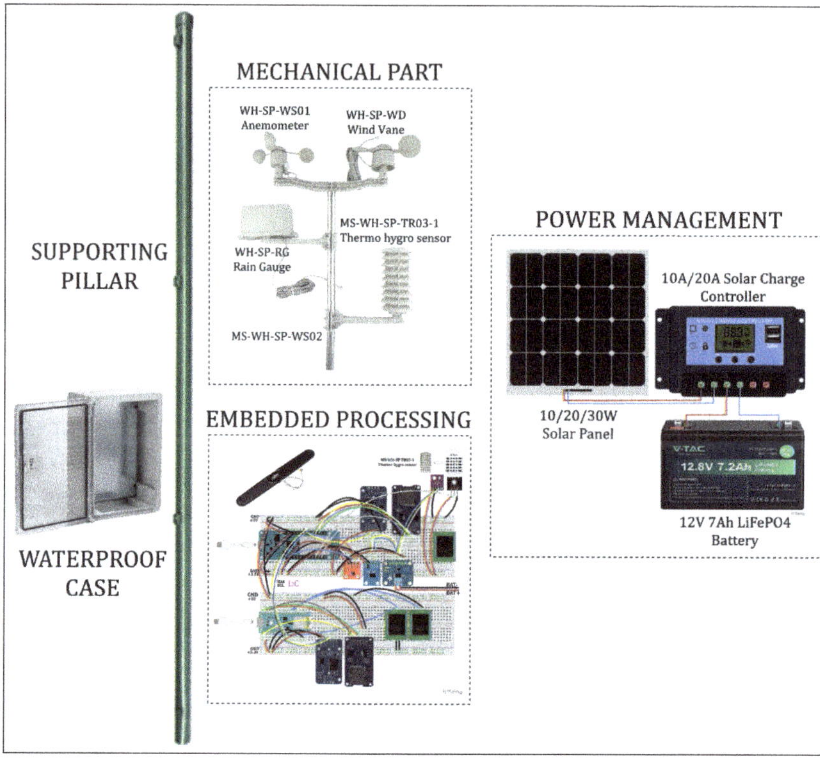

Figure 3. General system-level architecture of the proposed solar-powered environmental data collector. The platform integrates a mechanical sensing assembly (anemometer, wind vane, rain gauge, thermo-hygro module) mounted on a supporting pillar, a waterproof enclosure housing the dual-microcontroller hardware prototype (Arduino Nano 33 BLE for real-time sensing and TinyML-ready edge processing, Arduino MKR NB 1500 for LTE-M/NB-IoT communication), and a solar energy management subsystem composed of a 10–30 W photovoltaic panel, PWM charge controller, and 12 V $LiFePO_4$ battery (V-TAC SKU-11942, 12.8V 7.2AH, 150X63X93mm). The architecture highlights the modular separation between mechanical sensing, embedded processing, communication, and autonomous power management.

Beyond the physical decomposition of the platform, the system can also be described through a functional layered data-flow perspective, as shown in Figure 4. At the lowest level, the TinyML/Sensors layer acquires raw environmental measurements from both solid-state and mechanical sensors. This data is then processed locally by the sensing microcontroller and transferred to the communication layer, which is responsible for long-range wireless transmission through LTE-M or LoRaWAN technologies. At the upper level, cloud services support database storage, dashboard visualization, and future AI model training. An intermediate Edge AI layer is also reserved for future deployment of

https://doi.org/10.3390/app16073237

local inference capabilities, enabling on-device anomaly detection, adaptive sampling, and event-driven environmental intelligence.

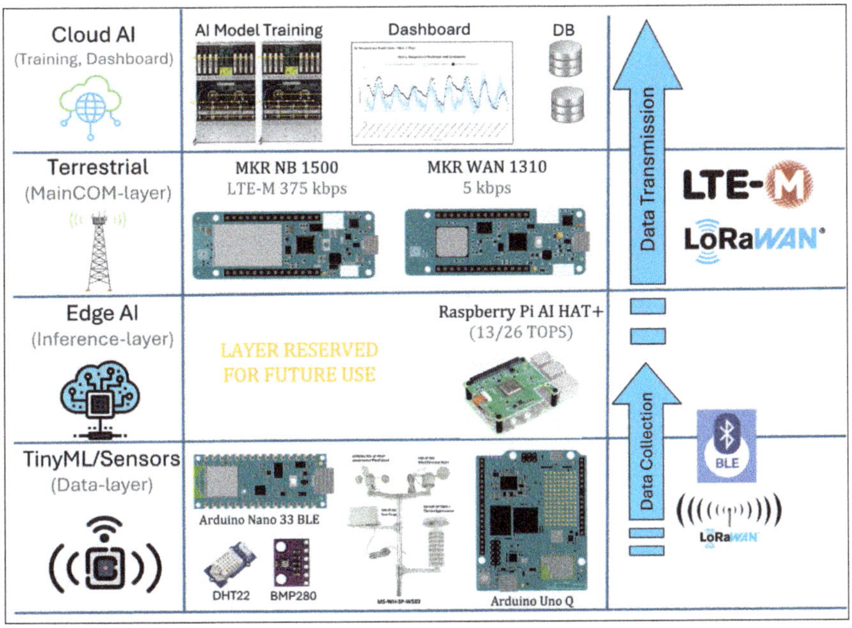

Figure 4. Layered architecture and end-to-end data flow of the proposed environmental monitoring platform. Environmental sensors connected to the sensing MCU collect measurements such as temperature, humidity, pressure, wind speed, and rainfall. These measurements are transferred through the embedded processing layer to the communication layer, where LTE-M or LoRaWAN modules transmit the data to cloud infrastructure. The cloud layer supports database storage, dashboard visualization, and future AI model training, while an intermediate Edge AI layer is reserved for future TinyML inference tasks.

The mechanical sensing layer comprises the meteorological instruments responsible for direct environmental interaction, including wind speed, wind direction, rainfall, temperature, and humidity measurement modules. These components are positioned at elevated height on a dedicated supporting structure to ensure unobstructed airflow exposure and representative microclimate measurements. Mechanical isolation from the electronics enclosure minimizes vibration coupling and reduces thermal interference between sensing elements and embedded circuitry.

The embedded processing layer houses the dual-microcontroller architecture within an IP-rated waterproof enclosure. This layer performs interrupt-driven acquisition of mechanical sensor signals, digital interfacing with solid-state sensors, local preprocessing, and LTE-M/NB-IoT data transmission. Physical separation of the sensing assembly from the electronics enclosure enhances maintainability, protects sensitive components from environmental exposure, and simplifies system diagnostics and upgrades.

The autonomous power management layer ensures energy independence through a photovoltaic panel, charge regulation circuitry, and $LiFePO_4$ battery storage. This subsystem is dimensioned to support multi-day autonomy under reduced solar irradiance conditions while maintaining sufficient energy reserves for communication bursts and edge computation tasks. The separation of energy management from sensing and processing layers allows for independent optimization of power budgeting and communication scheduling strategies.

https://doi.org/10.3390/app16073237

This layered decomposition improves modularity, simplifies maintenance, and enables independent optimization of sensing, computation, communication, and energy subsystems. Furthermore, the architecture supports straightforward sensor replacement, subsystem scaling, and future integration of additional edge intelligence capabilities without requiring structural redesign of the entire platform.

3.1.1. Mechanical Sensing Layer

The mechanical sensing components were adapted from commercially available weather station mechanical spare parts compatible with the Misol MS-WH-SP-WS02 platform, acquired from luminam.ro. These components include an anemometer for wind speed measurement, a wind vane for directional sensing, a tipping-bucket rain gauge for precipitation detection, and a thermo-hygro sensor module for temperature and humidity monitoring. The sensors are externally mounted on a rigid supporting pillar to ensure unobstructed exposure to ambient environmental conditions.

Although commercial modules were used in the current deployment, the proposed platform is designed as a hardware-agnostic solution. Sensing elements may be replaced with equivalent commercial devices or custom-designed mechanical assemblies without requiring architectural modification. This flexibility enables future integration of locally manufactured or 3D-printed sensor structures to reduce system costs and improve accessibility.

The anemometer and rain gauge generate pulse-based signals proportional to wind speed and rainfall events, respectively, while the wind vane provides directional information via discrete resistive or analog output states. These sensors rely on interrupt-driven signal generation, requiring accurate detection of high-frequency pulse transitions to ensure measurement reliability under rapidly changing environmental conditions.

3.1.2. Embedded Processing and Communication Layer

Real-time acquisition of mechanical sensor signals is handled by the Arduino Nano 33 BLE microcontroller. The Nano 33 BLE was selected due to its reliable interrupt-handling capabilities, sufficient computational performance, and low-power operating characteristics. The microcontroller continuously monitors sensor interrupt lines to ensure that all mechanical events are captured without data loss.

Although the Nano 33 BLE provides enhanced Flash memory, SRAM capacity, and processing frequency compared to traditional ultra-low-power microcontrollers, the present deployment phase primarily focuses on robust data acquisition and preprocessing. The available computational headroom is reserved for future integration of TinyML-based edge intelligence algorithms, including predictive energy management and adaptive sensing strategies.

Long-range communication and cloud connectivity are managed by the Arduino MKR NB 1500 module, which supports LTE-M/NB-IoT communication. The NB-IoT interface enables reliable low-power wide-area network (LPWAN) connectivity, allowing for sensor data transmission even in rural or geographically isolated environments characterized by limited cellular coverage. The communication subsystem supports bidirectional connectivity for remote device monitoring, configuration updates, and firmware management.

The dual-microcontroller architecture physically separates sensing and edge-processing tasks from communication functions. This separation enhances system scalability, improves energy efficiency by isolating high-consumption communication events, and provides computational flexibility for future intelligent processing extensions.

3.1.3. Autonomous Power Management Layer

The power subsystem ensures long-term autonomous operation through solar energy harvesting and battery storage. The architecture integrates a photovoltaic panel with

https://doi.org/10.3390/app16073237

configurable power ratings (10–30 W), a PWM solar charge controller for battery regulation, and a 12 V $LiFePO_4$ battery used as the primary energy storage unit.

This configuration enables sustained operation without external power infrastructure, supporting deployment in remote agricultural environments. The charge controller manages battery charging cycles, prevents overcharging and deep discharge conditions, and provides regulated power distribution to the embedded processing modules.

Detailed electrical modeling, battery dimensioning strategy, winter energy risk analysis, and charging stress evaluation are presented in Section 3.3.

3.1.4. System Integration and Deployment Considerations

All electronic components are housed inside an IP-rated waterproof enclosure designed to protect against environmental exposure while maintaining thermal stability. The enclosure supports modular integration of sensing, processing, and communication modules and allows for convenient maintenance access during field deployment.

In the current implementation phase, the primary objective is long-term environmental and system performance data collection, including battery state monitoring and communication reliability assessment. The collected datasets provide the foundation for future development of edge intelligence models aimed at optimizing energy consumption, adaptive sampling strategies, and communication scheduling.

The modular architecture enables flexible adaptation of the platform to multiple application domains, including precision agriculture, distributed environmental monitoring, renewable energy assessment, and future AI-native edge sensing applications.

The reference to adaptive sampling strategies in this work should be interpreted as an envisioned future capability supported by the proposed architecture rather than a function fully implemented in the present prototype. Adaptive sampling has been widely studied in wireless sensor networks as an energy-saving mechanism that dynamically adjusts sampling frequency while preserving data quality [23]. In the proposed platform, such a strategy could be realized by maintaining the sensing MCU in a low-power state during stable environmental periods and increasing the acquisition rate only when specific triggers are observed, such as rapid temperature or humidity variation, rainfall tipping events, or elevated wind pulse activity. Although this functionality is not yet deployed in the current implementation, the dual-microcontroller architecture was intentionally designed to support such future edge-intelligence extensions by decoupling local sensing and decision logic from communication tasks.

Although TinyML models are not yet deployed in the current prototype, the sensing architecture was intentionally designed to support future edge inference tasks. The sensing microcontroller (Arduino Nano 33 BLE) integrates a 64 MHz ARM Cortex-M4 processor with 256 kB RAM and 1 MB flash memory, which are commonly used for lightweight TinyML deployments. All environmental sensors and mechanical interrupt-driven components are connected to this sensing MCU, allowing for local processing of environmental data streams before transmission. This design reserves computational resources for future deployment of lightweight models performing tasks such as anomaly detection, adaptive sampling, or short-term environmental prediction.

3.2. Dual-Microcontroller Architecture Selection

To support both intelligent edge processing and reliable long-range communication, the proposed platform adopts a dual-microcontroller architecture. This design separates sensing and edge intelligence tasks from communication operations, improving system modularity, scalability, and energy efficiency. Figure 5 illustrates the comparison between several Arduino-compatible platforms considered during the design phase.

https://doi.org/10.3390/app16073237

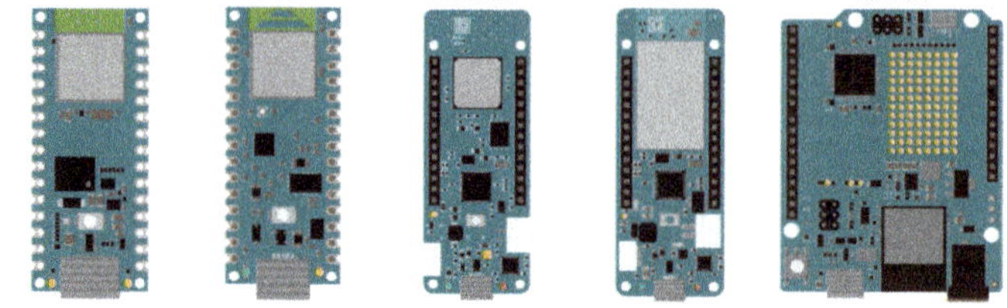

	Arduino Nano ESP32	Arduino Nano 33 BLE	Arduino MKR WAN 1310	Arduino MKR NB 1500	Arduino Uno R4 WiFi
Connectivity	WiFi, Bluetooth	Bluetooth	LoRaWAN	NB-IoT	WiFi, Bluetooth
Transmission Speed	150 Mbps / 2Mbps	2 Mbps	0.3 - 5 kbps	375 kbps	150 Mbps / 2 Mbps
Clock Speed	240 MHz	64 MHz	48 MHz	48 MHz	48 MHz / 250 MHz
Flash/ROM Memory	384 kB	1024 kB	256 kB	256 kB	256 kB / 384 kB
SRAM Memory	512 kB	256 kB	32 kB	32 kB	32 kB / 512 kB
Low Power Mode	7/240 µA	1 mA	104 µA	1 mA	5-18 mA / 8 µA
Operating Power I/O Pin	40 mA	10 mA	7 mA	7 mA	8 mA
Transmission Power	20 dBm / 10 dBm	8 dBm	20 dBm	23 dBm	20 dBm / 10 dBm
Receiver Sensitivity	-97/-98 dBm	-95 dBm	-137 dBm	-105 dBm	-97 dBm / -98 dBm

Figure 5. Comparison of several Arduino-compatible platforms considered for the system architecture, including connectivity, computational capability, memory resources, power consumption, and receiver sensitivity.

The sensing and edge-processing subsystem is implemented using the Arduino Nano 33 BLE. This platform was selected primarily due to its suitability for TinyML workloads and its ability to handle interrupt-driven sensing tasks generated by mechanical sensors such as rain gauges and anemometers. The board is based on the Nordic nRF52840 microcontroller, which provides sufficient SRAM (256 kB) and flash memory (1 MB) for lightweight machine learning inference models while maintaining relatively low power consumption. Additionally, the Nano 33 BLE supports efficient handling of high-frequency interrupts, enabling precise measurement of mechanical sensing events without compromising real-time performance.

While the Nano 33 BLE provides excellent capabilities for local processing, it lacks integrated long-range cellular connectivity. Conversely, the Arduino MKR NB 1500 integrates an NB-IoT/LTE-M cellular modem that enables direct communication with wide-area cellular networks. This board was therefore selected as the communication subsystem responsible for transmitting processed sensor data to cloud infrastructure.

Importantly, the separation of edge processing and communication functions offers several architectural advantages. First, it prevents communication tasks from interfering with real-time sensor acquisition and TinyML inference. Cellular communication operations can introduce latency, blocking events, or additional power consumption, which may negatively impact time-critical sensing processes if executed on a single microcontroller.

Second, this modular design allows for flexible communication backends. Although the current implementation utilizes NB-IoT connectivity through the MKR NB 1500, alternative communication modules such as WiFi (e.g., ESP32-based platforms) or LoRaWAN (e.g., MKR WAN 1310) can be substituted without modifying the sensing subsystem. This modularity enables the platform to adapt to different deployment scenarios, including rural environments without cellular coverage or installations requiring private long-range networks.

Finally, the dual-processor architecture improves system scalability and future extensibility. TinyML models can be executed locally on the sensing microcontroller to perform intelligent edge analytics such as anomaly detection, predictive maintenance, adaptive

https://doi.org/10.3390/app16073237

sampling, short-term weather prediction, frost risk detection, and heat stress monitoring for crops. These edge inference capabilities allow the system to react to environmental changes in real time while reducing the amount of data that must be transmitted to the cloud. For example, frost prediction models can trigger early-warning alerts for farmers, while temperature and humidity trend analysis can support early detection of plant stress conditions. By performing such inference tasks locally, the platform reduces communication overhead, improves responsiveness, and enables more energy-efficient operation of distributed environmental monitoring networks.

The overall system architecture resulting from this design decision is illustrated in Figure 6. The sensing and edge-processing subsystem, referred to as the TinyML/EdgeAI module, is responsible for real-time sensor acquisition, interrupt handling for mechanical sensing components, and local execution of lightweight machine learning models. This module may be implemented using platforms such as the Arduino Nano 33 BLE or other microcontrollers capable of running TinyML inference frameworks. These platforms provide sufficient computational capability and memory resources to support embedded inference tasks while maintaining low power consumption.

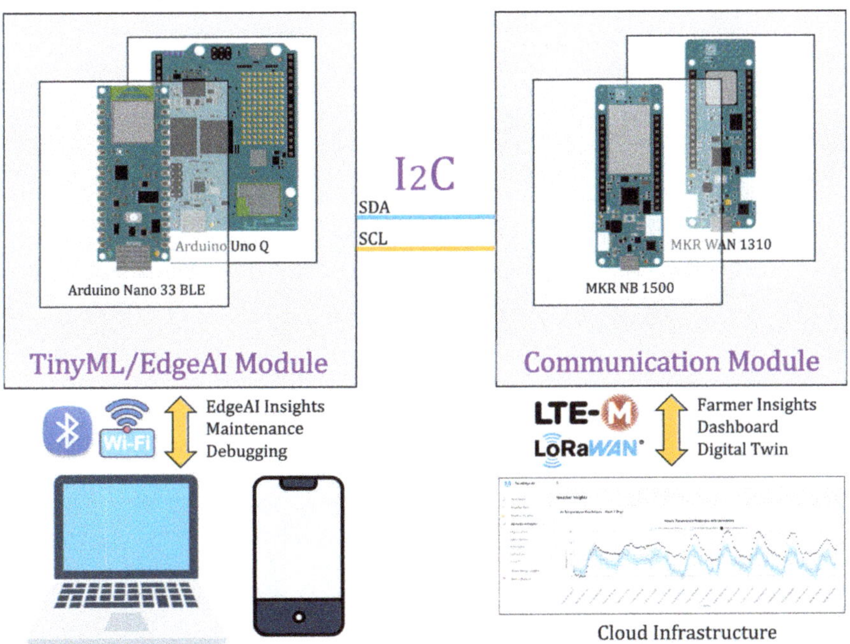

Figure 6. Dual-microcontroller architecture of the proposed environmental monitoring platform. The TinyML/EdgeAI module performs real-time sensor acquisition and local machine learning inference, while the communication module provides flexible connectivity through LTE-M/NB-IoT or LoRaWAN networks. The two subsystems communicate via an I^2C interface, enabling separation of sensing intelligence from network transmission and allowing modular adaptation of the communication layer.

In contrast, the communication module is responsible for long-range connectivity and remote data transmission. Depending on deployment requirements, different communication boards may be used, including the Arduino MKR NB 1500 for LTE-M/NB-IoT connectivity or the MKR WAN 1310 for LoRaWAN-based communication. This flexibility allows the system to adapt to different network infrastructures, enabling deployment in both

https://doi.org/10.3390/app16073237

cellular-covered areas and remote environments where low-power wide-area networks (LPWAN) are more suitable.

The two subsystems communicate through an inter-microcontroller interface implemented using the I^2C protocol. This lightweight communication channel enables the TinyML/EdgeAI module to transmit processed sensor data and inference results to the communication module, which subsequently handles cloud synchronization and remote monitoring. By isolating sensing and edge analytics from network communication tasks, the architecture prevents blocking communication events or network delays from interfering with real-time sensing operations.

This separation of responsibilities provides several practical advantages. First, it allows the edge-processing microcontroller to operate with deterministic timing when handling interrupts from mechanical sensors such as rain gauges or anemometers, which require precise event counting. Second, it enables independent optimization of computational and communication subsystems, allowing different microcontrollers to be selected depending on performance, power consumption, or connectivity requirements. Finally, the architecture improves system extensibility by allowing for future upgrades to either the edge-processing or communication subsystem without redesigning the entire platform.

The TinyML/EdgeAI module is therefore designed not only for raw sensor acquisition but also for local interpretation of environmental measurements before transmission. Rather than forwarding all sampled data directly to the cloud, this module can preprocess signals, extract relevant features, and generate compact event- or inference-based outputs for the communication subsystem. This approach supports more efficient use of bandwidth and energy resources while preserving the capability for real-time environmental awareness at the sensing node.

The sensing MCU also provides sufficient memory and computational resources for deploying lightweight TinyML models using frameworks such as TensorFlow Lite for Microcontrollers. This capability enables future integration of edge intelligence without requiring modifications to the sensing hardware architecture.

3.3. *Power Consumption Considerations of the Dual-Microcontroller Architecture*

A potential concern when adopting a dual-microcontroller architecture is the increase in baseline power consumption compared to a single-MCU design. To evaluate this trade-off, an illustrative duty-cycled power profile was generated based on the low-power characteristics of the selected boards (Arduino Nano 33 BLE and Arduino MKR NB 1500) and typical sensing and communication events observed in environmental monitoring systems.

Figure 7 presents the conceptual current consumption profile of the proposed architecture compared with a hypothetical single-MCU implementation capable of handling both sensing and communication tasks. The low-power baseline values used in the model were derived from the specifications summarized in Figure 5, where both the Nano 33 BLE and MKR NB 1500 operate at approximately 1 mA in low-power mode.

During normal operation, the sensing microcontroller remains in a low-power state and wakes only when interrupt-driven events occur. These short spikes correspond to mechanical sensing events such as anemometer rotations or rain gauge tipping events, which require immediate interrupt handling and event counting. Because these events are brief and infrequent relative to the overall duty cycle, their contribution to total energy consumption remains small.

In contrast, cellular communication events dominate the overall energy budget. The LTE-M transmission burst, shown in Figure 7, introduces a significantly higher current draw than the baseline operation of either microcontroller. This behavior is typical for IoT sensing platforms where communication energy greatly exceeds sensing and processing energy.

https://doi.org/10.3390/app16073237

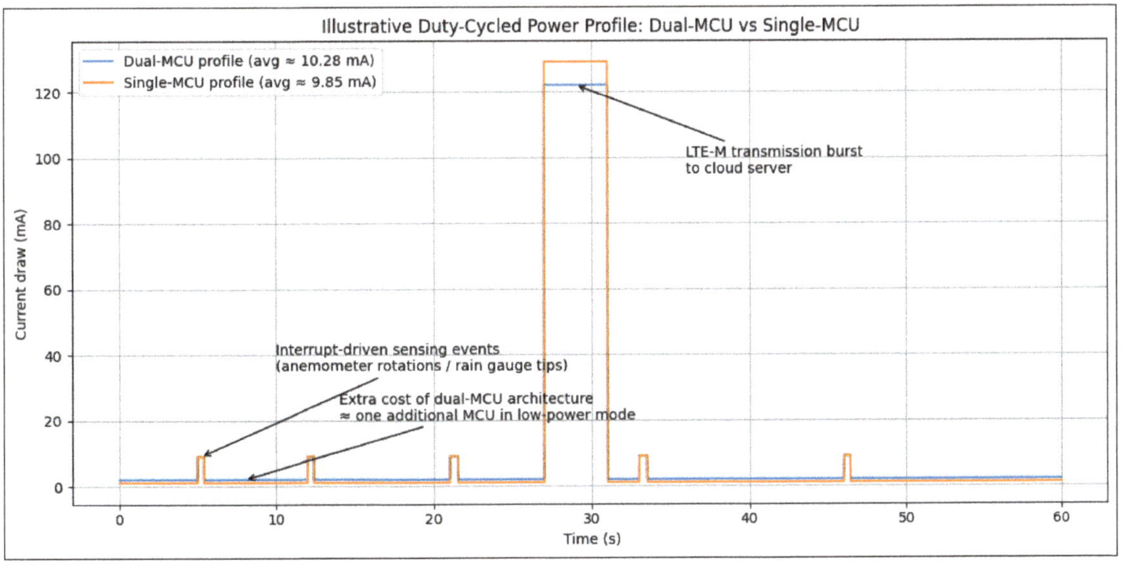

Figure 7. Illustrative duty-cycled current profile comparing the proposed dual-microcontroller architecture with a hypothetical single-MCU design. Small spikes correspond to interrupt-driven sensing events generated by mechanical sensors such as anemometer rotations and rain gauge tipping events, while the large spike represents LTE-M transmission to the cloud. The additional energy cost of the dual-MCU architecture is mainly the low-power baseline of the sensing microcontroller, whereas communication bursts dominate total energy consumption.

Consequently, the primary energy overhead introduced by the dual-microcontroller architecture is the additional low-power baseline of the sensing MCU. However, this increase is relatively small compared to the energy required for periodic communication bursts. In return, the dual-MCU architecture provides several advantages, including deterministic interrupt handling for mechanical sensors, separation of sensing and communication workloads, and modular support for alternative communication technologies such as LTE-M, LoRaWAN, or WiFi.

These results suggest that the dual-microcontroller architecture represents a reasonable design trade-off between energy consumption, sensing reliability, and system modularity, particularly for solar-powered environmental monitoring systems where communication energy dominates the overall power budget.

Future TinyML inference tasks are expected to be executed in a duty-cycled manner during scheduled sensing intervals or event-triggered conditions, ensuring that computational energy consumption remains negligible compared to the energy required for cellular communication.

3.4. Sensor Modules Integration and Prototype Wiring Architecture

To validate the proposed environmental monitoring platform under real operating conditions, a low-fidelity hardware prototype was developed and deployed directly in field monitoring locations (Figure 8). The prototype integrates sensing modules, microcontroller units, and communication interfaces while preserving sufficient hardware flexibility to support iterative system refinement and component replacement when necessary. This deployment strategy enables evaluation of signal integrity, communication reliability, and real-time data acquisition performance under actual environmental conditions while

https://doi.org/10.3390/app16073237

allowing for rapid adaptation of sensing and power management configurations based on field observations.

Figure 8 presents the detailed wiring layout of the sensing subsystem and microcontroller interconnections implemented using breadboard-based prototyping. The design enables rapid testing, modular sensor replacement, and flexible expansion of sensing capabilities.

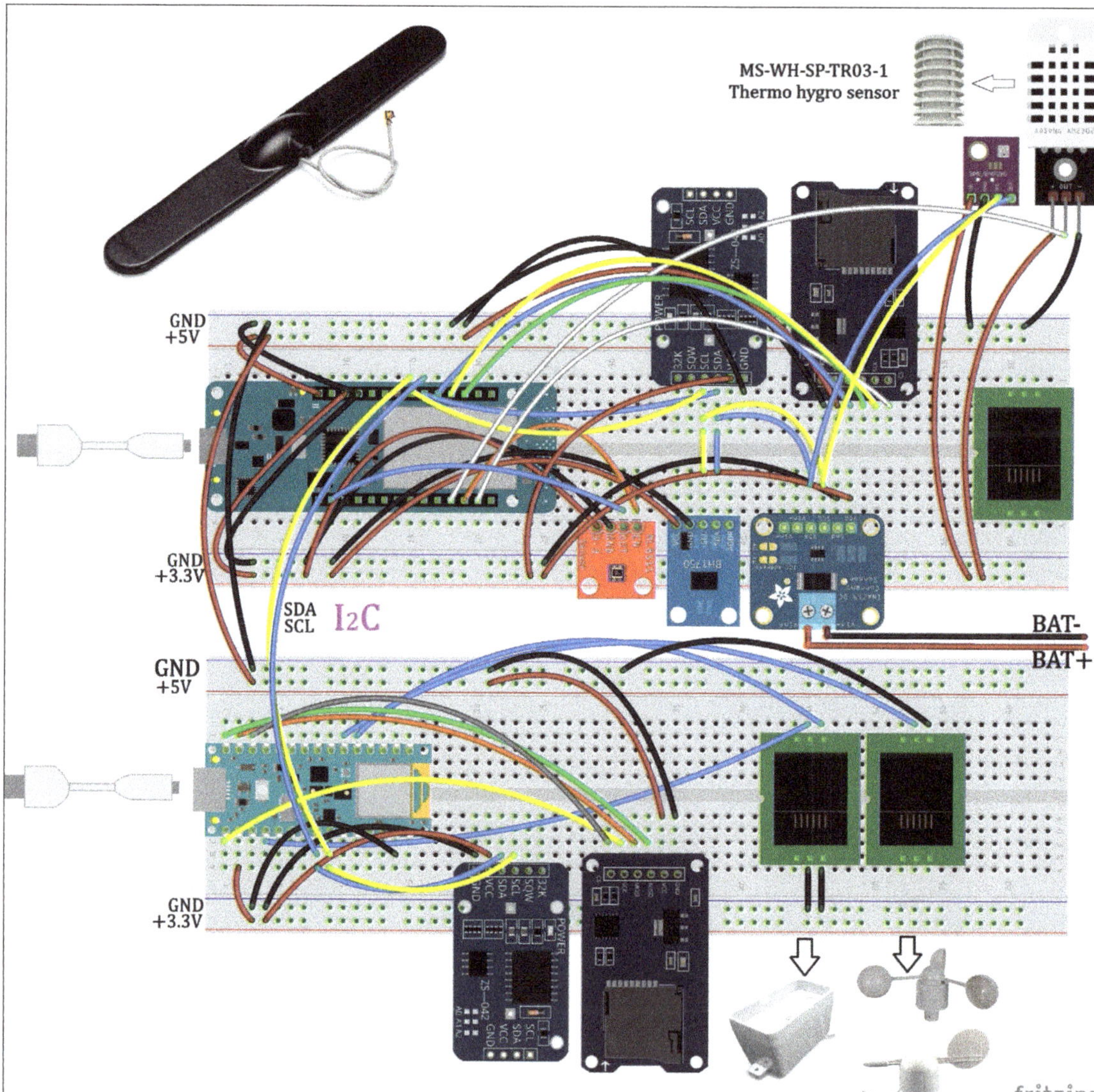

Figure 8. Low-fidelity prototype wiring architecture of the embedded processing unit. The breadboard-based implementation integrates environmental sensor modules, dual-microcontroller units, RJ11/RJ12 connectors for mechanical meteorological sensors, and USB-powered interfaces connected to the solar charge controller.

The sensing subsystem integrates multiple environmental monitoring modules, including temperature, humidity, atmospheric pressure, and inertial sensing units connected through standard digital communication interfaces such as I^2C and SPI. Additional mechanical meteorological sensors, including the anemometer, wind vane, and tipping-bucket rain gauge, are interfaced using dedicated RJ11/RJ12 connectors. These connectors provide a standardized and reliable interface between the data collector and externally mounted mechanical sensing elements. In the proposed configuration, three RJ11/RJ12 connectors are employed to support wind speed measurement, wind direction sensing, and rainfall detection.

The mechanical sensors generate pulse-based or resistive signals that are routed through the RJ connectors and processed by the Arduino Nano 33 BLE microcontroller using interrupt-driven acquisition routines. This configuration ensures accurate event counting and directional sensing while minimizing signal loss or timing inaccuracies associated with mechanical switching components.

The dual-microcontroller architecture is physically implemented on the prototype breadboard platform, where both the Arduino Nano 33 BLE and the Arduino MKR NB 1500 modules are mounted and interconnected with the sensing modules. The Nano 33 BLE performs real-time sensing and preprocessing, while the MKR NB 1500 manages NB-IoT (LTE-M) communication and cloud data transmission.

Power distribution for the microcontrollers is provided through USB interfaces connected to the solar charge controller. Two USB output ports from the charge controller are used to supply regulated power independently to each microcontroller unit. This approach simplifies power routing, enhances modularity, and supports independent debugging and firmware updates for each processing unit during development.

The breadboard-based wiring architecture provides a flexible and accessible testing platform that allows for rapid prototyping and sensor substitution without requiring printed circuit board fabrication. Although the prototype design is not optimized for long-term outdoor deployment, it enables comprehensive validation of sensing reliability, interrupt handling performance, and communication workflows prior to integration into the final weatherproof enclosure.

The modular wiring strategy also supports future system scalability, allowing additional sensing modules or custom-designed connectors to be integrated with minimal hardware modification.

3.4.1. LTE-M/Cat-M1 Communication Using Arduino MKR NB 1500

Long-range communication and cloud connectivity are implemented using the Arduino MKR NB 1500 platform, which integrates a u-blox SARA-R4 LTE modem supporting LTE-M (Cat-M1) and NB-IoT (NB1) standards. The board was selected due to its compatibility with low-power wide-area cellular communication, secure TCP/IP support, and seamless integration within Arduino-based embedded architectures.

Figure 9 presents the electrical characteristics and communication capabilities of the MKR NB 1500 module used in the proposed system.

Transmission power characteristics: the integrated u-blox SARA-R4 modem operates in 3GPP Power Class 3 with a maximum transmission power shown in Equation (1).

$$P_{TX,\max} = 23\ \text{dBm} \tag{1}$$

The equivalent linear power is presented in Equation (2).

$$P_{mW} = 10^{\frac{23}{10}} \approx 200\ \text{mW} \tag{2}$$

Unlike LoRa-based modules, transmission power in LTE-M systems is not manually configured at the application level. Instead, it is dynamically controlled by the cellu-

https://doi.org/10.3390/app16073237

lar network according to 3GPP uplink power control mechanisms. The modem adjusts its transmission power based on signal quality indicators such as RSRP and RSSI, link budget requirements, and network scheduling constraints. This adaptive behavior improves link robustness under heterogeneous rural coverage conditions while maintaining regulatory compliance.

Operating Bands

LTE's Cat M1/NB1 bands 1, 2, 3, 4, 5, 8, 12, 13, 18, 19, 20, 25, 26, 28

Power Settings

Input Voltage: 5V
Operating Voltage: 3.3V
Power Consumption:
Operating: 93mA
Low power: 30mA
DC Current per I/O pin: 3mA
LTE-M (Cat-M1): 23dBm

$$P_{mW} = 10^{\frac{P_{dBm}}{10}} = 10^{\frac{23}{10}} \approx 200\ mW$$

Battery

Minimum capacity: 700mAh
Maximum capacity: 1400mAh
Battery charging: 4h
Battery connector: JST S2B-PH-SM4-TB(LF)(SN)
Mating connector: JST PHR-2
Battery can be charged from USB

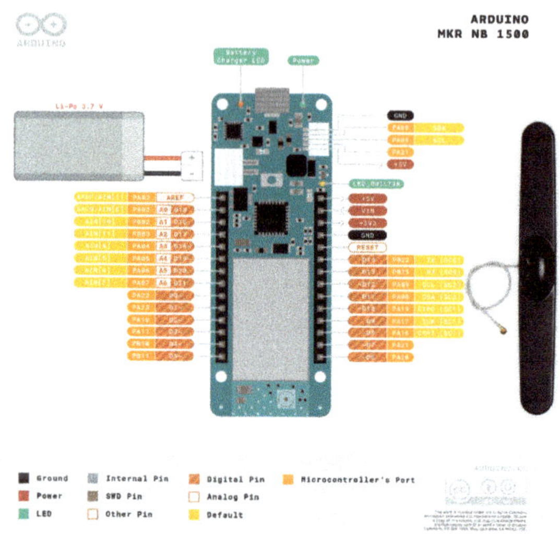

Figure 9. Arduino MKR NB 1500 platform used for LTE-M/Cat-M1 communication. The board integrates a u-blox SARA-R4 cellular modem supporting LTE Cat-M1/NB1 bands (1, 2, 3, 4, 5, 8, 12, 13, 18, 19, 20, 25, 26, 28). It operates at 3.3 V logic with 5 V input supply and supports LTE-M transmission at a maximum output power of 23 dBm (Power Class 3), corresponding to approximately 200 mW. The module supports Li-Po battery operation (700–1400 mAh typical range), USB charging, and low-power modes suitable for autonomous IoT deployments.

Electrical and Power Profile. The MKR NB 1500 operates with a 5 V input supply and 3.3 V logic levels. Typical current consumption is approximately:

- 93 mA during active communication;
- 30 mA in low-power idle mode.

However, LTE-M uplink transmission may generate short-duration current peaks exceeding 200–400 mA depending on network conditions and signal strength. These transient spikes are significantly higher than those of LoRa-based systems and must be considered during battery dimensioning and solar energy modeling (see Section 3.3).

The board supports external Li-Po batteries with recommended capacities between 700 mAh and 1400 mAh and includes integrated USB-based charging circuitry. In the proposed monitoring platform, regulated power is supplied through the solar charge controller, while long-term energy storage is provided by an external $LiFePO_4$ battery system for enhanced lifecycle stability and winter temperature resilience.

Auxiliary backup power strategy: The MKR NB 1500 platform supports direct connection of a 3.7 V Li-Po battery (700–1400 mAh range) through its integrated JST battery interface and onboard charging circuitry. In the proposed architecture, the board is primarily powered via its 5 V USB input, which is connected to the solar charge controller regulating the external 12 V $LiFePO_4$ energy storage system.

https://doi.org/10.3390/app16073237

This configuration enables the optional use of a 3.7 V, 1400 mAh Li-Po backup battery attached directly to the MKR NB 1500. The auxiliary battery provides local energy buffering during LTE-M transmission bursts, which may generate short-duration current peaks exceeding 200–400 mA. The onboard power management circuitry ensures seamless transition between USB supply and battery operation.

Such a layered power approach enhances system robustness by:

- Mitigating voltage dips during high-current cellular transmission;
- Maintaining modem operation during transient supply fluctuations;
- Enabling short-duration communication even if the primary 12 V battery is temporarily unavailable.

This auxiliary buffering strategy improves communication reliability and complements the main solar-powered $LiFePO_4$ storage system described in Section 3.3.

Communication workflow in the dual-MCU architecture: Within the proposed dual-microcontroller architecture, the MKR NB 1500 is exclusively responsible for LTE-M communication. The Arduino Nano 33 BLE performs real-time sensor acquisition and preprocessing, after which aggregated timestamped environmental measurements are transferred via I2C to the MKR NB 1500 for transmission.

Communication sessions are scheduled by the RTC module. During each transmission cycle, the modem:

- Wakes from low-power state;
- Establishes LTE-M connectivity;
- Uploads environmental data to the remote cloud platform;
- Returns to low-power mode.

This duty-cycled communication strategy minimizes active modem time, reduces average energy consumption, and supports long-term autonomous operation under solar-powered conditions.

Rationale for LTE-M selection: LTE-M was selected over alternative LPWAN technologies such as LoRa due to:

- Operation in licensed cellular spectrum;
- Higher receiver sensitivity and improved link budget;
- Native infrastructure support without private gateways;
- Bidirectional communication and QoS control;
- Seamless integration with existing cellular networks.

These characteristics are particularly advantageous in distributed agricultural deployments where reliable wide-area connectivity is required without additional gateway infrastructure. The integration of LTE-M communication within a modular solar-powered architecture enables scalable environmental monitoring while preserving energy autonomy and network robustness under variable rural coverage conditions.

3.4.2. Real-Time Clock Integration and Time-Synchronized Data Acquisition

Accurate time synchronization is essential for environmental monitoring systems that operate under low-power constraints and require periodic data acquisition and transmission. To ensure reliable timestamping and deterministic wake scheduling, the proposed platform integrates a DS3231 Real-Time Clock (RTC) module connected via the I^2C communication interface.

Figure 10 illustrates the hardware configuration and addresses the capabilities of the DS3231 RTC module used in the proposed system. The module provides stable local timekeeping with a typical drift of approximately ± 2 ppm (corresponding to approximately

https://doi.org/10.3390/app16073237

±63 s per year). While this level of accuracy is adequate for maintaining short-term sampling consistency, cumulative drift may become significant during long-term autonomous deployments, particularly in distributed multi-node monitoring scenarios where strict temporal alignment between stations is required.

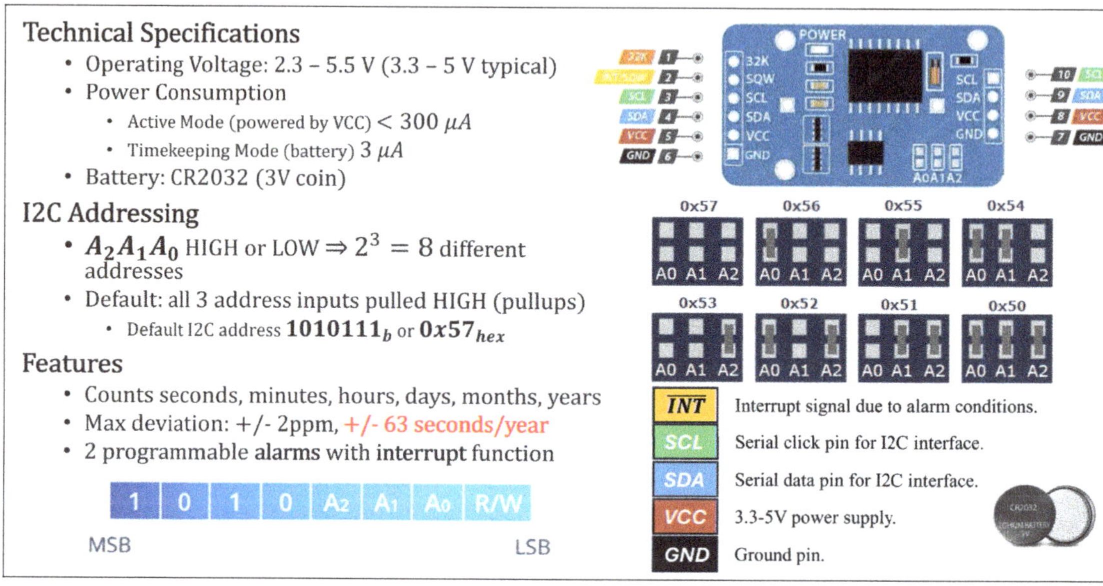

Figure 10. DS3231 real-time clock module used for time synchronization and wake scheduling. The module supports I^{2}C communication, programmable alarms, battery-backed timekeeping, and configurable addressing options.

The RTC supports programmable alarms, interrupt generation, and battery-backed timekeeping using an external CR2032 coin-cell battery, enabling continuous time tracking during power interruptions. In the proposed architecture, the DS3231 operates as the primary local timekeeper, while higher-precision long-term synchronization is achieved through periodic external calibration, as described in the following subsection.

In the proposed architecture, the RTC module is interfaced with the Arduino MKR NB 1500 and Arduino Nano 33 BLE microcontrollers through the I^{2}C bus using the default address configuration. The RTC provides precise timestamps for environmental measurements, communication scheduling, and data-logging operations. Time synchronization is initially established during device initialization, either by synchronizing the RTC with the system compilation time or by maintaining previously stored time information preserved by the RTC backup battery.

The RTC module plays a critical role in enabling energy-efficient operation by supporting deterministic wake-up scheduling. Instead of relying on internal microcontroller timers, which may accumulate drift during extended sleep intervals, the system periodically queries the RTC to determine the exact time and calculate the required sleep duration until the next acquisition interval. The monitoring platform supports configurable sampling intervals, typically ranging from one minute during testing phases to 15 min intervals during field deployment.

To ensure consistent sampling alignment, a first-boot synchronization mechanism is implemented. Upon system initialization, the device enters a synchronization phase in which data acquisition is delayed until the next scheduled interval boundary. This approach guarantees that all subsequent measurements are collected at fixed time slots,

https://doi.org/10.3390/app16073237

simplifying time-series data analysis and improving interoperability with external data processing systems.

During each wake cycle, the microcontroller retrieves the current timestamp from the RTC, performs environmental data acquisition from connected sensors, and stores the measurement results locally using an SD card storage module. When network connectivity is enabled, the timestamped measurements are transmitted to a remote cloud server using NB-IoT (LTE-M) communication. After completing data acquisition and transmission tasks, the system enters a low-power sleep mode until the next scheduled acquisition interval determined by the RTC.

The integration of the RTC module ensures reliable long-term timekeeping, enables deterministic sampling intervals, and supports aggressive power-saving strategies. This time-synchronized operation is essential for maintaining data consistency across distributed monitoring stations and for enabling future deployment of edge intelligence algorithms that rely on temporally aligned environmental datasets.

3.4.3. Atomic Time Synchronization Using DCF77 Radio Clock

In deployments using LTE-M/NB-IoT communication, accurate time synchronization can be obtained directly from the cellular network using mechanisms such as Network Identity and Time Zone (NITZ) or network time protocols. In such cases, the monitoring platform periodically synchronizes its internal clock with the network-provided time reference.

However, the proposed monitoring system was intentionally designed to support multiple communication technologies, including LTE-M/NB-IoT, LoRaWAN, and WiFi. In non-cellular deployments, particularly when using LoRaWAN networks or operating in offline environments, reliable network-based time synchronization may not always be available. For this reason, the platform incorporates a DS3231 real-time clock (RTC) module that provides stable local timekeeping independent of network connectivity.

Although the DS3231 RTC module provides stable local timekeeping, cumulative drift may occur during long-term autonomous deployments, potentially reaching approximately ± 63 s per year. For distributed environmental monitoring platforms that rely on synchronized multi-station datasets, long-term timing drift can introduce temporal inconsistencies in recorded environmental parameters. To address this limitation, the proposed monitoring platform integrates an external atomic time synchronization mechanism based on the DCF77 radio time signal.

The DCF77 system is a longwave radio time transmission service operating at 77.5 kHz and broadcast from Germany. The signal is derived from atomic clock references and provides highly accurate time synchronization across large geographical areas of Europe. The DCF77 receiver module periodically decodes amplitude-modulated time signals, enabling the monitoring platform to obtain absolute time references independent of local oscillator drift.

Figure 11 illustrates the integration of the DCF77 atomic clock receiver with the Arduino microcontroller and the DS3231 RTC module. The DCF77 receiver is connected using a dedicated digital input line that captures pulse-width encoded time information transmitted by the radio signal. Arduino processes the received time frame, validates signal integrity, and updates the RTC module when synchronization criteria are satisfied.

In the proposed architecture, the RTC module serves as the primary local timekeeping unit, while the DCF77 receiver operates as a periodic calibration source. This hierarchical time synchronization strategy minimizes energy consumption by avoiding continuous radio signal decoding, which can be power-intensive. Instead, DCF77 synchronization is performed at configurable intervals or during system initialization phases to correct accumulated RTC drift.

https://doi.org/10.3390/app16073237

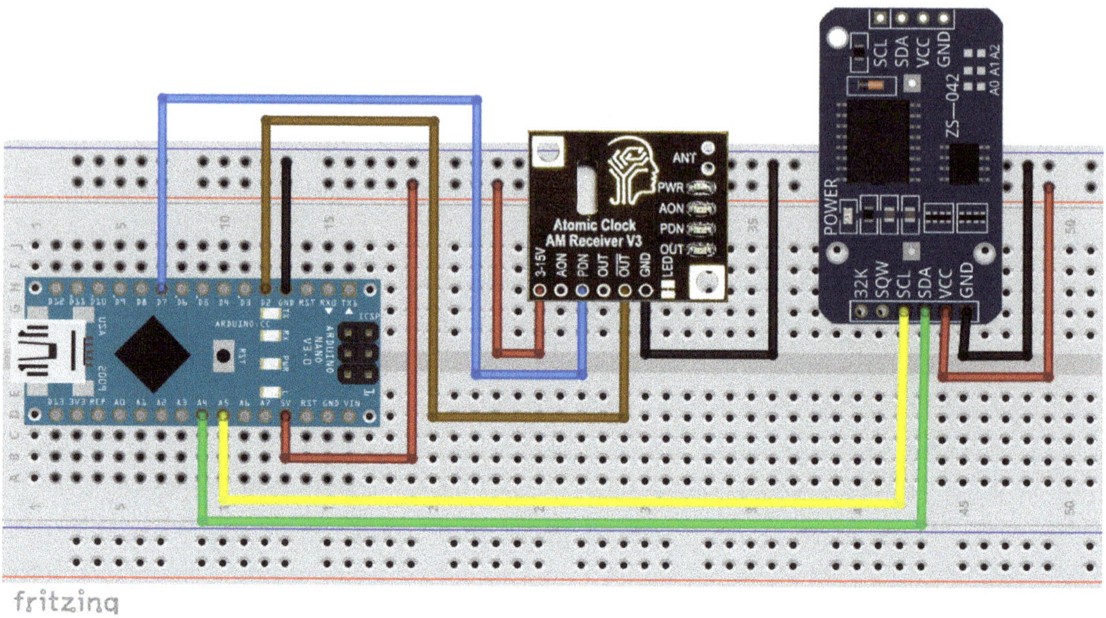

Figure 11. Integration of the DCF77 atomic clock receiver with the Arduino microcontroller and DS3231 RTC module. The DCF77 receiver provides periodic atomic time synchronization, while the RTC module maintains continuous local timekeeping for low-power operation.

Upon successful decoding of a valid DCF77 time frame, the microcontroller compares the received atomic reference time with the current RTC timestamp. If the time deviation exceeds a predefined correction threshold, the RTC is adjusted to the corrected atomic time reference. This approach ensures long-term temporal stability while preserving the low-power operational characteristics of the monitoring platform.

The combined use of RTC-based local timekeeping and periodic atomic synchronization enables the monitoring system to maintain accurate timestamping over extended deployment durations. This capability is particularly important for applications requiring high temporal alignment, such as multi-node environmental sensing, renewable energy resource analysis, and time-series machine learning model training.

The combined use of RTC-based local timekeeping and optional atomic synchronization enables the monitoring system to maintain accurate timestamping across a wide range of deployment scenarios. When cellular connectivity is available, time synchronization can be obtained directly from the LTE-M/NB-IoT network. In deployments using LoRaWAN or other non-cellular communication technologies, the RTC provides continuous timekeeping, while periodic DCF77 synchronization can correct long-term drift. This multi-layer time synchronization strategy increases the robustness and flexibility of the monitoring platform while supporting heterogeneous communication infrastructures.

3.4.4. Temperature and Humidity Sensing: DHT22 Selection Rationale

Accurate temperature and relative humidity measurements are essential for long-term environmental monitoring, microclimate analysis, and energy-aware agricultural management. Sensor precision directly impacts downstream analytics, including anomaly detection, crop stress modeling, and predictive environmental forecasting. In the proposed sensing architecture, the DHT22 digital temperature and humidity sensor was selected instead of the lower-cost DHT11 due to its extended measurement range, improved accuracy,

https://doi.org/10.3390/app16073237

higher resolution, and enhanced long-term stability, making it more suitable for outdoor autonomous deployments.

Figure 12 presents the pin configuration of both DHT11 and DHT22 sensors. Both devices share an identical four-pin layout (VCC, DATA, NC, GND) and operate using a single-wire digital communication protocol that transmits 40-bit data frames containing temperature and humidity information. This electrical and protocol compatibility enables seamless hardware replacement without requiring modifications to the microcontroller firmware logic. Consequently, system scalability and sensor upgrades can be implemented with minimal architectural impact.

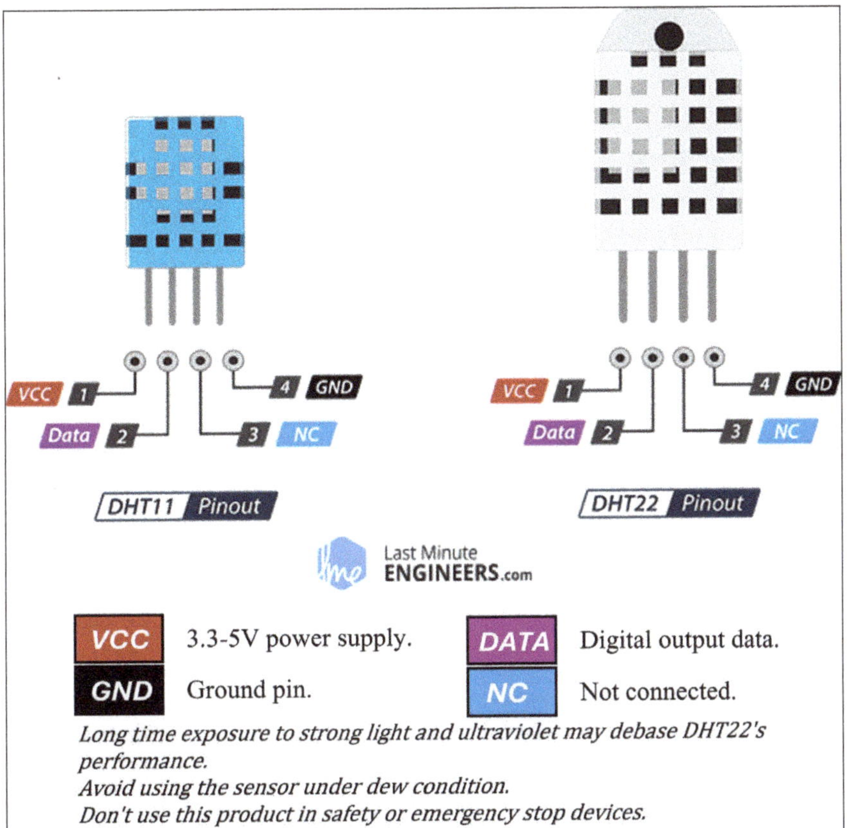

Figure 12. Pin configuration of DHT11 and DHT22 sensors. Both sensors share identical pin assignments and single-wire digital communication interfaces, enabling straightforward replacement at hardware level (figures adapted from lastminuteengineers.com).

The quantitative performance differences between the two sensors are summarized in Figure 13. The DHT22 provides a significantly extended temperature measurement range of −40–80 °C compared to 0–50 °C for the DHT11, which is critical for year-round outdoor agricultural deployments where winter sub-zero conditions and summer heat extremes may occur. Similarly, the humidity measurement range is expanded to 0–100% RH versus 20–90% RH, allowing for reliable operation in highly humid or near-saturation environments such as greenhouses or early-morning field conditions.

https://doi.org/10.3390/app16073237

Icon	Attribute	DHT11	DHT22
	Temperature Range	0°C to +50°C	-40°C to +80°C
	Temperature Accuracy	±1°C *(0°C)* ±2°C *(50°C)*	< ± 0.5°C
	Temperature Resolution	1°C	0.1°C
	Humidity Range	20% RH to 90% RH	0% RH to 100% RH *(-40°C to 80°C)*
	Humidity Accuracy	± 4% *(25°C)* ±5% *(0°C to 50°C)*	±2% to ±5% *(25°C)* ±5%C *(0°C to 50°C)*
	Humidity Resolution	1% RH	0.1% RH
	Voltage Range	3.0V – 5.5V	3.3V – 6.0V
	Current Consumption	0.5mA – 2.5mA *(measuring)* 0.1mA – 0.15mA *(standby)*	1mA – 1.5mA *(measuring)* 0.04mA – 0.05mA *(standby)*
	Long Term Stability	±1% RH/year	±0.5% RH/year
	Sensing Period	~4ms	~5ms
	Collection/Sensing Period	>6s	>2s
	Price	**1-2 €**	**5-10 €**

Figure 13. Technical comparison between the DHT11 and DHT22 temperature and humidity sensors. The figure summarizes key specifications including measurement range, accuracy, resolution, operating voltage, current consumption, long-term stability, sensing interval, and cost. The comparison highlights the improved accuracy, wider humidity range, finer resolution, and better long-term stability of the DHT22, justifying its selection for the proposed environmental monitoring platform.

Accuracy improvements are also substantial: the DHT22 specifies ±0.5 °C temperature accuracy and approximately ±2% RH humidity accuracy under nominal conditions, compared to ±1 °C and ±4% RH for the DHT11. Reduced measurement uncertainty directly enhances the reliability of long-term time-series datasets and improves the robustness of machine learning models trained on environmental variables.

Resolution differences further justify the selection. The DHT22 provides 0.1 °C and 0.1% RH resolution, whereas the DHT11 is limited to 1 °C and 1% RH increments. Higher resolution reduces quantization artifacts, improves sensitivity to subtle environmental fluctuations, and enables more precise detection of microclimate variations.

Long-term stability characteristics also favor the DHT22, which exhibits lower annual humidity drift compared to the DHT11 (see Figure 13). Improved stability reduces recalibration frequency and supports long-duration autonomous deployments powered by renewable energy sources, aligning with the design goals of the proposed monitoring platform.

Figure 14 illustrates the actual wiring configuration implemented in the hardware prototype. The DHT22 module is powered directly from the 3.3 V rail of the Arduino Nano 33 BLE, ensuring full logic-level compatibility without additional voltage regulation. The DATA pin is connected to a dedicated GPIO pin (D2 in the current implementation), configured for bidirectional communication according to the DHT timing protocol.

The wiring configuration shown in Figure 14 corresponds to the deployed field prototype used for validation. A pull-up resistor on the DATA line (integrated within the DHT22 module variant used in this study) ensures signal stability and reliable digital communication over short interconnection distances. The minimal three-wire interface reduces parasitic effects, simplifies sensor replacement, and supports the modular design philosophy of the overall monitoring platform.

https://doi.org/10.3390/app16073237

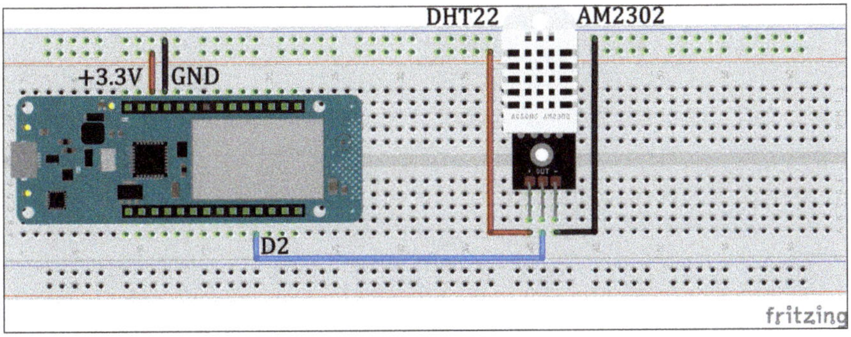

Figure 14. Breadboard implementation of the DHT22 sensor within the hardware prototype (designed with Fritzing). The sensor is powered from the 3.3 V rail, and the digital DATA line is connected to GPIO pin D2 of the Arduino Nano 33 BLE. The wiring shown corresponds to the actual configuration used during system validation.

Although the DHT22 has a slightly longer minimum sampling interval (>2 s) than the DHT11 (1 s), this limitation is irrelevant within the proposed architecture, where acquisition intervals are scheduled in the order of minutes. The improved performance characteristics justify the marginal increase in cost and make the DHT22 more suitable for long-term outdoor environmental deployments.

3.4.5. Atmospheric Pressure Sensing: Selection of the BMP280 Module

Accurate atmospheric pressure measurement is essential for altitude estimation, weather trend analysis, and environmental modeling in distributed monitoring systems. In the proposed architecture, the BMP280 digital barometric pressure sensor was selected instead of the earlier BMP180 due to its improved accuracy, higher resolution, and enhanced temperature compensation performance.

Figure 15 presents the pin configuration of both BMP180 and BMP280 modules. Both sensors support I^{2}C communication via SDA and SCL lines, enabling integration within the shared I^{2}C bus of the sensing subsystem. The BMP280 additionally supports configurable I^{2}C addresses (0×76 or 0×77), allowing for flexible bus configuration in multi-sensor environments.

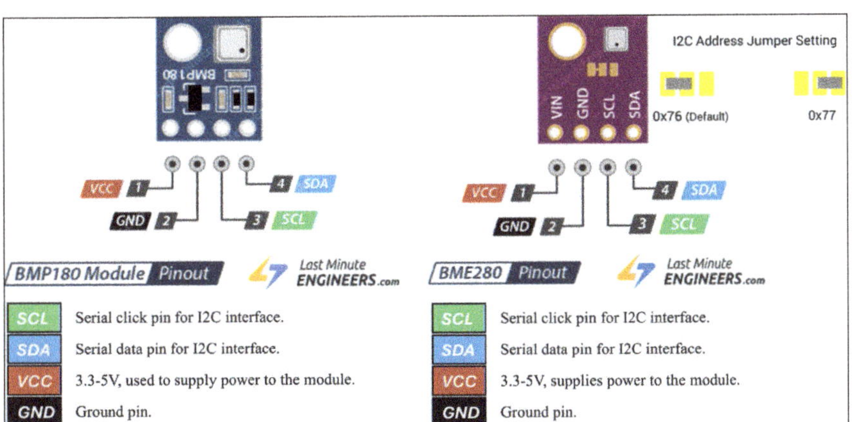

Figure 15. Pin configuration of BMP180 and BMP280 pressure sensor modules. Both devices support I^{2}C communication and operate at low voltage levels compatible with embedded microcontroller platforms (figures adapted from lastminuteengineers.com).

Figure 16 provides a detailed performance comparison between BMP180 and BMP280 sensors. Although both modules operate within the same pressure range (300–1100 hPa), the BMP280 offers improved absolute pressure accuracy (±1 hPa) compared to the BMP180 (±2 hPa). This improvement is significant for altitude estimation and atmospheric-trend-monitoring applications.

Although the BMP180 supports ultra-high-resolution oversampling modes capable of achieving internal pressure resolution on the order of 0.01 hPa, its absolute pressure accuracy remains ±2 hPa. In contrast, the BMP280 provides improved absolute accuracy (±1 hPa) and enhanced temperature compensation stability. For long-term environmental monitoring, absolute accuracy and thermal stability are more critical than raw digital resolution, particularly when evaluating atmospheric trends over extended periods.

Icon	Attribute	BMP 180	BMP 280
	Pressure Range	300 – 1100 hPa	300 – 1100 hPa *(-500 to +9000 m)*
	Pressure Relative Accuracy	±0.12 hPa (±1 m) *(950 – 1050 hPa @25°C-40°C)*	±0.12 hPa (±1 m) *(700 – 900 hPa @ 25°C-40°C)*
	Pressure Absolute Accuracy	± 2.0 hPa (± 4.5 hPa) *(300 – 1100 hPa @0°C-65°C)*	±1 hPa *(950– 1050 hPa @ 0°C-40°C)*
	Pressure Resolution	1.0 (0.01) hPa	0.16 hPa
	Temperature Range	-40°C to +85°C	-40°C to +85°C
	Temperature Accuracy	±1°C *(0 to 65°C)* ±1.5°C *(-40°C to 0°C)*	±0.5°C *(@ 25°C)* ±1°C *(0°C to 65°C)*
	Temperature Resolution	0.1°C	0.01°C
	Voltage Range	**3.3V – 5.5V**	**1.7V – 3.6V**
	Current Consumption	**0.6 mA**	**0.7-1.1 mA**
	Long Term Stability	±1 hPa/year	±1 hPa/year
	Price	**1-2 €**	**2-7 €**

The temperature measurement is used internally to calibrate the pressure and humidity sensors.
The maximum measurable humidity decreases at extremely high and low temperatures.

Figure 16. Performance comparison between BMP180 and BMP280 barometric pressure sensors, including pressure accuracy, resolution, temperature performance, voltage range, current consumption, and long-term stability. The improved resolution and accuracy of the BMP280 motivate its selection for the proposed monitoring platform.

Furthermore, effective measurement performance is influenced not only by digital resolution but also by noise characteristics and temperature-dependent compensation algorithms. The BMP280 incorporates improved internal filtering and calibration mechanisms, resulting in more stable pressure readings under varying environmental conditions.

Temperature measurement performance is also superior in the BMP280, providing improved accuracy and finer resolution. Since internal temperature compensation directly affects pressure calculation stability, enhanced temperature precision contributes to more reliable pressure readings under varying environmental conditions.

Although the BMP280 exhibits slightly higher active current consumption compared to the BMP180, the difference remains negligible within the overall energy budget of the solar-powered monitoring platform.

In addition to pressure measurement, the BMP280 integrates an internal temperature sensor used primarily for pressure compensation. While the device provides temperature readings with typical accuracy of approximately ±0.5 °C (at 25 °C), its primary design

https://doi.org/10.3390/app16073237

objective is barometric sensing rather than ambient temperature monitoring. In comparison, the DHT22 sensor employed in the sensing subsystem provides calibrated temperature and humidity measurements with comparable or superior temperature stability across the environmental range of interest.

Within the proposed architecture, temperature data from the DHT22 is therefore considered the primary ambient temperature reference, while the BMP280 temperature output is used for internal compensation and redundancy verification. This multi-sensor approach enhances robustness and enables cross-validation between independent sensing elements.

3.5. Wind Direction and Wind Speed Sensing Methodology

Wind measurements in the proposed platform are performed using the WH-SP-WD wind vane and the WH-SP-WS01 anemometer, which operate on complementary mechanical and electrical principles. Both sensors are physically mounted on the same mechanical assembly and electrically interconnected through a shared RJ11/RJ12 cable interface.

3.5.1. Wind Vane Operation Principle

The WH-SP-WD wind direction sensor operates using a mechanical magnet-based switching mechanism. Internally, the device contains eight reed switches, each connected to a resistor with a distinct resistance value. As the wind vane rotates, an embedded magnet activates one or two reed switches depending on the blade position. This design allows up to 16 discrete angular positions to be detected, corresponding to the principal and intermediate compass directions.

Each angular position produces a specific equivalent resistance value. When combined with an external fixed resistor (10 kΩ in the reference configuration), the wind vane forms a voltage divider circuit. The resulting output voltage is proportional to the selected resistance and can be measured using an analog-to-digital converter (ADC). In the proposed implementation, the analog output of the wind vane is directly connected to an analog input pin of the Arduino Nano 33 BLE, which samples the voltage and maps it to the corresponding wind direction angle.

Figure 17 illustrates the directional mapping and RJ11 routing configuration used in the sensor assembly. The diagram highlights the discrete directional sectors and the shared cable architecture.

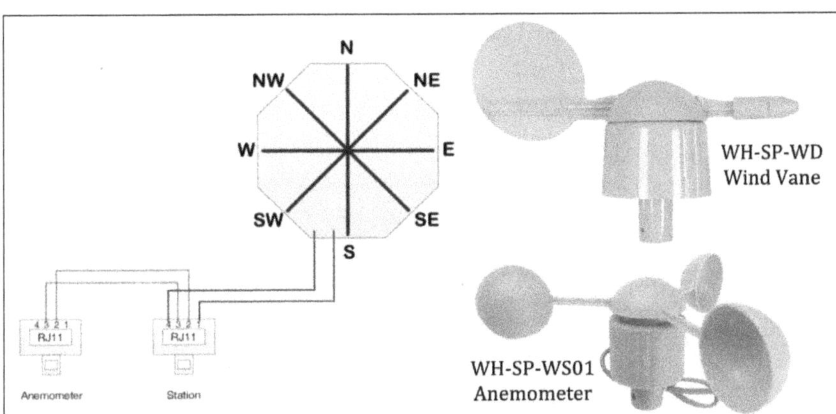

Figure 17. Wind vane directional sectors and RJ11 routing configuration. The sensor contains eight magnetically actuated switches connected to distinct resistors, allowing for discrete angular detection through resistance-based voltage division. The anemometer signal is routed through the wind vane assembly via the same cable interface.

https://doi.org/10.3390/app16073237

3.5.2. Anemometer Pulse-Based Measurement

The WH-SP-WS01 anemometer measures wind speed using a mechanical cup assembly coupled with a magnetic reed switch. Each full or partial rotation of the cup mechanism generates a pulse as the magnet passes the reed contact. The pulse frequency is directly proportional to wind speed.

The anemometer is electrically integrated into the wind vane module through a specially fitted connector. The RJ11/RJ12 cable connecting the wind vane to the embedded processing unit carries both:

- The analog wind direction signal (resistive voltage divider output);
- The digital pulse signal generated by the anemometer.

In the proposed hardware configuration, only the two central conductors of the RJ11/RJ12 cable are used for the anemometer signal, while the remaining conductors serve the wind vane resistive network. The anemometer pulse line is connected to a digital interrupt-capable input of the Arduino Nano 33 BLE. Interrupt-driven counting ensures that high-frequency pulse events are captured accurately without polling overhead.

Wind speed is calculated by counting pulse transitions over a predefined time interval and applying the manufacturer-provided conversion factor between pulse frequency and linear wind velocity. This interrupt-based acquisition approach ensures reliable measurement even under rapidly changing wind conditions.

3.5.3. Integrated Signal Acquisition Strategy

The combined routing of wind direction and wind speed through a single cable simplifies mechanical assembly and reduces wiring complexity on the supporting pillar. At the embedded processing layer, the Arduino Nano 33 BLE performs simultaneous analog sampling (for wind direction) and interrupt-driven pulse counting (for wind speed).

This dual-acquisition strategy enables:

- Real-time wind direction estimation via ADC conversion and lookup mapping;
- Precise wind speed measurement through edge-triggered pulse counting;
- Minimal power consumption by avoiding continuous polling;
- Scalable integration within the broader TinyML-enabled edge processing framework.

The separation of mechanical sensing from embedded electronics, combined with interrupt-driven acquisition, enhances reliability, reduces signal noise, and ensures stable long-term operation under outdoor environmental conditions.

3.6. Rain Gauge Wiring and Measurement Configuration

Precipitation measurement is performed using the WH-SP-RG tipping-bucket rain gauge. The sensor operates on a self-emptying mechanical principle in which collected rainwater fills one side of a calibrated bucket. When a predefined volume threshold is reached, the bucket tips, empties, and simultaneously actuates an internal magnetic reed switch. This event generates a short-duration electrical pulse corresponding to a fixed rainfall increment.

As illustrated in Figure 18, the rain gauge provides a pulse-based output via an RJ11 connector. The internal reed switch is connected to the two middle pins of the RJ11 plug, forming a normally-open contact. When the bucket tips, the contact momentarily closes, generating a digital pulse detectable by a microcontroller.

In the proposed architecture, the two central conductors of the RJ11 cable are connected to an interrupt-capable digital input pin of the Arduino Nano 33 BLE. One conductor is referenced to ground, while the second is connected to the input configured with an internal pull-up resistor. Under idle conditions, the input remains in a logic HIGH state.

During a tipping event, the reed switch closes and pulls the line to ground, producing a falling-edge interrupt.

Manufacturer's marking	MS-WH-SP-RG
Jack	RJ11
Material	Plastic
Color	light gray
Output	Pulse
Sensor type	Rainfall

Figure 18. WH-SP-RG tipping-bucket rain gauge used in the proposed environmental monitoring platform. The device provides a reed–switch pulse output through an RJ11 connector, where each tipping event corresponds to approximately 0.2794 mm of accumulated rainfall.

This interrupt-driven configuration enables accurate pulse detection without continuous polling, reducing computational load and minimizing energy consumption in the solar-powered system.

3.7. Inter-Microcontroller Communication via I²C

Communication between the sensing microcontroller and the communication microcontroller is implemented using the Inter-Integrated Circuit (I^2C) protocol. In the proposed architecture, the Arduino MKR NB 1500 operates as the I^2C master responsible for requesting sensor data, while the Arduino Nano 33 BLE operates as an I^2C slave device responsible for aggregating measurements from mechanical sensors such as the anemometer and tipping-bucket rain gauge.

The sensing MCU exposes a structured data packet through the I^2C interface at slave address `0x08`. During each data acquisition cycle, the communication MCU performs a request operation to retrieve the latest aggregated sensor measurements. This approach allows the sensing MCU to continuously process interrupt-driven events from the wind and rainfall sensors while the communication MCU focuses on network connectivity and data transmission tasks.

The data exchanged between the two microcontrollers is organized as a fixed-size packed structure containing wind speed, accumulated rainfall, wind direction, and status flags. Using a fixed-size data structure simplifies the communication protocol and reduces overhead, allowing the master MCU to retrieve all relevant sensor information in a single I^2C transaction.

To improve communication robustness in outdoor deployments, the I^2C bus operates at a conservative clock frequency of 100 kHz using the standard Arduino `Wire` library. The receiving MCU verifies that the number of bytes received matches the expected structure size before accepting the data. If a mismatch occurs, the packet is discarded and the I^2C bus is reset before the next acquisition cycle. Additional range validation checks are applied to sensor values in order to detect potentially corrupted measurements.

To further improve robustness, basic range validation checks are applied to the received measurements before they are accepted by the communication MCU. These checks ensure that the values fall within physically plausible limits for the monitored environmental parameters. Measurements outside these bounds may indicate communication corruption, partial packet transmission, or sensor malfunction and are therefore flagged as invalid.

https://doi.org/10.3390/app16073237

Table 1 summarizes the validation thresholds applied to the wind and rainfall measurements received from the sensing MCU.

Table 1. Range validation thresholds applied to I^2C sensor data received from the sensing MCU. Values outside these limits are considered potentially corrupted and are flagged for rejection or further validation.

Parameter	Valid Range	Unit	Rationale
Wind speed	0–100	m/s	The upper bound exceeds realistic extreme wind conditions and is used to detect corrupted or misaligned values.
Rainfall accumulation	0–1000	mm	The threshold prevents overflow effects and rejects implausible accumulated rainfall values.
Wind direction	0–360	degrees	The limits reflect the physical measurement domain of wind direction sensors.

From a hardware perspective, the I^2C bus operates over short internal connections within the sealed enclosure, typically shorter than 10 cm. This minimizes susceptibility to electromagnetic interference and ensures reliable signal integrity. Furthermore, the firmware performs periodic I^2C bus reinitialization after deep sleep cycles to prevent potential bus lock conditions.

Figure 19 illustrates the physical connection between the two microcontrollers, highlighting the SDA and SCL lines used for data exchange.

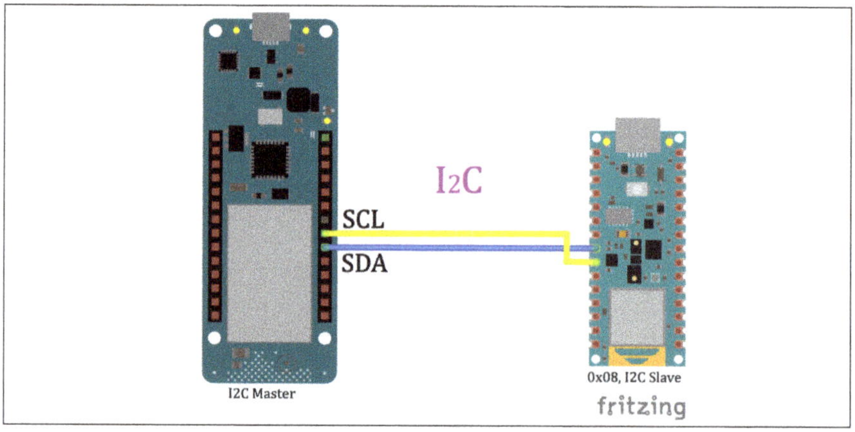

Figure 19. I^2C communication architecture between the Arduino MKR NB 1500 (master) and the Arduino Nano 33 BLE (slave at address `0x08`). The master MCU periodically requests aggregated wind and rainfall measurements through the SDA and SCL lines, allowing the sensing MCU to remain dedicated to interrupt-driven sensor acquisition.

Rainfall Computation Model

Each tipping event corresponds to approximately 0.2794 mm of precipitation according to the manufacturer specification. Let N denote the number of detected pulses within a measurement interval. The accumulated rainfall R (in millimeters) is computed as follows:

$$R = N \times 0.2794\ \text{mm} \tag{3}$$

https://doi.org/10.3390/app16073237

Rainfall intensity (mm/h) is estimated by counting pulses within a defined temporal window and extrapolating to an hourly rate. Cumulative precipitation is obtained by summing incremental measurements over longer observation periods.

The simplicity of the reed–switch pulse interface enhances robustness and long-term reliability under outdoor conditions. Since the output is purely digital, no analog calibration or signal conditioning circuitry is required, making the sensor particularly suitable for low-power IoT deployments.

3.8. Communication Security Considerations

The current prototype focuses on validating sensing reliability, communication robustness, and system power management in real-world deployments. For simplicity during early-stage experimentation, sensor data is transmitted using HTTP over port 80. This lightweight implementation facilitates rapid system debugging and integration during prototype development.

For production-grade deployments, secure communication mechanisms are planned for future system revisions. In particular, HTTPS-based communication over port 443 using TLS encryption will be adopted to ensure the confidentiality and integrity of transmitted data. Additionally, future platform iterations will consider secure firmware management mechanisms, including authenticated over-the-air (OTA) update capabilities, to allow for remote patching of firmware vulnerabilities and long-term maintenance of deployed devices.

3.9. Scalability Considerations for Large-Scale Deployments

The current cloud implementation employs a lightweight PHP–MySQL backend deployed on shared hosting infrastructure. This configuration was intentionally selected to support rapid prototyping, simple deployment, and early-stage validation of the sensing platform during experimental field trials.

For large-scale agricultural monitoring networks involving hundreds or thousands of distributed sensing nodes, more scalable cloud architectures would be required. In such scenarios, message-oriented communication protocols such as MQTT could be adopted to efficiently manage high-frequency sensor streams and device messaging. Similarly, scalable storage solutions including NoSQL or time-series databases (e.g., InfluxDB or TimescaleDB) could replace the traditional relational database layer in order to handle large volumes of time-series environmental data.

Because the proposed environmental monitoring platform separates sensing, communication, and cloud processing layers, the backend infrastructure can be upgraded without requiring modifications to the embedded hardware architecture. This design choice enables the system to evolve from a prototype deployment to a large-scale agricultural sensing network while maintaining compatibility with existing sensing devices.

3.10. Sensor Calibration and Pressure Reference

The environmental sensors used in the proposed monitoring platform were operated using their factory calibration parameters provided by the manufacturer. No additional on-site calibration procedure was performed during the experimental deployments. This design choice reflects the intended use of the platform as a low-cost environmental monitoring solution where sensors are typically deployed in distributed field locations without access to laboratory calibration equipment.

The temperature and humidity measurements were obtained using the DHT22 sensor, which provides a specified accuracy of approximately ±0.5 °C for temperature and ±2–5% for relative humidity depending on environmental conditions. During the experimental comparison with the regional meteorological station, the observed average differences of

https://doi.org/10.3390/app16073237

−0.71 °C for temperature and +4.98% for humidity fall within the expected accuracy range of the sensor and are therefore considered consistent with manufacturer specifications. Additionally, the local sensor was positioned at approximately 2 m above ground level within a residential environment, while the regional weather station measurements are typically obtained in standardized meteorological locations at greater heights and open terrain. These differences may introduce additional microclimate variations.

Atmospheric pressure measurements were obtained using the BMP280 barometric pressure sensor. The sensor reports local station pressure, whereas regional meteorological stations commonly publish pressure values normalized to mean sea-level pressure. The observed pressure offset of approximately −9.58 hPa between the monitoring node and the regional weather station is therefore primarily attributed to altitude differences between the two measurement locations.

In the current prototype implementation, no altitude-based pressure normalization was applied. The system records the raw station pressure values measured by the BMP280 sensor. Future versions of the platform may incorporate altitude-based pressure correction using the barometric formula in order to allow for direct comparison with sea-level pressure values reported by regional meteorological stations.

3.11. Power Management Module

3.11.1. High-Level Design

Long-term autonomous operation represents a critical requirement for distributed environmental monitoring systems deployed in rural or remote locations. To support energy-independent operation, the proposed monitoring platform integrates a solar-powered energy-harvesting subsystem combined with battery-based energy storage and charge management circuitry.

The power management architecture of the proposed system is illustrated in Figure 20. The subsystem consists of a photovoltaic solar panel, a solar charge controller, and a rechargeable lithium iron phosphate ($LiFePO_4$) battery. The solar panel, with selectable power ratings of 10 W, 20 W, or 30 W depending on deployment conditions, converts solar radiation into electrical energy. The generated energy is regulated by a 20 A solar charge controller responsible for managing battery charging cycles, preventing overcharging and deep discharge conditions, and stabilizing power delivery to the sensing and communication modules.

Energy storage is provided by a 12 V $LiFePO_4$ battery with a nominal capacity of 7.s Ah. $LiFePO_4$ battery technology was selected due to its improved thermal stability, extended lifecycle, and enhanced safety compared to conventional lithium-ion battery technologies. The battery supplies regulated power to both the Arduino Nano 33 BLE sensing module and the Arduino MKR NB 1500 communication module via USB, ensuring continuous system operation during low solar irradiance periods and night-time conditions.

The power management design prioritizes energy efficiency by enabling low-power operation modes in both microcontroller modules and optimizing data transmission intervals. This approach reduces overall system power consumption while maintaining reliable environmental data acquisition and communication performance. The modular design of the energy subsystem also allows for adaptation of solar panel capacity and battery size depending on geographical deployment conditions and seasonal solar radiation availability.

The implemented power management architecture enables long-term autonomous deployment of the environmental monitoring platform while supporting scalable sensing and communication requirements in distributed agricultural and environmental monitoring scenarios.

https://doi.org/10.3390/app16073237

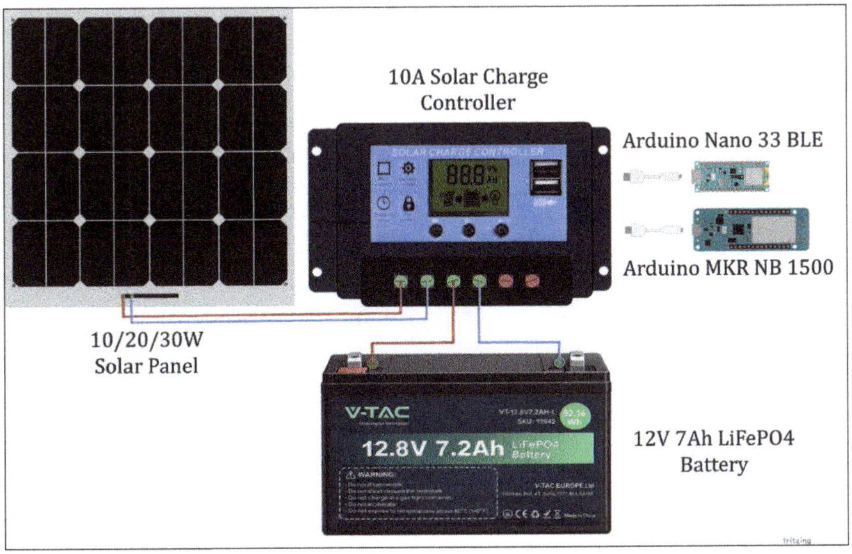

Figure 20. Power management architecture of the proposed monitoring platform. The subsystem integrates a photovoltaic solar panel, charge controller, and $LiFePO_4$ battery to provide autonomous energy supply for sensing and NB-IoT communication modules.

3.11.2. Winter Energy Risk Analysis and Battery Dimensioning

Although the selected $LiFePO_4$ battery capacity may appear oversized relative to the average system power consumption, energy storage sizing is primarily influenced by worst-case seasonal operating conditions. In temperate continental climates like Romania, winter operation introduces significant risks related to reduced solar irradiance and sub-zero ambient temperatures, which may affect both solar energy harvesting and battery-charging performance.

To evaluate these risks, a machine-learning-based temperature prediction model was developed using historical meteorological data for the deployment region. The model estimates hourly ambient temperature trends during winter months, allowing for the identification of prolonged freezing periods that may impact system energy availability.

Figure 21 presents the predicted hourly temperature evolution during the winter period between December and February for one of the monitoring locations. The shaded red regions indicate periods where the ambient temperature drops below 0 °C. During these intervals, $LiFePO_4$ batteries may experience reduced charging efficiency or charging restrictions due to internal battery protection mechanisms designed to prevent degradation and ensure safe operation.

Extended freezing periods may coincide with reduced solar radiation levels, particularly during overcast weather, snow accumulation on photovoltaic panels, or short daylight intervals typical for winter months. Snow and frost formation may partially or completely obstruct solar panel surfaces, further reducing energy-harvesting efficiency. These combined environmental factors increase the probability of prolonged low-energy input conditions. Consequently, sufficient battery capacity is required to maintain uninterrupted system operation during these periods of limited solar energy availability.

It should be noted that the internal temperature within the device enclosure may remain slightly higher than the external ambient temperature due to thermal insulation and heat generated by electronic components. Additionally, advanced battery management strategies, such as temperature-controlled charging protection or low-temperature battery heaters, may further mitigate cold-weather charging limitations.

https://doi.org/10.3390/app16073237

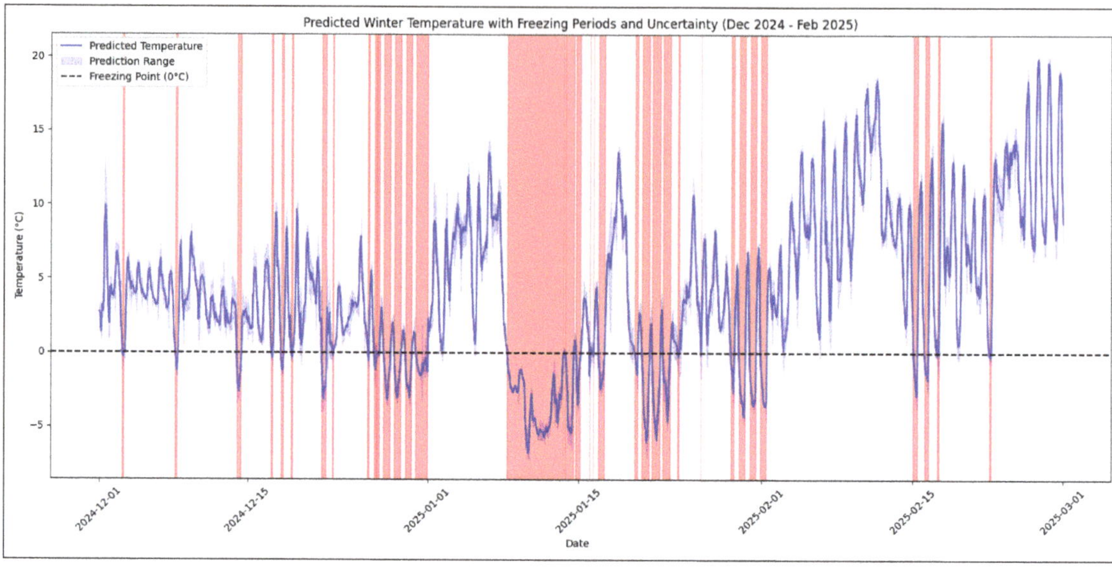

Figure 21. Machine-learning-based hourly winter temperature prediction for one deployment location between December 2024 and February 2025. The blue curve represents predicted hourly temperature, while shaded red regions indicate sub-zero temperature intervals where battery charging efficiency may be reduced or temporarily disable due to battery protection constraints.

In addition to temperature-related charging limitations, solar radiation availability during winter months was also evaluated to assess seasonal energy harvesting constraints. Historical solar radiation data and predictive modeling were used to estimate hourly solar irradiance levels during winter deployment periods.

Figure 22 illustrates the predicted hourly solar radiation levels between December 2025 and March 2026 during daylight hours (06:00–18:00). The dashed line represents the median solar radiation level across the analyzed period. The results indicate significant variability in solar irradiance, with extended intervals characterized by low radiation levels caused by overcast weather conditions, reduced solar elevation angles, and shorter daylight durations typical for winter months.

The analysis demonstrates that solar energy harvesting during winter may be highly intermittent and insufficient to fully sustain continuous system operation without adequate energy storage capacity. These findings further justify the selection of a higher-capacity battery to ensure reliable system performance during prolonged periods of reduced solar input.

The combined evaluation of temperature constraints and seasonal solar radiation variability enables risk-aware battery dimensioning and supports reliable long-term autonomous operation of the environmental monitoring platform under challenging winter environmental conditions.

3.11.3. Charge Regulation and Power Distribution

To regulate charging and ensure stable power delivery, the platform employs a 10 A PWM solar charge controller in a 12 V battery system. The current rating (10 A) represents the controller's maximum supported battery-side charge current, i.e., the upper bound of charging current delivered to the battery under peak photovoltaic (PV) input conditions.

https://doi.org/10.3390/app16073237

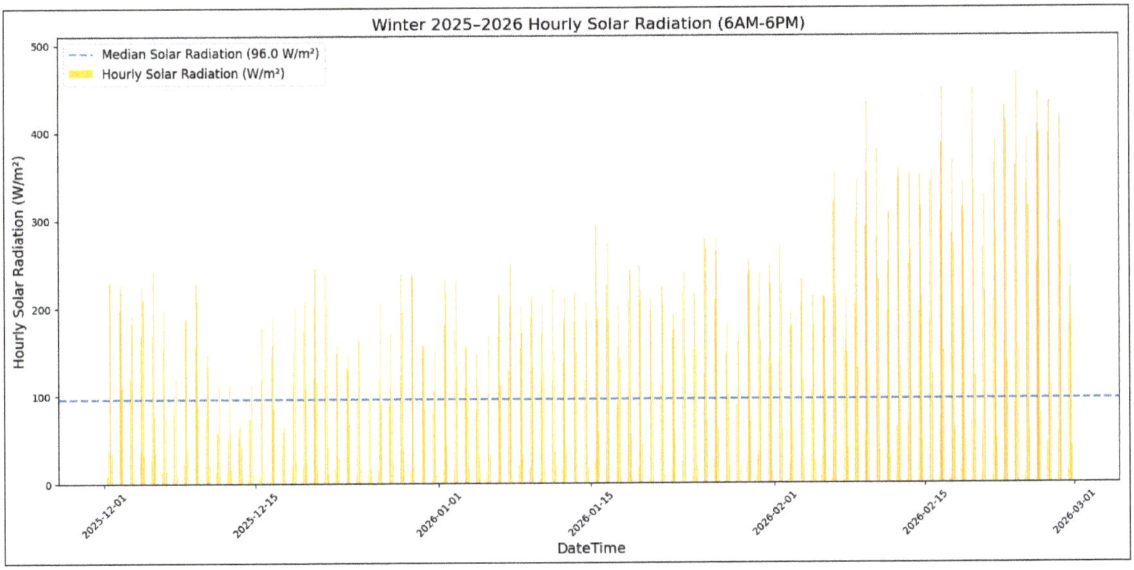

Figure 22. Predicted hourly solar radiation levels during winter months (December 2025—March 2026) for one deployment location. The dashed line represents the median solar radiation level. The results highlight significant variability and prolonged low-irradiance intervals that may limit photovoltaic energy harvesting during winter operation (see Appendix A.1).

For PWM controllers, the PV array is effectively operated close to the battery charging voltage during the bulk charging phase. Therefore, the maximum supported PV power can be approximated as follows:

$$P_{\max} \approx I_{\max} \cdot V_{\text{chg}}, \tag{4}$$

where $I_{\max}$ is the controller current rating and V_{chg} is the battery-charging voltage. For $LiFePO_4$ batteries, a typical charging voltage is $V_{\text{chg}} \approx 14.2$ V (depending on battery management system constraints and charging profile). With $I_{\max} = 10$ A, the theoretical upper PV power limit is:

$$P_{\max} \approx 10 \cdot 14.2 \approx 142 \text{ W}. \tag{5}$$

In practice, conversion losses, temperature effects, and irradiance variability reduce available power; thus, PV sizing below this limit is recommended for robust operation.

Given a PV rated power P_{PV}, the idealized battery charge current during bulk charging can be estimated as follows:

$$I_{\text{chg}} \approx \min\left(\frac{P_{\text{PV}}}{V_{\text{chg}}}, I_{\max}\right). \tag{6}$$

For the PV modules supported by the proposed platform (10/20/30 W), the expected peak charging currents are approximately:

$$I_{\text{chg}}(10\text{W}) \approx \frac{10}{14.2} \approx 0.70 \text{ A}, \tag{7}$$

$$I_{\text{chg}}(20\text{W}) \approx \frac{20}{14.2} \approx 1.41 \text{ A}, \tag{8}$$

$$I_{\text{chg}}(30\text{W}) \approx \frac{30}{14.2} \approx 2.11 \text{ A}, \tag{9}$$

which remain well below the 10 A controller limit.

https://doi.org/10.3390/app16073237

In addition to controller limits, battery charging stress is commonly expressed using the C-rate, defined as follows:

$$C_{rate} = \frac{I_{chg}}{C_{Ah}}, \quad (10)$$

where I_{chg} is the battery charge current and C_{Ah} is the nominal battery capacity in ampere-hours. Higher C-rates generally imply faster charging but may increase thermal and electrochemical stress depending on the battery chemistry and battery management system (BMS) constraints.

To illustrate the influence of battery capacity on charge stress under worst-case controller output, Figure 23 shows the theoretical C-rate if the controller were to deliver its full rated current ($I_{max} = 10$ A). For small battery capacities, the implied C-rate increases rapidly, motivating the use of moderate charge currents and/or sufficiently sized storage for long-term outdoor deployments.

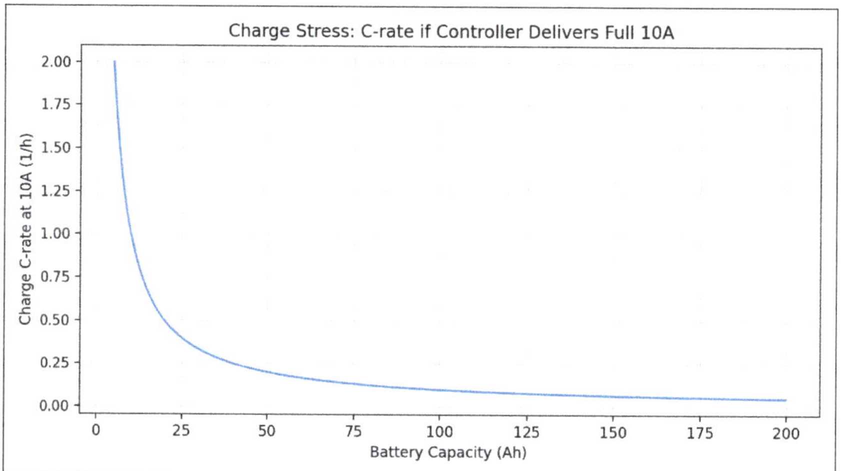

Figure 23. Charge stress expressed as C-rate if the PWM charge controller delivers its full rated current ($I_{max} = 10$ A). Smaller battery capacities correspond to higher implied C-rates.

A joint feasibility view relating PV sizing and battery capacity is presented in Figure 24. The figure maps the implied C-rate under ideal peak irradiance as a function of PV rated power and battery capacity (up to 50 Ah), while the vertical boundary indicates the maximum PV power beyond which the 10 A controller current limit would be exceeded under idealized conditions. In practice, winter irradiance variability, panel temperature effects, and conversion losses reduce effective charge current; however, the map provides a conservative design guideline for selecting PV and battery combinations that remain within controller limits and avoid excessive charge stress.

For the proposed system configuration, the selected PV modules (10–30 W) generate peak charging currents between approximately 0.7 A and 2.1 A. When combined with the selected 12 V 7.2 Ah $LiFePO_4$ battery, the resulting charge stress corresponds to an approximate C-rate of $C_{rate} \approx 2.1/7.2 \approx 0.29$ C under ideal peak charging conditions. This charging level remains well within the typical recommended operating range for $LiFePO_4$ batteries, ensuring safe and reliable battery operation.

These results confirm that battery stress is primarily governed by effective charging current rather than photovoltaic power alone. Proper controller current limiting and conservative PV sizing represent essential design strategies for protecting low-capacity $LiFePO_4$ batteries in autonomous solar-powered IoT deployments.

https://doi.org/10.3390/app16073237

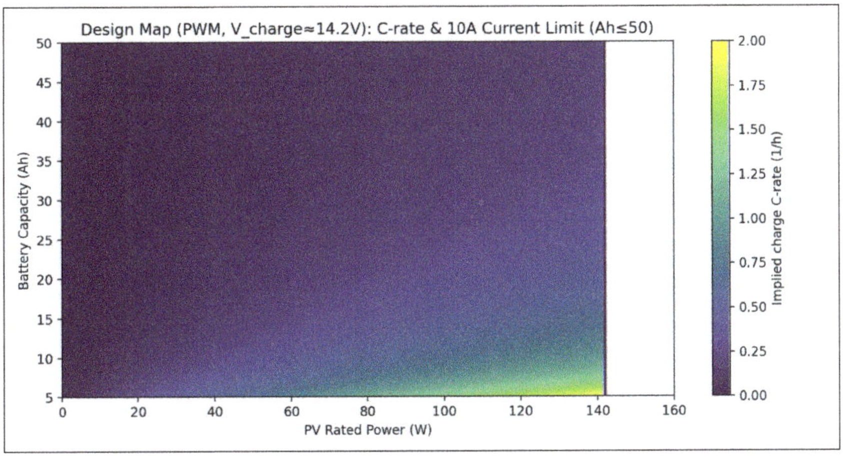

Figure 24. Design map for a 10 A PWM controller in a 12 V $LiFePO_4$ system ($V_{chg} \approx 14.2$ V), showing implied charging C-rate as a function of PV rated power and battery capacity (up to 50 Ah). The boundary indicates the theoretical PV power above which the controller charge current limit (10 A) would be exceeded under ideal peak conditions.

Finally, PV module voltage constraints must satisfy the controller's PV input voltage limit (maximum open-circuit voltage, $V_{OC,max}$), as specified by the manufacturer. In 12 V PWM systems, "12 V nominal" PV panels (typically $V_{mp} \approx 17$–18 V) are commonly used to ensure effective charging at V_{chg} while maintaining safe voltage margins under cold-weather increases in V_{OC}.

3.12. Cloud Database Architecture and Data Management

To support scalable storage, device management, and real-time data visualization, a relational database was deployed in the cloud using MySQL and administered via phpMyAdmin. The database schema was designed to ensure referential integrity, efficient time-series querying, and multi-user device management. The entity–relationship (ER) structure of the system is illustrated in Figure 25.

The `users` table stores authentication and role information for dashboard access. Each user record contains a unique `id`, `username`, `email`, a `password_hash` and a `role` field (`admin` or `user`). Indexes on `username` and `email` ensure efficient login queries. This design supports multi-user management of deployed monitoring devices.

The `devices` table maintains metadata for each deployed weather station. Each device is identified by a globally unique `device_id` (UUID string), along with descriptive fields such as `name`, `location`, GPS coordinates (`latitude`, `longitude`), operational `status`, and `last_seen` timestamp.

A foreign key constraint links `devices.user_id` to `users.id`, implementing a one-to-many relationship where a single user can manage multiple devices. The `ON DELETE SET NULL` rule ensures that devices remain stored even if a user account is removed, preserving historical data consistency.

The `weather_data` table represents the central time-series storage component of the system. Each record corresponds to a single measurement timestamp and contains:

- Atmospheric variables: temperature, humidity, pressure;
- Precipitation and wind parameters: rainfall, wind speed, wind direction;
- Soil measurements: soil moisture, soil temperature;
- Solar-related parameters: light intensity, UV index;
- GPS coordinates at measurement time.

https://doi.org/10.3390/app16073237

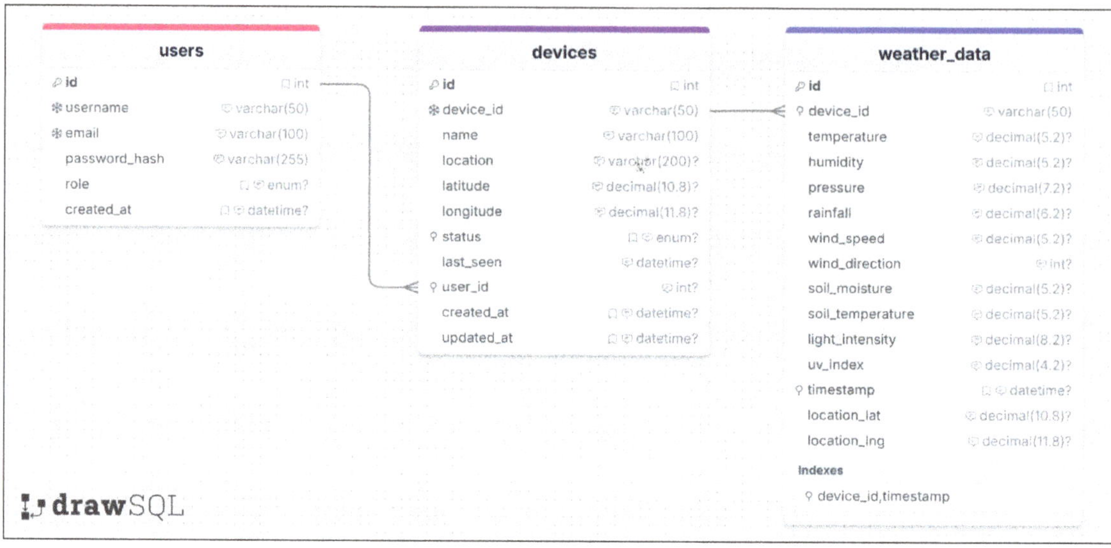

Figure 25. Entity–relationship diagram of the cloud database deployed in phpMyAdmin version 5.2.1, MariaDB version 10.6.19, PHP version 8.1.31 (https://www.mysql.com/, accessed on 16 March 2026). The schema includes three main entities: `users`, `devices`, and `weather_data`, with foreign-key constraints ensuring referential integrity between device ownership and time-series measurements.

Each measurement is linked to a specific device via a foreign key constraint referencing `devices.device_id`. The `ON DELETE CASCADE` rule ensures that removing a device automatically removes its associated measurements, preventing orphaned records.

To optimize analytical and dashboard queries, composite indexing was implemented:

- `INDEX (device_id, timestamp)` for fast retrieval of time-series data per device;
- `INDEX (timestamp)` for chronological queries.

This structure enables efficient filtering for operations such as:

- Retrieving the latest data point per device;
- Aggregating daily or monthly statistics;
- Exporting winter datasets for machine learning pipelines.

The relational design was selected over a NoSQL approach due to:

- Strong referential integrity requirements between users, devices, and measurements;
- Structured meteorological schema with consistent measurement types;
- Efficient indexing for time-series queries;
- Compatibility with phpMyAdmin and shared-hosting cloud environments.

By separating device metadata from high-frequency measurement data, the system ensures scalability for long-term deployments while maintaining efficient query performance. The schema supports both real-time monitoring and historical data extraction for downstream analytics and machine learning model training.

Furthermore, the designed relational database schema is fully integrated with a cloud-based web application that enables real-time data access, visualization, device management, and AI-driven analytics. As illustrated in Figures A2–A4, the platform provides a centralized *Dashboard* for system-level monitoring, a *Weather Data* module for structured tabular access to time-series measurements, and a *Data Collectors* interface for managing field-deployed devices, including their operational status, connectivity metrics (e.g., RSSI), and last communication timestamps.

In addition, dedicated analytics modules such as *Weather Insights*, *Agricultural Insights*, and *Green Energy Insights* enable the integration and deployment of machine learning algorithms for predictive modeling, anomaly detection, and domain-specific decision support. Detailed implementation aspects of the web application architecture, user management, device orchestration mechanisms, and interface components are provided in Appendix B. This modular cloud architecture ensures seamless interaction between edge devices, centralized storage, and AI services, thereby supporting scalable deployment of intelligent environmental monitoring systems across multiple industries.

4. Results

4.1. Lte-M/NB-IoT Signal Strength Evaluation in Field Deployment

To evaluate the communication reliability of the proposed environmental monitoring platform, field measurements of the received signal strength indicator (RSSI) levels were collected during data collector deployment in Sânandrei, Timiș County, Romania.

Figure 26 shows the statistical distribution of the NB-IoT RSSI measurements recorded by the deployed monitoring node. A total of 4306 signal strength readings were collected during routine environmental data transmissions. The measured RSSI values ranged from −93 dBm to −57 dBm, with an average RSSI of −75.51 dBm and a median RSSI of −77 dBm.

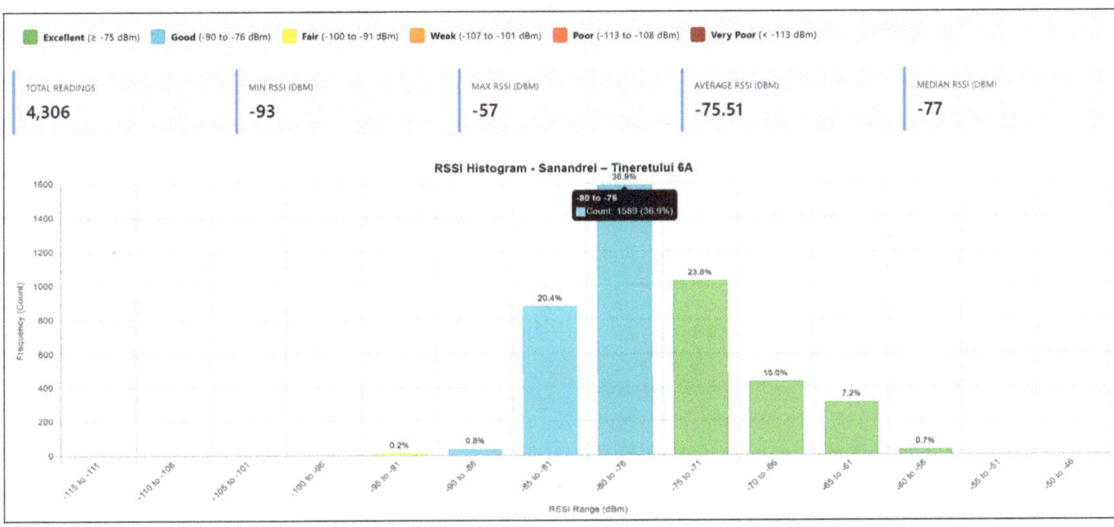

Figure 26. Distribution of NB-IoT (Orange LTE-M) RSSI measurements collected during field deployment in Sânandrei, Timiș County, Romania. The histogram shows the signal strength frequency distribution and statistical indicators, including the minimum, maximum, average, and median RSSI values.

The histogram distribution indicates that the majority of RSSI measurements fall within the interval between −85 dBm and −71 dBm. Approximately 36.9% of the measurements were concentrated within the −80 dBm to −76 dBm range, while 23.8% of the samples were recorded between −75 dBm and −71 dBm. These signal strength intervals correspond to good-to-excellent NB-IoT connectivity levels according to commonly accepted cellular signal quality classifications.

https://doi.org/10.3390/app16073237

Lower signal strength intervals, categorized as fair or weak communication conditions (below −90 dBm), were rarely observed, representing less than 1% of the total measurements. No measurements were recorded within the very poor signal strength range below −113 dBm, indicating stable network coverage at the deployment location.

The observed RSSI distribution confirms that NB-IoT connectivity provides sufficient link reliability for periodic environmental data transmission using low-power communication intervals. Stable signal conditions also reduce retransmission overhead, thereby contributing to the improved energy efficiency of the solar-powered monitoring system.

Furthermore, the collected RSSI dataset provides valuable insights for future adaptive communication strategies. Signal strength statistics can be used to dynamically adjust transmission intervals, optimize modem power states, and support machine-learning-based communication scheduling to further extend battery autonomy under adverse environmental or network conditions.

4.2. LTE-M Signal Quality in Remote Deployment

To evaluate the reliability of LTE-M communication in rural environments, additional signal quality measurements were conducted at a remote deployment location in Rogoz de Beliu, Romania. This location represents a typical agricultural monitoring scenario, characterized by limited cellular coverage and a significant distance from urban infrastructure.

The data collector installed in Rogoz de Beliu was deployed on a hilltop location overlooking a village area situated in a valley between two surrounding hills. Such terrain conditions may partially obstruct cellular propagation paths and can lead to signal attenuation and variability owing to terrain shadowing effects. These geographical characteristics provide a realistic test scenario for evaluating the behavior of the monitoring platform under marginal connectivity conditions commonly encountered in rural agricultural deployments.

During the experimental campaign, the monitoring node periodically recorded the received signal strength indicator (RSSI) values reported by the cellular modem for each transmission cycle. A total of 122 RSSI measurements were collected over the observation period.

Figure 27 presents the distribution of the recorded RSSI values. The measurements indicate that the majority of the received signal strength values fall within the range of −95 dBm to −91 dBm, representing approximately 67.2% of the observations. An additional 29.5% of the measurements fall within the −90 dBm to −86 dBm interval. Only a small fraction of the readings (3.3%) were recorded in the weaker −100 dBm to −96 dBm range.

Overall, the observed signal statistics indicate a median RSSI value of −91 dBm and an average RSSI of −90.79 dBm, with recorded values ranging from −97 dBm to −87 dBm. According to common cellular signal quality classifications, this range corresponds to fair-to-weak signal conditions typical of rural or semi-remote deployments.

Under these conditions, intermittent transmission gaps were occasionally observed, which are likely caused by temporary signal degradation approaching the receiver sensitivity limits of the cellular modem. The MKR NB 1500 module used in the proposed system typically operates reliably down to approximately −100 to −105dBm, depending on the network conditions. When the instantaneous signal quality drops near or below this threshold, packet transmission attempts may fail or require retransmission by the cellular network stack.

In the current prototype implementation, explicit retransmission algorithms or adaptive transmission interval adjustments have not yet been implemented at the application level. Instead, the system incorporates local data buffering through an SD card storage mechanism that records all collected sensor data independently of network availability.

https://doi.org/10.3390/app16073237

This approach ensures that environmental measurements are preserved, even during temporary communication interruptions. Future versions of the platform may incorporate adaptive transmission scheduling or retransmission strategies based on observed signal quality metrics in order to further improve communication reliability in challenging connectivity environments.

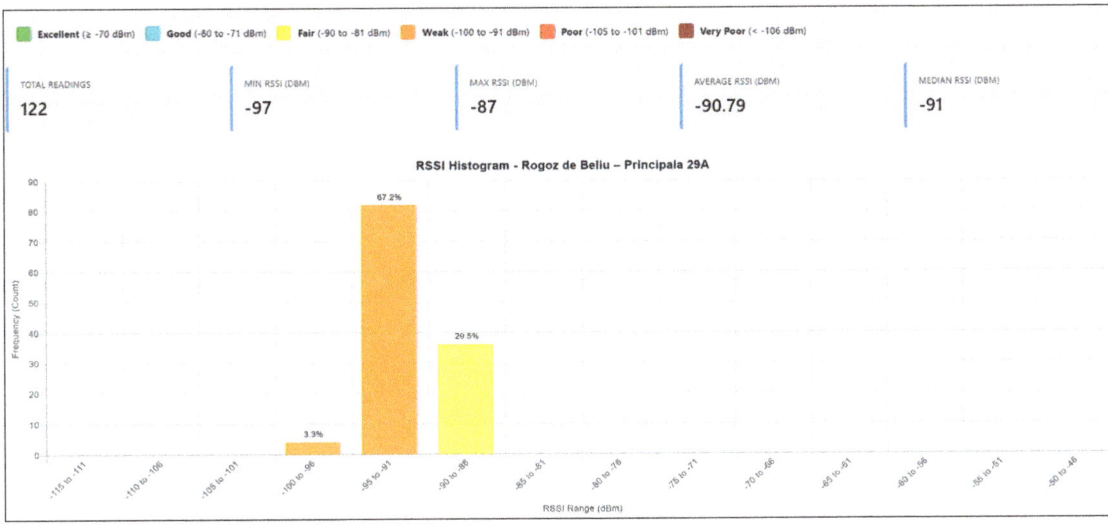

Figure 27. Distribution of LTE-M RSSI measurements recorded at the Rogoz de Beliu, Arad, RO deployment site. Most signal levels fall within the −95 to −91 dBm range, indicating fair-to-weak connectivity, typical of rural agricultural environments.

4.3. Microclimate Analysis: Comparison with Regional Weather Station Data

To validate the performance of the IoT data collector and assess microclimate variations, the measurements from the backyard installation (2 m altitude) were compared with data from the official weather station in Sanandrei (10 m altitude) for the period from January 16 to January 31, 2026. The weather station data, obtained from Visual Crossing, represent standard meteorological measurements at 10 m height, whereas the data collector captures local microclimate conditions at 2 m elevation within a residential backyard environment characterized by surrounding houses, trees, and garden vegetation.

During this observation period, the temperature, humidity, and pressure sensors were positioned outside the data collector enclosure and directly exposed to ambient air at 2 m altitude. This sensor placement represents an improvement over earlier configurations, in which sensors were housed inside the collector case with only a ventilation hole, because direct exposure ensures more accurate measurement of ambient conditions and better agreement with standard meteorological measurements.

Hourly data points were extracted from the 15-min interval collector dataset (filtering for measurements where the minute equals zero) and matched with corresponding hourly weather station observations. This temporal alignment enabled direct comparison of temperature, relative humidity, and atmospheric pressure between the two measurement locations.

4.3.1. Temperature Comparison

Figure 28 presents a comparison of temperatures recorded by the backyard data collector and those at the weather station. The analysis reveals a mean temperature difference of −0.71 °C (collector minus station), with a standard deviation of 1.05 °C, indicating that

https://doi.org/10.3390/app16073237

the backyard location was, on average, slightly cooler than the regional weather station. The temperature differences ranged from −3.90 °C to +4.10 °C, demonstrating temporal variability in microclimate conditions.

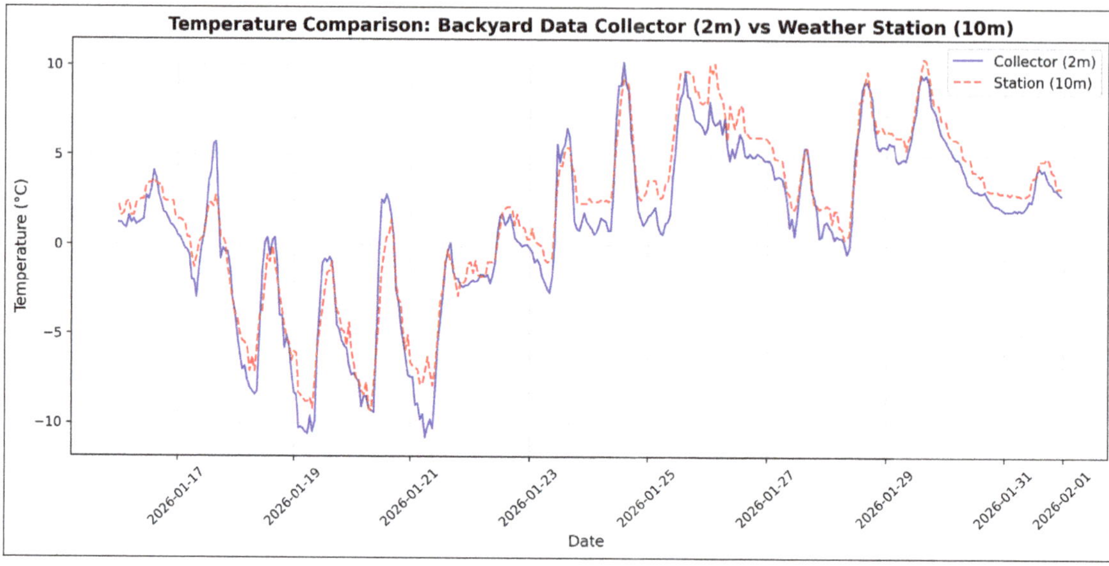

Figure 28. Temperature comparison between a data collector (2 m altitude) and a regional weather station (10 m altitude) in Sanandrei, Romania, from January 16 to 31, 2026.

The observed variations can be attributed to several microclimatic factors.

(1) The lower measurement height (2 m vs. 10 m), which places the sensor closer to the ground surface, potentially experiencing stronger radiative cooling effects during night-time and reduced solar heating during daytime;
(2) The sheltered location among buildings and vegetation, which may create localized cooling effects through shading and reduced wind exposure;
(3) The proximity to ground-level heat sources and sinks, including soil thermal properties and vegetation evapotranspiration.

Despite these local variations, the temperature measurements obtained from the data collector demonstrated a strong temporal correlation with the regional weather station data, following the same diurnal and synoptic patterns. The temperature profile of the collector closely tracked the evolution of temperature at the weather station throughout the observation period, confirming that the device accurately captured the underlying meteorological trends. The observed differences, which remained within the standard deviation range of −3.90 °C to +4.10 °C, can be attributed to local microclimate factors, such as shading from surrounding structures, ground-level thermal effects, and reduced wind exposure, rather than systematic measurement errors. This alignment validated the capability of the data collector to monitor local environmental conditions while maintaining consistency with regional weather patterns.

4.3.2. Humidity Comparison

The relative humidity comparison, shown in Figure 29, demonstrates a mean difference of 4.98% (collector minus station), with a standard deviation of 5.95% and a range from −10.99% to 24.45%. The positive mean difference indicates that the backyard location was, on average, more humid than the weather station measurements. The variability

https://doi.org/10.3390/app16073237

in humidity differences reflects the complex interactions between local vegetation, soil moisture, and micro-scale atmospheric processes.

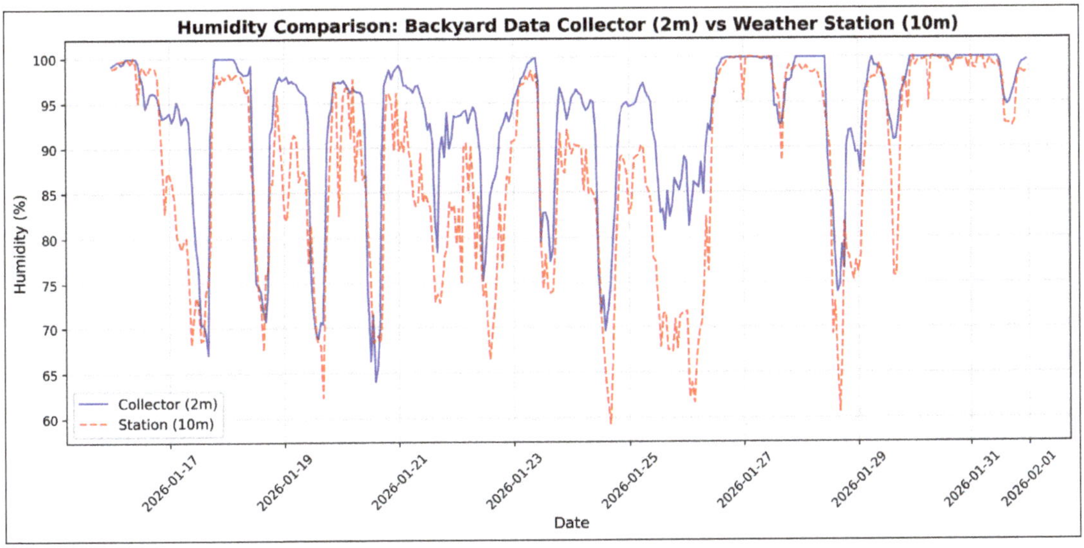

Figure 29. Comparison of relative humidity between a data collector (2m altitude) and a regional weather station (10m altitude) in Sanandrei, Romania, from January 16 to 31, 2026.

The higher average humidity at the backyard location may result from several factors:

(1) Reduced air circulation due to the sheltered positioning among buildings and vegetation, which may trap moisture near the ground;
(2) Local evapotranspiration patterns from garden vegetation that may create micro-scale humidity gradients;
(3) The influence of surrounding structures, which may affect local air circulation and moisture distribution.

The range of differences (>35 percentage points) highlights the importance of microclimate monitoring because local conditions can deviate significantly from regional averages, particularly in heterogeneous environments with mixed land cover.

The solid blue line in Figure 28 represents measurements from the Internet of Things (IoT) data collector with sensors directly exposed to ambient air, whereas the dashed red line shows data from the official weather station. The collector's temperature profile closely tracks the weather station's temporal patterns, demonstrating excellent agreement (mean difference: -0.71 °C, $\sigma = 1.05$ °C) with local microclimate variations, resulting in differences within the range of -3.90 °C to 4.10 °C.

The solid blue line in Figure 29 represents measurements from the IoT data collector with sensors directly exposed to ambient air, whereas the dashed red line shows data from the official weather station. The mean difference of 4.98% (collector minus station) with a standard deviation of 5.95% reflects local microclimate influences from surrounding vegetation and built structures, with the improved sensor placement ensuring an accurate measurement of ambient conditions.

4.3.3. Pressure Comparison

Figure 30 illustrates the atmospheric pressure comparison between the two measurement locations. The analysis shows a consistent negative pressure difference with a mean of -9.58 hPa (standard deviation: 0.28 hPa), ranging from -10.38 hPa to -8.93 hPa. This

https://doi.org/10.3390/app16073237

systematic offset is primarily attributed to the 8 m altitude difference between the two sensors (2 m vs. 10 m), as atmospheric pressure decreases with elevation according to the barometric formula.

The solid blue line in Figure 30 represents measurements from the Internet of Things (IoT) data collector with sensors directly exposed to ambient air, whereas the dashed red line shows data from the official weather station. The consistent offset of approximately −9.58 hPa is primarily attributed to the 8 m altitude difference between the two measurement locations, with minimal temporal variation ($\sigma = 0.28$ hPa), confirming both sensor calibration accuracy and the effectiveness of direct sensor exposure.

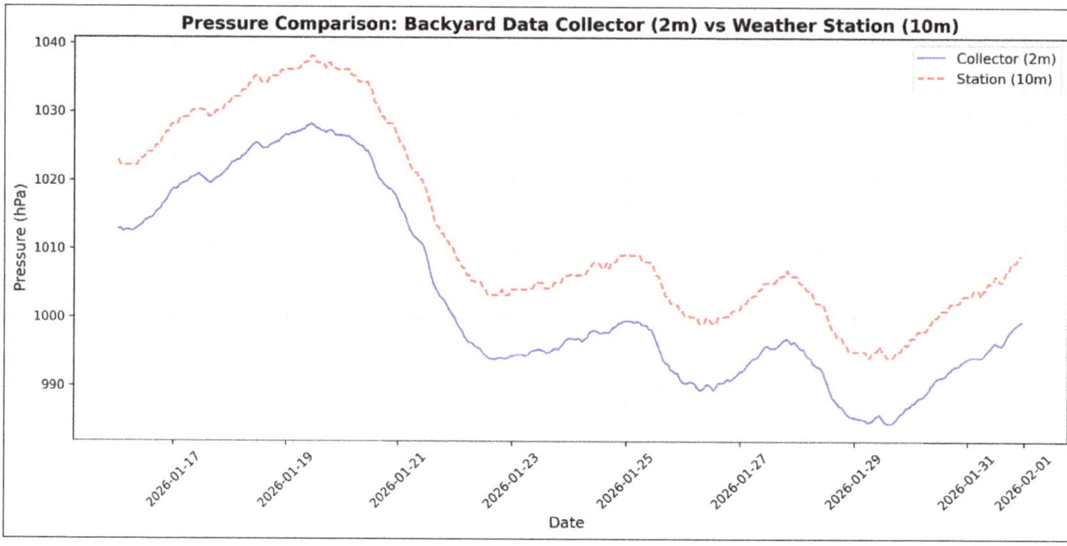

Figure 30. Atmospheric pressure comparison between the data collector (2 m altitude) and the regional weather station (10 m altitude) in Sanandrei, Romania, from 16 to 31 January 2026.

The small standard deviation (0.28 hPa) indicates that the pressure difference remained remarkably stable throughout the observation period, confirming that the offset was predominantly due to the altitude difference rather than the measurement error or local pressure anomalies. This consistency validates the pressure sensor calibration and demonstrates that when corrected for altitude, the data collector provides reliable atmospheric pressure measurements that align with the regional weather station data.

4.4. Cost-Effective Sensor Performance and Validation

A key objective of this research was to demonstrate that accurate microclimate monitoring can be achieved using low-cost, commercially available sensors. The hardware components selected for the IoT data collector represent the most economical options available on the market, with a total system cost of €315.00 (Table 2). Despite the minimal investment, the validation results demonstrate that these budget sensors provide measurements of exceptional quality that closely match those from professional weather station equipment.

The performance of the pressure sensor provides compelling evidence of the accuracy of the system. As shown in Figure 30, the atmospheric pressure measurements from the data collector follow the pressure patterns of the weather station with remarkable precision. The temporal evolution of pressure, including subtle variations and minor fluctuations, is captured with such fidelity that the two datasets appear nearly indistinguishable when overlaid, differing only by the consistent altitude-related offset of approximately −9.58 hPa

https://doi.org/10.3390/app16073237

(σ = 0.28 hPa). This exceptional agreement validates that even the most economical pressure sensors (BMP280, €7.00) can deliver professional-grade measurements when properly calibrated and positioned.

Table 2. Hardware cost breakdown of the proposed AI-ready NB-IoT data collector.

Item	Description	Price
MCU & COMMUNICATION		
Arduino Nano 33 BLE	EdgeAI-capable light-weight sensor controller	€31.00
MKR NB 1500	NB-IoT Data transmission module	€80.00
Dipole Pentaband Antenna	MKR NB 1500 Antenna	€6.00
SENSORS		
Weather station	Mechanical part	€50.00
Thermo/hygro sensor	Thermo hygro sensor case	€20.00
DHT22	Temperature & humidity	€12.00
BMP280	Barometric pressure sensor	€7.00
POWER MANAGEMENT		
30W Solar Panel	Breckner Germany, 440 × 425 × 45 mm	€12.00
Solar Charge Controller	12/24 V, 20A, 2× USB ports	€5.00
2× LiFePo4 Battery 7Ah	V-TAC SKU-11942 12.8 V 7.2 Ah	€30.00
CASINGS		
Distribution Panel	Starke ST01411 30 × 20 × 13 cm IP65	€11.00
Battery Case	Starke ST01438 30 × 40 × 17 cm IP65	€35.00
Sonoff case	UV & light sensors	€5.00
WIRING & CONNECTORS		
Cable RJ12 6P6C	1× Cable Rj12 6 wires for DHT22 & BMP280	€3.00
Connector PIC-ICSP	2× OLIMEX-ICSP, OLIMEX-ICSP-mini and MICROCHIP-RJ11	€8.00
Total		€315.00

Similarly, the temperature and humidity sensors (DHT22, €12.00) demonstrated excellent performance, with mean differences of −0.71 °C (σ = 1.05 °C) and 4.98% (σ = 5.95%), respectively, compared those with of the regional weather station. These small differences are primarily attributable to genuine microclimate variations between the 2 m backyard location and the 10 m weather station height, rather than sensor limitations. The strong temporal correlation observed across all parameters confirms that the low-cost sensor suite accurately captures both diurnal patterns and synoptic-scale weather variations.

The validation results demonstrate that cost-effective sensor solutions can achieve measurement quality comparable to that of professional meteorological equipment, making distributed microclimate monitoring economically viable for agricultural applications. This finding is particularly significant for precision agriculture, where the deployment of multiple monitoring stations across fields requires affordable and reliable sensing technology.

5. Limitations

5.1. Limitations of Temperature and Humidity Measurement

Although the DHT22 sensor provides a cost-effective solution for environmental monitoring, several limitations must be considered for long-term autonomous deployment.

5.1.1. Humidity Long-Term Drift

According to the manufacturer, the DHT22 exhibits a long-term humidity stability of approximately ±0.5% RH per year. Assuming a conservative worst-case linear accu-

https://doi.org/10.3390/app16073237

mulation model, the total humidity error after N years can be approximated as follows:

$$E_{N,\mathrm{RH}} = E_{0,\mathrm{RH}} + N \cdot D_{\mathrm{RH}} \tag{11}$$

where $E_{0,\mathrm{RH}}$ represents the initial accuracy (typically $\pm 2\%$ RH at 25 °C) and $D_{\mathrm{RH}} = 0.5\%$ RH/year denotes the annual drift.

After five years, the worst-case accumulated humidity error is expressed as:

$$E_{5,\mathrm{RH}} = \pm(2\% + 5 \times 0.5\%) = \pm 4.5\%\mathrm{RH} \tag{12}$$

Such a cumulative deviation may influence long-term humidity trend analysis, irrigation control thresholds, and disease prediction models that rely on precise relative humidity estimation.

5.1.2. Estimated Temperature Long-Term Drift

The DHT22 datasheet does not explicitly specify long-term temperature stability. However, considering its initial temperature accuracy of approximately ± 0.5 °C and its sensor grade, a conservative engineering approximation assumes a temperature drift on the order of:

$$D_T \approx 0.05\ ^\circ\mathrm{C/year} \tag{13}$$

Under a worst-case linear accumulation assumption:

$$E_{5,T} = \pm(0.5\ ^\circ\mathrm{C} + 5 \times 0.05\ ^\circ\mathrm{C}) = \pm 0.75\ ^\circ\mathrm{C} \tag{14}$$

Although a sub-degree drift remains acceptable for general environmental monitoring, gradual bias accumulation may affect multi-year datasets used for training machine learning models, particularly in applications sensitive to subtle temperature variations.

5.1.3. Implications for Long-Term Environmental Monitoring

In extended deployments, cumulative sensor drift may lead to:

- Gradual offset bias in humidity and temperature records;
- Artificial long-term trend distortion;
- Reduced precision in threshold-based control strategies;
- Decreased robustness of ML models trained on absolute measurements.

For applications that primarily rely on relative changes or short-term dynamics, the DHT22 sensor is suitable for cost-effective monitoring. Nevertheless, periodic cross-validation with reference meteorological data or software-based drift compensation strategies should be considered in multi-year intelligent sensing systems.

Figure 31 illustrates the projected long-term degradation of temperature and humidity accuracy for the DHT22 sensor over a five-year deployment period under a conservative linear drift assumption. The temperature accuracy was assumed to degrade from an initial ± 0.5 °C to approximately ± 0.75 °C after five years, based on an estimated drift of ± 0.05 °C/year. Similarly, the humidity accuracy was assumed to degrade from an initial $\pm 2\%$ RH to approximately $\pm 4.5\%$ RH after five years, based on the specified long-term stability of $\pm 0.5\%$ RH/year.

5.2. Limitations of Atmospheric Pressure Measurement

Although the BMP280 sensor provides reliable and cost-effective barometric pressure measurements suitable for environmental monitoring, several accuracy and long-term stability considerations must be acknowledged.

According to the manufacturer's specifications (Figure 16), the absolute pressure accuracy of the BMP280 varies with pressure and temperature. Within the 700–900 hPa interval at 25–40 °C, the typical accuracy is approximately ±0.12 hPa (equivalent to approximately ±1 m altitude). However, within the 950–1050 hPa range at 0–40 °C, corresponding to typical sea-level atmospheric conditions, the accuracy decreases to approximately ±1 hPa. This error margin corresponds to an altitude uncertainty of approximately ±8–±9 m when applying the barometric formula.

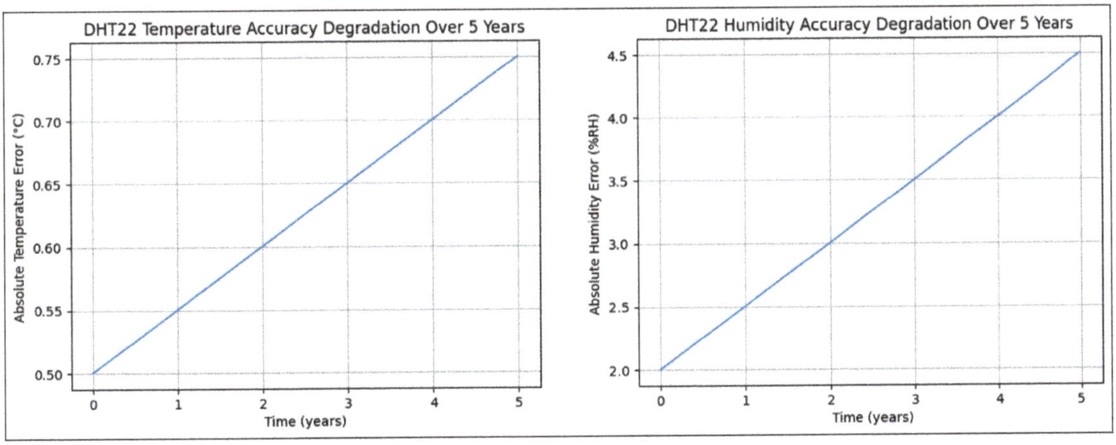

Figure 31. Projected five-year linear accuracy degradation of the DHT22 sensor. Left: Absolute temperature error growth from ±0.5 °C to ±0.75 °C, assuming ±0.05 °C/year drift. Right: Absolute humidity error growth from ±2% RH to ±4.5% RH, assuming ±0.5% RH/year drift. The plots illustrate the potential long-term uncertainty accumulation in autonomous multi-year deployments.

Although such deviations are acceptable for short-term meteorological trend monitoring, they may introduce bias when high-precision altitude normalization or pressure-gradient analysis is required. In particular, when comparing measurements across distributed nodes deployed at slightly different elevations, accumulated systematic offsets can impact cross-station consistency if not properly calibrated.

In addition to the instantaneous accuracy limits, the BMP280 exhibits a specified long-term stability of approximately ±1 hPa per year. This drift corresponds to a gradual altitude-equivalent deviation of approximately ±8 m per year. For short-term environmental monitoring, this drift is generally negligible. However, in long-term deployments extending over multiple years, cumulative drift may introduce systematic bias into historical datasets.

Such drift can be particularly relevant in machine learning applications. Supervised learning models trained on multi-season pressure data may implicitly learn sensor-specific offsets rather than purely atmospheric dynamics. In distributed deployments, heterogeneous drift behavior across multiple nodes could lead to model inconsistencies if pressure values are used as direct predictive features. Therefore, periodic recalibration against a trusted reference (e.g., nearby meteorological stations or known altitude correction models) is recommended.

Furthermore, temperature-dependent accuracy variations may influence pressure readings during seasonal transitions. Although the BMP280 incorporates internal temperature compensation, residual thermal effects can still contribute to small deviations, particularly under rapid ambient temperature changes or enclosure-induced thermal gradients.

To mitigate these limitations in future deployments, several strategies can be adopted:

- Periodic cross-calibration using regional meteorological reference data.
- Altitude normalization using standardized barometric correction models.
- Drift-aware preprocessing pipelines before ML training.

https://doi.org/10.3390/app16073237

- Feature engineering strategies that emphasize pressure gradients rather than absolute values.

While the BMP280 provides a cost-effective and sufficiently accurate solution for trend-based environmental monitoring, future system iterations should investigate higher-accuracy barometric sensors with improved long-term stability characteristics. Sensors offering lower absolute pressure error margins and reduced annual drift may enhance reliability in multi-year deployments and distributed sensing networks. Additionally, the integration of automatic or semi-automatic calibration strategies, such as periodic cross-referencing with regional meteorological stations, GNSS-assisted altitude normalization, or adaptive model-based offset correction, could further mitigate long-term drift effects. Such enhancements would be particularly beneficial for machine learning applications, where cumulative systematic bias may influence model training and long-horizon prediction performance.

Although the BMP280 sensor provides cost-effective and stable short-term barometric pressure measurements, long-term accuracy degradation must be considered in multi-year deployments. According to the manufacturer's specifications, the absolute pressure accuracy varies depending on the pressure and temperature ranges. In the 700–900 hPa interval at 25–40 °C, the typical accuracy is approximately ±0.12 hPa, whereas in the 950–1050 hPa range at 0–40 °C, corresponding to typical sea-level conditions, the accuracy decreases to approximately ±1 hPa. In addition, the specified long-term stability is approximately ±1 hPa per year.

5.2.1. Worst-Case Linear Drift Model

Assuming a conservative worst-case scenario in which long-term drift accumulates linearly over time, the total absolute pressure error after N years can be approximated as follows:

$$E_{N,\text{worst}} = E_0 + N \cdot D \tag{15}$$

where E_0 represents the initial absolute accuracy (hPa) and D denotes the annual drift (hPa/year).

For $E_0 = \pm 1$ hPa and $D = \pm 1$ hPa/year, the worst-case accumulated error after five years becomes:

$$E_{5,\text{worst}} = \pm(1+5) = \pm 6\ \text{hPa} \tag{16}$$

Using the barometric approximation near sea level, where 1 hPa corresponds to approximately 8–9 m of altitude variation, this translates into an altitude-equivalent uncertainty of approximately ±48–±54 m after five years.

5.2.2. Stochastic Drift Model

In practice, long-term sensor drift may not accumulate strictly linearly but instead behave as a bounded random process. Assuming that the drift follows a random-walk model, the expected accumulated deviation can be approximated as follows:

$$E_{N,\text{typ}} \approx E_0 + D\sqrt{N} \tag{17}$$

For $N = 5$ years and $D = 1$ hPa/year:

$$E_{5,\text{typ}} \approx \pm(1+\sqrt{5}) \approx \pm 3.24\ \text{hPa} \tag{18}$$

This corresponds to an altitude-equivalent deviation of approximately ±26–±29 m.

Figure 32 visualizes both models over a 5-year horizon for $E_0 = 1$ hPa and $D = 1$ hPa/year. The left panel shows the expected growth of absolute pressure er-

https://doi.org/10.3390/app16073237

ror, while the right panel expresses the same degradation as a relative error percentage normalized by a representative sea-level reference pressure $P_{\text{ref}} = 1013$ hPa. Under the worst-case model, the error reaches ± 6 hPa after five years (approximately 0.59%), they represent systematic offsets an expected error of ± 3.24 hPa (approximately 0.32%). Although these relative deviations remain below 1%, they represent systematic offsets that can bias long-horizon learning if raw absolute pressure is used without correction.

To reduce drift-induced bias in future TinyML tasks, pressure features should preferentially be expressed in drift-robust forms, such as temporal differences:

$$\Delta P(t) = P(t) - P(t - \Delta t) \tag{19}$$

or trend estimators computed over fixed windows:

$$S(t) = \frac{P(t) - P(t - T)}{T} \tag{20}$$

These formulations largely cancel long-term baseline shifts and emphasize meteorologically meaningful dynamics. For multi-year deployments and multi-node learning scenarios, future work should evaluate higher-grade barometric sensors with improved long-term stability or implement periodic calibration and adaptive offset-correction strategies.

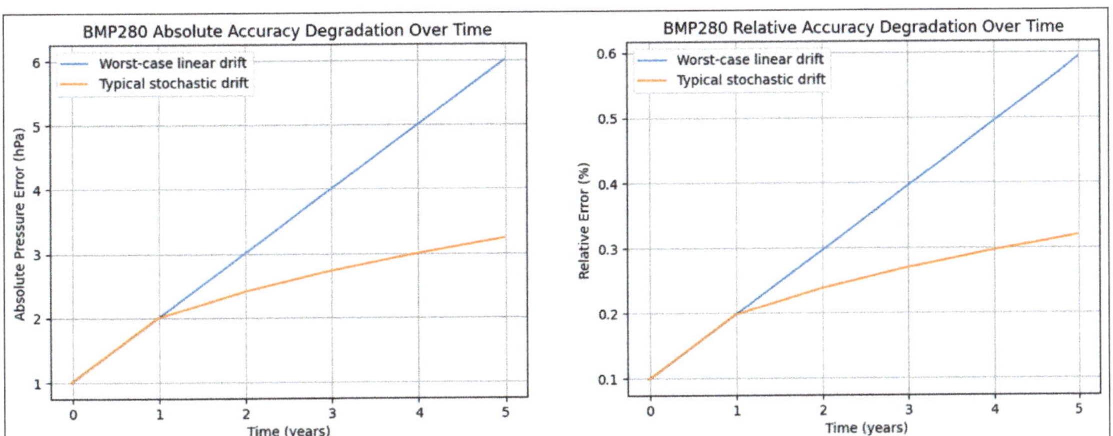

Figure 32. Simulated degradation of BMP280 pressure accuracy over time using two drift models ($E_0 = 1$ hPa, $D = 1$ hPa/year). (**Left**) Absolute pressure error growth (hPa). (**Right**) Relative error percentage normalized by $P_{\text{ref}} = 1013$ hPa. The plots highlight that multiyear deployments may experience gradual baseline shifts, which can impact machine learning models if absolute pressure is used directly as an input feature.

6. Discussion

6.1. Sensor Validation and Microclimate Measurement Accuracy

The validation results demonstrate that the proposed IoT data collector achieves exceptional measurement accuracy using the most economical sensors available on the market, with a total hardware cost of only €315.00 (Table 2). A comparison between our data collector and the regional weather station revealed distinct microclimate characteristics at the 2 m measurement height while simultaneously validating the performance of low-cost sensor technology.

https://doi.org/10.3390/app16073237

The sensors, directly exposed to ambient air at an altitude of 2 m, provide accurate measurements that closely track regional weather patterns. The mean temperature difference of −0.71 °C ($\sigma = 1.05$ °C) demonstrated excellent agreement with the weather station, with the remaining differences attributable to genuine microclimate variations rather than measurement artifacts. The humidity measurements showed a positive mean difference (4.98%, $\sigma = 5.95\%$), reflecting the influence of local vegetation and built structures on moisture distribution. The relatively small differences observed across all parameters validated the sensor performance and confirmed that direct exposure to ambient conditions provided reliable microclimate monitoring.

The pressure sensor performance provides compelling evidence of the accuracy of the system. As shown in Figure 30, the atmospheric pressure measurements from the data collector followed the weather station pressure patterns with remarkable precision. The temporal evolution of pressure, including subtle variations and minor fluctuations, is captured with such fidelity that the two datasets appear nearly indistinguishable when overlaid, differing only by a consistent altitude-related offset of approximately −9.58 hPa ($\sigma = 0.28$ hPa). This exceptional agreement validates that even the most economical pressure sensors (BMP280, €7.00) can deliver professional-grade measurements when they are properly calibrated and positioned. Similarly, the temperature and humidity sensors (DHT22, €12.00) demonstrated excellent performance, with a strong temporal correlation observed across all parameters, confirming that the low-cost sensor suite accurately captured both diurnal patterns and synoptic-scale weather variations.

These findings underscore the value of distributed microclimate monitoring systems for agricultural applications, where local environmental conditions at the crop level (typically 1–2 m height) may differ substantially from standard meteorological measurements taken at 10 m height. The ability to capture these microclimate variations is particularly important for precision agriculture, where management decisions benefit from site-specific environmental data rather than regional averages. The validation results demonstrate that cost-effective sensor solutions can achieve measurement quality comparable to that of professional meteorological equipment, making distributed microclimate monitoring economically viable for large-scale agricultural deployment. This finding is particularly significant for precision agriculture, where the deployment of multiple monitoring stations across fields requires affordable and reliable sensing technology.

The combination of low cost, high accuracy, and reliable performance positions the proposed system as an accessible solution for farmers and agricultural researchers seeking to implement distributed environmental monitoring networks in the future. The demonstrated capability to achieve professional-grade measurements with budget sensors opens new possibilities for the widespread adoption of precision agriculture technologies, particularly in resource-constrained agricultural regions where cost-effectiveness is paramount.

6.2. *Lifecycle Cost and Sensor Performance Considerations*

The hardware cost of approximately €315 reported for the proposed monitoring platform corresponds to a prototype implementation that was assembled using development boards and commercially available modules. In a production-oriented design based on a custom-printed circuit board and batch component procurement, the per-unit hardware cost can be further reduced. This approach enables the deployment of a larger number of monitoring nodes across agricultural environments at a fraction of the cost of traditional meteorological stations.

An important aspect of long-term environmental monitoring systems is the lifecycle performance of the sensing components. Low-cost digital sensors typically exhibit measurable long-term drifts and may require periodic recalibration or replacement during

https://doi.org/10.3390/app16073237

extended deployments. For example, commonly used temperature and humidity sensors such as the DHT22 exhibit long-term stability on the order of approximately ±0.5% RH per year, while more advanced sensors such as the Sensirion SHT45 provide significantly improved stability of less than 0.2% RH per year and temperature drift below 0.03 °C per year.

To provide context for the sensing components used in the proposed platform, Table 3 presents an indicative comparison between representative low-cost sensors used in this study and the specifications of environmental probes commonly employed in commercial meteorological stations (in this particular example, €7000+).

As shown in Table 3, recent advances in MEMS-based sensing technologies have allowed low-cost environmental sensors to achieve nominal accuracy levels comparable to those reported for some commercial environmental probes. However, professional meteorological stations typically incur higher costs not only from the sensing element itself but also from additional system-level components, such as calibrated radiation shields, aspirated housings, certified calibration procedures, and long-term maintenance services.

The energy system design also differs significantly between professional weather stations and low-power IoT monitoring platforms. Commercial meteorological stations frequently rely on higher-power telemetry technologies, such as GSM or cellular communication modules, which require larger photovoltaic panels (often tens of watts) and higher-capacity battery systems.

Table 3. Indicative comparison between sensors used in the proposed data collector and representative commercial meteorological probes.

Parameter	DHT22	SHT45	Commercial Probe (RHT2/AT2 Example)
Temperature range	−40 to 80 °C	−40 to 125 °C	−20 to 60 °C
Temperature accuracy	±0.5 °C	±0.1 °C	±0.5 °C
Temperature long-term drift	Not specified	<0.03 °C/year	Not always specified
Humidity range	0–100% RH	0–100% RH	0–100% RH
Humidity accuracy	±2–5% RH	±1% RH	±2–3% RH
Humidity long-term drift	±0.5% RH/year	<0.2% RH/year	~1–2% first year
Response time (typical)	~5 s	~1.8–8 ms	<10 s (90% RH step)
Approximate sensor cost	€5–10	~€17	Significantly higher

Commercial probe specifications are based on representative industrial meteorological sensors used in professional weather stations.

In contrast, the proposed monitoring platform adopts low-power communication technologies, such as NB-IoT or LoRaWAN, enabling reliable long-range communication while operating with smaller solar panels and reduced energy storage capacity. These design differences reflect the distinct deployment objectives. Professional meteorological stations prioritize standardized measurements, traceable calibrations, and long-term stability for scientific and regulatory applications. The proposed platform focuses on enabling dense, low-cost distributed sensing networks capable of capturing microclimate variability across agricultural environments.

7. Conclusions

This study presents the design, implementation, and field validation of a modular, solar-powered environmental monitoring platform that integrates LTE-M/NB-IoT communication and TinyML-enabled edge processing. The proposed architecture combines a dual-microcontroller approach, where the Arduino Nano 33 BLE performs real-time sensor

https://doi.org/10.3390/app16073237

acquisition and local processing, and the Arduino MKR NB 1500 ensures reliable long-range communication. This separation of sensing, edge intelligence, and communication enhances modularity, energy efficiency, and scalability of the system.

Field deployment in two distinct environments in Romania demonstrated stable LTE-M connectivity, with RSSI measurements ranging from −93 dBm to −57 dBm and an average signal strength of −75.51 dBm, confirming a reliable rural communication performance. Microclimate validation against an official regional weather station showed a strong temporal correlation for temperature, humidity, and pressure measurements. The observed differences were primarily attributed to local environmental conditions and altitude variations, rather than sensor inaccuracies. In particular, the atmospheric pressure comparison revealed a consistent altitude-related offset of −9.58 hPa with minimal variance ($\sigma = 0.28$ hPa), which validated the sensor stability and calibration.

The results confirm that low-cost, commercially available sensors, such as the DHT22 and BMP280, can achieve measurement performance comparable to that of professional meteorological stations when properly integrated and calibrated. With a total hardware cost of approximately €315, the proposed platform demonstrates that distributed microclimate monitoring is economically viable for precision agriculture applications.

In addition to sensing, the integration of TinyML capabilities enables local data filtering and event-driven processing, reducing transmission overhead and improving energy efficiency in solar-powered deployments. The modular architecture further allows adaptation to additional sensing domains, renewable energy assessments, and smart city environmental monitoring.

Future work will focus on adaptive communication scheduling based on signal quality indicators, extended multi-season deployment analysis, integration of additional energy-aware machine learning models, and large-scale distributed deployment across agricultural regions to support data-driven farm management.

8. Future Work and Next Steps

The dual-microcontroller architecture adopted in this study opens up significant opportunities for extending the platform beyond conventional environmental monitoring toward intelligent, adaptive, edge-based decision systems. The separation between the sensing and communication functions provides a foundation for distributed learning, adaptive communication strategies, and energy-aware system optimization.

8.1. Large-Scale Data Collection and Dataset Expansion

The next development phase will focus on extended multisession data acquisition across diverse environmental conditions. The continuous logging of meteorological parameters, communication metrics (RSSI, RSRP, and transmission latency), battery voltage levels, and solar charging behavior enabled the construction of a comprehensive multi-domain dataset. Such a dataset will support supervised and self-supervised learning approaches for communication optimization, anomaly detection, and predictive energy management in smart buildings.

Scaling the deployment to multiple nodes across heterogeneous rural environments will further enable the spatial analysis of microclimate variability and cellular signal dynamics, forming the basis for distributed learning strategies and federated edge intelligence.

8.2. Adaptive LTE-M Communication via TinyML

The primary objective of future research is the implementation of adaptive LTE-M communication control using TinyML models deployed on the Arduino Nano 33 BLE.

https://doi.org/10.3390/app16073237

Instead of relying on fixed transmission intervals, the edge node dynamically adjusts the communication parameters based on

- Signal strength indicators (RSSI, RSRP);
- Battery state-of-charge and charging rate;
- Solar energy availability forecasts;
- Environmental event detection (e.g., rainfall, wind spikes);
- Network stability statistics.

Machine learning models trained offline using the collected datasets were quantized and deployed on the Nano 33 BLE to enable real-time inference. The model outputs may control:

- Transmission interval adaptation;
- Modem power state selection;
- Data aggregation strategies;
- Event-triggered communication.

This adaptive mechanism aims to minimize energy consumption while maintaining the data reliability and quality of service.

8.3. Migration Toward High-Precision Humidity and Temperature Sensing

Although the current implementation employs the DHT22 sensor for temperature and relative humidity monitoring, future system iterations may benefit from migration toward higher-precision digital sensing platforms, such as the Sensirion SHT45 (Figure 33).

Icon	Attribute	DHT11	DHT22	SHT45
	Temperature Range	0°C to +50°C	-40°C to +80°C	-40°C to +125°C
	Temperature Accuracy	±1°C *(0°C)* ±2°C *(50°C)*	< ±0.5°C	±0.1°C
	Temperature Resolution	1°C	0.1°C	0.01°C
	Humidity Range	20% RH to 90% RH	0% RH to 100% RH *(-40°C to 80°C)*	0% RH to 100% RH
	Humidity Accuracy	± 4% *(25°C)* ±5% *(0°C to 50°C)*	±2% to ±5% *(25°C)* ±5%C *(0°C to 50°C)*	±1% RH *(±0.5% long-term production)*
	Humidity Resolution	1% RH	0.1% RH	0.01% RH
	Voltage Range	3.0V – 5.5V	3.3V – 6.0V	1.1V – 3.6V
	Current Consumption	0.5mA – 2.5mA *(measuring)* 0.1mA – 0.15mA *(standby)*	1mA – 1.5mA *(measuring)* 0.04mA – 0.05mA *(standby)*	0.3mA – 0.5mA *(measuring)* 0.08uA – 3.4mA *(standby)*
	Long Term Stability	±1%RH/y	±0.5%RH/y	<0.2%RH/y, <0.03°C/y
	Sensing Period	~4ms	~5ms	~1.8-8ms
	Collection/Sensing Period	>6s	>2s	>2s
	Price	**1-2 €**	**5-10 €**	**17 €**

Figure 33. Comparison of DHT11, DHT22, and SHT45 temperature and humidity sensor specifications (information taken from the datasheets).

The DHT22 provides acceptable performance for low-cost environmental monitoring, offering ±0.5 °C temperature accuracy and ±2–5% RH) accuracy, with a long-term drift of approximately ±0.5%RH/year. However, several limitations affect its suitability for precision agriculture and long-term autonomous deployment:

https://doi.org/10.3390/app16073237

- Limited humidity stability over time;
- Slow single-wire communication protocol;
- Relatively high measurement current (1–1.5 mA);
- Moderate resolution (0.1 °C, 0.1% RH).

In contrast, the SHT45 represents a next-generation CMOSens® platform, offering substantial improvements:

- Temperature accuracy: ±0.1 °C;
- Humidity accuracy: ±1% RH;
- Resolution: 0.01 °C and 0.01% RH;
- Long-term drift: <0.2%RH/year, <0.03 °C/year;
- Standby current: 0.08 μA;
- Fast I^2C digital interface with CRC integrity.

Expected Impact of Migration

Replacing the DHT22 with the SHT45 would:

1. Improve measurement fidelity by reducing systematic temperature error from ±0.5 °C to ±0.1 °C, enhancing evapotranspiration modeling and microclimate monitoring.
2. Increase long-term deployment stability by lowering humidity drift (<0.2%RH/year).
3. Reduce power consumption due to ultra-low standby current, improving autonomous solar-battery operation.
4. Enable higher sampling rates (millisecond-scale measurement times).
5. Improve communication robustness through I^2C with CRC validation.

Despite the higher unit cost compared to the DHT22, the improved accuracy, stability, and energy efficiency make the SHT45 a strong candidate for research-grade and precision agriculture deployments.

8.4. Migration Toward Higher-Accuracy Barometric Sensors

Although the BMP280 sensor provides an excellent balance between cost and performance for distributed environmental monitoring, future iterations of the platform will investigate the integration of higher accuracy pressure sensors, such as the BMP388. Figure 34 summarizes the comparative characteristics of BMP180, BMP280, and BMP388 modules.

The BMP388 offers improved metrological performance, including enhanced absolute and relative pressure accuracy and superior long-term stability. While the BMP280 specifies an absolute accuracy of approximately ±1 hPa (950–1050 hPa @ 0–40 °C) and a long-term stability of ±1 hPa/year, the BMP388 reduces the absolute accuracy error to approximately ±0.5 hPa and improves the long-term stability to approximately ±0.33 hPa/year. Over multi-year deployments, this reduction in drift can significantly limit cumulative bias, particularly in applications involving altitude estimation, pressure-based weather pattern classification, or long-term machine learning model training.

In addition to improved stability, the BMP388 provides higher pressure and temperature resolution, which may enhance the detection of subtle atmospheric variations. Although the module cost is moderately higher (approximately €12–14 compared to €2–7 for BMP280), the performance-to-cost ratio remains highly favorable, especially for deployments targeting long-term autonomous operation with minimal recalibration.

Future research should evaluate the trade-offs between sensor cost, long-term drift behavior, and machine learning model robustness. Experimental campaigns will be conducted to quantify whether the improved stability of the BMP388 translates into measurable gains in the predictive accuracy of pressure-based ML models, adaptive communica-

https://doi.org/10.3390/app16073237

tion strategies, and energy optimization algorithms implemented on the Arduino Nano 33 BLE platform.

Icon	Attribute	BMP 180	BMP 280	BMP 388
	Pressure Range	300 – 1100 hPa	300 – 1100 hPa *(-500 to +9000 m)*	300 – 1250 hPa *(-500 to +9000 m)*
	Pressure Relative Accuracy	±0.12 hPa (±1 m) *(950 – 1050 hPa @25°C-40°C)*	±0.12 hPa (±1 m) *(700 – 900 hPa @ 25°C-40°C)*	±0.08 hPa (±66 cm) *(900– 1100 hPa @ 25°C-40°C)*
	Pressure Absolute Accuracy	± 2.0 hPa (± 4.5 hPa) *(300 – 1100 hPa @0°C-65°C)*	±1 hPa *(950– 1050 hPa @ 0°C-40°C)*	±0.5 hPa *(300– 1100 hPa @-20°C-40°C)*
	Pressure Resolution	1.0 (0.01) hPa	0.0018 hPa	0.0066 hPa (0.00085 hPa)
	Temperature Range	-40°C to +85°C	-40°C to +85°C	-40°C to +85°C
	Temperature Accuracy	±1°C *(0 to 65°C)* ±1.5°C *(-40°C to 0°C)*	±0.5°C *(@ 25°C)* ±1°C *(0°C to 65°C)*	±0.3°C *(@ 25°C)* ±0.5°C *(0°C to 65°C)*
	Temperature Resolution	0.1°C	0.01°C	0.005°C (0.00015 °C)
	Voltage Range	3.3V – 5.5V	1.7V – 3.6V	1.65V – 3.6V
	Current Consumption	0.6 mA	0.7 - 1.1 mA	0.7 - 0.8 mA
	Long Term Stability	±1 hPa/year	±1 hPa/year	±0.33 hPa/year
	Price	1-2 €	2-7 €	12-14 €

The temperature measurement is used internally to calibrate the pressure and humidity sensors.
The maximum measurable humidity decreases at extremely high and low temperatures.

Figure 34. Comparative specifications of BMP180, BMP280, and BMP388 barometric pressure sensors. The figure summarizes pressure range, relative and absolute accuracy, resolution, temperature characteristics, supply voltage, current consumption, long-term stability, and approximate market price. The BMP388 demonstrates improved absolute accuracy (±0.5 hPa), enhanced relative accuracy (±0.08 hPa), and superior long-term stability (±0.33 hPa/year) compared to BMP280 and BMP180, making it a strong candidate for multi-year autonomous environmental monitoring deployments.

Figure 35 illustrates the projected long-term degradation of both the absolute and relative pressure accuracy of the BMP280 and BMP388 sensors over a five-year deployment horizon. Two drift models were considered: a conservative worst-case linear accumulation model and a stochastic random-walk model representing more typical long-term behavior.

As shown in Figure 35(left), the BMP280 may reach an absolute error of approximately ±6 hPa after five years under worst-case linear drift assumptions, whereas the BMP388 remains below approximately ±2.2 hPa under the same conditions. Under the random-walk model, the expected degradation was significantly lower for both sensors; however, the BMP388 consistently demonstrated improved long-term stability.

Figure 35(right) shows the corresponding relative error evolution (expressed as the percentage of the nominal atmospheric pressure near 1000 hPa). The BMP388 maintains a substantially lower long-term relative deviation, which is particularly relevant for machine learning applications that rely on the multi-year consistency of environmental features.

These results highlight the potential benefits of adopting higher-stability pressure sensors in future long-term ML-driven environmental monitoring deployments.

https://doi.org/10.3390/app16073237

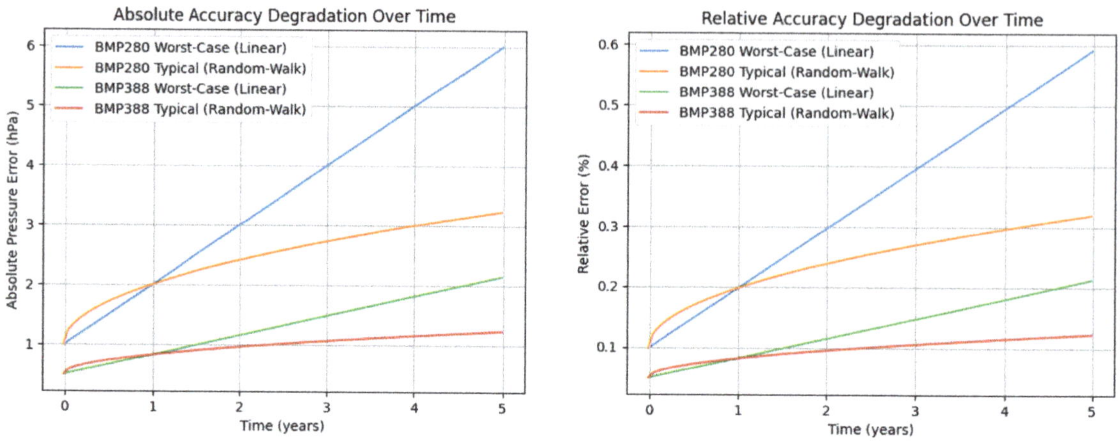

Figure 35. Projected long-term degradation of pressure measurement accuracy for BMP280 and BMP388 sensors over a five-year deployment period. (left) Absolute pressure error evolution (hPa) under the worst-case linear drift and stochastic random-walk models. (right) Corresponding relative error expressed as a percentage of the nominal atmospheric pressure (1000hPa). The results highlight the improved long-term stability of the BMP388 compared with that of the BMP280, particularly in extended autonomous environmental monitoring scenarios.

Author Contributions: Conceptualization, E.-C.T. and V.N.; methodology, E.-C.T. and V.N.; software, E.-C.T.; validation, E.-C.T., V.N. and C.S.-C.; formal analysis, E.-C.T. and V.N.; investigation, E.-C.T. and V.N.; resources, V.N., C.S.-C., C.A., R.M.M. and C.P.S.; data curation, E.-C.T.; writing—original draft preparation, E.-C.T. and V.N.; writing—review and editing, V.N., C.S.-C., C.A., R.M.M. and C.P.S.; visualization, E.-C.T.; supervision, C.A. and C.S.-C.; project administration, C.S.-C.; funding acquisition, C.S.-C., R.M.M. and C.P.S. All authors have read and agreed to the published version of the manuscript.

Funding: This study received no external funding. The development of the prototype was partially supported by hardware resources and technical support provided by Orange collaborators.

Institutional Review Board Statement: Not applicable.

Informed Consent Statement: Not applicable.

Data Availability Statement: The data presented in this study are available upon request from the corresponding author, due to privacy restrictions.

Acknowledgments: The authors would like to thank Orange collaborators for their technical support and for providing hardware resources used during the development and testing of the environmental monitoring platform. The authors used Paperpal (web-based academic writing assistant) and GPT v5.4 Thinking from OpenAI to assist with drafting, language refinement, and improvement of English clarity in certain sections of the manuscript. The AI tools were used solely for editorial support and for paragraph structuring. All scientific content, experimental design, data analysis, figures, and conclusions were developed and verified by the authors. The authors take full responsibility for the accuracy, integrity, and originality of the work.

Conflicts of Interest: Authors R.M.M. and C.P.S. were employed by the company Orange Romania S.A. The remaining authors declare that this research was conducted in the absence of any commercial or financial relationships that could be construed as potential conflicts of interest.

https://doi.org/10.3390/app16073237

Abbreviations

The following abbreviations are used in this manuscript:

AI	Artificial Intelligence
BMS	Battery Management System
Cat-M1	LTE Category M1 (LTE-M)
CR2032	20 mm diameter, 3.2 mm thickness lithium coin cell battery
DCF77	German longwave atomic time signal (77.5 kHz)
GPIO	General Purpose Input/Output
I2C	Inter-Integrated Circuit
IoT	Internet of Things
$LiFePO_4$	Lithium Iron Phosphate Battery
Li-Po	Lithium Polymer Battery
LPWAN	Low Power Wide Area Network
LTE-M	Long Term Evolution for Machines
MCU	Microcontroller Unit
NB-IoT	Narrowband Internet of Things
PWM	Pulse Width Modulation
PV	Photovoltaic
QoS	Quality of Service
RJ11/RJ12	Registered Jack 11/12 Connector
RSSI	Received Signal Strength Indicator
RTC	Real-Time Clock
SD	Secure Digital (memory card)
SPI	Serial Peripheral Interface
SRAM	Static Random-Access Memory
TinyML	Tiny Machine Learning

Appendix A. Winter Solar Radiation Prediction

Appendix A.1. Sanandrei Winter Solar Radiation Dataset and Splitting Strategy

This appendix describes the Sanandrei dataset used to train and evaluate the winter-time solar radiation prediction model. The dataset was built from a multi-year historical weather time series (CSV format) containing hourly records with a unified timestamp column (`datetime`) and meteorological variables. In this study, the prediction target was `solarradiation`, whereas the input feature set included calendar context and weather predictors: `dayofyear`, `hour`, `temp`, `feelslike`, `dew`, `windgust`, `windspeed`, `winddir`, and `visibility`. To focus on the winter solar resource, we filtered the dataset to the winter months {December, January, and February} and further restricted samples to daytime hours between 06:00 and 18:00 (inclusive). After filtering, the samples were sorted chronologically to preserve the natural temporal ordering of the time series. Solar-derived missing values (when present in the source file) were conservatively imputed with zero for `solarradiation`, `solarenergy`, and `uvindex`, reflecting the fact that these variables may be absent or null during the night or data gaps, while the remaining required predictors were validated and rows containing NaNs in the used columns were removed.

Appendix A.2. Chronological Train/Validation/Test Split

To avoid temporal leakage and emulate real deployment conditions (training on past seasons to predict future seasons), the dataset was split strictly by year using a chronological hold-out strategy. Specifically, the training set included winter daytime data from 2019 to 2023, the validation set used the subsequent year 2024, and the test set used the most recent year 2025. This corresponds to a 5-year/1-year/1-year partition, as illustrated in Figure A1. Under this configuration, the split represented approximately 66.67% of the training data

https://doi.org/10.3390/app16073237

and 16.67% each for validation and testing (assuming comparable winter daytime sampling density across years). This design supports robust hyperparameter tuning in the validation year (2024) while providing an unbiased performance estimate for a strictly unseen future year (2025).

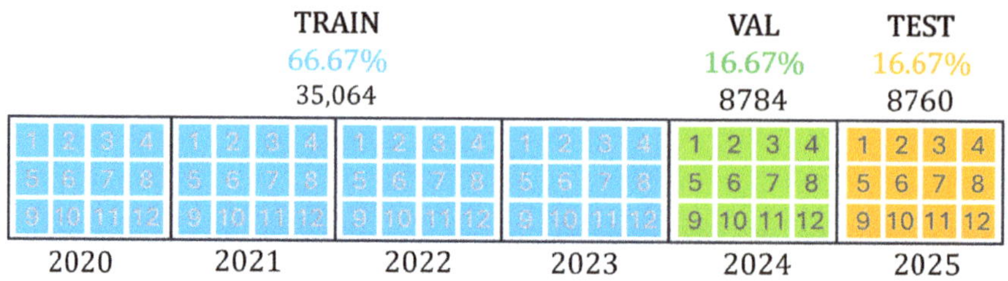

Figure A1. Chronological dataset splitting strategy used for winter daytime solar radiation forecasting in Sânandrei. Winter daytime samples are partitioned by year into training (2019–2023, 66.67%), validation (2024, 16.67%), and testing (2025, 16.67%) subsets to prevent temporal leakage and to evaluate generalization on a future year.

Appendix A.3. Normalization and Sliding-Window Sequence Construction

After the year-based split, feature scaling was applied using min–max normalization. Importantly, scalers were fit on the training subset only and then applied to the validation and test subsets, ensuring that no statistical information from 2024 or 2025 was used during training-time preprocessing. Formally, let $\mathbf{x}_t \in \mathbb{R}^d$ be the feature vector at time t and y_t the solar radiation target; min–max scaling maps each feature dimension to $[0,1]$ using training-set extrema.

To model the temporal dependencies, the normalized time series was transformed into supervised learning samples using a sliding-window strategy. With a sequence length of `SEQ_LEN` $= 24$, each input tensor was constructed from the previous 24 time steps:

$$X_t = [x_{t-24}, x_{t-23}, \ldots, x_{t-1}] \in \mathbb{R}^{24\times d}, \qquad y_t = y_t.$$

This procedure was applied independently within the training, validation, and test subsets (without crossing year boundaries), producing three sequence datasets used to train and evaluate various ML models.

Appendix A.3.1. Analysis of Random Forest Configurations and Performance

This section analyzes the performance of the Random Forest (RF) models under three different temporal filtering strategies: (i) winter daytime only, (ii) winter full-day, and (iii) all-year daytime. The objective of this study was to evaluate the influence of seasonal filtering and diurnal constraints on model generalization and predictive stability.

(1) Winter Daytime Model (December–February, 06:00–18:00).

As shown in Table A1, the relatively high training score compared to the validation score indicates moderate overfitting. Restricting the dataset to daylight hours reduces the noise from nighttime zero-radiation values but also significantly reduces the sample size and variability. The use of a deeper tree structure (Table A2, max_depth = 20) contributes to a stronger fitting on the training set but slightly weaker validation generalization.

(2) Winter Full-Day Model (December–February, 00:00–23:00).

Interestingly, despite including zero-radiation nighttime values, this configuration achieved lower MAE and RMSE on validation. The trees were allowed to grow without depth restriction (max_depth=None), but the reduced number of estimators (25) acted as

https://doi.org/10.3390/app16073237

an implicit regularization. This improvement suggests that including full daily patterns may help the model better learn transition dynamics (sunrise/sunset behavior).

(3) All-Year Daytime Model (Full Year, 06:00–18:00).

The all-year daytime configuration exhibited the strongest overall performance. This significant improvement is primarily due to the following reasons:

- Larger dataset size;
- Increased seasonal variability;
- Broader solar radiation patterns.

Table A1. Performance comparison of the three best-performing Random Forest configurations under different temporal filtering strategies.

Metric	Winter Daytime	Winter Full Day	All-Year Daytime
R^2_{train}	0.9733	0.9781	0.9890
R^2_{val}	0.7951	0.8261	0.9121
R^2_{test}	0.8415	0.8420	0.9059

Table A2. Comparison of best-performing Random Forest architectures across temporal filtering strategies.

Parameter	Winter Daytime	Winter Full Day	All-Year Daytime
n_estimators	50	25	100
max_depth	20	None	None
min_samples_split	5	5	5
min_samples_leaf	1	1	1
max_features	log2	sqrt	sqrt

Although the validation RMSE appears higher than the winter-only full-day case, this must be interpreted relative to the increased dynamic range of solar radiation across all the seasons. Higher R^2 values confirm superior generalization capability.

Comparative Discussion.

Several important insights have emerged.

1. Expanding the temporal coverage (all-year) substantially improves generalization.
2. Including night-time winter data reduces validation error compared to winter daytime-only filtering.
3. Hyperparameter differences (e.g., number of trees and tree depth) significantly impact overfitting behavior.
4. Shallower ensembles (fewer trees or no depth constraint with fewer estimators) may generalize better under limited seasonal data.

These findings demonstrate that dataset design and temporal filtering strategies influence performance as much as hyperparameter tuning. The difference between $R^2_{val} = 0.795$ and $R^2_{val} = 0.826$ under the same seasonal restriction highlights that architectural tuning alone can produce measurable improvements, even when the underlying dataset remains unchanged.

Appendix A.3.2. Comparison of Random Forest Architectures

The comparison in Table A2 shows that the best-performing configuration for the largest dataset (all-year) required a higher number of trees, whereas winter-restricted datasets performed optimally with fewer estimators. This suggests that the ensemble capacity should scale proportionally with dataset diversity and seasonal variability.

https://doi.org/10.3390/app16073237

Appendix B. Cloud Web Application Architecture

Appendix B.1. Overview

To support scalable data management, device orchestration, and AI-driven analytics, a cloud-based web application was developed and deployed alongside the environmental monitoring infrastructure (Figure A2). The platform acts as an intermediary layer between edge devices (Arduino-based data collectors), a centralized MySQL database hosted in the cloud, and end-users accessing the system through a browser interface.

Figure A2. Cloud Dashboard interface of the EdgeAI Management platform showing system-wide monitoring and device management features, including geographic visualization of deployed data collectors, high-level performance indicators, and navigation modules for Weather, Agricultural, and Green Energy Insights.

The web application was implemented using a PHP–MySQL backend architecture and deployed via a cloud hosting environment with phpMyAdmin database administration. The system enables secure authentication, real-time visualization of measurements, device lifecycle management, alert handling, and integration of Machine Learning inference modules.

Appendix B.2. System Architecture

The cloud platform follows a three-tier architecture:

1. **Edge layer**: solar-powered environmental data collectors transmitting measurements via LTE-M/NB-IoT to the cloud API.
2. **Backend layer**: REST-based PHP services interfacing with a MySQL relational database.
3. **Frontend layer**: responsive dashboard for visualization, analytics, and device management.

Incoming measurements were transmitted by each device using a unique `device_id` identifier. The backend validates, stores, and indexes time-series data in the `weather_data` table, enabling efficient chronological retrieval and filtering of data.

Appendix B.3. User and Device Management

The platform supports role-based access control through the `users` table, allowing both administrative and standard-user roles. Administrators can:

https://doi.org/10.3390/app16073237

- Register and manage devices;
- Assign devices to specific users;
- Monitor connectivity and operational status;
- Review alerts and system notifications.

The `Data Collectors` interface allows monitoring of deployed devices, including:

- Device name and geographic location;
- GPS coordinates;
- Operational status (active, inactive, maintenance);
- Last communication timestamp;
- RSSI statistics and connectivity quality.

This structure ensures traceability and accountability for each field-deployed node in the system.

Appendix B.4. Weather Data Visualization

The *Weather Data* module provides structured access to time-series measurements (see Figure A3). Users can:

- Filter data by device;
- Sort by timestamp;
- Search specific intervals;
- Inspect temperature, humidity, pressure, rainfall, wind, soil, and radiation parameters.

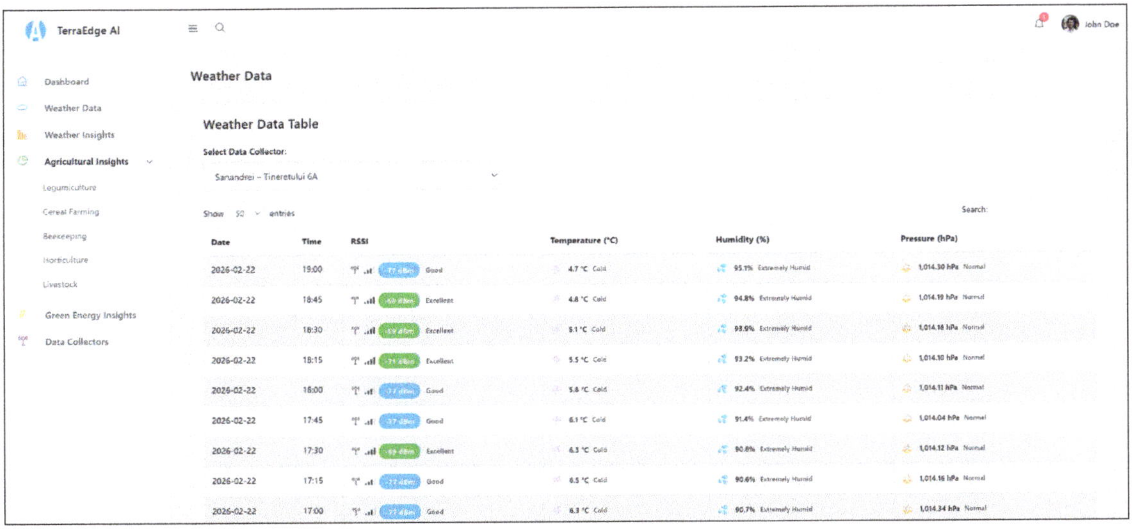

Figure A3. Weather Data module of the EdgeAI cloud platform showing structured time-series measurements, device selection interface, and tabular visualization of environmental parameters (temperature, humidity, pressure, and RSSI).

Measurements are displayed with contextual interpretation (e.g., "Cold", "Extremely Humid", "Normal Pressure") to enhance usability for non-technical stakeholders.

Efficient database indexing on `(device_id, timestamp)` ensures an optimized query performance even for multi-year datasets.

https://doi.org/10.3390/app16073237

Appendix B.5. Dashboard and System Monitoring

The main *Dashboard* page (Figure A2) provides system-level insights, including the following:

- Total readings and device activity;
- Connectivity statistics (RSSI distribution);
- Geographic visualization of deployed stations; (Sanandrei, Timis county RO; Rogoz de Beliu, Arad county RO);
- Summary indicators and performance metrics.

This centralized overview allows for a rapid assessment of the network health and spatial distribution of devices.

Appendix B.6. AI Integration and Insight Modules

The cloud platform integrates predictive and analytical Machine Learning modules under dedicated sections (Figure A4):

- **Weather insights**: time-series forecasting (e.g., temperature prediction with uncertainty bands)
- **Agricultural insights**: soil moisture prediction, irrigation advisory support, crop stress indicators
- **Green energy insights**: solar radiation prediction, energy yield estimation, hybrid renewable modeling

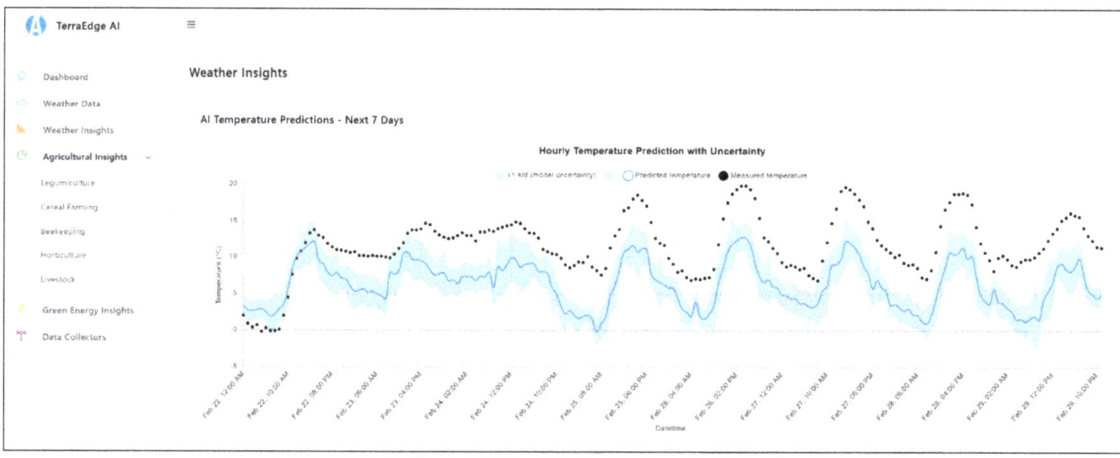

Figure A4. Weather Insights module illustrating AI-based temperature forecasting with uncertainty estimation. The plot presents the predicted temperature values, measured observations, and confidence intervals (±1 standard deviation), enabling the interpretability and reliability assessment of the deployed Machine Learning model.

Machine learning models can be executed in two ways:

1. Directly in the cloud (high-capacity inference);
2. Or partially at the edge (TinyML-based inference on Arduino Nano 33 BLE).

The cloud dashboard serves as a visualization and orchestration interface for the AI outputs.

https://doi.org/10.3390/app16073237

Appendix B.7. Scalability and Multi-Industry Applicability

The modular database design and API-driven backend enable a horizontal scalability. Additional sensor types, new device categories, and industry-specific analytics modules can be incorporated without redesigning the core schema.

The platform architecture supports the following applications:

- Precision agriculture;
- Renewable energy optimization;
- Environmental monitoring;
- Smart farming and IoT ecosystems.

Appendix B.8. Summary

The cloud dashboard is a critical component of the overall environmental monitoring architecture. It bridges edge intelligence and centralized analytics, enabling data acquisition, storage, visualization, and Machine Learning integration within a unified, scalable ecosystem.

This integrated design supports both research-oriented experimentation and practical deployment in the agricultural, environmental, and renewable energy domains.

References

1. Wolfert, S.; Ge, L.; Verdouw, C.; Bogaardt, M.J. Big Data in Smart Farming—A review. *Agric. Syst.* **2017**, *153*, 69–80. [CrossRef]
2. Kamilaris, A.; Prenafeta-Boldú, F.X. Deep learning in agriculture: A survey. *Comput. Electron. Agric.* **2018**, *147*, 70–90. [CrossRef]
3. Liakos, K.G.; Busato, P.; Moshou, D.; Pearson, S.; Bochtis, D. Machine Learning in Agriculture: A Review. *Sensors* **2018**, *18*, 2674. [CrossRef] [PubMed]
4. Atzori, L.; Iera, A.; Morabito, G. The Internet of Things: A survey. *Comput. Netw.* **2010**, *54*, 2787–2805. [CrossRef]
5. Gubbi, J.; Buyya, R.; Marusic, S.; Palaniswami, M. Internet of Things (IoT): A vision, architectural elements, and future directions. *Future Gener. Comput. Syst.* **2013**, *29*, 1645–1660. [CrossRef]
6. Ratasuk, R.; Mangalvedhe, N.; Zhang, Y.; Robert, M.; Koskinen, J.P. Overview of narrowband IoT in LTE Rel-13. In *Proceedings of the 2016 IEEE Conference on Standards for Communications and Networking (CSCN)*; IEEE: Berlin, Germany, 2016; pp. 1–7. [CrossRef]
7. Mekki, K.; Bajic, E.; Chaxel, F.; Meyer, F. A comparative study of LPWAN technologies for large-scale IoT deployment. *ICT Express* **2019**, *5*, 1–7. [CrossRef]
8. Banbury, C.R.; Reddi, V.J.; Lam, M.; Fu, W.; Fazel, A.; Holleman, J.; Huang, X.; Hurtado, R.; Kanter, D.; Lokhmotov, A.; et al. Benchmarking TinyML Systems: Challenges and Direction. *arXiv* **2021**, arXiv:2003.04821. [CrossRef]
9. Warden, P.; Situnayake, D. *TinyML: Machine Learning with TensorFlow Lite on Arduino and Ultra-Low-Power Microcontrollers*; O'Reilly Media: Sebastopol, CA, USA, 2019.
10. Nallusamy, R.; Duraiswamy, K. Solar Powered Wireless Sensor Networks for Environmental Monitoring. *Inf. Technol. J.* **2011**, *10*, 1–10. [CrossRef]
11. Helmy, H.A.; El-Rifaie, A.M.; Youssef, A.A.F.; Haggag, A.; Hamad, H.; Eltokhy, M. Improving Solar Energy-Harvesting Wireless Sensor Network (SEH-WSN) with Hybrid Li-Fi/Wi-Fi, Integrating Markov Model, Sleep Scheduling, and Smart Switching Algorithms. *Technologies* **2025**, *13*, 437. [CrossRef]
12. Voyant, C.; Notton, G.; Kalogirou, S.; Nivet, M.L.; Paoli, C.; Motte, F.; Fouilloy, A. Machine learning methods for solar radiation forecasting: A review. *Renew. Energy* **2017**, *105*, 569–582. [CrossRef]
13. Kalaany, C.M.A.; Kimaita, H.N.; Abdelmoneim, A.A.; Khadra, R.; Derardja, B.; Dragonetti, G. The Potential of Low-Cost IoT-Enabled Agrometeorological Stations: A Systematic Review. *Sensors* **2025**, *25*, 6020. [CrossRef] [PubMed]
14. Ganesan, S.; Lean, C.; Chen, L.; Yuan, K.; Ng, P.K.; Basir Khan, M.R. IoT-enabled Smart Weather Stations: Innovations, Challenges, and Future Directions. *Malays. J. Sci. Adv. Technol.* **2024**, *4*, 180–190. [CrossRef]
15. Khan, S.; Mahi, M.; Rasheduzzaman, M. Design and Implementation of a Low-Cost Weather Monitoring System using ESP-NOW. In *2024 13th International Conference on Electrical and Computer Engineering (ICECE)*; IEEE: Dhaka, Bangladesh, 2024; pp. 437–442. [CrossRef]
16. Jasso-Reyes, D.A.; Cabrera-Perdomo, C.I.; Reyes-Villagrana, R.A. On the Architecture of a Low-Cost Meteorological Station Based on the Internet of Things (IoT): Preliminary Results. *Environ. Earth Sci. Proc.* **2025**, *34*, 14. [CrossRef]
17. Eyasin, M.S.H.; Sobhani, M.E.; Nasrin, S.; Al Rafi, A.S.; Muzahidul Islam, A. CropSynergy: Harnessing IoT solutions for smart and efficient crop management. *Crop Des.* **2026**, *5*, 100127. [CrossRef]

18. Zhurakovskyi, B.; Pliushch, O.; Saiko, V.; Shutenko, V. Machine Learning-based Environmental Monitoring and Analysis System. In Proceedings of the Cybersecurity Providing in Information and Telecommunication Systems, Kyiv, Ukraine, 28 February 2025.
19. Zhao, B.; Zheng, D.; Yang, C.; Wang, S.; Mansurova, M.; Jomartova, S.; Kunicina, N.; Zabasta, A.; Beliaev, V.; Caiko, J.; et al. Design and Optimization of an Internet of Things-Based Cloud Platform for Autonomous Agricultural Machinery Using Narrowband Internet of Things and 5G Dual-Channel Communication. *Electronics* **2025**, *14*, 1672. [CrossRef]
20. Lukic, M.; Sobot, S.; Mezei, I.; Vukobratovic, D.; Danilovic, D. In-depth Real-World Evaluation of NB-IoT Module Energy Consumption. In *Proceedings of the 2020 IEEE International Conference on Smart Internet of Things (SmartIoT)*; IEEE: Beijing, China, 2020; pp. 261–265. [CrossRef]
21. Michelinakis, F.; Al-selwi, A.S.; Capuzzo, M.; Zanella, A.; Mahmood, K.; Elmokashfi, A. Dissecting Energy Consumption of NB-IoT Devices Empirically. *arXiv* **2020**, arXiv:2004.07127. [CrossRef]
22. Trabelsi, S.; Gontara, S.; Bougharriou, S.; Mtibaa, A. Advancing NB-IoT communication: Performance analysis and novel gap-aware hybrid scheduling for delay-sensitive traffic. *Wirel. Netw.* **2025**, *32*, 243–284. [CrossRef]
23. Masoum, A.; Meratnia, N.; Havinga, P.J. An energy-efficient adaptive sampling scheme for wireless sensor networks. In *Proceedings of the 2013 IEEE Eighth International Conference on Intelligent Sensors, Sensor Networks and Information Processing*; IEEE: Melbourne, VIC, Australia, 2013; pp. 231–236. [CrossRef]

https://doi.org/10.3390/app16073237

applied sciences

MDPI

Article

Optimized Scheduling of IoT Devices in Healthcare Facilities: Balancing Cost and Quality of Care

Francesco Nucci [1,*], Gabriele Papadia [1] and Emiliano Fedeli [2]

1 Department of Engineering for Innovation, University of Salento, 73100 Lecce, Italy; gabriele.papadia@unisalento.it
2 Laser Romae S.r.l., 00144 Roma, Italy; emiliano.fedeli@laserromae.it
* Correspondence: francesco.nucci@unisalento.it

Featured Application: This study optimizes the allocation and scheduling of IoT devices for patient monitoring in healthcare. Utilizing NSGA-II, it minimizes costs while maximizing quality of care, ensuring efficient resource use. The findings assist healthcare facility administrators in improving patient tracking and operational efficiency in dynamic healthcare settings.

Abstract: This paper addresses the critical challenge of optimal allocation and scheduling of Internet of Things (IoT) tracking devices for patient monitoring in healthcare facilities, where limited resources must be efficiently distributed to minimize cost and maximize care quality. We formulate this healthcare management problem as a specialized variant of the Resource-Constrained Scheduling Problem that incorporates patient-specific factors such as duration of stay and priority. After establishing the computational complexity of the problem, we propose a Non-dominated Sorting Genetic Algorithm II (NSGA-II) to address the complex problem of balancing multiple objectives: cost minimization and quality of care maximization. Our approach offers a set of optimal trade-offs, enabling informed decision-making to select the best final solution. Computational experiments conducted on both simulated scenarios and real-world healthcare facility datasets demonstrate that our approach outperforms existing methods, achieving between 1.2 and 3.0 times more solutions than the state of the art. Moreover, in comparison to manual scheduling by medical center managers, our method achieves cost savings of up to 12% (with an average of 6.3%) and quality improvements of up to 20% (with an average of 10%) across the tested experiments. The proposed method scales effectively to realistic healthcare settings with varying numbers of patients and tracking devices, maintaining solution quality while keeping computational time within practical limits for daily operational use. Our findings contribute to both healthcare operations research and clinical practice by providing an efficient methodology for optimizing the use of limited monitoring resources while prioritizing patient safety.

Keywords: healthcare monitoring; internet of things; scheduling; bi-objective optimization; metaheuristic

1. Introduction

The rapid advancement of Information Technology (IT) has fundamentally transformed healthcare, particularly in patient monitoring within hospital settings. As hospitals and medical facilities increasingly adopt digital solutions, the ability to continuously track patients' vital signs, predict potential complications, and optimize healthcare operations has improved significantly. Advanced IT solutions, including cloud computing, IoT, AI, and edge computing, enable real-time data collection, remote monitoring, and predictive analytics, enhancing both patient outcomes and hospital efficiency [1]. The incorporation of AI-driven decision support systems to enhance patient care is studied in [2,3].

IT-based monitoring solutions bring clear benefits to healthcare. They boost workflow efficiency, improve early disease detection, and reduce human error. One key use is indoor positioning systems, which track patients and equipment in real time. These rely on wireless networks and cloud computing to support hospital navigation and emergency response [4,5]. Wearable IoT devices and sensor-based systems also allow continuous monitoring of vital signs. This supports personalized care and cuts down on manual checks [6,7]. A review in [8] explores Industry 4.0 in healthcare, while [9] focuses on IoT-based medical devices. As noted in [10], the Healthcare IoT (H-IoT) enables real-time monitoring and quicker interventions, improving patient outcomes. It also simplifies data collection and analysis, making healthcare more efficient. According to [11], IoT helps reduce hospital readmissions and supports remote care. Finally, AI-driven predictive analytics is transforming decision-making. It detects early warning signs and suggests timely actions [12,13]. These advancements have not only improved patient care but also reduced operational costs for healthcare providers.

Despite growing adoption of IoT and AI in healthcare, most existing scheduling solutions focus on general aspects like task timing, system responsiveness, or network performance. For instance, optimized scheduling models have been proposed to reduce delays and task failure rates [14], while others introduced decision support systems to prioritize urgent care when resources are limited [15]. Some approaches integrate deep learning or predictive analytics to improve sensing accuracy and tailor device usage based on patient needs [16,17]. However, these models often overlook the specific challenge of assigning individual IoT devices to patients in a way that balances cost with quality of care.

Studies from different regions highlight critical contextual considerations. For example, research in Japan shows that elderly users benefit from voice-based IoT interfaces due to ease of use [18], while work in India emphasizes the need for scalable, cost-effective solutions in resource-limited healthcare environments [19]. European reviews also stress the importance of adapting device allocation strategies to diverse care models and patient needs [20].

Although these contributions have advanced the field, none offer a comprehensive framework that integrates operational cost, device characteristics, and patient well-being. This underscores the need for a new approach—one that formulates device–patient allocation as a multi-objective scheduling problem, explicitly balancing economic efficiency with high-quality, personalized care.

How can IoT medical devices be optimally allocated to patients in healthcare settings while simultaneously minimizing operational costs and maximizing quality of care? Specifically, we investigated whether a bi-objective scheduling approach can effectively balance these competing objectives while accounting for real-world constraints such as device compatibility, setup times, availability windows, and battery limitations.

This study aims to develop a comprehensive optimization framework for the allocation of IoT medical devices to patients that explicitly addresses the trade-off between cost efficiency and care quality. Our specific objectives are as follows:

- Formulate the IoT device allocation problem as a bi-objective scheduling model that captures essential real-world constraints.
- Design and implement an efficient heuristic solution approach based on NSGA-II that generates high-quality Pareto-optimal solutions within practical time constraints.

- Evaluate the proposed approach against both existing methods and manual scheduling practices to demonstrate its practical value in healthcare settings.

This paper proposes a novel bi-objective optimization model that explicitly addresses the trade-off between operational costs and quality of care in IoT device scheduling. We develop a tailored heuristic solution based on the NSGA-II algorithm, enhanced with domain-specific constraints such as device compatibility, setup durations, availability windows, and battery lifespan.

Experimental results demonstrate the effectiveness of our approach. Compared to baseline heuristics and manual scheduling, our method achieves up to a 12% reduction in operational costs (with an average of 6.3%) and care quality improvements of up to 20% (with an average of 10%) based on weighted patient-priority metrics. The system rapidly produces diverse high-quality solutions within just a few seconds, and within less than a minute, it reliably approximates an accurate Pareto front—making it well suited for real-time decision support. These findings significantly advance the field by demonstrating that intelligent, constraint-aware scheduling can simultaneously optimize for clinical and economic outcomes in dynamic healthcare environments.

To address the challenge of allocating IoT medical devices in healthcare, we formulated the problem as a bi-objective scheduling model. This allowed us to represent key real-world elements—such as patients, devices, time windows, and care priorities—within a structured optimization framework, aligning them with classic scheduling constructs like jobs, machines, and processing times.

The model incorporates essential operational constraints, including device–patient compatibility, setup times, availability windows, continuous monitoring requirements, and battery limitations. These constraints ensure the formulation realistically captures the complexities of hospital environments. By modeling the trade-offs between cost and quality of care, the framework generates a Pareto front of optimal solutions. This empowers healthcare decision-makers with flexible, data-driven options that support efficient resource use and improved patient outcomes.

The proposed IoT device allocation model, which balances cost and quality of care, falls within the class of computationally intensive multi-objective scheduling problems. Hard constraints—such as time windows, device compatibility, battery limits, and setup times—further increase its complexity. As even single-objective variants are NP-hard, solving the bi-objective version requires navigating a large, non-convex solution space. Due to the limitations of exact methods for large instances, heuristic and metaheuristic approaches like evolutionary algorithms are preferred for efficiently approximating the Pareto front under realistic time constraints.

To address the complexity of allocating IoT medical devices in healthcare, this study presents a heuristic approach based on the NSGA-II algorithm, tailored for bi-objective scheduling. The method uses genetic representations to explore large solution spaces, optimizing for both operational cost and care quality. NSGA-II's evolutionary operators—crossover, mutation, and elitism—refine solutions to generate a diverse Pareto front, giving decision-makers flexible, high-quality options.

Unlike single-objective or rigid heuristic methods, our approach dynamically adjusts NSGA-II parameters and integrates real-world constraints like device compatibility and battery limits. Its multi-run, time-bounded design ensures practicality in time-sensitive hospital environments. This enables scalable, interpretable scheduling with better resource use, improved patient–device matching, and transparent trade-off evaluation.

This paper makes several key contributions to the field of healthcare resource optimization through the design, formulation, and implementation of a bi-objective scheduling model for IoT device allocation. First, it introduces a novel optimization framework that explicitly balances operational costs with quality of care—two often conflicting objectives rarely addressed together in prior work. By modeling real-world constraints such as patient priority, device compatibility, setup times, and availability windows, the proposed formulation reflects the complexity of clinical environments more accurately than existing approaches. Second, the paper develops and tailors a heuristic algorithm based on NSGA-II, capable of generating a diverse set of high-quality solutions under realistic time constraints, which is essential given the NP-hard nature of the problem. Third, the method is designed to support real-time, adaptive re-optimization, allowing healthcare facilities to respond dynamically to changes such as new admissions or evolving patient conditions.

From a practical standpoint, the system has broad applicability in modernizing healthcare facility operations, offering a scalable and interpretable decision support tool that enhances efficiency and patient outcomes. It can be deployed across various healthcare settings—from small outpatient facilities to large multi-ward hospitals—where it automates complex planning tasks, reduces human error, and improves responsiveness to clinical needs.

By integrating intelligent scheduling into real-world medical center workflows, this work extends current scientific understanding of IoT-enabled healthcare optimization and bridges the gap between theoretical modeling and operational decision-making in digital healthcare environments.

The topic of this paper strongly aligns with the scope and objectives of *"Applied Sciences"* and its Special Issue *"The Internet of Things (IoT) and Its Application in Monitoring"*. By addressing a real-world challenge at the nexus of IoT deployment, healthcare optimization, and intelligent scheduling, our proposed framework directly contributes to the advancement of practical, data-driven solutions for patient monitoring. This work not only highlights the increasing importance of IoT in enhancing clinical operations but also introduces methodological innovations that support the journal's mission of connecting applied research with tangible technological impact.

2. Background

Healthcare IoT software management is vital for hiding complexity and enabling easy deployment [21]. Smart resource allocation is equally crucial for cost control and performance amid fluctuating device demand. Poor allocation can harm care during peaks and waste resources during lulls. Effective resource management ensures efficient and cost-effective device use. Proper system design is key for successful IoT adoption and better healthcare service [22]. Strong resource allocation is also essential for reliable remote monitoring [23]. Management must balance scalability and cost within financial and performance limits. IoT's healthcare benefits come with rising operating costs [24], making efficient resource use critical. Device variety in cost and comfort impacts patient acceptance, requiring scheduling to balance cost, comfort, and clinical needs.

Recent studies address IoT scheduling in healthcare, especially for home visits and monitoring. The authors of [14] presented a smart PHMS with optimized scheduling, reducing task starvation (14%) and failure (17%). A review in [25] analyzed real-time IoT healthcare scheduling, comparing approaches and outlining future directions. The authors of [26] proposed Prioritized Scheduling (PS) for delay-sensitive tasks, outperforming EDF variations. The study in [15] presented a decision support system to allocate limited devices, prioritizing critical cases. The architecture described in [16] combines IoT with deep learning to improve sensing accuracy and personalize resource allocation based on patient needs. Finally, the authors of [17] integrated machine learning with IoT to predict demand, enhancing care and operations.

To present a well-rounded view of the global research landscape, it is essential to highlight key contributions from international research centers, especially those in Europe and Asia.

For instance, a study by [18] in Japan evaluated various user interfaces for IoT devices among senior citizens, finding that voice interfaces were more suitable for elderly users due to shorter setting times and higher usability scores. In India, [19] discussed the impact of IoT in healthcare, emphasizing the challenges and opportunities in adopting digital healthcare solutions in resource-constrained environments. Additionally, the authors of [20] reviewed IoT-based ambient assisted living solutions for the growing elderly population and their care needs, categorizing them by health focus, IoT technologies, aims, and experimental evaluation. The work in [27] performed heart disease prediction using an IoT-based framework and an improved deep learning approach, applied to the Hungarian dataset.

While this body of work demonstrates significant advancements in IoT-based healthcare scheduling, most studies focus on general resource use, network performance, or task timing. Crucially, none directly address the problem of assigning specific IoT devices to patients in a way that balances operational cost with quality of care. This gap in the literature highlights the need for novel approaches that integrate clinical priorities, device characteristics, and patient comfort. Even recent international studies, while innovative in their respective domains, do not provide comprehensive frameworks for patient-specific device allocation that optimizes both economic and clinical outcomes.

The systematic analysis of this expanded literature reveals several methodological patterns crucial to our research design. First, successful implementations consistently incorporate multi-objective optimization techniques that balance technical efficiency with patient-centered outcomes. Second, regional variations in healthcare delivery models significantly impact device allocation strategies, necessitating adaptable frameworks. This methodological synthesis directly informs our research approach by establishing the assessment metrics, constraint parameters, and evaluation frameworks employed in our study. Our proposed multi-objective optimization framework for IoT device allocation therefore builds upon a comprehensive understanding of global research trends. Unlike prior work, it explicitly considers both financial constraints and the delivery of high-quality care through appropriate device assignment, addressing the identified gaps in current approaches.

3. Materials and Methods

3.1. Research Problem

In the context of our study, a healthcare facility accommodates patients for defined periods, and IoT devices must be allocated to patients throughout their stay to optimize both operational costs and quality of care.

Each patient requires a specific class of IoT device tailored to monitor particular parameters. The allocation of these devices incurs costs related to their operational expenses, which vary depending on the type of device used. In addition, the devices' quality and characteristics—such as weight, size, and battery life—directly influence patient quality of care. These factors affect the ease with which patients can wear and use the devices, thereby impacting their overall experience. Consequently, it is essential—particularly when considering the patient's priority level—to utilize devices that maximize the patient experience. However, it is important to recognize that cost minimization and quality of care are often competing objectives.

The overarching goal is to effectively schedule the allocation of available IoT devices to patients over time in a manner that minimizes operational costs while simultaneously maximizing patient well-being.

The mathematical formulation of the scheduling problem is described as follows.

A list of patients is provided, with each patient assigned a priority level by healthcare professionals based on medical assessments, urgency, and institutional protocols. Additionally, each patient specifies their stay duration in the facility, including start and end times, as well as the required device class.

A set of IoT devices is available, each characterized by a specific quality level that impacts the comfort and well-being of the wearer. Each device is also associated with an hourly operational cost, a limited operational lifespan (battery duration), and a predefined availability window (start and end times) during which it can be utilized. Additionally, the device's class parameter specifies the subset of patients for whom it is suitable, while the setup time parameter represents the time required to transfer the device from one patient to another.

The constraints are of various types. First, the device–patient allocation is valid only if it falls within the availability window of both the device and the patient. Second, the allocation is valid if the device class matches the patient class. If the device is reassigned to another patient, a setup activity must occur between the two allocations. Within the time window that identifies the patient's stay in the facility, the patient must always be assigned to a device. Therefore, if a device needs to be replaced because it has reached its operational lifespan, a new device must be immediately allocated to the patient. Finally, the total periods during which a device is allocated to multiple patients must not exceed the device's operational lifespan.

3.2. Research Model

Our approach transforms the scheduling challenge into a bi-objective optimization problem, a methodology that simultaneously addresses two potentially competing goals. In bi-objective optimization, improving one performance metric can necessitate a trade-off in another, which is particularly characteristic of complex systems in manufacturing, logistics, and project management.

In our context, efficiency is quantified by minimizing assignment costs, while quality of care is defined by the level of benefit patients receive from the assigned devices. Specifically, higher quality of care is achieved by allocating patients to more advanced devices that offer enhanced features directly impacting their experience and well-being. For instance, lighter and more compact models improve patient comfort and ease of use, thus contributing to a higher quality of care. The system prioritizes allocating the most suitable devices, especially those with superior features, to high-priority patients whenever feasible. This dual-objective optimization framework mirrors the complex realities of medical device scheduling, where financial limitations must be carefully balanced with the imperative to maximize positive clinical outcomes and patient experience.

Mathematically formulating the two-objective scheduling problem requires a precise definition of variables, constraints, and objective functions, which are comprehensively detailed in the accompanying parameters in Table 1. Variables are listed in Table 2.

Table 1. Problem parameters.

Name	Description
$P = \{j \| j = 1, \ldots, N\}$	patient set
r_j	patient j requested device class
p_j	patient j priority
f_j	patient j service window start
g_j	patient j service window end
$D = \{i \| i = 1, \ldots, M\}$	device set
q_i	device i quality
c_i	device i cost rate
d_i	device i class
s_i	device i setup time
l_i	device i lifespan
b_i	device i availability window start
e_i	device i availability window end

Table 2. Problem variables.

Name	Description
Γ_i	ordered list of patients assigned to device $i \in D, \Gamma_i \subseteq P$
Λ_j	ordered list of devices assigned to patient $j \in P, \Lambda_j \subseteq D$
$x_{ij_1j_2}$	binary variable representing whether device i is assigned, after patient j_1, to j_2
$y_{ji_1i_2}$	binary variable representing whether patient j is assigned, after device i_1, to i_2
z_{ij}	start of assignment of device i to patient j
w_{ij}	end of assignment of device i to patient j

Constraints are a core component of our optimization model, as they determine which scheduling solutions are feasible. They ensure compliance with device availability windows (Equations (1) and (2)) and patient availability windows (Equations (3) and (4)), enforce device–patient class compatibility (Equation (5)), incorporate setup times between assignments (Equation (6)), maintain continuous device coverage throughout a patient's stay (Equation (7)), and respect device lifespan constraints (Equation (8)).

It is important to highlight that constraints enforce distinct availability requirements for devices and patients. Specifically, device–patient allocations must fall within the device's availability window (Equations (1) and (2)), while each patient must be continuously assigned to a device throughout their entire availability window (Equations (3), (4) and (7)). This distinction is critical: devices may remain idle during their availability, but patients require uninterrupted device coverage.

$$b_i \leq \min_{j \in \Gamma_i} z_{ij} \qquad \forall i \in D \tag{1}$$

$$\max_{j \in \Gamma_i} w_{ij} \leq e_i \qquad \forall i \in D \tag{2}$$

$$f_j = \min_{i \in \Lambda_j} z_{ij} \qquad \forall j \in P \tag{3}$$

$$\max_{i \in \Lambda_j} w_{ij} = g_j \qquad \forall j \in P \tag{4}$$

$$d_i = r_j \qquad \forall i \in D \quad \forall j \in \Gamma_i \tag{5}$$

$$w_{ij_1} + s_i \leq z_{ij_2} \qquad \forall i \in D \quad \forall j_1, j_2 \in \Gamma_i \quad x_{ij_1j_2} = 1 \tag{6}$$

$$w_{i_1j} \leq z_{i_2j} \qquad \forall j \in P \quad \forall i_1, i_2 \in \Lambda_j \quad y_{ji_1i_2} = 1 \tag{7}$$

$$\sum_{j \in \Gamma_i} (w_{ij} - z_{ij}) \leq l_i \qquad \forall i \in D \quad \forall j \in \Gamma_i \tag{8}$$

Regarding the bi-objective function, the two key performance indicators (KPIs) are the total cost γ and the overall quality of care σ.

Equation (9) calculates γ, which represents the total operational cost of device usage across all patients. For each device i, the formula sums the durations of all assignments $(w_{ij} - z_{ij})$ across all patients j to which the device was assigned (set Γ_i). Each device's total usage time is then multiplied by its hourly cost c_i. The final value γ is obtained by summing these cost calculations across all devices in the system. In summary, γ provides a comprehensive measure of the economic cost incurred from device utilization throughout the scheduling period, accounting for both assignment durations and device-specific operational costs.

Equation (10) calculates σ, which represents a weighted measure of the quality of service provided to patients. For each patient j, the algorithm computes the sum of quality-weighted assignment durations $(w_{ij} - z_{ij}) \cdot q_i$ across all devices i assigned to that patient. This sum is then normalized by the patient's total stay duration $(g_j - f_j)$ and weighted by the patient's priority p_j. The final value σ is obtained by summing these weighted quality measures across all patients. Notably, if a patient j is assigned only a single device i during their stay, the summation naturally reduces to a single term, and the normalized, weighted quality for that patient's assignment simplifies to $p_j \cdot q_i$. In essence, σ serves as a comprehensive service quality metric, integrating factors such as assignment durations, the inherent quality of the assigned devices, and the clinical priority of the patients. A higher value of σ signifies an improved overall service quality, reflecting a greater emphasis on accommodating the needs of higher-priority patients and the allocation of devices with superior features and functionalities.

This metric is designed to capture the multifaceted nature of service quality in our context, ensuring that both the efficiency of the assignment and the tangible benefits experienced by patients are appropriately valued.

$$\gamma = \sum_{i \in D} c_i \sum_{j \in \Gamma_i} (w_{ij} - z_{ij}) \quad (9)$$

$$\sigma = \sum_{j \in P} \frac{p_j}{g_j - f_j} \sum_{i \in \Lambda_j} q_i (w_{ij} - z_{ij}) \quad (10)$$

3.3. Solution Method

The bi-objective nature of the proposed IoT device allocation model—balancing operational cost and quality of care—places it within the class of multi-objective scheduling problems, which are well known for their computational complexity. The inclusion of hard constraints such as time windows, device compatibility, battery limitations, and setup times further increases the problem's difficulty. Even in single-objective forms, many variants of scheduling problems are classified as NP-hard. Extending these to a bi-objective framework significantly compounds the computational burden, as it requires exploring a large, non-convex solution space to identify a diverse set of Pareto-optimal solutions.

Given this complexity, exact methods (e.g., integer programming or branch-and-bound) often become infeasible for realistic problem sizes due to exponential runtime. As a result, heuristic and metaheuristic approaches, such as evolutionary algorithms, are commonly adopted to provide high-quality solutions within acceptable time frames. These methods are especially suited for multi-objective problems, as they can efficiently approximate the Pareto front while navigating complex constraint landscapes.

In [28], a Mixed Integer Linear Programming (MILP) model was proposed to address critical scheduling challenges, including staff assignments, patient distribution, resource allocation, and overtime management. The primary objective was to control healthcare costs while enhancing the quality of patient care.

In [29], the Genetic Algorithm (GA), a metaheuristic inspired by natural selection, is applied to various healthcare scheduling problems, including patient admission scheduling, nurse scheduling, operating room scheduling, surgery scheduling, and other related tasks.

In [30], the authors investigate the application of biomimicry concepts in cancer treatment to improve appointment scheduling and therapeutic outcomes. Their approach leverages automation through three nature-inspired algorithms: Wolf Optimization, Firefly Optimization, and Genetic Algorithm.

Simulated Annealing (SA), a probabilistic technique for approximating the global optimum of a function, is introduced in [29]. This method is particularly effective for evaluating a broad set of potential schedules, iteratively refining them to achieve an optimal or near-optimal solution.

Multi-Objective Particle Swarm Optimization (MOPSO) enhances the Particle Swarm Optimization (PSO) algorithm to handle multiple objectives [31]. It maintains a repository of non-dominated solutions and employs a leader selection mechanism to guide the swarm toward optimal outcomes. MOPSO is particularly effective in exploring the solution space and identifying a set of Pareto-optimal schedules.

Pareto Simulated Annealing (PSA), an adaptation of SA for multi-objective optimization, applies a Pareto dominance criterion to accept or reject solutions, as discussed in [32]. PSA is valuable for balancing competing objectives by evaluating different scheduling configurations.

Non-dominated Sorting Genetic Algorithm II (NSGA-II) is a widely adopted approach for multi-objective optimization, designed to identify a diverse set of optimal solutions. It is particularly useful for balancing conflicting objectives, such as minimizing travel time and reducing patient visit delays, while generating Pareto-optimal schedules. In [31], NSGA-II is applied to scheduling problems through a simulation-based approach.

To address the inherent complexity of allocating IoT medical devices in healthcare environments, this study introduces a heuristic optimization approach based on the NSGA-II algorithm, tailored to solve bi-objective scheduling problems. At its core, the method leverages genetic representations of patient–device assignments, enabling the intelligent exploration of vast solution spaces that traditional methods struggle to handle. Each candidate solution encodes device assignments across time windows, with objectives that aim to minimize operational costs while maximizing the quality of care based on patient priorities and device capabilities. Through evolutionary mechanisms—such as crossover, mutation, and elitism—NSGA-II continuously refines the population of solutions, ultimately producing a Pareto front that captures a range of trade-offs. This allows decision-makers to choose from multiple high-quality solutions rather than being forced to accept a single, potentially suboptimal result.

Unlike existing methods that often optimize a single objective or rely on rigid heuristics, this approach offers several key innovations. By dynamically adjusting NSGA-II parameters across multiple runs and incorporating domain-specific constraints—such as device compatibility, setup time, and battery limits—the algorithm adapts to the real-world variability of clinical environments. Its multi-run design and time-bound execution also make it highly practical for deployment in resource-constrained healthcare settings, where timely decisions are crucial. In doing so, the approach overcomes the limitations of static or overly simplified models, offering a flexible, scalable, and interpretable solution framework. The anticipated benefits include more efficient use of healthcare facility resources, improved patient outcomes through better device matching, and greater transparency in the decision-making process through access to a spectrum of optimal solutions.

Algorithm 1 outlines the optimization process for assigning IoT devices to patients using the NSGA-II algorithm. The procedure begins by receiving input lists of patients and devices, along with a time constraint (line 1). The goal is to produce an optimized set of device–patient assignments and a final Pareto-optimal front (line 2). The algorithm first defines the attributes of both patients and devices (line 3) and introduces an assignment class to manage their pairings (line 4). A multi-objective fitness function is then defined (lines 5–8), which aims to minimize the overall cost (γ), maximize quality of care (σ)—based on patient priority and device quality—and respect time window constraints. The genetic representation of a solution is set up next (lines 9–11): each chromosome is a list of assignment objects, where each gene includes the device ID, patient ID, and corresponding assignment time window. Storage for Pareto-optimal solutions is initialized (line 12), and a timer is started (line 13). The main loop runs until the specified time limit is reached (line 14). Within this loop, NSGA-II parameters—*pop_size*, *num_gen*, *p_c*, *p_m*, *cross_op*, *mut_op*, and *sel_method* —are randomly generated as defined in Equations (11)–(17) (line 15), and the algorithm (as detailed in Algorithm 2) is executed using these parameters (line 16). The resulting Pareto front and logbook from each execution are stored (line 17).

Once the time limit expires, the algorithm returns the accumulated set of Pareto-optimal solutions and the complete logbook of all evolutionary runs (line 19).

$$pop\_size \sim \mathcal{U}_d\{50, 100, 150, 200, 250, 300\} \tag{11}$$

$$num\_gen \sim \mathcal{U}_d\{50, 100, 150, 200, 250, 500\} \tag{12}$$

$$p_c \sim \mathcal{U}(0.7, 0.9) \tag{13}$$

$$p_m \sim \mathcal{U}(0.01, 0.1) \tag{14}$$

$$cross\_op \sim \mathcal{U}_d\{\text{OX}, \text{PMX}, \text{PBX}, \text{PPX}\} \tag{15}$$

$$mut\_op \sim \mathcal{U}_d\{\text{Swap}, \text{Insertion}, \text{Inversion}\} \tag{16}$$

$$sel\_method \sim \mathcal{U}_d\{\text{Binary Tournament}, \text{Random}, \text{Roulette Wheel}\} \tag{17}$$

Algorithm 1 Optimization of IoT device assignment using NSGA-II.

1: **Input:** List of patients, List of devices, Time limit *time_limit*
2: **Output:** List of optimized assignments of devices to patients and Pareto optimal set
3: Define the patient and device classes with attributes
4: Define an **Assignment** class to store device-patient assignments
5: Define the **fitness function**:
6:     Minimize total cost of device usage γ
7:     Maximize quality of care σ, based on patient priority and device quality
8:     Respect time window constraints
9: Define the **genetic representation** of a solution:
10:     A chromosome is a list of device-patient assignments
11:     Each gene represents an assignment (device ID, patient ID, start time, end time)
12: Initialize storage for Pareto optimal solutions
13: Initialize the timer *clock*
14: **while** $clock < time\_limit$ **do**
15:     Randomly generate the NSGA-II parameters *pop_size, num_gen, p_c, p_m, cross_op, mut_op,* and *sel_method* according to Equations (11)–(17).
16:     Run **Execution of NSGA-II** with the generated parameters as detailed in Algorithm 2
17:     Store the Pareto front and logbook obtained from the execution
18: **end while**
19: Return the final Pareto optimal set and logbook containing all evolutionary results

Algorithm 2 details the practical implementation of the NSGA-II optimization, including specific parameters such as population size and number of generations, and more. It methodically walks through the evolutionary process, highlighting how NSGA-II applies tournament selection with Pareto dominance ranking to effectively navigate the multi-objective solution space. The genetic operators—crossover, mutation, and elitism—work in concert to explore diverse assignment possibilities while preserving high-quality solutions.

This implementation demonstrates how evolutionary algorithms can tackle complex healthcare resource allocation problems by mimicking natural selection processes to iteratively improve assignments across multiple competing objectives. For further details regarding the developed code, refer to Appendix A. For a comprehensive description of the system architecture and workflow, consult Appendix B.

A systematic benchmark analysis was conducted, comparing our proposed NSGA-II-based heuristic algorithm against the exact solver SCIP in terms of solution quality, computational efficiency (runtime), and scalability (performance on increasing problem sizes).

SCIP was chosen as a benchmark for comparison against the metaheuristic algorithm due to its capability to find high-quality, and ideally provably optimal, solutions for mixed integer programming problems [33]. Unlike metaheuristics, which provide approximate solutions, SCIP strives to find the absolute best possible outcome within the given time constraints. However, it also allows a maximum time limit to be set, enabling the retrieval of a high-quality solution even if its optimality is not fully proven.

Algorithm 2 Execution of NSGA-II.

```
Input: Population size pop_size, Number of generations num_gen, Crossover probability p_c, Mutation probability p_m, Crossover operator cross_op, Mutation operator mut_op, Selection method sel_method
Output: Optimized solutions and logbook of evolutionary process
Step 1: Define Genetic Algorithm Components
   Register the individual structure: List of assignments
   Register the fitness function: Multi-objective (min cost γ, max quality of care σ)
   Register genetic operators: cross_op, mut_op, sel_method
   Set NSGA-II parameters: pop_size, num_gen, p_c, p_m
Step 2: Initialize the Population
   Create an initial population of pop_size individuals
   Each individual is randomly generated with assignments
Step 3: Evolutionary Process
for generation = 1 to num_gen do
   Evaluate the fitness of each individual in the population
   Apply NSGA-II selection using sel_method:
   Apply Crossover with probability p_c using cross_op:
   Apply Mutation with probability p_m using mut_op:
      Randomly modify some assignments (change device or time slot)
   Apply Elitism:
end for
Return the final population and logbook containing evolutionary data
```

Solving a multi-objective problem with a primarily single-objective MILP solver like SCIP presents challenges due to the need to handle multiple conflicting objectives simultaneously. While SCIP is designed for single-objective optimization, various techniques can be employed to adapt it for multi-objective problems. One effective approach is the ϵ-constraint method, a well-established technique in multi-objective optimization, as described in [34]. This method transforms a multi-objective problem into a series of single-objective optimizations by iteratively reformulating the problem: one objective is selected as the primary function to minimize, while the remaining objectives are converted into constraints with dynamically adjusted bounds. This allows the solver to systematically explore the trade-offs between competing objectives and generate a set of Pareto-optimal solutions. We refer to the method of employing the SCIP solver to solve a bi-objective optimization problem using the ϵ-constraint method as 'SCIP 2-OBJ'.

4. Results

4.1. Example

An example is provided below to illustrate the problem-solving process. Table 3 shows the data for two patients requesting IoT devices. Both patients belong to the same class ($r_j = 1$) and have the same priority ($p_j = 1$), but they have different time window durations ($g_1 - f_1 = 15$ and $g_2 - f_2 = 12$). Table 4 contains information about three devices, each with availability windows and classes suitable for both patients. The first device has very low quality $q_1 = 30$ and cost $c_1 = 5$, but its lifespan is only $l_1 = 9$ time units, rendering it insufficient for complete coverage. The second device provides complete coverage for both patients ($l_2 = 15$) and has a quality of $q_2 = 60$, but its cost, $c_2 = 10$, is double that of the first device. The last device has the highest values for quality ($q_3 = 90$), cost ($c_3 = 20$), and duration ($l_3 = 30$). The decision-maker may assign up to three devices to the two patients, balancing cost and quality.

Table 3. Example patient data.

j	r_j	p_j	f_j	g_j
1	1	1	6	21
2	1	1	2	14

Table 4. Example device data.

i	q_i	c_i	d_i	s_i	l_i	b_i	e_i
1	30	5	1	1	9	1	50
2	60	10	1	2	15	1	50
3	90	20	1	2	30	1	40

The best solutions appear in the Pareto diagram in Figure 1. The four solutions have divergent costs and qualities, with no single solution dominating the others. The Pareto-optimal zone is situated in the upper-left quadrant of the diagram, symbolizing a combination of low costs and high-quality healthcare services. Solution 1 prioritizes cost minimization, while Solution 2 focuses on maximizing quality of care. Solutions 3 and 4 represent trade-off solutions, balancing cost and quality of care objectives.

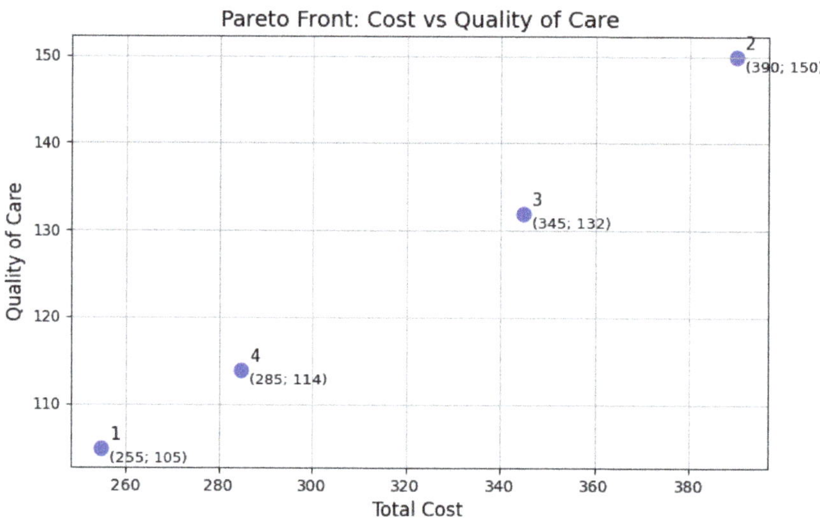

Figure 1. Example Pareto front.

Solution 1 achieves cost minimization, as can be seen in Figure 2, which gives specific detail to the assignments made. Initially, Device 1, the cheapest option, is assigned to Patient 2. However, to achieve complete coverage for Patient 2, the more costly Device 3 is subsequently required for the remaining time window. In contrast, Device 2, which has a medium cost, is assigned to Patient 1.

Solution 2 (Figure 3) prioritizes maximizing quality of care by using only the two highest-quality devices, leading to the highest cost.

As depicted in Figure 4, Solution 3 assigns the cheapest device (Device 1) to Patient 1, supplemented by Device 2 for the final segment, and the most expensive device (Device 3) to Patient 2. Instead, Solution 4 (Figure 5) reduces costs by switching Devices 2 and 3. Consequently, Solution 4 uses the most expensive device for less time than Solution 3.

With these objective insights, the decision-maker is actively involved in guiding the final outcome to achieve an optimal trade-off between cost and quality of care. The process begins by specifying the allowable runtime for the algorithm, which balances the need for timely results with solution accuracy. Once the NSGA-II algorithm completes its execution, the system presents the decision-maker with the Pareto front (as shown in Figure 1), offering a visual and analytical summary of the best trade-off solutions found. Based on institutional budget constraints and qualitative considerations—such as care standards—the decision-maker can interactively explore this set of non-dominated solutions. By selecting individual points on the Pareto front, they can inspect corresponding detailed schedule (as shown in Figure 2). After evaluating these options, the decision-maker chooses the most suitable solution and commits the final scheduling decision, which is then forwarded to the hospital information system for implementation.

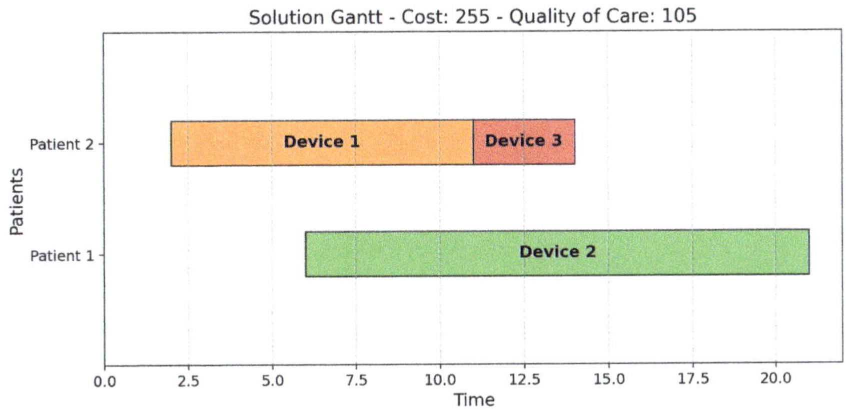

Figure 2. Example Solution 1 Gantt.

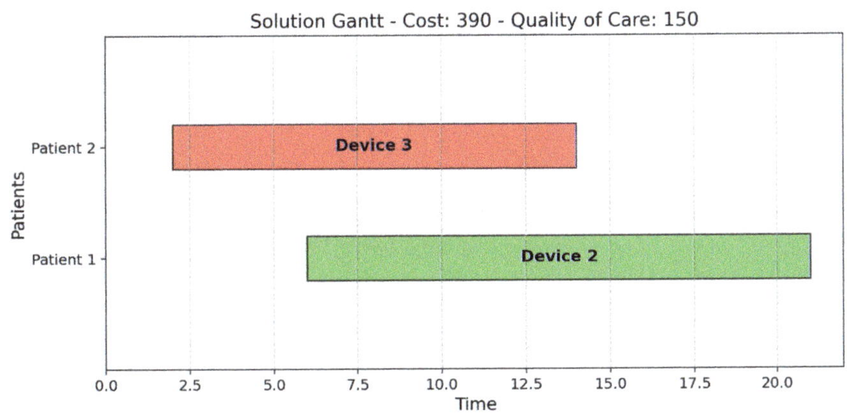

Figure 3. Example Solution 2 Gantt.

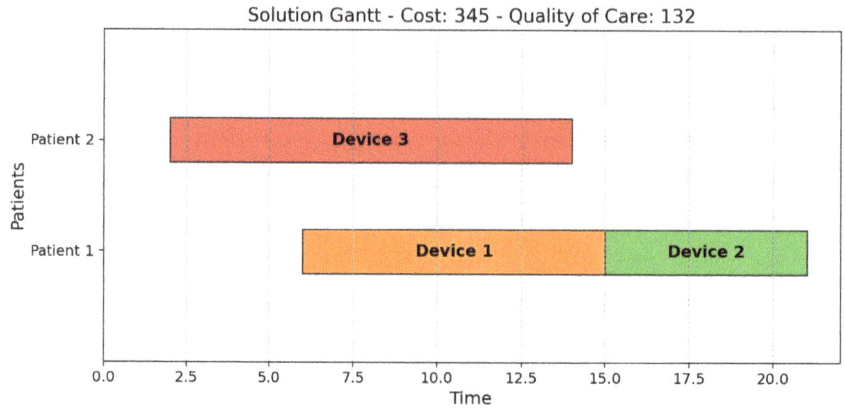

Figure 4. Example Solution 3 Gantt.

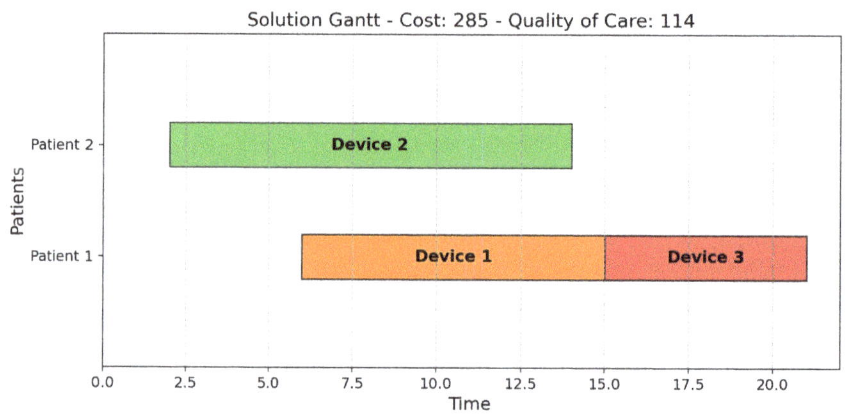

Figure 5. Example Solution 4 Gantt.

4.2. Experimental Campaign

To validate the effectiveness of our proposed heuristic, we conducted a comprehensive experimental campaign. Our code implementation, written in Python v3.12.10 https://www.python.org/downloads/release/python-31210 (accessed on 17 March 2025), was executed on a macOS system (MacBook Pro with Apple M2 Pro chip and 32 GB of RAM).

We evaluate and compare the performance of two multi-objective optimization algorithms (NSGA-II and SCIP 2-OBJ) by analyzing their respective Pareto-optimal solution sets. We identify dominated solutions, compute the hypervolume indicator (a widely used metric for assessing Pareto front quality), and visualize the results using scatter plots and hypervolume areas. The hypervolume metric quantifies the region of objective space dominated by a solution set relative to a reference point. This provides an intuitive measure of solution quality. By comparing the Pareto fronts and their hypervolume values, we provide insights into the relative effectiveness of the algorithms in producing diverse and high-quality trade-off solutions.

Table 5 presents the case studies employed in our experimental evaluation. These studies are derived from actual patient and device scenarios, with sensitive details obscured through data normalization to comply with non-disclosure agreements. These confidentiality measures mandated by data protection requirements do not affect the significance of the findings. Key parameters, such as patient and device counts, define these scenarios. To maintain consistent evaluation conditions across experiments, a maximum execution time (time limit) was implemented, as shown in the final column of Table 5.

The findings from these case studies are systematically presented in Table 6, facilitating comparative analysis and insightful deductions. Our analysis focuses on three key aspects: the distribution of solutions, the Pareto front's spread, and the most significant solutions within the convex hull (detailed in Appendix C).

Both algorithms generate their respective Pareto-optimal solution sets. To determine the overall Pareto-optimal front, these sets are combined, as solutions from one algorithm may be dominated by those from the other. Performance is evaluated using several metrics. First, we count the number of solutions from each algorithm that are included in the final Pareto front (see column 'No. Pareto-Optimal Solutions' in Table 6). Second, we determine the number of solutions from each algorithm that are excluded from the final Pareto front due to the dominance of solutions from the other (refer to column 'No. Dominated Solutions' in Table 6). Next, the final convex hull is computed, and the number of solutions from each algorithm within it is tallied ('No. Solutions in the Convex Hull' column). Finally, we calculate the hypervolume associated with each algorithm's Pareto front. For comprehensive details, please refer to the provided complete dataset.

Table 5. Experimental campaign.

Exp. ID	No. Patients	No. Devices	Time Limit (s)
1	2	4	60
2	4	8	120
3	5	10	240
4	10	30	360
5	20	30	600
6	20	40	900

In the first experiment (Table 5), we visually compare the Pareto fronts produced by NSGA-II (blue circles) and SCIP 2-OBJ (red squares) in Figure 6. This comparison helps evaluate solution performance. NSGA-II generated a front with 10 solutions, while SCIP 2-OBJ produced 15. The dominated regions (hypervolumes) for each front are shaded in blue and red, respectively. Solutions dominated by those from the other front are marked with crosses and were excluded from further analysis for clarity. For example, at a cost of 350, the NSGA-II solution dominates its SCIP counterpart due to higher quality of care. The final combined Pareto front includes only non-dominated solutions: 9 from NSGA-II and 12 from SCIP 2-OBJ. The convex hull, representing the most promising subset, is indicated by green-filled markers and a dashed line (see Appendix C).

A qualitative comparison suggests NSGA-II performs better. It produced fewer dominated solutions (one crossed blue marker vs. three crossed red ones at cost values of 250, 270, and 350). Moreover, NSGA-II contributes five solutions to the convex hull, compared to just two from SCIP 2-OBJ (at the extreme left and right). This is further supported by the hypervolume measure, where NSGA-II dominates a larger area. Overall, these results indicate that NSGA-II is more effective at identifying well-balanced, high-performance solutions. Numerical confirmation is provided in row 1 of Table 6.

The second experiment (see row 2 in Tables 5 and 6), which scaled the number of patients and devices, along with the time limit, to double the initial values, reinforced the findings from the first experiment. Although 'SCIP 2-OBJ' generated a larger set of Pareto-optimal solutions, these solutions exhibited a lower overall quality, as evidenced by the reduced number of solutions in the convex hull and hypervolume. In contrast, NSGA-II effectively identified a more selective set of higher-quality solutions. This disparity in performance is attributed to the sampling methodology inherent in the 'SCIP 2-OBJ' ϵ-

constraint approach, compounded by the time limit, which prevented the algorithm from fully converging to certified optimal solutions.

The results of the third experiment (Tables 5 and 6, row 3), which increased complexity and doubled the time limit, showed that the exact approach, despite generating more solutions, failed to produce any of high quality, as none were within the convex hull. Our proposed approach, in contrast, effectively produced a slightly larger number of solutions with significantly higher quality, as demonstrated by the improved convex hull representation and hypervolume.

In the last three experiments, we significantly increased the complexity, which led to different observations compared to the first three experiments.

Regarding the fourth experiment represented in Table 5, we observed (Table 6, row 4) that a significantly higher number of solutions from our algorithm were dominated within the final Pareto front. Despite the low number of solutions generated by the exact method, these were of higher quality, as evidenced by the small difference between our method and the exact method in convex hull participation and hypervolume value. This occurred because the sampling process of the 'SCIP 2-OBJ' method, when conducted in a very large solution space, achieved better performance by exploring the solution domain more effectively than in the previous experiments. Additionally, the 'NSGA-II' algorithm, having to search for Pareto-optimal solutions within a broader domain, faced greater difficulty in finding numerous high-quality solutions, although it still managed to achieve better results than the exact method and locate solutions in the early generations.

In the fifth experiment, we doubled the number of patients while keeping the number of devices constant, attempting to simulate a common real-world situation of resource scarcity. In this case, the exact method found many more solutions compared to the previous experiment and produced results comparable to our approach, both in terms of convex hull participation and hypervolume.

In the final experiment (Tables 5 and 6, row 6), we increased the number of devices compared to the previous one. In this case, the performance advantage of the heuristic became more pronounced due to the greater problem complexity, which led the NSGA-II method to quickly find many interesting solutions while the exact approach found fewer good solutions. Consequently, in this last case, we observed equivalent results between the two methods in terms of convex hull participation, but due to the lower number of Pareto-optimal solutions generated, the exact method was outperformed in terms of the hypervolume parameter.

In conclusion, the increased available time allowed the exact method (SCIP 2-OBJ) to find many more solutions, while the heuristic (NSGA-II) was very fast in the early generations but failed to improve significantly with increased time, which instead benefited the exact method in sampling the solution domain more precisely. This demonstrates that for practical applications where time is critical, the heuristic approach is preferable as it rapidly produces good-quality solutions before converging asymptotically.

Table 6. Experimental campaign results.

Exp.	No. Pareto-Optimal Solutions		No. Dominated Solutions		No. Solutions in the Convex Hull		Hypervolume	
ID	NSGA-II	SCIP 2-OBJ	NSGA-II	SCIP 2-OBJ	NSGA-II	SCIP 2-OBJ	NSGA-II	SCIP 2-OBJ
1	9	12	1	3	4	2	1279	1187
2	16	30	4	2	6	2	5328	5074
3	19	34	0	31	8	0	6620	5078
4	24	3	2	1	5	2	66,691	57,348
5	27	11	7	1	6	5	240,599	223,702
6	32	9	6	1	6	5	808,678	630,125

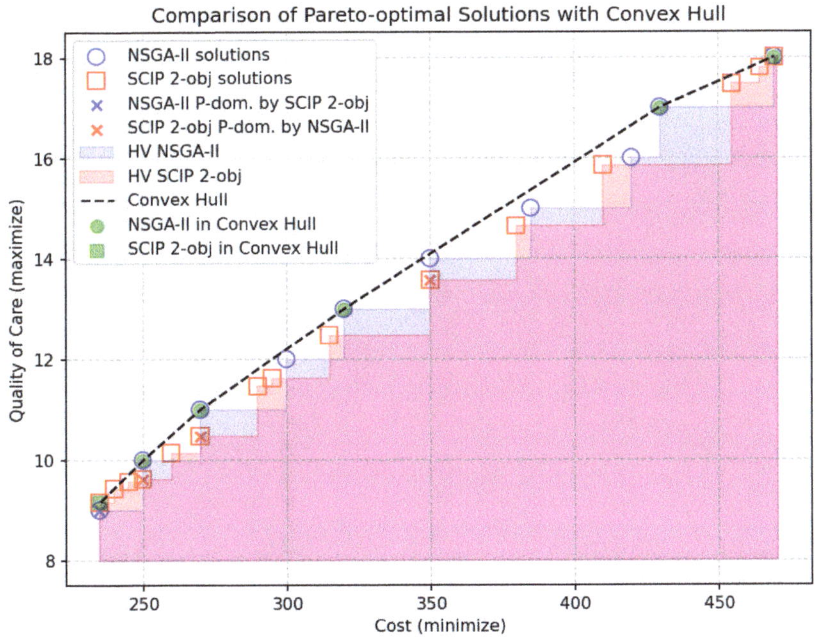

Figure 6. Exp 1 Pareto comparison.

Lastly, to evaluate the benefits of our automated method for resource allocation and scheduling in healthcare, we conducted a comparative analysis against the manual practices currently used by managers. Due to data confidentiality constraints (DoD), the manual solution is not disclosed, as it would reveal the decision-making strategies currently adopted by healthcare managers. Instead, we focus on demonstrating the relative improvements achieved by our approach. Specifically, we compare the manual solution provided by experienced managers with the Pareto-optimal solutions generated by our automated system. Since the Pareto-optimal solutions generated by our method outperform the manual one, we report the percentage of cost reduction and quality improvement achieved by the specific solution that dominates the manual schedule. This provides a clear numerical assessment of the advantages of our method, both in terms of financial efficiency and schedule quality, over traditional decision-making practices.

The results in Table 7 highlight the clear benefits of moving from manual scheduling to the automated NSGA-II approach. Because managers previously allocated resources manually, the data now show that this automated method can lead to significant gains. Although the first test scenario shows no difference, subsequent scenarios consistently demonstrate cost savings (between 2% and 12%) and improved quality outcomes (between 3% and 20%). These benefits become more pronounced as the scenarios grow more complex, with more patients and devices involved. This trend reflects the increasing difficulty for human managers to juggle the many variables needed for optimal scheduling at larger scales. Adopting automated tools like NSGA-II offers healthcare facilities a strong opportunity to cut costs while improving patient care—especially in complex, high-demand environments.

Table 7. Comparison between automated method (NSGA-II) and manual scheduling.

Exp.	Cost Saving with Automatic Method	Quality Improvement with Automatic Method
1	0%	0%
2	2%	3%
3	5%	7%
4	8%	12%
5	11%	18%
6	12%	20%

5. Discussion

The experimental results offer significant insights into the comparative performance of the NSGA-II heuristic and the SCIP 2-OBJ exact approach for multi-objective healthcare resource allocation. These findings contribute to our understanding of algorithmic performance in complex decision-making and provide practical guidance for real-world applications.

Consistently, NSGA-II outperformed SCIP 2-OBJ regarding solution quality, as indicated by superior hypervolume and convex hull representation, particularly in moderate complexity scenarios (experiments 1–3). This aligns with previous research highlighting NSGA-II's efficacy in navigating complex Pareto fronts [31].

However, in highly complex scenarios (experiments 4–6), the exact method showed improved relative performance, especially in solution quality, supporting the theoretical notion that exact methods may excel in certain complex domains [35].

A key observation was the distinct convergence patterns. NSGA-II demonstrated rapid initial convergence, ideal for time-sensitive healthcare applications, as emphasized in previous studies [36]. Conversely, the exact method exhibited gradual improvement with increased computational resources, suggesting its suitability for offline analysis, consistent with observed time–performance trade-offs [37].

Scalability experiments (experiments 4–6) revealed that NSGA-II maintained its ability to find high-quality solutions with increasing complexity, though with some relative performance degradation, extending previous scalability studies [38]. Interestingly, the exact method's sampling improved in larger solution spaces, suggesting that the ϵ-constraint approach benefits from increased solution diversity, mitigating time constraints.

The dominance of NSGA-II solutions in the convex hull underscored the importance of comprehensive evaluation metrics. Combining hypervolume analysis with convex hull representation, building on previous hypervolume indicator work [39], provided a more robust evaluation framework.

Practically, NSGA-II's rapid high-quality solution generation makes it ideal for time-critical healthcare resource allocation. Its ability to balance competing objectives suits dynamic healthcare environments.

The proposed system has several practical implications for real-world healthcare operations. First, it streamlines the patient monitoring workflow by automating the assignment of IoT devices, which reduces reliance on manual planning and minimizes the risk of human error. This leads to more accurate and efficient resource use, especially in high-demand or time-sensitive scenarios. Second, the dynamic re-optimization feature allows the system to adapt in real time to changes such as new patient admissions or shifts in clinical conditions. This ensures that device allocation remains optimal even in unpredictable or rapidly evolving environments, supporting better responsiveness in patient care. Finally, the scalable architecture makes the solution suitable for a wide range of healthcare settings—from small medical centers to large hospitals—offering long-term benefits in terms of operational efficiency, cost savings, and improved patient outcomes. This positions the system as a valuable tool for modernizing healthcare resource management and delivering higher-quality care with reduced administrative burden.

6. Conclusions

This study addressed the complex challenge of optimally allocating IoT medical devices to patients in healthcare environments by formulating the task as a bi-objective scheduling problem that explicitly balances operational cost with quality of care. We incorporated a rich set of real-world constraints—such as device compatibility, setup durations, time availability windows, and battery limitations—into a novel optimization framework. To solve this NP-hard problem efficiently, we developed a tailored heuristic based on the NSGA-II algorithm.

The results of our study confirm the successful achievement of all research objectives. First, the proposed model offers a realistic and flexible structure that captures the trade-offs inherent in clinical scheduling, enabling decision-makers to make data-driven choices. Second, the NSGA-II-based approach generates diverse high-quality solutions rapidly: meaningful options appear within seconds, and a refined Pareto front is available in under a minute, making it suitable for real-time use. Third, our evaluation shows that the method outperforms both baseline heuristics and manual scheduling approaches, with an average reduction of 6.3% in operational costs (reaching up to 12%) and improvements in care quality of up to 20% (with an average of 10%) based on patient-priority metrics. These findings provide a clear and positive answer to our research question, demonstrating that a bi-objective scheduling strategy can effectively balance economic and clinical considerations, even under realistic constraints.

The practical implications of this research are considerable. Healthcare facilities can deploy the system as part of real-time scheduling dashboards to assist staff in planning and revising device assignments efficiently. In high-pressure environments like emergency rooms or intensive care units, the system's rapid re-optimization capability can support immediate responses to shifting clinical needs. Moreover, by embedding the algorithm into medical center information systems, healthcare providers can automate the scheduling of connected devices in smart healthcare settings. In mobile or remote care environments, where resource constraints are more severe, the model supports strategic, data-driven allocation to maximize both coverage and impact.

Despite promising results in optimizing IoT medical device allocation via bi-objective scheduling, limitations exist. The simulation might not fully reflect real-world unpredictability like sudden patient changes or device failures. The model's accuracy depends on reliable input data, potentially limiting it in data-scarce settings. While NSGA-II performed well, its scalability for much larger systems needs further study. Lastly, user adoption and integration into current hospital workflows were not evaluated, which could affect real-world implementation.

Looking ahead, the proposed framework opens up multiple promising avenues for both theoretical advancement and practical deployment in the broader context of smart and connected healthcare. Beyond immediate healthcare facility scheduling needs, this approach can serve as a foundation for developing fully autonomous healthcare logistics systems, where device assignment, personnel scheduling, and patient flow are coordinated in real time. Its adaptability positions it as a core component in next-generation hospital management platforms, potentially integrating with electronic health records (EHRs), remote monitoring systems, and AI-driven clinical decision support. Furthermore, the methodology is applicable to other resource-constrained domains beyond healthcare, such as eldercare facilities, disaster response units, or home-based telehealth services, where balancing efficiency with service quality is equally critical.

Future research will focus on investigating how priority configurations influence the trade-offs between cost and quality of care, with the goal of identifying optimal weight settings and dynamic adjustment strategies. Understanding these relationships is essential for tailoring the system to different medical contexts, where clinical priorities, patient demographics, and resource availability may vary. Building on these insights, future versions of the system could incorporate adaptive priority calibration mechanisms, enabling scheduling policies to dynamically respond to real-time clinical needs and patient conditions.

Beyond this, further research should explore richer and more dynamic scheduling environments. Integrating patient mobility data, urgency updates, and predictive analytics could transform the framework into a proactive system capable of anticipating needs and reallocating resources before bottlenecks arise. The use of reinforcement learning, hybrid metaheuristics, or adaptive online optimization techniques may further enhance system performance under high-uncertainty conditions. Additionally, extending the scope to multi-hospital networks or regional healthcare systems could support collaborative device sharing and cross-institution scheduling, bringing added value to public health infrastructure. Incorporating human-centered factors—such as caregiver fatigue, ethical prioritization, and patient comfort—would also broaden the framework's applicability and acceptance.

To realize this potential, strong collaboration with healthcare professionals, IT developers, and policymakers will be essential. Pilot studies in diverse healthcare settings—from technologically advanced hospitals to under-resourced clinics—will help validate the system's effectiveness, uncover real-world challenges, and guide further refinement. Ultimately, this work not only offers a solution to a complex and timely healthcare problem, but also establishes a flexible, extensible platform for future innovations in intelligent, patient-centered resource optimization.

Author Contributions: Conceptualization, F.N.; methodology, F.N. and G.P.; validation, F.N. and G.P.; resources, G.P. and E.F.; writing—original draft preparation, F.N.; writing—review and editing, F.N.; supervision, F.N. and G.P.; software, F.N.; project administration, G.P. and E.F.; funding acquisition, G.P. and E.F. All authors have read and agreed to the published version of the manuscript.

Funding: This work was funded by Puglia Region (Italy)—Project "SMILE&SCALETECH" (P.O. PUGLIA FESR 2014-2020).

Institutional Review Board Statement: Not applicable.

Informed Consent Statement: Not applicable.

Data Availability Statement: The data analyzed in this manuscript are available at https://github.com/fnuni/2025applsci (accessed on 17 March 2025).

Acknowledgments: The authors express their gratitude for the administrative and technical assistance provided by the company Advantech S.r.l. in Lecce, Italy. The authors appreciate the reviewer's thorough evaluation and insightful comments, which have significantly contributed to improving the paper quality.

Conflicts of Interest: The author E.F. was employed by the company Laser Romae S.r.l. in Rome, Italy. The remaining authors declare that the research was conducted in the absence of any commercial or financial relationships that could be construed as potential conflicts of interest. The funder had no role in the design of this study; in the collection, analyses, or interpretation of data; in the writing of the manuscript; or in the decision to publish the results.

Abbreviations

The following abbreviations are used in this manuscript:

IoT	Internet of Things
IT	Information Technology
AI	Artificial Intelligence
H-IoT	Healthcare Internet of Things
PHMS	Patient Health Monitoring System
PS	Prioritized Scheduling
EDF	Earliest Deadline First
IoMT	Internet of Medical Things
MILP	Mixed Integer Linear Programming
GA	Genetic Algorithm
SA	Simulated Annealing
MOPSO	Multi-Objective Particle Swarm Optimization
PSO	Particle Swarm Optimization
NSGA-II	Non-dominated Sorting Genetic Algorithm II
SCIP 2-OBJ	SCIP solver for bi-objective optimization problem

Appendix A. Class and Dependency Diagram

The UML diagram in Figure A1 illustrates the main classes involved in an IoT-based scheduling system, highlighting their attributes, methods, and relationships. The Patient class represents individuals requiring medical device assignments, while the Device class models the available equipment. The Assignment class links patients to devices for a specific time period. The Schedule class manages assignments and computes relevant objectives, such as cost and quality of care. Finally, the IoTSchedulingProblem class orchestrates the scheduling process, providing methods for problem initialization, optimization, and result visualization. The relationships between classes illustrate dependencies, ensuring a structured and logical representation of the scheduling framework.

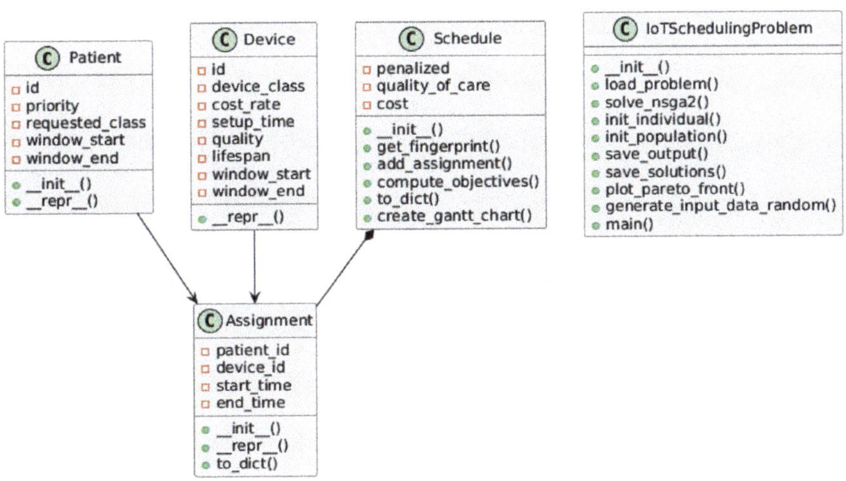

Figure A1. UML class diagram.

The dependency relationships are reported in the dependency diagram in Figure A2. Patient and Device both contribute to creating Assignment. Schedule contains multiple Assignment instances. IoTSchedulingProblem references and manages all other classes, acting as the central coordination point. The diagram suggests a modular, flexible system designed to optimize medical device scheduling using the NSGA-II advanced computational technique for multi-objective optimization.

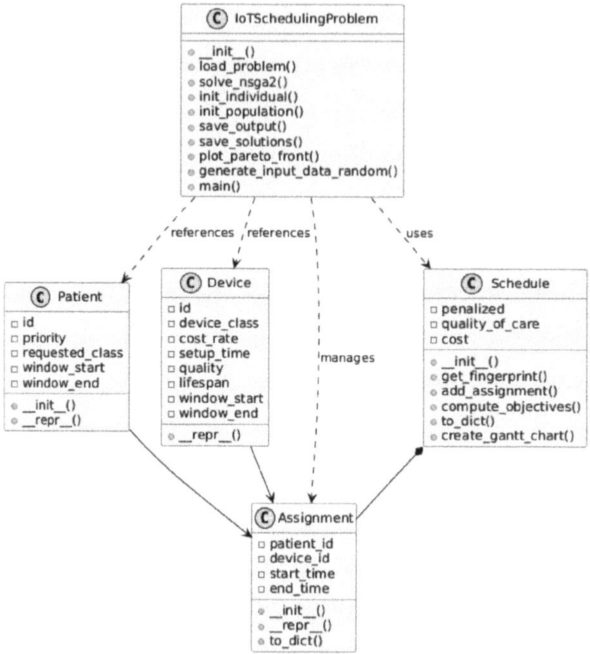

Figure A2. UML dependency diagram.

Appendix B. System Architecture and Workflow

The system employs a distributed architectural paradigm, as depicted in Figure A3, to efficiently manage and schedule IoT devices for patient monitoring. This architecture consists of several key components, each serving a specific role in optimizing data flow and processing. Client nodes (user terminals) act as the primary interface for healthcare professionals, including nurses and administrative staff, allowing them to input data, retrieve optimized schedules, and monitor device assignments. IoT devices, which are medical-grade and deployed to patients, continuously capture real-time physiological data and transmit them to the backend for further processing. Backend processing is responsible for executing an optimization algorithm, such as NSGA-II, to determine the most efficient allocation of IoT devices while adhering to predefined constraints and objectives. To ensure seamless data management, a distributed database stores patient records, device availability, scheduling results, and historical data, guaranteeing data integrity and easy retrieval of past assignments.

The sequence diagram in Figure A4 visually represents the operational workflow for IoT-based patient monitoring. It illustrates how different system components interact throughout the workflow, from data input to real-time re-optimization.

The operational workflow begins with data acquisition, where healthcare personnel input relevant information, including available IoT device inventories and patient monitoring requirements. The optimization procedure follows, in which the backend processes the input data and applies the optimization algorithm to generate an efficient device-to-patient assignment, taking into account factors such as patient priority, device availability, and clinical conditions. The final decision is made by the decision-maker, who considers all the generated alternatives. The result storage and distribution phase ensures that the optimized schedule is persistently stored in the distributed database and made accessible to authorized healthcare personnel. User interaction allows nurses and healthcare staff to retrieve assigned schedules via client terminals, ensuring adherence to the proposed plan for each patient. Lastly, the system supports dynamic updating, which allows real-time re-optimization in response to new patient admissions or evolving clinical conditions.

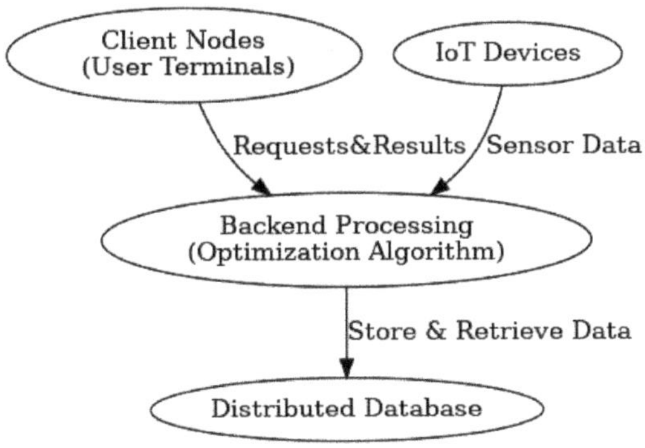

Figure A3. System architecture and workflow.

This architecture establishes a scalable and automated approach for managing patient–device assignments, reducing manual errors, and enhancing overall healthcare operational efficiency.

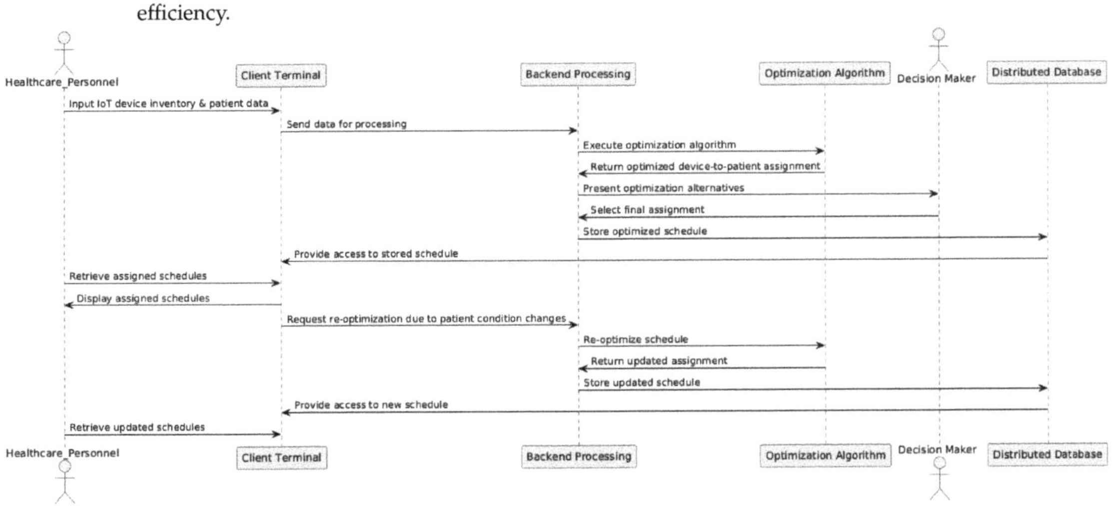

Figure A4. Sequence diagram.

Appendix C. Pareto Front and Convex Hull

In multi-objective optimization, the Pareto front represents the set of non-dominated solutions. The Pareto-optimal solutions are those that cannot be enhanced in one aspect without compromising another. The convex hull is the smallest convex shape that encloses all Pareto-optimal points. It highlights the most significant trade-offs between objectives and helps identify the most promising solutions among the Pareto-optimal ones, as they represent the extreme and most interesting choices within the optimal set. This filtering is particularly useful when the Pareto front consists of a large number of solutions, making it easier to focus on the most relevant trade-offs.

Figure A5 illustrates a set of solutions in a multi-objective optimization problem, where the first objective is minimized, and the second objective is maximized. Dominated points (which do not belong to the Pareto front) are shown in blue, while Pareto-optimal solutions are highlighted in red. The convex hull, representing the most significant trade-offs among the Pareto-optimal solutions, is outlined with a green dashed line.

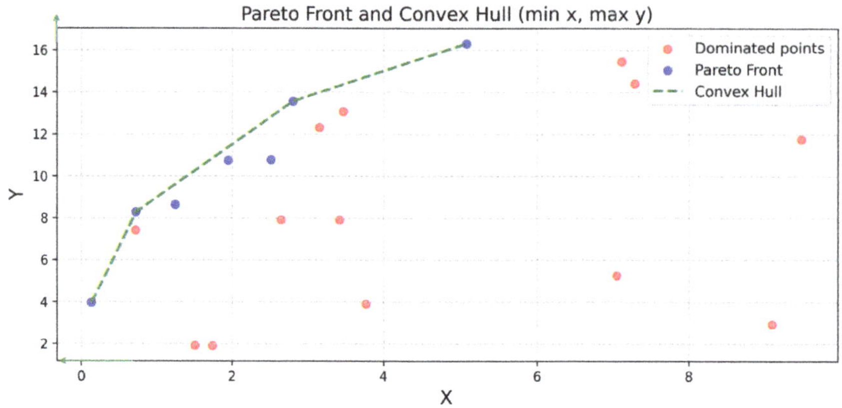

Figure A5. Example of Pareto front and convex hull.

References

1. Stolojescu-Crisan, C.; Butunoi, B.P.; Crisan, C. IoT Based Intelligent Building Applications in the Context of COVID-19 Pandemic. In Proceedings of the 2020 14th International Symposium on Electronics and Telecommunications, ISETC 2020—Conference Proceedings, Timișoara, Romania, 5–6 November 2020. [CrossRef]
2. Rajasekar, S.J.S. An Enhanced IoT Based Tracing and Tracking Model for COVID -19 Cases. *SN Comput. Sci.* **2021**, *2*, 42. [CrossRef] [PubMed]
3. Bai, C.; Dallasega, P.; Orzes, G.; Sarkis, J. Industry 4.0 technologies assessment: A sustainability perspective. *Int. J. Prod. Econ.* **2020**, *229*, 107776. [CrossRef]
4. Khanh, T.T.; Nguyen, V.D.; Pham, X.Q.; Huh, E.N. Wi-Fi indoor positioning and navigation: A cloudlet-based cloud computing approach. *Hum.-Centric Comput. Inf. Sci.* **2020**, *10*, 32. [CrossRef]
5. Seo, W.J.; Evans, N. Internet of Things Adoption Challenges in Enterprise Asset Management Organisations. In *Proceedings of the 14th WCEAM Proceedings. WCEAM 2019. Lecture Notes in Mechanical Engineering*; Springer: Cham, Switzerland, 2019.
6. Wichmann, J.; Leyer, M. Factors Influencing the Intention of Actors in Hospitals to Use Indoor Positioning Systems: Reasoned Action Approach. *J. Med. Internet Res.* **2021**, *23*, e28193. [CrossRef]
7. Bazo, R.; da Costa, C.A.; Seewald, L.A.; da Silveira, L.G.; Antunes, R.S.; da Rosa Righi, R.; Rodrigues, V.F. A Survey About Real-Time Location Systems in Healthcare Environments. *J. Med. Syst.* **2021**, *45*, 1–13. [CrossRef]
8. Paul, S.; Riffat, M.; Yasir, A.; Mahim, M.N.; Sharnali, B.Y.; Naheen, I.T.; Rahman, A.; Kulkarni, A. Industry 4.0 applications for medical/healthcare services. *J. Sens. Actuator Netw.* **2021**, *10*, 43. [CrossRef]
9. Pradhan, B.; Bhattacharyya, S.; Pal, K. IoT-Based Applications in Healthcare Devices. *J. Healthc. Eng.* **2021**, *2021*, 6632599. [CrossRef]
10. Kumar, M.; Kumar, A.; Verma, S.; Bhattacharya, P.; Ghimire, D.; Kim, S.H.; Hosen, A.S. Healthcare Internet of Things (H-IoT): Current Trends, Future Prospects, Applications, Challenges, and Security Issues. *Electronics* **2023**, *12*, 2050. [CrossRef]
11. Rahman, M.H.; Islam, T.; Amjad, M.H.H.; Shovon, M.S.S.; Chowdhury, M.E.; Ashakin, M.R.; Hossain, B.; Bhowmik, P.K.; Nurullah, M.; Sunny, A.R. Impact of Internet of Things (IoT) on Healthcare in Transforming Patient Care and Overcoming Operational Challenges. *J. Angiother.* **2024**, *8*, 1–8. [CrossRef]
12. Kishor, A.; Chakraborty, C. Artificial intelligence and internet of things based healthcare 4.0 monitoring system. *Wirel. Pers. Commun.* **2022**, *127*, 1615–1631. [CrossRef]
13. Wu, C.; Tang, Y.M.; Kuo, W.T.; Yip, H.T.; Chau, K.Y. Healthcare 5.0: A secure and distributed network for system informatics in medical surgery. *Int. J. Med. Inform.* **2024**, *186*, 105415. [CrossRef]
14. Iqbal, N.; Imran; Ahmad, S.; Ahmad, R.; Kim, D.H. A Scheduling Mechanism Based on Optimization Using IoT-Tasks Orchestration for Efficient Patient Health Monitoring. *Sensors* **2021**, *21*, 5430. [CrossRef] [PubMed]

15. Secundo, G.; Shams, S.M.R.; Nucci, F. Digital technologies and collective intelligence for healthcare ecosystem: Optimizing Internet of Things adoption for pandemic management. *J. Bus. Res.* **2021**, *131*, 563–572. [CrossRef] [PubMed]
16. Ahila, A.; Dahan, F.; Alroobaea, R.; Alghamdi, W.Y.; Mohammed, M.K.; Hajjej, F.; mohammed alsekait, D.; Raahemifar, K. A smart IoMT based architecture for E-healthcare patient monitoring system using artificial intelligence algorithms. *Front. Physiol.* **2023**, *14*, 1125952. [CrossRef]
17. Gowda, V.D.; Sharma, A.; Mukherjee, S.; Rahman, M.; Barshe, S.B. Optimizing Resource Allocation in Healthcare Facilities Through IoT and Machine Learning Predictive Analysis. *Lect. Notes Netw. Syst.* **2024**, *1007 LNNS*, 177–187. [CrossRef]
18. Yoshioka, D.; Kogami, H.; Kang, S.I.; Yoshizaki, R.; Sakurai, Y.; Nakano, K.; Wu, J.; Fujisaki-Sueda-Sakai, M.; Sugawara, I.; Miura, T.; et al. *Evaluation of IoT-Setting Method Among Senior Citizens in Japan*; Lecture Notes in Computer Science (including subseries Lecture Notes in Artificial Intelligence and Lecture Notes in Bioinformatics); Springer: Washington, DC, USA, 2021; Volume 12786 LNCS, pp. 278–292. [CrossRef]
19. Dash, S.P. The Impact of IoT in Healthcare: Global Technological Change—The Roadmap to a Networked Architecture in India. *J. Indian Inst. Sci.* **2020**, *100*, 773–785. [CrossRef]
20. Stavropoulos, T.G.; Papastergiou, A.; Mpaltadoros, L.; Nikolopoulos, S.; Kompatsiaris, I. Iot wearable sensors and devices in elderly care: A literature review. *Sensors* **2020**, *20*, 2826. [CrossRef]
21. Belcastro, L.; Marozzo, F.; Presta, A.; Varchera, R.; Vinci, A. Developing Platform-Agnostic IIoT Applications in Edge-Cloud Environments. *Procedia Comput. Sci.* **2025**, *253*, 2106–2115. [CrossRef]
22. Dziak, D.; Jachimczyk, B.; Kulesza, W.J. IoT-Based Information System for Healthcare Application: Design Methodology Approach. *Appl. Sci.* **2017**, *7*, 596. [CrossRef]
23. Park, K.H.; Park, J.; Lee, J.W. An IoT System for Remote Monitoring of Patients at Home. *Appl. Sci.* **2017**, *7*, 260. [CrossRef]
24. Kelly, J.T.; Campbell, K.L.; Gong, E.; Scuffham, P. The Internet of Things: Impact and Implications for Health Care Delivery. *J. Med. Internet Res.* **2020**, *22*, e20135. [CrossRef]
25. Khajeh, S.A.; Saberikamarposhti, M.; Rahmani, A.M. Real-Time Scheduling in IoT Applications: A Systematic Review. *Sensors* **2022**, *23*, 232. [CrossRef]
26. Asingwire, B.K.; Sibomana, L.; Ngenzi, A.; Kabiri, C. Delay and size-dependent priority-aware scheduling for IoT-based healthcare traffic using heterogeneous multi-server priority queueing system. *IET Commun.* **2023**, *17*, 1877–1887. [CrossRef]
27. Rajkumar, G.; Devi, T.G.; Srinivasan, A. Heart disease prediction using IoT based framework and improved deep learning approach: Medical application. *Med Eng. Phys.* **2023**, *111*, 103937. [CrossRef]
28. Yinusa, A.; Faezipour, M. Optimizing Healthcare Delivery: A Model for Staffing, Patient Assignment, and Resource Allocation. *Appl. Syst. Innov.* **2023**, *6*, 78. [CrossRef]
29. Abdalkareem, Z.A.; Amir, A.; Al-Betar, M.A.; Ekhan, P.; Hammouri, A.I. Healthcare scheduling in optimization context: A review. *Health Technol.* **2021**, *11*, 445–469. [CrossRef]
30. Kumar, K.; Narasimham, N.; Prasad, A.R. Biomimicry in Radiation Therapy: Optimizing Patient Scheduling for Improved Treatment Outcomes. *Adv. Artif. Intell. Mach. Learn. Res.* **2024**, *4*, 2452–2467. [CrossRef]
31. Ala, A.; Alsaadi, F.E.; Ahmadi, M.; Mirjalili, S. Optimization of an appointment scheduling problem for healthcare systems based on the quality of fairness service using whale optimization algorithm and NSGA-II. *Sci. Rep.* **2021**, *11*, 1–19. [CrossRef]
32. Han, X.; Dong, Y.; Yue, L.; Xu, Q.; Xie, G.; Xu, X. State-transition simulated annealing algorithm for constrained and unconstrained multi-objective optimization problems. *Appl. Intell.* **2021**, *51*, 775–787. [CrossRef]
33. Achterberg, T. SCIP: Solving constraint integer programs. *Math. Program. Comput.* **2009**, *1*, 1–41. [CrossRef]
34. YV, H.; LS, L.; DA, W. On a bicriterion formation of the problems of integrated system identification and system optimization. *IEEE Trans. Syst. Man Cybern.* **1971**, *SMC-1*, 296–297. [CrossRef]
35. Ehrgott, M.; Gandibleux, X.; Przybylski, A. Exact Methods for Multi-Objective Combinatorial Optimisation. *Int. Ser. Oper. Res. Manag. Sci.* **2016**, *233*, 817–850. [CrossRef]
36. Bertsimas, D.; Goyal, V. On the approximability of adjustable robust convex optimization under uncertainty. *Math. Methods Oper. Res.* **2013**, *77*, 323–343. [CrossRef]
37. Talbi, E.G. *Metaheuristics: From Desing to Implementation*; John Wiley and Sons, Inc.: Hoboken, NJ, USA, 2009; p. 624.
38. Nebro, A.J.; Durillo, J.J. On the Effect of Applying a Steady-State Selection Scheme in the Multi-Objective Genetic Algorithm NSGA-II. *Stud. Comput. Intell.* **2009**, *193*, 435–456. [CrossRef]
39. Zitzler, E.; Brockhoff, D.; Thiele, L. *The Hypervolume Indicator Revisited: On the Design of Pareto-Compliant Indicators Via Weighted Integration;* Lecture Notes in Computer Science (including subseries Lecture Notes in Artificial Intelligence and Lecture Notes in Bioinformatics); Springer: Berlin/Heidelberg, Germany, 2007; Volume 4403 LNCS, pp. 862–876. [CrossRef]

applied sciences

Article

IoT-Driven Resilience Monitoring: Case Study of a Cyber-Physical System

Ali Aghazadeh Ardebili [1,2,*], Cristian Martella [1,*], Antonella Longo [1,*], Chiara Rucco [1], Federico Izzi [1] and Antonio Ficarella [1]

[1] Department of Engineering for Innovation, University of Salento, 73100 Lecce, Italy; chiara.rucco@unisalento.it (C.R.); federico.izzi@studenti.unisalento.it (F.I.); antonio.ficarella@unisalento.it (A.F.)
[2] Department of Research and Development, HSPI SpA, 00185 Rome, Italy
[*] Correspondence: ali.a.ardebili@unisalento.it (A.A.A.); cristian.martella@unisalento.it (C.M.); antonella.longo@unisalento.it (A.L.)

Abstract: This study focuses on Digital Twin-integrated smart energy systems, which serve as an example of Next-Generation Critical Infrastructures (CI). The resilience of these systems is influenced by a variety of internal features and external interactions, all of which are subject to change following cyber-physical disturbances. This necessitates real-time resilience monitoring for CI during crises; however, a significant gap remains in resilience monitoring. To address this gap, this study leverages the role of Internet of Things (IoT) in monitoring complex systems to enhance resilience through critical indicators relevant to cyber-physical safety and security. The study empirically implements Resilience-Key Performance Indicators (R-KPIs) from the domain, including Functionality Loss, Minimum Performance, and Recovery Time Duration. The main goal is to examine real-time IoT-based resilience monitoring in a real-life context. A cyber-physical system equipped with IoT-driven Digital Twins, data-driven microservices, and a False Data Injection Attack (FDIA) scenario is simulated to assess the real-time resilience of this smart system. The results demonstrate that real-time resilience monitoring provides actionable insights into resilience performance based on the selected R-KPIs. These findings contribute to a systematic and reusable model for enhancing the resilience of IoT-enabled CI, advancing efforts to ensure service continuity and secure essential services for society.

Keywords: IoT-based monitoring; cyber-physical resilience; real-Time; digital twins; empirical study; sustainable energy; smart energy systems; safety-critical systems

1. Introduction

The rise of cyber-physical critical infrastructures (CIs) with advanced features like Artificial Intelligence (AI) integration highlights the importance of assessing and overseeing resilience [1]. These infrastructures require a comprehensive approach to resilience measurement and monitoring due to their complex and interconnected nature. CIs play a crucial role in contemporary societies, covering a wide range of sectors essential for maintaining operations and safeguarding public well-being [2]. These infrastructures are fundamental for the functioning of society and are responsible for delivering essential services to the public. From energy grid CIs to transportation systems, these infrastructures provide essential services that facilitate daily life [3]. Consequently, disruptions in critical systems, such as transportation, communication, and energy, can have far-reaching consequences. For example, disruption in the transportation system could lead to delays in the delivery of goods and services, resulting in economic losses for businesses and consumers [4]. Similarly, a disruption in the communication system could hinder emergency response efforts and jeopardize public safety [5]. Additionally, disruptions in the energy system could lead to power outages, impacting businesses, hospitals, and individuals who rely on electricity for their daily activities [6,7]. Overall, disruptions in such systems can have cascading effects that threaten public safety and security, as well as causing significant economic losses.

Recognizing the interconnectivity and vulnerability inherent in CIs, it is essential to prioritize resilience in order to mitigate risks and enhance societal resilience when faced with unforeseen challenges. With this approach, communities and societies can better prepare for and respond to various threats and crises, ultimately ensuring their ability to bounce back and recover more effectively [8].

The resilience of CIs is influenced by a wide range of internal characteristics and external interactions, all of which are subject to dynamic changes following cyber-physical disturbances [9,10]. Consequently, resilience must be regarded as a dynamic concept that requires continuous study during crises triggered by extreme events, such as earthquakes or terrorist attacks, and even their aftermath [11,12]. This highlights the critical importance of leveraging IoT technologies for the real-time monitoring of CIs.

In this context, resilience quantification emerges as a crucial approach to understanding, assessing, and enhancing the resilience of CIs. While existing methodologies often rely on metrics and indicators derived from historical data [13–15], a significant gap persists in real-time resilience monitoring. Addressing this gap is essential to effectively capture the dynamic behavior of CIs during crises.

To bridge this gap, this study seeks to answer a pressing and emerging question: ***Is it feasible to monitor the resilience of IoT-integrated CIs in real-time using sensor data for specific KPIs?***

By exploring this question, the study underscores the urgency and relevance of real-time resilience monitoring in advancing the safety and functionality of CIs. Therefore, this article presents an empirical study based on real-world data, observations, and experimentation to derive conclusions. The research design involves developing and operating a cyber-physical testbed to implement various data-driven algorithms for real-time resilience monitoring. The testbed is a smart PV panel, with its resilience being evaluated under a FDIA. The primary contributions of this empirical study are outlined as follows:

- The development and validation of a comprehensive method for real-time resilience monitoring of IoT-integrated CI.
- The implementation and testing of different data-driven algorithms tailored to R-KPIs, informed by observed system behavior.
- The construction and operation of a practical cyber-physical testbed for empirical resilience assessment using a Digital Twin-integrated smart PV system.

The remainder of the article is structured as follows: **Section 2 Research Landscape**: An overview of the current state of resilience assessment of CI. In **Section 3**, we explain the theoretical foundation of the resilience KPIs that are used in this article. **Section 4 Statistical and AI methods**: A detailed description of the cyber-physical system under study and methodology for implementing and measuring the selected R-KPIs. **Section 5 Cyber-Physical System**: A synthesis of the testbed results, with a validation of the resilience monitoring method based on sensor data in the real time. **Section 6 Case Study**: A detailed description of test configuration, and discussion of results from conducted tests results. **Section 7 Limitations, Challenges, and Future Research**: Discussion of study limitations, encountered challenges, and potential future research avenues. **Section 8**

Conclusions: Summarizes key findings and their implications for the resilience monitoring of IoT-enabled CI.

2. Research Landscape

Critical infrastructure (CI) encompasses physical assets and systems that provide a necessary service in national, regional, and local scopes. Because of the necessity of the service continuity of CIs, it is extremely important that the service can be delivered under challenging situations like natural disasters or disturbances from cyber-physical attacks [16].

The capacity to withstand or to recover quickly from risks is called resilience. CI should be resilient in all aspects, from governance to operational level [17].

Prior studies unveiled the efficiency of data-driven solutions to enhance the resilience of complex systems [1,18–20] and CI [21–23]. However, achieving a socio-technical transition towards more sustainable and resilient CIs necessitates substantial conceptual changes in the system architecture, coupled with the incorporation of new assets dedicated to collecting real-time data, communication, and computations. The integration of these new components into the system brings more complexity, consequently diminishing the resilience of the overall system. While this transition seems fundamental because of societal challenges of climate change and increasing natural disasters, emerging cyber-physical threats, and the changes in the service end users' behaviour [24], transforming entire socio-technical CI involves a novel resilience engineering approach [25] to guarantee the uninterrupted service continuity of emerging AI-integrated CIs.

Nevertheless, at present, the technologies supporting these transitions are either under study or in the developmental stage, typically confined to laboratory-scale implementations. Additionally, the majority of existing CIs continue to operate using traditional monitoring and control systems. Therefore, the body of knowledge in AI-integrated CIs resilience engineering is not fully defined, and there is a gap in standardized models and performance metrics to quantify the resilience of AI-integrated CIs.

Next-Gen Energy Systems Resilience

The energy sector is transitioning towards a Next-Gen model, characterized by intelligent energy infrastructures that leverage renewable energy sources [26] and distributed generation [26]. This transformation is further enhanced by emerging technologies such as Digital Twins [19,27,28], IoT, data-driven solutions [28], real-time anomaly detection [29], and big data analytics [30–32], collectively shaping a smart grid that promises a sustainable and efficient future. However, this evolution is not without challenges. Ensuring the resilience of these advanced systems poses a significant challenge, requiring innovative and adaptive solutions. This study is motivated by these challenges and focuses on Next-Gen energy CIs with these defining characteristics.

One key concern lies in the growing dependence on renewables [33,34]. While solar and wind power offer significant environmental benefits, their inherent variability and intermittency pose challenges [35]. Unlike traditional, reliable power plants, renewable sources are not always available, demanding robust energy storage and sophisticated grid management systems to function effectively [36]. Furthermore, extreme weather events can disrupt these already fluctuating sources [37], potentially cascading into power outages and grid instability.

Smart grids, another cornerstone of Next-Gen energy systems, introduce a different set of vulnerabilities. These intelligent networks, enabling two-way communication between utilities and consumers, offer real-time monitoring, dynamic pricing, and improved efficiency. However, the increased complexity creates a larger attack surface for cyber threats [38,39]. Malicious actors targeting communication networks or control systems could disrupt critical operations, leading to widespread blackouts [40].

The rise of distributed generation, where power is produced closer to consumption points through rooftop solar panels or microgrids, presents a double-edged sword. While it fosters energy independence and reduces reliance on centralized power plants, it also introduces complexities in managing the grid and maintaining stability. Additionally, a cyber-attack targeting a single distributed generation unit could have a ripple effect, impacting the entire grid.

3. Theoretical Foundation of Resilience Curve and Its KPIs in This Domain

To quantify the resilience of smart energy systems, this study conducts a comprehensive literature review. The review identifies various measurable resilience indexes. From this pool of indexes, and various articles, the current study focuses on a case study within smart energy systems. To quantify CI resilience in this CIs, timeliness plays a vital role. Therefore, we prioritize time-related KPIs for this analysis. Other metrics also impact resilience monitoring, such as Age of Information (AoI), which quantifies data freshness and serves as a critical metric for real-time resilience monitoring [41–44]. However, these metrics are not derived from the resilience curve, and we leave their exploration for future studies.

Two reference articles form the foundation for the selection of R-KPIs and resilience curve construction in this study (see Section 3.1 for definitions). An empirical study conducted in the domain of smart PV panels, using a similar testbed [45], serves as a basis for selecting three specific KPIs: functionality loss, minimum performance, and recovery time. To calculate these R-KPIs, it is essential to first construct a resilience curve [46] (see Section 3.1). Given that the collected data are inherently noisy, we apply two methods empirically implemented and evaluated for noisy data in [47]: Support Vector Machine (SVM) and polynomial fitting via least squares (Polyfit) (see Section 3 for definitions). Although SVM was identified in the reference article as the superior method for accurately reflecting system behavior, both methods are employed in this study to allow for comparative analysis. As a practical recommendation for monitoring system resilience, it is advised that once a method is chosen, it should consistently be used throughout the system's lifecycle to construct its resilience curve.

3.1. Resilience Curve and Selected R-KPIs

Resilience curves are widely applied across various fields in resilience engineering, encompassing applications in critical infrastructure resilience [48,49], resilience index development [50–53], recovery reviews [54–57], system component criticality [58–60], post-disturbance activities [61–63], and measurements and/or benchmarking for resilience assessment [64–66].

In this article, the resilience curve will be used to calculate the selected R-KPIs. In the following section, the three R-KPIs that are chosen for further analysis will be defined in detail.

3.1.1. Recovery Time

The primary objective of resilience-enhancing metrics is to enhance the three core capacities of resilience: absorption, adaptation, and restoration. This goal is achieved through the implementation of diverse strategies aimed at strengthening the functionality and performance of critical infrastructure, such as incorporating redundancy.

Redundancy in critical infrastructure refers to integrating duplicate or backup components and systems to ensure that essential functions can persist even in the face of disruptions. By incorporating redundant elements, the system gains the ability to absorb shocks, adapt to unexpected challenges, and facilitate quicker restoration. Redundancy serves as a safeguard against single points of failure, minimizing the impact of disruptions and significantly contributing to reducing recovery time. It plays a pivotal role in enhancing overall resilience by providing alternative pathways and resources, thereby fortifying the infrastructure's ability to bounce back swiftly and effectively from unforeseen events. Moreover, shorter recovery times can also be achieved through the implementation of measures that prioritize the swift restoration and replacement of impaired infrastructure components. This proactive approach not only accelerates recovery but also contributes to the overall enhancement of resilience, as it minimizes downtime and fortifies the system against prolonged disruptions.

The recovery time after a disruption is a crucial index for critical infrastructure resilience, particularly in sectors like energy, due to its direct impact on overall operational resilience. In the aftermath of a disturbance within critical infrastructure, performance inevitably experiences a decline, reaching its minimum level. Following this critical decrease, there are essentially two potential outcomes. Firstly, the performance may reach zero, resulting in a complete system shutdown—a scenario that is universally deemed unacceptable in any disturbance situation for critical infrastructure.

Conversely, the system's response to the disturbance may trigger a recovery phase, characterized by an upward trajectory in performance levels. This recovery phase is crucial as it signifies the infrastructure's ability to rebound and stabilize after the initial level in performance. The stabilized performance level, as illustrated in Figure 1, can assume one of three forms: it may be equal to the prior stable level, higher than the pre-disturbance level, or lower than the pre-disturbance level. This phase is termed the recovery phase, representing a critical aspect of the system's resilience.

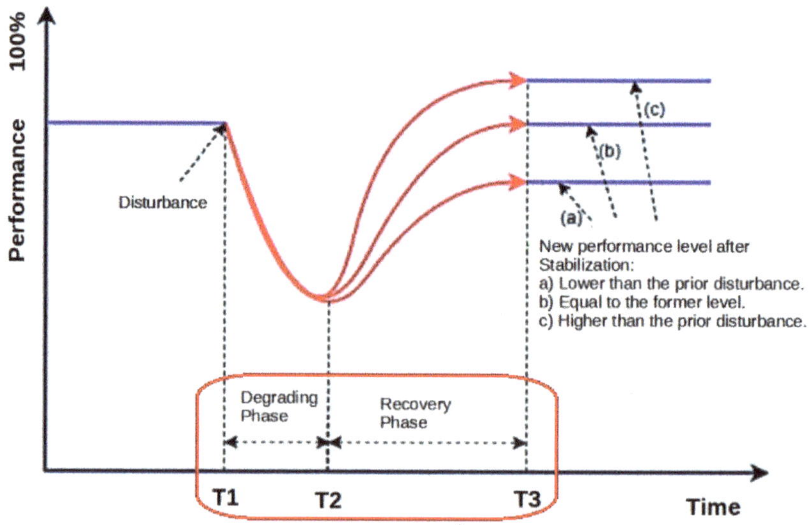

Figure 1. Illustration of recovery time. The red box highlights the point on the resilience curve where the recovery phases duration can be identified.

The concept of recovery time encompasses both the degrading phase, where performance declines, and the subsequent recovery phase, where performance improves and stabilizes. As illustrated in Figure 1, the recovery time spans from the occurrence of the disturbance to the point of stabilization after the recovery phase. The duration of this recovery time is indicative of the system's overall robustness and its ability to efficiently restore and stabilize its performance following disruptions, which is vital for the sustained and reliable operation of critical infrastructure systems, especially in the energy sector.

3.1.2. Minimum Performance Level

The determination of the minimum performance level in critical infrastructure depends on the inherent design features of the system and the severity of the encountered disturbance. Monitoring this minimum performance level holds crucial significance as it ensures the preservation of essential services vital for the system's proper functioning. The minimum performance level is intricately defined by the indispensable thresholds associated with the societal needs for that particular service. In the event that the minimum performance of a critical infrastructure (CI) descends below this predefined level following a disturbance, it becomes imperative to reassess the response strategy to this risk. Such a proactive approach is essential for safeguarding the reliability and functionality of the critical infrastructure system, aligning its performance with the crucial needs of the society it serves. Continuous monitoring and adaptive strategies are thus indispensable to maintain the resilience and effectiveness of critical infrastructure in the face of dynamic challenges. Figure 2 shows the minimum performance level after disturbance.

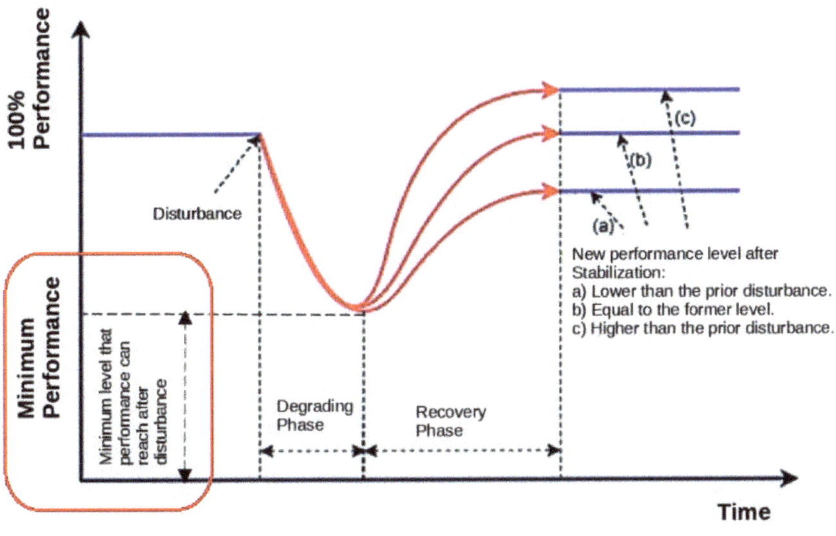

Figure 2. Illustration of minimum performance level. The red box highlights the point on the resilience curve where the minimum performance level can be identified.

3.1.3. Functionality Loss

Resilience curves are applied across the critical infrastructure literature this shows two kinds of curve: a typical representation with a semi-linear degradation and semi-linear recovery phase, or non-idealized system behavior (Figure 3). Since the complex systems can show the irregular behavior after disturbance because the interdependences between other CIs and the dynamic nature and natural complexity of the system, it is important to have a index to cover the loss during the lifecycle of recovery time. This loss is called Loss of Functionality [67]. Figure 4 shows a graphical illustration of Loss of Functionality.

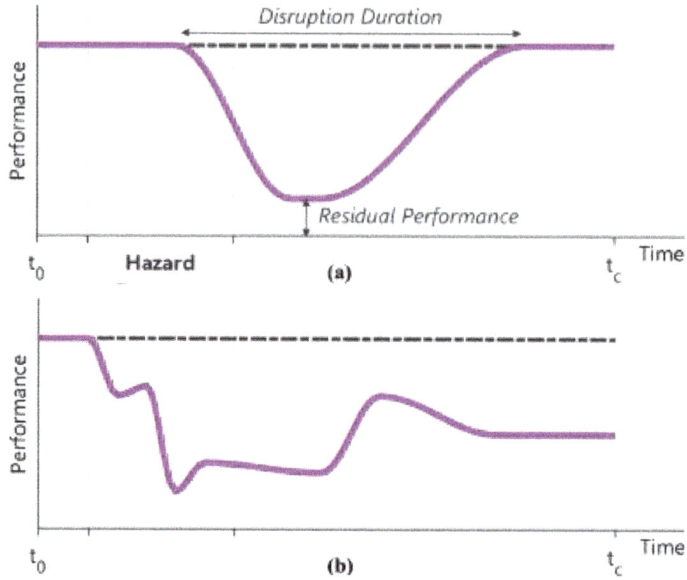

Figure 3. (**a**,**b**) Graphical illustration of different behaviors after disturbance [68].

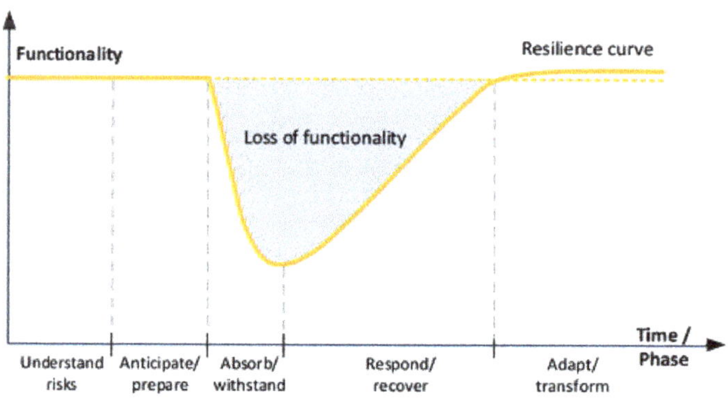

Figure 4. Graphical illustration of Loss of Functionality [67].

The method that is used in this research is adopted from a developed comprehensive framework for assessing the resilience of infrastructure in response to specific events, such as earthquakes [69]. The framework aims to measure the impact of an earthquake by estimating the predicted degradation in the quality of service provided by the infrastructure, denoted as $Q(t)$. We can break down the process:

Assuming a disturbance occurs at time t_0, the degradation in service quality is assessed from the moment of the shock (t_0) until the service quality ($Q(t)$) fully recovers to its pre-disturbance levels at time t_1. This period represents the recovery phase.

The measure of Loss of Functionality, denoted as LF, is determined by considering how much the service quality degrades during the recovery period, regardless of the behavior of the system shown in Figure 3. The calculation can be expressed as follows:

$$FL = \int_{t_0}^{t_1} [100 - Q(t)]\, dt$$

In simpler terms, Loss of Functionality is the difference between the initial service quality at the time of the disturbance (t_0) and the service quality once it has fully recovered (t_1). This provides a quantifiable metric for understanding the impact of the disturbance on the infrastructure's ability to maintain its continuity of service.

4. Implemented Statistical and AI Methods

In the current research, Rolling Average is used for raw data time series smoothing and Polynomial Fitting is employed to model a polynomial that accurately represents the dataset obtained from the testbed during disturbance scenario testing.

Polynomial fitting is a regression technique that fits a polynomial (a mathematical expression consisting of variables raised to powers and multiplied by coefficients) to a set of data points. The goal is to find the polynomial that best captures the relationship between the independent variable(s) and the dependent variable. The degree of the polynomial determines its complexity, and higher-degree polynomials can capture more complex relationships but may also be prone to overfitting.

For Polynominal Curve Fitting, Least Squares Regression and Support Vector Regression (SVR) with a Radial Basis Function (RBF) Kernel model are used. Support Vector Regression (SVR) is a regression algorithm that uses support vector machines to model the relationship between variables. In SVR, the goal is to find a hyperplane that best fits the data while allowing for a certain degree of error. The RBF kernel is a specific type of kernel function used in SVR, and it is particularly effective in capturing non-linear relationships. In the following section, the theoretical foundation of the methods is explained.

4.1. Moving Average

The moving average is a statistical technique used to analyze data trends by smoothing out short-term fluctuations, providing a clearer view of the underlying direction in a dataset [70]. It is particularly useful in time series analysis, where data may exhibit high volatility due to random variations. The most basic form, the Simple Moving Average (SMA), calculates the average of a fixed number of consecutive data points, or "window size". As new data points become available, the average recalculates by including the most recent observation and excluding the oldest one, effectively "moving" along the dataset [71]. For instance, the SMA over a window size N is calculated using the formula:

$$\mathrm{SMA}_t = \frac{X_t + X_{t-1} + \ldots + X_{t-N+1}}{N}$$

where X_t represents the current data point, and N is the window size.

Moving averages have extensive applications across various fields, such as finance, where they are used to identify stock price trends [72], and economics, where they help analyze indicators like GDP and inflation rates [73].

Sensor data from photovoltaic (PV) panels for DC power often exhibits noise due to environmental fluctuations, electromagnetic interference, and sensor limitations. Variations in sunlight, temperature, and shading cause inconsistencies, while electronic components introduce interference, affecting data stability. Sensor inaccuracies, often due to limited sensitivity issues, further contribute to this variability, making it challenging to obtain clean data directly from sensors [74,75].

Implementing a rolling average for smoothing time series data is a widely adopted technique (39,529 documents in SCOPUS used key term `rolling average OR moving average`) with its own set of pros and cons. Rolling averages are a commonly used method for data smoothing and trend analysis [76], offering distinct advantages. Rolling averages have been introduced as a convenient method for regulating power-time curves in renewable and conventional energy profiles [77–80], which served as the main motivation for considering rolling averages in the current study. Nevertheless, their simplicity may sometimes limit their ability to capture complex patterns in data, highlighting the need to explore alternative or complementary approaches for more intricate analyses.

Recent studies have demonstrated that implementing a rolling average is inefficient for resilience curve construction when data are affected by significant noise [47]. However, in this article, moving averages are used to provide essential smoothing for noisy datasets, making it easier to detect underlying patterns and inform forecasting models [81].

4.2. Least Squares Regression

The polyfit function in NumPy is used for polynomial fitting, which involves finding the coefficients of a polynomial that best fits a set of data points. The theoretical foundation of polynomial fitting lies in the concept of least squares regression.

The goal to minimize the sum of squared differences

$$\text{minimize} \sum_{i=1}^{N} (y_i - P(x_i))^2 \tag{1}$$

In the Matrix form, it can be represented in this way:

$$X = \begin{bmatrix} 1 & x_1 & x_1^2 & \dots & x_1^n \\ 1 & x_2 & x_2^2 & \dots & x_2^n \\ \vdots & \vdots & \vdots & \ddots & \vdots \\ 1 & x_N & x_N^2 & \dots & x_N^n \end{bmatrix} \quad C = \begin{bmatrix} c_0 \\ c_1 \\ \vdots \\ c_n \end{bmatrix} \quad Y = \begin{bmatrix} y_1 \\ y_2 \\ \vdots \\ y_N \end{bmatrix}$$

Finally, a solution is gained using least squares

$$C = (X^T X)^{-1} X^T Y \tag{2}$$

4.3. Support Vector Regression (SVR) Model with a Radial Basis Function (RBF) Kernel

$$f(x) = \sum_{i=1}^{n} \alpha_i K(x, x_i) + b \tag{3}$$

where $f(x)$ is the predicted output, n is the number of support vectors, α_i is the coefficients associated with the support vectors, $K(x, x_i)$ is the kernel function, which measures the similarity between x and the support vectors x_i, and b is a bias term. The RBF kernel is defined as follows:

$$K(x, x_i) = \exp\left(-\frac{\|x - x_i\|^2}{2\sigma^2}\right) \tag{4}$$

where σ is a parameter that controls the width of the Gaussian distribution.

This equation captures the non-linear relationship between input features and output in the SVR model. The specific form of the kernel function, in this case, the RBF kernel, contributes to the model's ability to capture complex patterns in the data.

It should be noted that the SVR model is designed to handle non-linear relationships and may not have a simple linear equation like traditional linear regression.

5. Cyber-Physical System

This section includes the discussion of a real case study that we have implemented to assess the energy CP framework that we propose. Being a prototype, the case study should be considered as an experiment in which the building blocks were implemented according to the essential functionalities and features they must provide. As already mentioned, our ambition is to perform a complete testbed of the proposed framework in order to assess the same framework. The architecture adopted for the case study is shown in Figure 5. According to the proposed energy CP framework, it includes the three main building blocks: Physical Asset, Data Infrastructure, and Digital Twin. The Physical Asset consists of a portable power-generating infrastructure in an autonomous Smart PhotoVoltaic Station that features a PV panel equipped with sensors to assess the placement surrounding's conditions, along with actuators to control the orientation of the panel. The Data Infrastructure is limited to implement two fundamental services for the framework, which are data streaming and data persistence. For the case study, the device we have adopted for deploying these services is a fog node implemented by a Raspberry PI 4B. Finally, the Digital Twin was implemented in the form of a virtual world interactive model of the SPVS. According to the proposed framework, the overall Digital Twin includes its four fundamental services, which are Dynamic Environment, Operation, Ideal State, and Demand. Considering the processing and storage resources the Energy DT needs, these services are deployed on a workstation. Such a workstation represents the cloud backend of the framework we propose, but with more limited resources in terms of processing and storage capabilities.

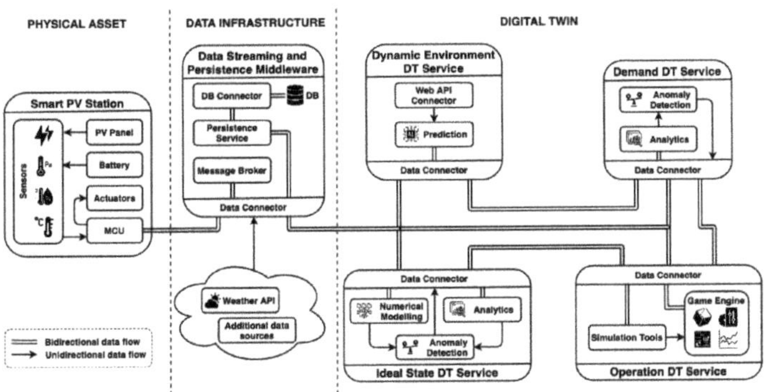

Figure 5. Conceptual model of the proposed system [82].

5.1. *Physical Asset: Smart PhotoVoltaic Station*

The models discussed in this case study are applied in the PV power generation system called a Smart PhotoVoltaic Station (SPVS). Such a system is part of the real testbed we have conducted and which is detailed in the present section. The list of components that are presented in Table 1 was used for assembling the CP infrastructure (Figure 6a,c) and for evaluating our experimental setup.

Table 1. List of sensors, actuators, and other components [45,82].

Category	Component	Specification
Sensors	Air quality	Bosch BME280 (Bosch Sensortec GmbH, Reutlingen, Germany)
	Power	INA3221
Actuators	Servo motors	2× (0°–180°)
Other Components	MCU	2× ESP32
	Voltage converter	2×
	MPPT	
	Battery	LiFePo4 12 V 6 Ah
	PV panel	20 W monocrystalline

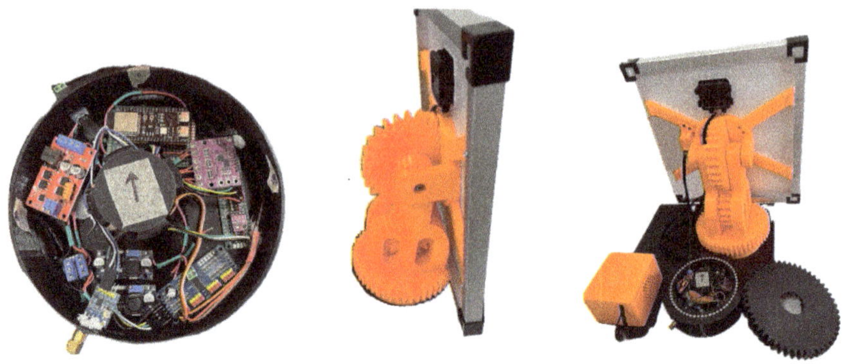

(a) (b) (c)

Figure 6. SPVS physical asset implementation. (**a**) Control system (Table 1). (**b**) Motion mechanism. (**c**) Assembled view (back view).

The logical model of the SPVS is shown in Figure 7, where the physical components and the connections between them are represented. In particular, it includes two types of physical connections: power delivery and data delivery. The former is used to highlight the electric circuit to power the SPVS components, whilst the latter maps the data streams between the components.

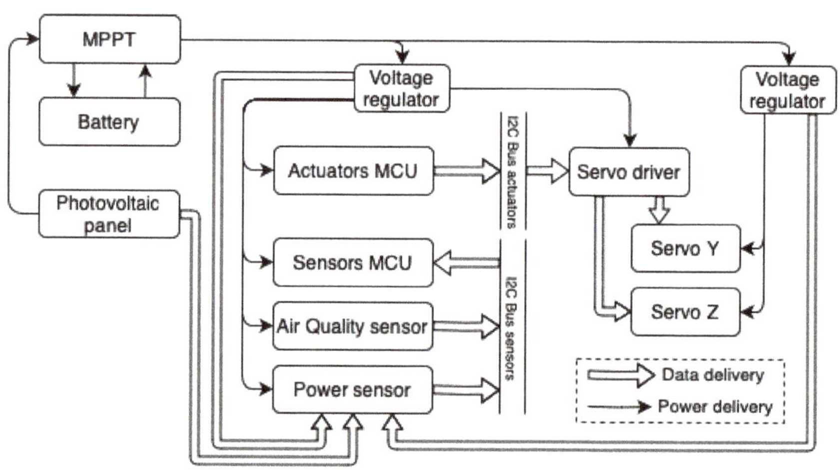

Figure 7. The logical model of the smart PV system [45,82].

5.1.1. PV Panel

For the purposes of this work, the choice of a suitable PV panel plays a critical role. Since the module is used for a portable SPVS as a testbed, a 20 W monocrystalline solar module has been chosen. Moreover, durable ESG glass is another relevant requirement to avoid the degradation of the module due to microfractures during installation and movements of the PV panel.

The 20 W Mono Solar Module from Offgridtec (MPN 3-01-001560), whose datasheet is shown in Table 2, operates with high-efficiency monocrystalline solar cells (>18%), and thanks to its operating voltage of 20 V, it is ideal for 12 V systems. "Monocrystalline" refers to a type of solar cell or module where the silicon used in the construction is made up of a single crystal structure. In contrast, polycrystalline solar cells are made from multiple crystals, and thin-film solar cells are made using different materials altogether. Monocrystalline solar cells are known for their higher efficiency and greater space-efficiency compared to other types.

Table 2. Offgridtec Mono20W3-01-001560 PV module specifications.

Parameter	Value
Maximum Power (Pmax)	20 W
Open Circuit Voltage (Voc)	22.3 V
Short Circuit Current (Isc)	1.21 A
Voltage at Maximum Power (Vmpp)	17.8 V
Current at Maximum Power (Impp)	1.12 A
Module Efficiency of Voc	−0.45%
Module Efficiency of Isc	−0.45%
Module Efficiency of power	−0.45%
Nominal Operating Cell Temperature (NOCT)	45 (± 2) °C
Operating Temperature Range	−40 °C to +85 °C
Cells type/Array	2 × 18
Maximum system voltage	600 VDC

Values are measured at Standard Test Conditions (STC), with Irradiance 1000 Wm^{-2}, Air Mass (AM) 1.5 Spectrum and Temperature 25 °C.

5.1.2. Sensors and Actuators

The SPVS features a set of sensors and actuators used to perceive and interact with the surrounding environment. On the sensors side, the device is equipped with sensors to assess the air quality (temperature, atmospheric pressure, and relative humidity) and a DC power sensor that is used to collect data on the live power production of the PV panel, the power stored in the battery, and the power used by the system in performing its operations.

The station is also capable of tracking a desired orientation. To do so, on the actuators side, the device's mechanical gear work is actuated through a couple of servo motors. One of them is devoted to control the pitch angle of the panel, whilst the other one controls its yaw angle (as shown in Figure 8).

5.1.3. Service Modules

The brain of the SPVS physical asset is implemented through ESP32 micro-controller units (MCU). The choice of this chip is motivated by its good performance, relative to the requirements posed by tasks it is intended to perform and the services it should expose, at a low price and bundled in a tiny board. The ESP32 board also includes an antenna module that allows it to establish wireless communication (either WiFi or Bluetooth) on the 2.4 GHz band.

The device is powered using the energy generated by the PV panel and stored in the accumulation system. In particular, a Maximum Power Point Tracker (MPPT) is used to monitor the output of the PV panel and adjust the voltage and current so as to keep the system always at the point of maximum power. The output of the MPPT feeds the battery, but it is too high to power the logical components that require at most 5 volts. Additionally, it is also important to split the power sources to use for low power (sensors and control devices) and high power (servo motors) devices, respectively. Therefore, two step-down voltage converters are installed between the system's power source output (the battery) and the modules that need to be powered. These step-down voltage converters are tuned to output constant 5 volts. By keeping the power sources separated, it is possible to avoid undesired power drops when performing power intensive tasks that would result in the reboot of the MCU board or even the damage of the most sensitive components.

Figure 8. Dynamic 3D model with 2 degrees of freedom (Dof) that is used to visualize the current gradient of the PV module [45,82].

5.2. *Data Infrastructure: Data Streaming and Persistence Middleware*

For the purpose of the present case study, the Data Infrastructure component of the proposed framework is delegated to the exclusive management of data streaming and data persistence. The Data Streaming and Persistence Middleware (DSPM) is crucial because it allows the exchange of data within the CP system by determining how these data must persist and how they must be made available to both the Energy DT's services and the SPVS. Moreover, the DSPM is responsible for retrieving additional data by issuing specific requests to external data sources. For the present case study, the contributions obtained by these external data sources are related to services like open weather APIs (for obtaining instantaneous weather metrics), but also additional IoT sensors, such as local weather stations and pyranometers. The software module that implements the interface with external data sources is called Web API Connector.

A detailed discussion about the services corresponding to data streaming and data persistence is reported below.

5.2.1. Data Streaming

The data streaming service makes it possible the interaction between the SPVS and the virtual world interactive model. Such an interaction was implemented by adopting the Message Queuing Telemetry Transport (MQTT) protocol that enables the publish/subscribe paradigm. The efficiency of MQTT at an industrial scale has been demonstrated in previous studies [83]. In this regard, an instance of message broker was made available to support the communication between MQTT publishers and subscribers. Clients subscribe to MQTT topics to secure sensor data payloads, ensuring timely data reception, concurrent with the publishing activities. Incoming messages undergo a deserialization process, transforming payloads into manipulable JSON objects for data extraction and subsequent processing.

On the service side, the software module of the case study architecture that is delegated to support data streaming between services is called *Data Connector*. The Data Connector operations flowchart is reported in Figure 9. So, all the services of the framework that must be enabled for the data streaming needs to integrate such a module. In addition, the data streaming service is responsible for managing communication via the message broker and the reference database instance, as well as acquiring data from the SPVS and the Energy DT's services. This result is achieved by using an approach to a data fetching request that can be configured to be synchronous or asynchronous, as needed. In this way, it is possible to integrate a controller to the software components of the edge device which can regulate the data transmission rate by monitoring specific indicators related to the state of the system, such as the battery level of charge. A specific service of the middleware called *persistence service* intercepts the MQTT traffic between the SPVS and the virtual world interactive model in order to persist the corresponding data entities.

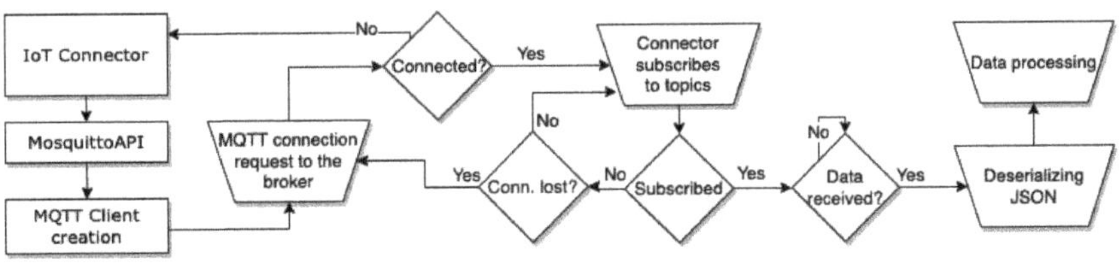

Figure 9. Data Connector flowchart.

5.2.2. Data Persistence

The Data Persistence service consists of two microservices that make it possible to store historical records of data flowing back and forth between the the SPVS and the Energy DT's services, namely sensor readings and action commands. These two microservices implement the interface and the interaction with the reference DBMS instance. Among the possible database solutions, MongoDB was identified as the most suitable for the case study, thanks to its document-based nature that fosters high performance querying of IoT data [84] alongside an efficient handling of several insert queries. When comparing to relational DBMSs such as MySQL, MongoDB allows to outperform in terms of resources usage and overall latency [85,86].

MongoDB's document-based approach allows to store and process heterogeneous data types, such as sensor data, time-series data, and metadata, in a single document. Supporting an efficient and effective local data storage on edge devices, MongoDB allows to reduce the need to stream data towards remote servers or cloud infrastructures. Concerning the DBMS interface microservice, a Python script represents the most suitable solution for the present case study in terms of disk usage and responsiveness performance. Indeed, the usage of state-of-the-art software solutions, such as Apache NiFi, can be counterproductive and challenging due to the high computational needs they require to run on the resource-constrained fog device used for the testbed. A Python script provides a subscription for each MQTT topic related to both the physical and the digital counterpart, acting as a man in the middle. In this sense, it intercepts the corresponding data flows exchanged by the two counterparts and prepares the carried data entities for storage by interacting with the MongoDB microservice.

5.3. *Energy Digital Twin: Virtual World Interactive Model*

According to the CP framework proposed in this work, the DT corresponds to the digital counterpart of the physical asset. For the aim of the case study, we have implemented the DT as the Virtual World Interactive Model of the SPVS. Such a model corresponds to an interactive and graphical representation of the SPVS within the Unreal Engine virtual world. By following the specification of the framework we propose, the Energy DT provides four interconnected services called *Dynamic Environmental Service* (DES), *Operation Service* (OS), *Ideal State Service* (ISS), and *Demand Service* (DS), respectively. A detailed description for each of these services is provided in the following section.

5.3.1. Dynamic Environment Service

For the present case study, the DES service is delegated to gather environmental data detected by the sensors installed on the SPVS, along with meteorological data retrieved by the DSPM, using a Web API Connector. Regarding this former aspect, DES collects basic environmental parameters like temperature, pressure, and humidity, but also additional weather information, including cloud coverage and solar irradiance relative to the location where the SPVS is installed. The DES service processes the collected data to perform predictions on temperature and irradiation using ML approaches. Finally, it assimilates solar radiation metrics, which encompass values related to Direct Radiation, Diffuse Radiation, and Direct Normal Irradiance.

5.3.2. Operation Service

The OS service is driven by the system's functioning based on embedded sensors and real-time data to simulate production and the current state of the physical asset. Such a service carries out a series of tasks such as the following: (1) ensuring the real-time simulation of dynamic environmental conditions by referring to environmental data detected from its deployment location, (2) employing AI methods to forecast the values of environmental parameters, and (3) feeding these predicted values to the ISS to estimate both the ideal state of the system and the corresponding actual production, using real-time data analytics. The OS service represents a central node for the CP system that interfaces with the SPVS's physical components and synthesizes data from various Energy DT services, external APIs, and embedded sensors. The OS service utilizes software modules for implementing system interaction and data visualization. By observing Figure 5, it is possible to note that the OS includes a software module called *Game Engine* (GE). The GE consists of an instance of Unreal Engine and is responsible for rendering the high-fidelity virtual model. It offers a real-time graphical representation of the physical asset's digital counterpart. This graphical representation is more than a mere visual representation, considering that it enables functional simulations, providing an interactive platform that mirrors the SPVS's physical state and behavior. The GE component plays a pivotal role for the proposed framework because it provides a graphical representation of the DT and the corresponding digital representation of the current state of the physical asset at the same time. It merges field data obtained from the SPVS and data received from other Energy DT's services to process and exhibit the corresponding results, using intuitive dashboards and illustrative charts. These dashboards and charts provide a detailed snapshot of real-time data, enriched by the valuable predictions generated by the Energy DT's services dedicated to the delegated predictive analytics to achieve this goal.

The OS service operates a convergence between data directly obtained from embedded sensors of the SPVS and data streams coming from other Energy DT's services. It orchestrates this information into detailed analytical visualizations and an accurate representation of the physical state. Among the assimilated data, the OS receives detailed anomaly effects such as shading and soiling on the PV panel. This specific information, coupled with weather-related data retrieved from the DSPM component, prompts the OS service to render an approximate cloud condition and its consequent impact on light physics. Moreover, it utilizes forecast data from the other services of the Energy DT to perform simulations predicting future conditions. This predictive information is effectively used to generate visual comparisons through specialized graphics and dashboards (see Figure 10). These visualizations enable a direct comparison of real-time operational data with predicted outcomes, providing a layered and comprehensive perspective on the system's functionality.

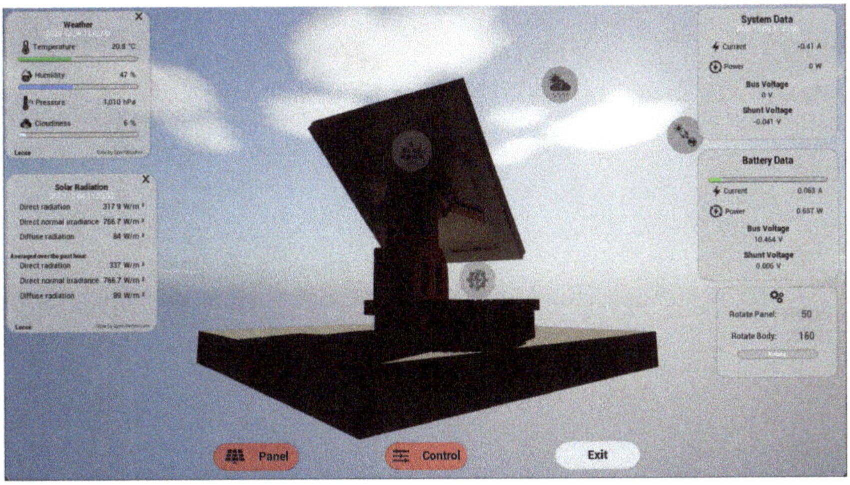

Figure 10. Interactive Platform Interface [82].

The OS service establishes a real-time bi-directional communication with the SPVS to facilitate the monitoring of the current state of the physical asset and the manual tuning of a set of parameters. In this way, both the state of the digital and physical assets are synchronized and it is possible to interact with the physical SPVS by executing direct commands through the dashboard made available by the user interface rendered in the Unreal virtual world.

Finally, the OS service facilitates bidirectional communication with the SPVS, enabling its direct control. In this way, it becomes possible to (1) accentuate the synergy within the CP infrastructure, (2) empower the dynamic interaction with the SPVS, and (3) ensure optimized performance through continuous monitoring and immediate control adjustments, based on the system's data-driven insights.

5.3.3. Ideal State Service

The ISS provides anomaly detection functionality within the SPVS. Anomalies are characterized by a number of factors such as soiling, shading, CP attacks, and component malfunctions, which require fast and accurate detection in order to optimize the performance of the system and guarantee the service continuity.

The ISS is meant to estimate the ideal production parameters for a given set of real-time factors, including temperature, solar irradiation, and energy demand. Such an estimate can be carried out either analytically, i.e., using a mathematical model of the SPVS equivalent circuit [87], illustrated in Figure 11, or using a ML model trained on real-world data.

The ISS compares the estimated values of current (I), voltage (V), and power (P) with the measured set of corresponding parameters provided by the OS. If a gap between the two sets of parameters crosses certain defined tolerance thresholds, an anomaly is detected. The event diagram illustrated in Figure 12 illustrates the process of estimation and comparison implemented by the present service.

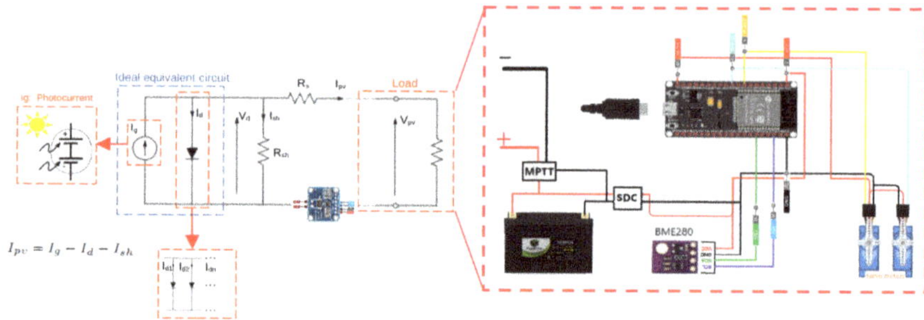

Figure 11. The equivalent circuit of the PV module with the load.

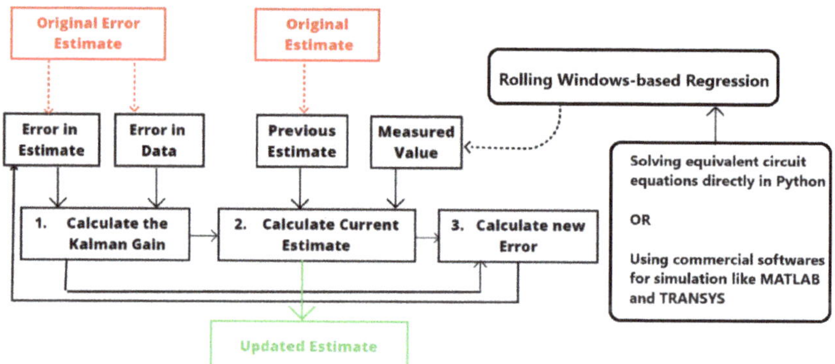

Figure 12. The block diagram of Kalman filter method that is used in current approach.

In particular, the estimation of production values involves numerical models based on the solution of the set of differential equations reported below (note: In Equation (5), I_{pv} is the output current of the PV cell, I_g is the actual photocurrent, I_d is the current of the diode, and I_{sh} is the current of the shunt resistor, K_i is a parameter provided in the datasheet or technical documentation of a specific photovoltaic device or solar cell, I_{gn} is photocurrent STC (Standard Test Condition), G is the actual irradiance, $G_n = 1000$ [W/m^2], the irradiance at STC, K_i is the temperature coefficient, and T is the actual temperature in Kelvin. T_0 is the temperature STC (typically 298 Kelvin), V_T is the thermal voltage, calculated as $(K * T)/q$, K is the Boltzmann constant = $1.3806503 \times 10^{-23}$, J/K, T is the actual temperature of the p-n junction in Kelvin, and q is the elementary charge = $1.60217646 \times 10^{-19}$, C).

$$\begin{aligned} I_{pv} &= I_g - I_d - I_{sh} \\ I_{\mathrm{d}} &= I_0\left(e^{\frac{V}{nV_T}} - 1\right) \\ I_{\mathrm{g}} &= I_{\mathrm{gn}}\left(\frac{G}{G_n}\right)(1 + K_i(T - T_0)) \\ I_{\mathrm{sh}} &= \frac{V_{\mathrm{oc}}}{R_{\mathrm{sh}}}\left(1 - \exp\left(\frac{qV}{nKT}\right)\right) \end{aligned} \tag{5}$$

By solving these equations, it is possible to assess the data for the system functioning in totally ideal conditions. However, real-world data are inherently dynamic and non-linear. Data collected from real-world systems inevitably contains noise, introducing uncertainty around the signal value. To enhance the robustness of the estimation process, a real-world-similar synthetic data generation approach is employed, based on the methodology introduced and described in [88,89]. This approach helps with ensuring that there is a more reliable estimation of production values, simulating the impact of noise in data acquisition systems into data. In particular, the process involves a Rolling Window Regression algorithm that is initially trained with noise-free synthetic data. Noise is then introduced to the estimated data using various distributions and, subsequently, a Kalman filter is applied to filter the noisy data, as illustrated in the flowchart in Figure 12. Finally, the optimal distribution is selected based on the best Mean Squared Error of the AI algorithm, recognizing that different distributions may better suit each parameter. As a result, a dataset that contains I, V, and P values for different temperatures and irradiation is built. Then, by using a Python script, the nearest temperature and irradiation in the dataset are identified and the corresponding ideal I, V, and P for the given conditions are extracted. Eventually, these values are compared with the actual values from OS to discern disturbances in the system and trigger anomaly detection warnings in the interactive platform's interface (Figure 10).

5.3.4. Demand Service

The DS is responsible for forecasting the energy consumption of appliances and attached AC devices and inferring the configuration of the SPVS to optimize a given cost function, improving the energy management task. This data-driven approach requires means to collect valuable field data to be used, in turn, as the input for properly tuned ML models. To enable this functionality, on the physical asset side, the basic setup of the SPVS described in Section 5.1 should be expanded with an inverter module connected to the output of the MPPT module. The inverter enables DC to AC current conversion, allowing to feed AC loads. An AC power sensor can be installed on the load to monitor and collect data regarding the energy demand footprint.

Data from DES and OS (discussed in Sections 5.3.1 and 5.3.2, respectively) are merged with field data from AC power sensors to feed ML models capable of forecasting the evolution of the power demand and enabling the analysis of what-if scenarios to support the decision-making process and optimize the power generation in different conditions.

5.3.5. Service Deployment

The framework services of the SPVS architecture (see Figure 13a) were organized and distributed by following the principles of the edge cloud continuum [82] and according to the European Scope of the Cloud-Edge computing [90]. In particular, the CP infrastructure was developed in the works of [82,91] as a testbed and features the physical asset, an on-premise edge node, and a desktop data center (as illustrated in the simplified logical schema in Figure 13b).

By following the original approach, data monitored by the SPVS are upstreamed to the on-premise edge node, which acts as a proxy between upstream data consumers and downstream physical entities. The role of such node is to perform the preliminary data preparation pipelines, enhancing the data quality and making data available in the right format. Upstream, the desktop data center models a far edge (near-premise) data center, as presented in [90]. Offering more computational resources, this data center can perform heavy and complex analyses and predictions on relatively limited batches of data streamed by on-premise edge nodes. Following this approach, it becomes possible to implement a local-level policy decision tool, whose purpose is to perform informed decisions based on analyses, other than implementing fine-grained strategic actions. The results obtained by these strategic actions can be then translated to commands for the managed downstream physical devices.

When required, heavier analyses can be delegated to the cloud infrastructures and eventually using the corresponding results to provide global insights and assess optimization policies on an aggregated level-scale.

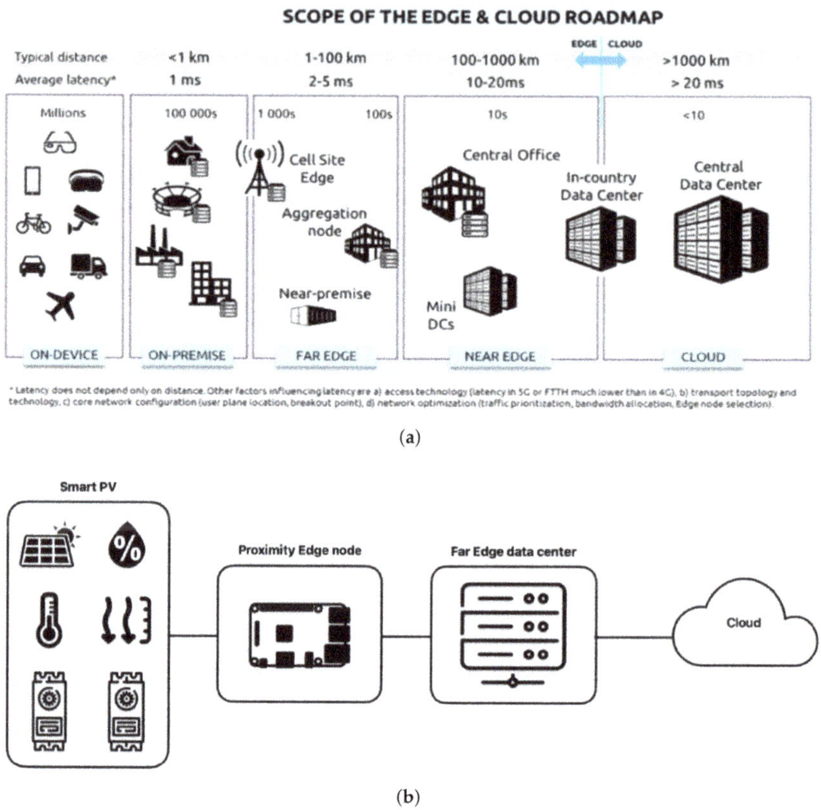

Figure 13. Mapping of the Edge-cloud architectural framework. (**a**) Scope of the European Industrial cloud and edge Roadmap [90]. (**b**) Edge-cloud architecture of the system [82].

Furthermore, the high flexibility and scalability of such a distributed design fosters the development and deployment of resilient cyber-physical systems, encouraging the implementation of efficient resilience boost techniques tailored to the requirements of the specific edge-to-cloud layer that they are applied to.

The R-KPIs encompass three key metrics, as reported in Table 3.

Table 3. Selected R-KPIs.

R-KPI	Definition	Significance
Recovery Time (T)	Represents the duration required for the system to recover from a disturbance occurrence.	Provides a quantitative measure, shedding light on the system's ability to rebound following an event.
Functionality Loss (FL)	Illustrates the extent of functionality loss in the system, irrespective of the system's behavior during degradation and recovery.	Offers insights into the overall impact on system functionality, encompassing both observable and latent effects.

Table 3. *Cont.*

R-KPI	Definition	Significance
Minimum Performance (Pmin)	Indicates the minimum level of performance achievable by systems.	The rationale for utilizing this index lies in the complexity of fitting the resilience curve to the dataset derived from IoT sensors embedded in the system. The intricate behavior of the system post-disturbance may lead to the loss of local and global minimums in performance degradation during the polynomial fitting of the curve (refer to Figure 2). The Minimum Performance Index is instrumental for decision-makers, enabling them to consider the critical threshold of minimum acceptable performance in crucial infrastructures.

The justification for employing the Minimum Performance Index underscores the challenges associated with fitting resilience curves to IoT sensor data and the intricate behavior of the system post-disturbance. This index serves as a vital reference point for decision-makers, allowing them to factor in the minimum performance crucial for the resilience of CI.

6. Case Study

In the present section, we analyze the outcomes of the implementation of the selected R-KPIs to evaluate the overall functionality of the system by examining data gathered from the embedded sensors of a smart PV panel. Various tests were conducted during brief periods throughout the day, encompassing diverse time frames and varying weather conditions. The current section synthesizes the data collected on December 18th. The remainder of this section is structured as follows: Section 6.1 presents the daylight and other pertinent environmental conditions on the test day; the test procedure is documented in Section 6.2 and the disturbance scenario is detailed in Section 6.3; Section 6.4 discusses the testbed functionality validation; finally, the resilience quantification is analyzed in Section 6.5.

6.1. Test Condition

The date of 18 December 2023 was selected for the tests because the weather remained generally clear with occasional cloud cover. We go into more detail in the following section:

Overall, the weather conditions were suitable, with no significant variations in temperature or visibility. The day featured mostly clear skies, transitioning to partly cloudy in the afternoon, and the wind speeds remained moderate throughout the observed period. These conditions were favorable for conducting tests and collecting data as part of the system implementation (the detailed environmental data are collected from https://weatherspark.com/).

- **Temperature:** Ranged from 11 °C to 14 °C.
- **Atmospheric Pressure:** Maintained at around 1030 to 1034 hPa.
- **Wind:** Predominantly from the NW direction, with speeds varying from 17 to 31 km/h.
- **Visibility:** $\geq$10 km throughout the day.
- **Cloud Cover:** Mostly clear and partly cloudy, with occasional cloud layers at 450 to 600 m.

- **Dew Point:** Varied between 9 °C and 11 °C.

Figure 14 shows the elevation of the center of the Sun above (positive) or below (negative) the horizon (black line). Yellow and gray fills indicate day and night, respectively. Light gray lines are the corresponding curves for the winter and summer solstices. Civil twilight and night are indicated by shaded overlays. Figure 15 provides more details related to Monday, 18 December 2023 in Lecce (Italy) (the portable smart PV power station testbed is situated within the Ecotekne complex, located in Lecce, Italy. The geographical coordinates are 40°19′59.2″ N latitude and 18°06′51.3″ E longitude). These details can be defined as follows: cloud coverage (color coded by percentage of sky covered), height of dominant cloud layer (black dots: report time; lines: inferred duration), and any other cloud layers (gray dots and lines). Finally, Figure 16 details the following: measured temperature at approximately 2 meters above the surface of an open field (black dots); 6-, 12-, and 24-hour lows (horizontal blue lines) and highs (red lines), placed above the hourly average temperature (faint purple line), with 25th to 75th and 10th to 90th percentile bands. The thin dotted line is the perceived temperature. Civil twilight and night are indicated by shaded overlays.

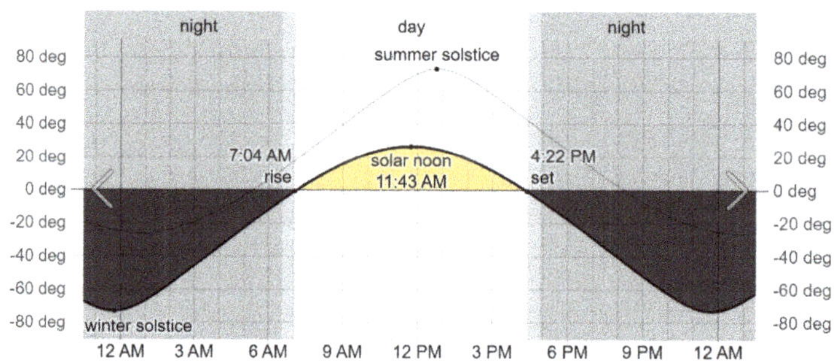

Figure 14. Solar Elevation on Monday, 18 December 2023 in Lecce.

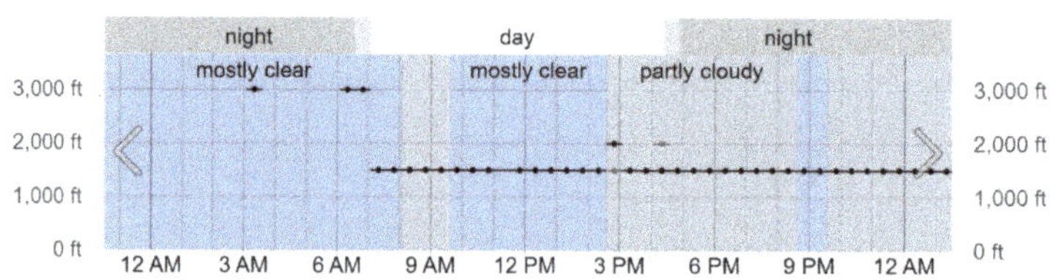

Figure 15. Cloud Cover on Monday, 18 December 2023 in Lecce.

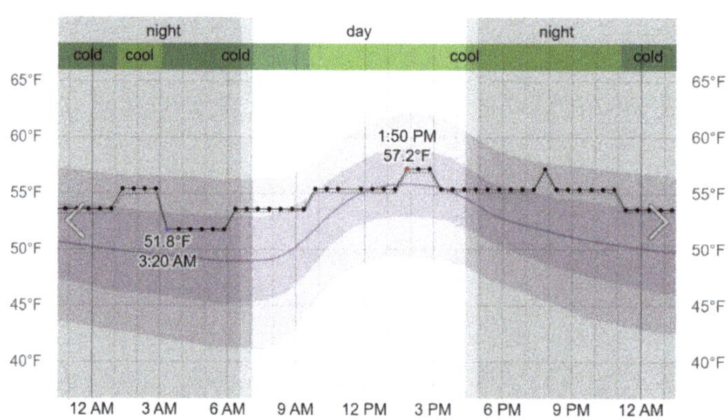

Figure 16. Temperature on Monday, 18 December 2023 in Lecce.

6.2. Test Procedure

The smart PV panel is positioned at the position that is in Section 6.1 for evaluating its general functionality. The testing procedure involves comprehensive data collection throughout the day, which is subsequently compared against solar energy availability and prevailing weather conditions. This comparative analysis aims to ascertain whether energy production aligns with daylight patterns and adapts to the dynamic environmental factors such as the cloudiness.

Given the system's design to trace the sun's trajectory, the hypothesis posits that the smart PV panel is supposed to achieve peak capacity throughout the day until sunset, coinciding with a general reduction in irradiation. Correspondingly, a decline in energy production is expected along with diminishing irradiation. Conversely, during periods of cloudiness or partial cloud cover, an observable oscillation in energy production is anticipated.

The verification of these hypotheses in the experiment involves a visual examination of the dynamic environmental conditions alongside energy production. Future studies to assess production accuracy could involve constructing data-driven or physical models of the system, utilizing tools such as MATLAB Simscape or PVlib Python toolbox. The comparison of actual production against the model-based simulation of production will provide a method for evaluating system performance.

Furthermore, these future studies will offer the potential to gain insights into the noise present in data originating from embedded sensors. Therefore, such further exploration can unveil the real-world behavior of the system under dynamic environmental conditions, shedding light on the impact of various sources of noise. In the next subsection, the results of the tests and the collected data are reported and discussed.

The test began at 7:46 in the morning and ended at 17:08, involving continuous data collection. Figure 17 illustrates the bus voltage values of the panel in volts. The data were recorded at a frequency of every 30 seconds. In Figure 18, the original dataset is depicted alongside a line plot that incorporates a rolling average (with a window size of 10). This rolling average ensures a smoother curve, facilitating a more nuanced analysis of the data.

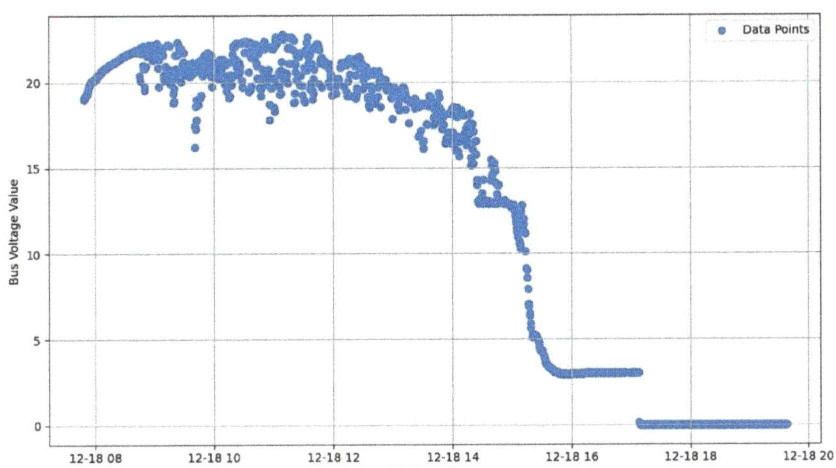

Figure 17. The voltage of the panel on Monday, 18 December 2023 in Lecce influenced by a dynamic environment including sunrise and sunset Figure 14, cloud cover Figure 15, and temperature Figure 16.

The sunrise, occurring at 7:04 (Figure 14), leads to an initial surge in voltage as the test begins, eventually stabilizing at 22 volts, albeit with noticeable noise. This gradual increase can be attributed to the soft, ambient light during the early stages of sunrise, characterized by the sun on the horizon and the lingering twilight effect resulting from the sun's rays reflecting in the atmosphere. This stable condition persists until noon.

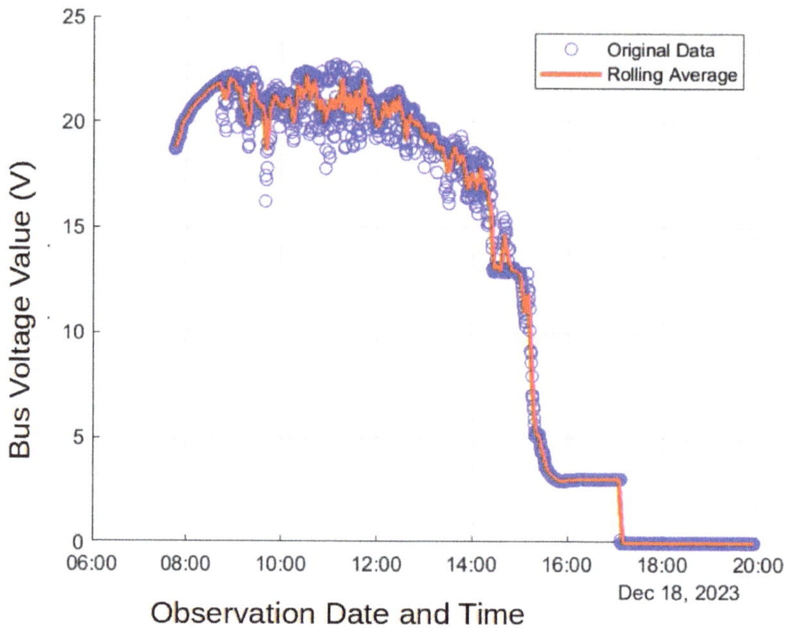

Figure 18. Panel voltage (on Monday, 18 December 2023): comparison between original data and rolling average.

Around 12:00 p.m., cloud cover emerges, introducing a decline in production. By 2:40 p.m., the sky becomes partly cloudy, further impacting the voltage, causing a decrease. As the test progresses towards sunset at 4:22 p.m., and twilight ensues, there is a dramatic effect on production, ultimately stabilizing at 3 volts.

The nocturnal production, observed post-sunset, is attributed to light contamination from the building's surroundings. Yet, such a contamination does not yield any significant contribution to the power output and the system, no longer being able to sustain itself, and keeps operating until the residual battery power is no longer sufficient. At that point, observable at about 17:00, the power suddenly drops as an effect of the lack of power to feed the system. This synthesis affirms the system's functionality under real-world dynamic environmental conditions.

In a nutshell, the comprehensive analysis of the smart PV panel's functionality under real-world dynamic environmental conditions provides a robust understanding of its behavior throughout the day. The system's ability to adapt to varying light intensities, to respond to cloud cover, and to exhibit stability in the presence of noise and light contamination poses it as a reliable and resilient solution for solar energy production in diverse settings. The findings also pave the way for future studies, such as building data-driven or physical models, in order to further enhance our understanding and optimize the system's performance.

In next section, we will identify the disturbance scenario and quantify the resilience of the system using the method detailed in Section 3.1. The Resilience KPIs are scenario-based indices. For each risk, the R-KPI must be calculated separately. This is essential because the behavior of complex systems following disturbances of varying natures will differ across different scenarios. In this section, the R-KPIs of the system are calculated in the presence of the scenario that is detailed in Section 6.3.

The disturbance was applied at 9:00 a.m. on 18 December 2023. The environmental conditions of the test day are described in Section 6.1. Subsequent subsections provide an explanation of the disturbance scenario and the calculation of R-KPIs for resilience quantification.

6.3. Disturbance Scenario

For the testing phase, we have chosen the False Data Injection risk [92], a scenario characterized by its cybersecurity nature. This selection is motivated by the pervasive adoption of distributed computing in decentralized energy systems, where IoT device networks and smart grids play a crucial role in automating industrial control, modern power systems, and other CIs. This risk is pivotal, as attacks on power systems operating within smart grids lead to the loss of control over management devices, causing operational issues, power outage, and significant power disruptions [93]. These systems heavily rely on sensors and actuators to generate and transmit sensory data through various nodes. While providing substantial benefits for different industries, these systems are vulnerable to cyber-attacks.

False Data Injection Attacks (FDIA) represent a specific category of malicious data attacks targeting CIs managed by Cyber-Physical Information Systems [94], including Digital Twins. FDIA strategies involve attackers compromising sensor readings, introducing undetected corrupt data into calculations of values and variables crucial for defining the system's state. In this particular scenario, the focus is on injecting false angle data into the system.

To simulate the attack, we manually alter the angle of the panel (the direction in which the panel rotates around the horizontal axis) and force the panel to return to its rest angle—the position it assumes when the system is turned off. Following this command, the panel undergoes a change in orientation that deviates from the optimal angle. Consequently, the ideal state service of the Digital Twin, as elucidated in Section 6, should recognize this erroneous position and issue a command to the system to optimize its orientation.

In the subsequent section, we will present and discuss the test results, accompanied by the calculation of R-KPIs.

6.4. Testbed Functionality Validation

The system has been validated in various scenarios, reflecting the impact of variable real-world conditions on the performance of power generation along with validation of mDTs integration with each other and with sensor readings and action commands along with the Communication and Persistence Layer. In the validation scenario discussed in this work, the DT has been set up to update the panel orientation in near real-time to make it face the sun directly (rotating with two DoF in Figure 8). Command messages travel from the Digital Twin to its physical counterpart every minute, and the MPPT is tuned to keep the battery LoC between 10.25 and 10.5 volts. The observations were gathered at a frequency of one batch of sensor data every 30 s over a time span of 30 min. These collections occurred at various times of different days, encompassing an external perimeter, and were conducted under sunny weather conditions, sunny weather conditions with occasional periods of partial cloudiness, and cloudy conditions. As a result, the panel orientation was updated to match the (solar azimuth, solar elevation) couples of angles. For instance, in the sunny sky scenario, the panel spans from (175°, 27°), respectively, to (183°,

27°). The plot illustrated in Figure 19 is a sample of the evolution of PV output voltage and battery level of charge (LoC). The irregular pattern of the PV curve reflects the disturbance introduced by obstacles that cause shading phenomena on the PV panel's surface, which are mainly characterized by the passage of clouds and some external obstacles (a tree). As a result, the curve features a series of steep descents and ascents, but the range of the PV output voltage is still kept relatively small (less than 1 volt) by the MPPT. On the other hand, the curve representing the battery LoC exhibits a saw-tooth profile. In particular, slow descents caused by the execution of edge tasks are interleaved by steep ascents, which will represent the intervention of the MPPT in feeding the battery enough to keep its LoC between the above-mentioned thresholds. A second scenario was simulated to observe the evolution of PV voltage output when the panel's pose is fixed. This test is conducted to have a focused evaluation of the functionality of integrated mDTs with DBMS and IoT elements and to validate the efficacy of the proposed architecture. Figure 20 plots this curve during sunset. The temperature curve is arguably related to the solar exposition intensity, as it smoothly goes down as the position of the sun concerning the solar panel changes. On the other hand, the PV voltage output curve resembles a discrete descending staircase function. This profile is given by the action of the MPPT component, whose function is to regularize the output voltage by tracking the maximum power intensity provided by the PV panel. The results demonstrate that the system of systems yields the anticipated outcomes, and the overall complex system functions efficiently. However, the system is subject to certain limitations, which will be elaborated upon in the next section along with the proposed future steps.

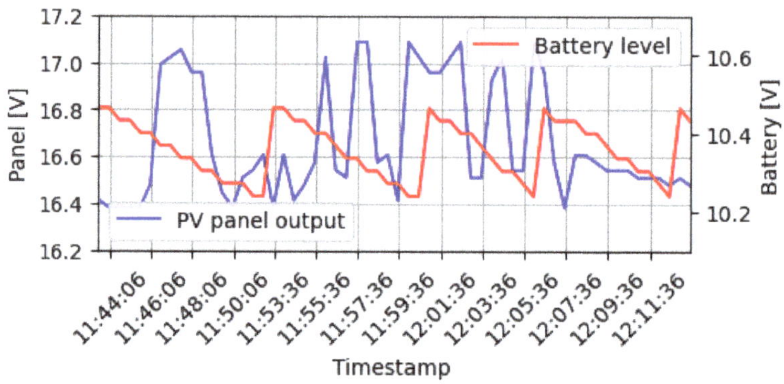

Figure 19. PV panel output and battery level.

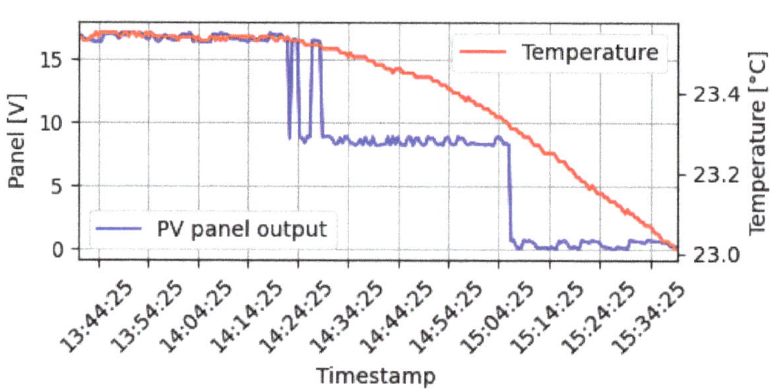

Figure 20. Sunset: PV output and air temperature.

6.5. Resilience Quantification and Synthesis Results

The false position was applied at 9:00 a.m., and as shown in Figure 21, the collected data after the disturbance reveals a decline in voltage starting from 9:00 p.m. Figure 21 provides a clearer depiction of the system's behavior post-disturbance, unveiling its irregular response (Figure 3).

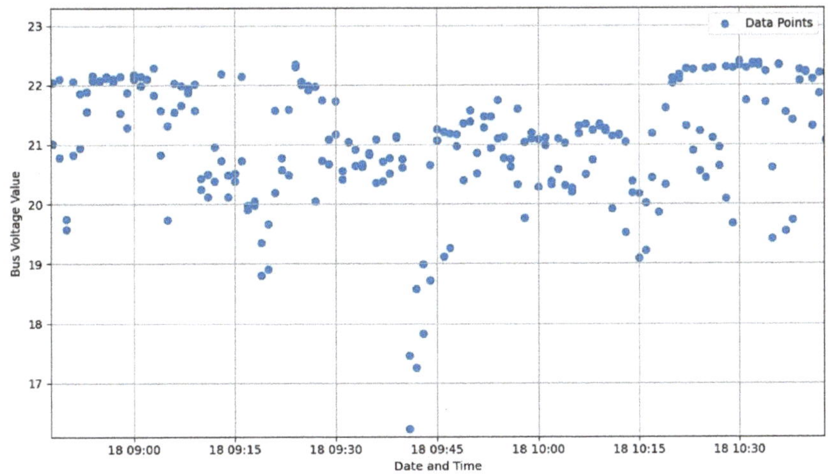

Figure 21. Bus voltage measurement during the disturbance (voltate in volts).

In the initial phase, we can determine the recovery time using Figure 22 as around 10:20 p.m.; the system's behavior stabilizes again, hovering around a panel voltage value of 22 volts. The observed recovery time of 80 min appears to be lengthy. However, it is essential to note that the test was conducted on a testbed constructed with basic elements, with the primary goal being to assess the functionality of the Digital Twin (DT) and establish a sample process for quantifying resilience. Conducting the test in a facility equipped with industrial hardware would likely result in a shorter recovery time.

Figure 22. The irregular behaviour of the system after disturbance.

The minimum production level the system reached after the disturbance was 16.1 volts. Although the decrease was dramatic, the system quickly initiated the recovery period and did not linger at the minimum level, showcasing a positive characteristic for a critical infrastructure system.

In this stage, two types of polynomial fitting to the dataset are employed: Support Vector Regression (SVR) and Least Squares. The utilization of these two methods aims to highlight the difference between the straightforward second-degree polynomial least squares calculation and the more intricate SVR, with the objective of overfitting the resilience curve to demonstrate its behavior and calculate the Functionality Loss (Figure 23).

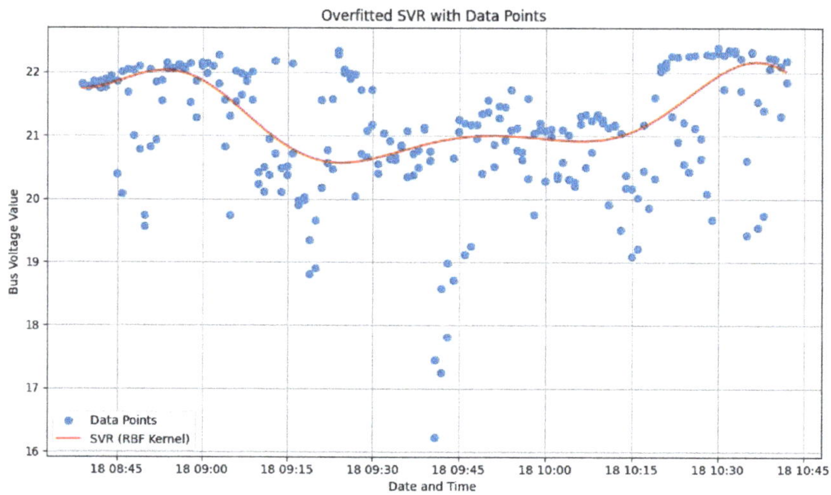

Figure 23. The resilience curve (fitted by SVR).

Even though SVR attempts to fit the curve to the dataset more precisely than least squares, measurements lower than 20.5 volts still do not have an impact on the fitted curve (Figure 23). This is attributed to the closeness of the points and congestion of the measurements above 20.5 volts. However, a more complex solution could involve using the moving average to decrease the density and incorporate the effects of global and local minimums into the fitted curve. Nevertheless, since the system starts to recover very quickly—the global minimum occurs in less than 10 min with values under 19 volts—this additional modification is deemed unnecessary.

Considering that the stable value before the disturbance was 22 volts and the system stabilized again at 22 volts after 10:30 a.m., a horizontal line is considered on the Bus Voltage Value axis (shown in green), and the area between the fitted curve and the horizontal area is calculated (in the figures the area that shows the Functionality Loss is highlighted in yellow). Figures 24 and 25 depict the results.

The results of calculating the Functionality Loss for the Least Squares-fitted resilience curve is 6957.07, and for SVR is 5385.83. The Least Squares-fitted resilience curve shows higher Functionality Loss; however, it does not represent the behavior of system. On the other hand, the SVR curve shows less Functionality Loss. Considering the absence of the global minimum voltage in the SVR curve, the the Least Squares-fitted resilience curve sounds closer to reality. However the graphical representation of the behavior is crucial, and in this case, we select the SVR-fitted resilience curve.

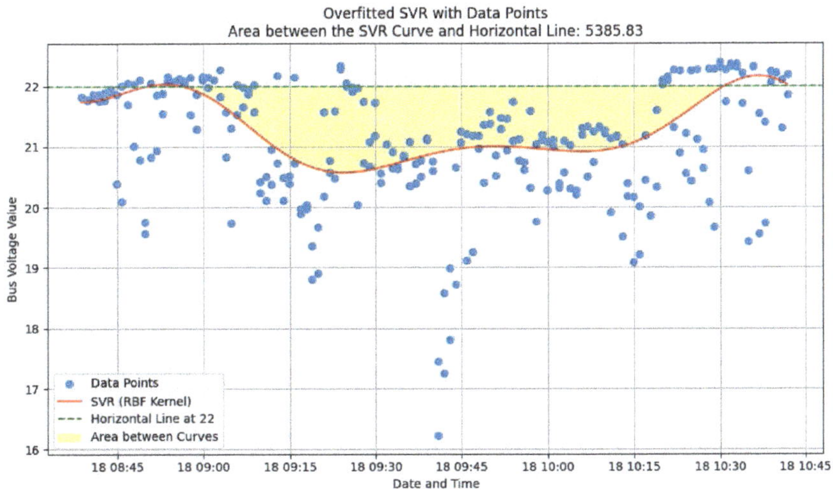

Figure 24. Functionality Loss calculation using the resilience curve fitted by SVR.

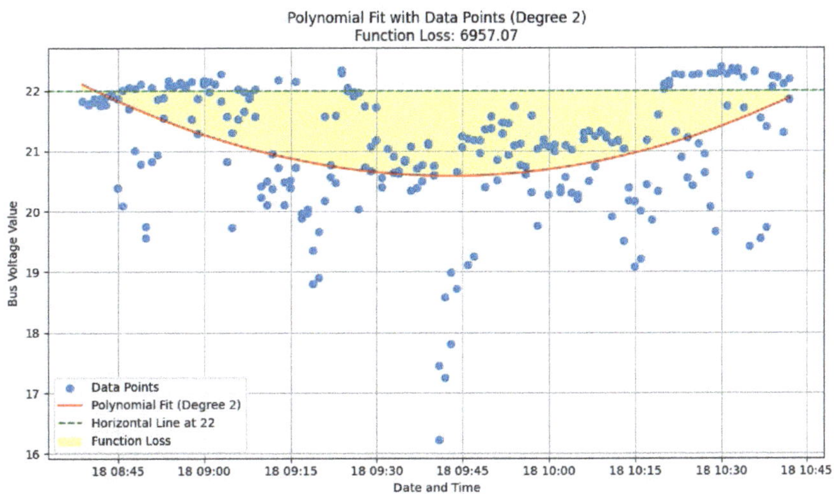

Figure 25. Functionality Loss calculation using the resilience curve fitted by Least Squares.

7. Limitations, Challenges, and Future Study

The current article represents a scoping review of knowledge synthesis. It employs a systematic and iterative approach to identify and report on the existing or emerging body of literature related to the quantification of R-KPIs for modeling critical infrastructure resilience. However, for a more comprehensive analysis, a deeper exploration of real-life cases, extensive discussion, and validation of the reported R-KPIs in the literature require scenario-based validations. This, therefore, stands as a potential avenue for future research.

Similarly, the prioritization of R-KPIs also necessitates a scenario-based approach and an in-depth examination through real-life case studies, criteria extraction, and R-KPI prioritization. Unfortunately, there is currently no literature available that identifies the criteria for critical infrastructure resilience in a general context. This study has the potential to pave the way for future research to fill this gap and further enrich the knowledge base for the quantitative modeling of critical infrastructure resilience.

Finally, future studies should investigate the challenges associated with highly noisy real-time data from embedded sensors, as this is a common occurrence in real-world scenarios involving diverse machine types. In the current study, the sensors provide data with relatively low natural noise. However, the issue of highly noisy data is a potential topic for future research.

8. Conclusions

In conclusion, this study has successfully addressed the critical question of real-time resilience monitoring for IoT-integrated CIs. By developing and validating a robust framework, this research contributes significantly to the resilience engineering domain. The integration of R-KPIs, including Functionality Loss, Minimum Performance, and Recovery Time, has enabled a targeted approach to resilience quantification. Using a Digital Twin-integrated smart PV panel, we demonstrated the effectiveness of IoT-based, real-time monitoring for assessing the resilience of cyber-physical systems under simulated disturbances.

The findings underscore the importance of continuous, real-time data acquisition in supporting actionable insights for resilience enhancement, providing a systematic approach to resilience quantification for CIs. This framework and testbed model are not only practical but also reusable, offering researchers and industry professionals a solid foundation for further resilience studies in IoT-integrated infrastructures. These contributions advance resilience monitoring, support secure service continuity, and address the growing need for robust resilience in essential services, paving the way for more resilient, IoT-enabled infrastructures that can better withstand and recover from future disturbances.

Author Contributions: A.A.A. contributed in the research project from inception to final manuscript preparation, including conceptualization, experimental design, data analysis, and drafting along with coordination of the team. A.L. provided essential supervision and guidance throughout the study, shaping its direction. C.M. constructed and managed the experimental testbed, ensuring functionality, reliability, and overseeing data collection. C.R. conducted the state-of-the-art review and contributed to manuscript drafting. A.F. supported the project through supervision and administrative oversight. F.I. contributed to the development of immersive environments and user interfaces in Unreal Engine. All authors have read and agreed to the published version of the manuscript.

Funding: This research received no external funding.

Institutional Review Board Statement: Not applicable.

Informed Consent Statement: Not applicable.

Data Availability Statement: The data presented in this study are available on request from the corresponding author. The raw data supporting the conclusions of this article will be made available on request.

Conflicts of Interest: Author Ali Aghazadeh Ardebili was employed by the company HSPI SpA. The remaining authors declare that the research was conducted in the absence of any commercial or financial relationships that could be construed as a potential conflict of interest.

References

1. Radanliev, P.; De Roure, D.; Van Kleek, M.; Santos, O.; Ani, U. Artificial intelligence in cyber physical systems. *AI Soc.* **2020**, *36*, 783–796. [CrossRef] [PubMed]
2. Batista e Silva, F.; Forzieri, G.; Marin Herrera, M.A.; Bianchi, A.; Lavalle, C.; Feyen, L. HARCI-EU, a harmonized gridded dataset of critical infrastructures in Europe for large-scale risk assessments. *Sci. Data* **2019**, *6*, 126. [CrossRef] [PubMed]
3. Cantelmi, R.; Di Gravio, G.; Patriarca, R. Reviewing qualitative research approaches in the context of critical infrastructure resilience. *Environ. Syst. Decis.* **2021**, *41*, 341–376. [CrossRef] [PubMed]

4. Akakura, Y.; Sasaki, T.; Ono, K.; Watanabe, T. An Assessment of the Impacts on the International Container Transport and the World Economy Resulting from the 2014/15 U.S. West Coast Port Disruption. *J. Integr. Disaster Risk Manag.* **2018**, *8*, 1–21. [CrossRef]
5. Gallarno, G.; Muniz, J.; Parnell, G.S.; Pohl, E.A.; Wu, J. Development and assessment of a resilient telecoms system. *J. Def. Model. Simul. Appl. Methodol. Technol.* **2023**, *21*, 405–420. [CrossRef]
6. Koks, E.; Pant, R.; Thacker, S.; Hall, J.W. Understanding Business Disruption and Economic Losses Due to Electricity Failures and Flooding. *Int. J. Disaster Risk Sci.* **2019**, *10*, 421–438. [CrossRef]
7. Avordeh, T.K.; Salifu, A.; Quaidoo, C.; Opare-Boateng, R. Impact of power outages: Unveiling their influence on micro, small, and medium-sized enterprises and poverty in Sub-Saharan Africa - An in-depth literature review. *Heliyon* **2024**, *10*, e33782. [CrossRef]
8. Zhu, Q.; Başar, T. Disentangling Resilience From Robustness: Contextual Dualism, Interactionism, and Game-Theoretic Paradigms. *IEEE Control. Syst. Mag.* **2024**, *44*, 95–103. [CrossRef]
9. Xu, L.; Guo, Q.; Sheng, Y.; Muyeen, S.; Sun, H. On the resilience of modern power systems: A comprehensive review from the cyber-physical perspective. *Renew. Sustain. Energy Rev.* **2021**, *152*, 111642. [CrossRef]
10. Kwasinski, A. Modeling of Cyber-Physical Intra-Dependencies in Electric Power Grids and Their Effect on Resilience. In Proceedings of the 2020 8th Workshop on Modeling and Simulation of Cyber-Physical Energy Systems, Sydney, Australia, 21 April 2020; pp. 1–6. [CrossRef]
11. Urlainis, A.; Ornai, D.; Levy, R.; Vilnay, O.; Shohet, I.M. Loss and damage assessment in critical infrastructures due to extreme events. *Saf. Sci.* **2022**, *147*, 105587. [CrossRef]
12. Loveček, T.; Straková, L.; Kampová, K. Modeling and Simulation as Tools to Increase the Protection of Critical Infrastructure and the Sustainability of the Provision of Essential Needs of Citizens. *Sustainability* **2021**, *13*, 5898. [CrossRef]
13. Carrington, N.K.; Ma, S.; Dobson, I.; Wang, Z. Extracting Resilience Statistics from Utility Data in Distribution Grids. In Proceedings of the 2020 IEEE Power & Energy Society General Meeting (PESGM), Montreal, QC, Canada, 2–6 August 2020; pp. 1–5. [CrossRef]
14. Fuggini, C.; Bolletta, F. Identification of indicators, metrics and level of service for the resilience of transport critical infrastructure. *Int. J. Sustain. Mater. Struct. Syst.* **2020**, *4*, 330. [CrossRef]
15. Achillopoulou, D.V.; Mitoulis, S.A.; Argyroudis, S.A.; Wang, Y. Monitoring of transport infrastructure exposed to multiple hazards: A roadmap for building resilience. *Sci. Total Environ.* **2020**, *746*, 141001. [CrossRef] [PubMed]
16. Aghazadeh Ardebili, A.; Ficarella, A.; Longo, A.; Mazzeo, O. Critical Infrastructure Resilience. 2023. Available online: https://iris.unisalento.it/handle/11587/503626 (accessed on 3 December 2024).
17. Aghazadeh Ardebili, A.; Padoano, E. A literature review of the concepts of resilience and sustainability in group decision-making. *Sustainability* **2020**, *12*, 2602. [CrossRef]
18. Chaterji, S.; Naghizadeh, P.; Alam, M.A.; Bagchi, S.; Chiang, M.; Corman, D.; Henz, B.; Jana, S.; Li, N.; Mou, S.; et al. Resilient cyberphysical systems and their application drivers: A technology roadmap. *arXiv* **2019**, arXiv:2001.00090.
19. Ardebili, A.A.; Longo, A.; Ficarella, A. Implementing Digital Twins in Energy Systems: Meta Analysis of the State of Art and Evolution. 2021. Available online: https://www.semanticscholar.org/paper/Implementing-Digital-Twins-in-Energy-Systems%3A-Meta-Ardebili-Longo/16e088485affb69bd5c5b4f88bb7b68c08bd8a4a (accessed on 3 December 2024).
20. Ardebili, A.A.; Longo, A.; Ficarella, A. Digital Twins bonds society with cyber-physical Energy Systems: A literature review. In Proceedings of the 2021 IEEE International Conferences on Internet of Things (iThings) and IEEE Green Computing & Communications (GreenCom) and IEEE Cyber, Physical & Social Computing (CPSCom) and IEEE Smart Data (SmartData) and IEEE Congress on Cybermatics (Cybermatics), Melbourne, Australia, 6–8 December 2021; pp. 284–289.
21. Habibi Rad, M.; Mojtahedi, M.; Ostwald, M.J. Industry 4.0, disaster risk management and infrastructure resilience: A systematic review and bibliometric analysis. *Buildings* **2021**, *11*, 411. [CrossRef]
22. Ye, X.; Du, J.; Han, Y.; Newman, G.; Retchless, D.; Zou, L.; Ham, Y.; Cai, Z. Developing human-centered urban digital twins for community infrastructure resilience: A research agenda. *J. Plan. Lit.* **2023**, *38*, 187–199. [CrossRef]
23. Argyroudis, S.A.; Mitoulis, S.A.; Chatzi, E.; Baker, J.W.; Brilakis, I.; Gkoumas, K.; Vousdoukas, M.; Hynes, W.; Carluccio, S.; Keou, O.; et al. Digital technologies can enhance climate resilience of critical infrastructure. *Clim. Risk Manag.* **2022**, *35*, 100387. [CrossRef]
24. Geels, F.W. Transformative innovation and socio-technical transitions to address grand challenges. *Eur. Comm. R&I Pap. Ser. Work. Pap.* **2020**, *2*, 1–39.
25. Rohracher, H. 45Analyzing the Socio-Technical Transformation of Energy Systems: The Concept of Sustainability Transitions. In *Oxford Handbook of Energy and Society*; Oxford University Press: Oxford, UK, 2018.
26. Guelpa, E.; Bischi, A.; Verda, V.; Chertkov, M.; Lund, H. Towards future infrastructures for sustainable multi-energy systems: A review. *Energy* **2019**, *184*, 2–21. [CrossRef]

27. Aghazadeh Ardebili, A.; Zappatore, M.; Ramadan, A.I.H.A.; Longo, A.; Ficarella, A. Digital Twins of smart energy systems: A systematic literature review on enablers, design, management and computational challenges. *Energy Inform.* **2024**, *7*, 94. [CrossRef]
28. Ardebili, A.A.; Longo, A.; Ficarella, A. Navigating the Future Data-Driven Automation Tools: State-of-the-Art and Research Roadmap for Digital Twins of Energy Systems. In Proceedings of the 2023 IEEE International Conference on Big Data (BigData), Sorrento, Italy, 15–18 December 2023; pp. 3888–3897.
29. Aghazadeh Ardebili, A.; Hasidi, O.; Bendaouia, A.; Khalil, A.; Khalil, S.; Luceri, D.; Longo, A.; Abdelwahed, E.H.; Qassimi, S.; Ficarella, A. Enhancing resilience in complex energy systems through real-time anomaly detection: A systematic literature review. *Energy Inform.* **2024**, *7*, 96. [CrossRef]
30. Zhou, K.; Yang, S. Understanding household energy consumption behavior: The contribution of energy big data analytics. *Renew. Sustain. Energy Rev.* **2016**, *56*, 810–819. [CrossRef]
31. Zhou, K.; Fu, C.; Yang, S. Big data driven smart energy management: From big data to big insights. *Renew. Sustain. Energy Rev.* **2016**, *56*, 215–225. [CrossRef]
32. Ma, Z.; Xie, J.; Li, H.; Sun, Q.; Si, Z.; Zhang, J.; Guo, J. The role of data analysis in the development of intelligent energy networks. *IEEE Netw.* **2017**, *31*, 88–95. [CrossRef]
33. Johansson, B. Security aspects of future renewable energy systems–A short overview. *Energy* **2013**, *61*, 598–605. [CrossRef]
34. Sadorsky, P. Some future scenarios for renewable energy. *Futures* **2011**, *43*, 1091–1104. [CrossRef]
35. Bessa, R.; Moreira, C.; Silva, B.; Matos, M. Handling renewable energy variability and uncertainty in power system operation. In *Advances in Energy Systems: The Large-Scale Renewable Energy Integration Challenge*; John Wiley & Sons: Hoboken, NJ, USA, 2019; pp. 1–26.
36. Jafarizadeh, H.; Yamini, E.; Zolfaghari, S.M.; Esmaeilion, F.; Assad, M.E.H.; Soltani, M. Navigating challenges in large-scale renewable energy storage: Barriers, solutions, and innovations. *Energy Rep.* **2024**, *12*, 2179–2192. [CrossRef]
37. Bremen, L.V. Large-scale variability of weather dependent renewable energy sources. In *Management of Weather and Climate Risk in the Energy Industry*; Springer: Berlin/Heidelberg, Germany, 2010; pp. 189–206.
38. Zhao, A.P.; Li, S.; Gu, C.; Yan, X.; Hu, P.J.H.; Wang, Z.; Xie, D.; Cao, Z.; Chen, X.; Wu, C.; et al. Cyber vulnerabilities of energy systems. *IEEE J. Emerg. Sel. Top. Ind. Electron.* **2024**, *5*, 1455–1469. [CrossRef]
39. Demertzis, K.; Iliadis, L. A computational intelligence system identifying cyber-attacks on smart energy grids. In *Modern Discrete Mathematics and Analysis: With Applications in Cryptography, Information Systems and Modeling*; Springer: Berlin/Heidelberg, Germany, 2018; pp. 97–116.
40. Sridhar, S.; Hahn, A.; Govindarasu, M. Cyber-Physical Systems Security for the Electric Power Grid. *Proc. IEEE* **2012**, *100*, 250–266. [CrossRef]
41. Yang, Y.; Du, H.; Xiong, Z.; Xu, R.; Niyato, D.; Han, Z. Exploring Impacts of Age of Information on Data Accuracy for Wireless Sensing Systems: An Information Entropy Perspective. *IEEE Trans. Mob. Comput.* **2025**, 1–18. [CrossRef]
42. Kahraman, I.; Köse, A.; Koca, M.; Anarim, E. Age of information in internet of things: A survey. *IEEE Internet Things J.* **2023**, *11*, 9896–9914. [CrossRef]
43. Zhang, T.; Zhou, J.; Chen, Z.; Tian, Z.; Wen, W.; Jia, Y. Information freshness optimization of multiple status update streams in Internet of things: Generation rate control and service rate reservation. *Digit. Commun. Netw.* **2023**, *9*, 971–980. [CrossRef]
44. Liu, X.; Liu, H.; Zheng, K.; Liu, J.; Taleb, T.; Shiratori, N. AoI-Minimal Clustering, Transmission and Trajectory Co-Design for UAV-Assisted WPCNs. *IEEE Trans. Veh. Technol.* **2025**, *74*, 1035–1051. [CrossRef]
45. Aghazadeh Ardebili, A.; Martella, C.; Martella, A.; Lazari, A.; Longo, A.; Ficarella, A. Smart critical infrastructures security management and governance: Implementation of cyber resilience kpis for decentralized energy asset. In Proceedings of the CEUR Workshop Proceedings-Italian Conference on Cyber Security 2024: Proceedings of the 8th Italian Conference on Cyber Security (ITASEC 2024), Salerno, Italy, 8–12 April 2024; Volume 3731.
46. Poulin, C.; Kane, M.B. Infrastructure resilience curves: Performance measures and summary metrics. *Reliab. Eng. Syst. Saf.* **2021**, *216*, 107926. [CrossRef]
47. Aghazadeh Ardebili, A.; Boscolo, M.; Ficarella, A.; Longo, A.; Padoano, E. Resilience Modeling of Cyber-Physical Systems: A Comparative Study of Statistical vs. AI Methods. In Proceedings of the XXIX AIDI Summer School "Francesco Turco" Industrial Systems Engineering, Lecce, Italy, 11–13 September 2024.
48. Fanucchi, R.; Bessani, M.; Camillo, M.H.; Soares, A.D.S.; London, J.B., Jr.; Desuó, L.; Maciel, C.D. Stochastic indexes for power distribution systems resilience analyzes. *IET Gener. Transmn. Distrib.* **2019**, *13*, 2507–2516. [CrossRef]
49. Ji, A.; He, R.; Chen, W.; Zhang, L. Computational methodologies for critical infrastructure resilience modeling: A review. *Adv. Eng. Inform.* **2024**, *62*, 102663. [CrossRef]
50. Ioannidis, C.; Pym, D.; Williams, J.; Gheyas, I. Resilience in information stewardship. *Eur. J. Oper. Res.* **2019**, *274*, 638–653. [CrossRef]

51. Rezvani, S.M.; Silva, M.J.F.; de Almeida, N.M. Urban Resilience Index for Critical Infrastructure: A Scenario-Based Approach to Disaster Risk Reduction in Road Networks. *Sustainability* **2024**, *16*, 4143. [CrossRef]
52. Kavousi-Fard, A.; Wang, M.; Su, W. Stochastic resilient post-hurricane power system recovery based on mobile emergency resources and reconfigurable networked microgrids. *IEEE Access* **2018**, *6*, 72311–72326. [CrossRef]
53. Bao, S.; Zhang, C.; Ouyang, M.; Miao, L. An integrated tri-level model for enhancing the resilience of facilities against intentional attacks. *Ann. Oper. Res.* **2019**, *283*, 87–117. [CrossRef]
54. Wang, C. Role of recovery profile dependency in time-dependent resilience. *Eng. Rep.* **2024**, *6*, e12716. [CrossRef]
55. Miles, S.; Ly, M.; Terry, N.; Choe, Y. Restimate: Recovery Estimation Tool for Resilience Planning. *J. Saf. Sci. Resil.* **2024**, *5*, 47–63. [CrossRef]
56. Zhang, J.; Li, G.; Zhang, M. Multi-objective optimization for community building group recovery scheduling and resilience evaluation under earthquake. *Comput.-Aided Civ. Infrastruct. Eng.* **2023**, *38*, 1657–1676. [CrossRef]
57. Liang, H.; Xie, Q. Resilience-based sequential recovery planning for substations subjected to earthquakes. *IEEE Trans. Power Deliv.* **2022**, *38*, 353–362. [CrossRef]
58. Lee, S.; Shin, S.; Judi, D.; McPherson, T.; Burian, S. Criticality analyzes of a water distribution system considering both economic consequences and hydraulic loss using modern portfolio theory. *Water* **2019**, *11*, 1222. [CrossRef]
59. Liu, X.; Ferrario, E.; Zio, E. Identifying resilient-important elements in interdependent critical infrastructures by sensitivity analyzes. *Reliab. Eng. Syst. Saf.* **2019**, *189*, 423–434. [CrossRef]
60. Li, R.; Gao, Y. On the component resilience importance measures for infrastructure systems. *Int. J. Crit. Infrastruct. Prot.* **2022**, *36*, 100481. [CrossRef]
61. Lin, S.; El-Tawil, S. Time-dependent resilience assessment of seismic damage and restoration of interdependent lifeline systems. *J. Infrastruct. Syst.* **2020**, *26*, 04019040. [CrossRef]
62. Nozhati, S.; Ellingwood, B.; Chong, E. Stochastic optimal control methodologies in risk-informed community resilience planning. *Struct. Saf.* **2020**, *84*, 101920. [CrossRef]
63. Trucco, P.; Petrenj, B. Characterisation of resilience metrics in full-scale applications to interdependent infrastructure systems. *Reliab. Eng. Syst. Saf.* **2023**, *235*, 109200. [CrossRef]
64. Ouyang, M.; Liu, C.; Xu, M. Value of resilience-based solutions on critical infrastructure protection: Comparing with robustness-based solutions. *Reliab. Eng. Syst. Saf.* **2019**, *190*, 106506. [CrossRef]
65. Panteli, M.; Trakas, D.; Mancarella, P.; Hatziargyriou, N. Power systems resilience assessment: Hardening and smart operational enhancement strategies. *Proc IEEE* **2017**, *105*, 1202–1213. [CrossRef]
66. Pagano, A.; Pluchinotta, I.; Giordano, R.; Vurro, M. Drinking water supply in resilient cities: Notes from L'Aquila earthquake case study. *Sustain. Cities Soc.* **2017**, *28*, 435–449. [CrossRef]
67. Jovanović, A.; Klimek, P.; Renn, O.; Schneider, R.; Øien, K.; Brown, J.; DiGennaro, M.; Liu, Y.; Pfau, V.; Jelić, M.; et al. Assessing resilience of healthcare infrastructure exposed to COVID-19: Emerging risks, resilience indicators, interdependencies and international standards. *Environ. Syst. Decis.* **2020**, *40*, 252–286. [CrossRef]
68. Rosales-Asensio, E.; Elejalde, J.L.; Pulido-Alonso, A.; Colmenar-Santos, A. Resilience framework, methods, and metrics for the prioritization of critical electrical grid customers. *Electronics* **2022**, *11*, 2246. [CrossRef]
69. González, C.; Niño, M.; Ayala, G. Functionality Loss and Recovery Time Models for Structural Elements, Non-Structural Components, and Delay Times to Estimate the Seismic Resilience of Mexican School Buildings. *Buildings* **2023**, *13*, 1498. [CrossRef]
70. Brown, R.G. *Smoothing, Forecasting and Prediction of Discrete Time Series*; Prentice-Hall: Hoboken, NJ, USA, 1963.
71. Chatfield, C. *Time-Series Forecasting*; CRC Press: Boca Raton, FL, USA, 2000.
72. Murphy, J.J. *Technical Analysis of the Financial Markets: A Comprehensive Guide to Trading Methods and Applications*; Penguin: London, UK, 1999.
73. Maddala, G.S. *Introduction to Econometrics*; Wiley: Hoboken, NJ, USA, 2001.
74. Shaker, H.; Alba, E. Noise modeling for photovoltaic systems using real-world data. *IEEE Trans. Sustain. Energy* **2017**, *8*, 1–10.
75. Korpela, T.; Rossi, M.; Lehtonen, M. Noise and signal interference in photovoltaic power data. *Renew. Energy* **2016**, *92*, 139–150.
76. Pratama, I.; Prasetyaningrum, P.T.; Setyaningsih, P.W. Time-Series Data Forecasting and Approximation with Smoothing Technique. In Proceedings of the 2019 International Conference on Information and Communications Technology (ICOIACT), Yogyakarta, Indonesia, 24–25 July 2019; pp. 439–444.
77. Li, D.; Yu, X.; Chen, J.; Lin, Z.; He, S.; Liu, J.; Yao, Y.; Wu, Y. Typical Load Analysis and Forecast of a Provincial Power Grid in Mid-Southern China. In Proceedings of the 2021 IEEE 5th Conference on Energy Internet and Energy System Integration (EI2), Taiyuan, China, 22–24 October 2021; pp. 3352–3357.
78. Raj, R.P.; Kowli, A. Characterizing the ramps and noise in solar power imbalances. *Sol. Energy* **2022**, *247*, 531–542. [CrossRef]
79. Ernst, B.; Wan, Y.H.; Kirby, B. *Short-Term Power Fluctuation of Wind Turbines: Analyzing Data from the German 250-MW Measurement Program from the Ancillary Services Viewpoint*; Technical Report; National Renewable Energy Lab.(NREL): Golden, CO, USA, 1999.

80. Chhabra, M.; Lim, M.; Barnes, F. Frequency stabilization using solar smoothing, leveling and time shifting in a hybrid renewablenetwork. In Proceedings of the ISGT2011-India, Kollam, Kerala, India, 1–3 December 2011; pp. 275–281.
81. Hyndman, R.J.; Athanasopoulos, G. *Forecasting: Principles and Practice*; OTexts: Melbourne, Australia, 2018.
82. Ardebili, A.A.; Martella, A.; Martella, C.; Longo, A.; Ficarella, A. Digital Twins: Case Study of Energy Metaverse and Edge-Cloud Integration. In Proceedings of the 2024 IEEE International Conference on Big Data (BigData), Washington, DC, USA, 15–18 December 2024; pp. 5476–5485. [CrossRef]
83. Chai, B.X.; Gunaratne, M.; Ravandi, M.; Wang, J.; Dharmawickrema, T.; Di Pietro, A.; Jin, J.; Georgakopoulos, D. Smart industrial internet of things framework for composites manufacturing. *Sensors* **2024**, *24*, 4852. [CrossRef] [PubMed]
84. Yılmaz, N.; Alatlı, O.; Çiloğlugil, B.; Erdur, R.C. Evaluation of storage and query performance of sensor based Internet of Things data with MongoDB. In Proceedings of the 2018 International Conference on Artificial Intelligence and Data Processing (IDAP), Malatya, Turkey, 28–30 September 2018; pp. 1–6.
85. Pandey, R. Performance Benchmarking and Comparison of Cloud-Based Databases MongoDB (NoSQL) vs. MySQL (Relational) Using YCSB. *Electron. Resour.* **2020**. Available online: https://www.researchgate.net/publication/344047197_Performance_Benchmarking_and_Comparison_of_Cloud-Based_Databases_MongoDB_NoSQL_Vs_MySQL_Relational_using_YCSB (accessed on 3 December 2024).
86. Eyada, M.M.; Saber, W.; El Genidy, M.M.; Amer, F. Performance evaluation of IoT data management using MongoDB versus MySQL databases in different cloud environments. *IEEE Access* **2020**, *8*, 110656–110668. [CrossRef]
87. Ardebili, A.A.; Longo, A.; Ficarella, A. Digital twinning of PV modules for smart systems-A comparison between commercial and open-source simulation models. In Proceedings of the 2023 IEEE International Conference on Dependable, Autonomic and Secure Computing, International Conference on Pervasive Intelligence and Computing, Intl Conf on Cloud and Big Data Computing, Intl Conf on Cyber Science and Technology Congress (DASC/PiCom/CBDCom/CyberSciTech), Abu Dhabi, United Arab Emirates, 14–17 November 2023; pp. 1045–1050.
88. Aghazadeh Ardebili, A.; Ficarella, A.; Longo, A.; Khalil, A.; Khalil, S. Hybrid Turbo-Shaft Engine Digital Twinning for Autonomous Aircraft via AI and Synthetic Data Generation. *Aerospace* **2023**, *10*, 683. [CrossRef]
89. Aghazadeh Ardebili, A.; Longo, A.; Ficarella, A.; Khalil, A.; Khalil, S. Exploring Synthetic Noise Algorithms for Real-World Similar Data Generation: A Case Study on Digitally Twining Hybrid Turbo-Shaft Engines in UAV/UAS Applications. In *Model and Data Engineering: Proceedings of the 12th International Conference (MEDI 2023), Sousse, Tunisia, 2–4 November 2023*; Springer: Cham, Switzerland, 2023; pp. 87–101.
90. The European Commission. European Industrial Technology Roadmap for the Next Generation Cloud-Edge Offering. Technical Report. 2021. Available online: https://ec.europa.eu/newsroom/repository/document/2021-18/European_CloudEdge_Technology_Investment_Roadmap_for_publication_pMdz85DSw6nqPppq8hE9S9RbB8_76223.pdf (accessed on 3 December 2024).
91. Somma, A.; Benedictis, A.D.; Zappatore, M.; Martella, C.; Martella, A.; Longo, A. Digital Twin Space: The Integration of Digital Twins and Data Spaces. In Proceedings of the 2023 IEEE International Conference on Big Data (BigData), Sorrento, Italy, 15–18 December 2023; pp. 4017–4025. [CrossRef]
92. Yong, S.Z.; Zhu, M.; Frazzoli, E. Switching and data injection attacks on stochastic cyber-physical systems: Modeling, resilient estimation, and attack mitigation. *ACM Trans. Cyber-Phys. Syst.* **2018**, *2*, 1–2. [CrossRef]
93. Tan, R.; Nguyen, H.H.; Yau, D.K. Collaborative load management with safety assurance in smart grids. *ACM Trans. Cyber-Phys. Syst.* **2017**, *1*, 1–27. [CrossRef]
94. Matei, I.; Piotrowski, W.; Perez, A.; de Kleer, J.; Tierno, J.; Mungovan, W.; Turnewitsch, V. System resilience through health monitoring and reconfiguration. *ACM Trans. Cyber-Phys. Syst.* **2024**, *8*, 1–27. [CrossRef]

applied sciences

MDPI

Article

An Artificial Intelligence-Based Digital Twin Approach for Rejection Rate and Mechanical Property Improvement in an Investment Casting Plant

Javier Nieves [1,*], David Garcia [1], Jorge Angulo-Pines [1], Fernando Santos [1] and Pedro Pablo Rodriguez [2]

[1] Azterlan Member of Basque Research Team Alliance (BRTA), Aliendale Auzunea 6, 48200 Durango, Spain; dgarcia@azterlan.es (D.G.); jangulo@azterlan.es (J.A.-P.); fsantos@azterlan.es (F.S.)

[2] EIPC Research Center, AIE, Torrekua 3, 20600 Eibar, Spain; prodriguez@eipc.es

* Correspondence: jnieves@azterlan.es

Abstract: The manufacturing process carried out in the investment casting industry suffers from problems similar to other production processes. In addition, the high requirements of the customers and the industries that require these parts mean that high quality standards must be met. If those requirements are not achieved, this leads to the rejection of the manufactured parts. Therefore, given the current technology revolution (i.e., Industry 4.0) and the possibilities offered by tools such as digital twins and artificial intelligence, it is possible to work on a generation of intelligent systems that can reduce and even avoid these problems. Therefore, this study proposes the creation of a digital twin based on artificial intelligence to work on proactively identifying problems before they happen and, if they are detected, launch an optimization process that offers corrective actions to solve them. More specifically, this work focuses on the analysis of the manufacturing process (definition, KPI extraction, capture, distribution, and visualization), the creation of a base system for the integral management of process optimization, and experiments developed for determining the best method for making predictions. Additionally, we propose a recommender system to (i) avoid the appearance of porosities and (ii) keep the elongation of the parts in the ranges desired by the customer.

Keywords: investment casting; artificial intelligence; digital twin; system of system; machine learning; process optimization

1. Introduction

Society has been evolving for years and increasing its population; thus, the demand for products is increasing. Specifically, many products need metal parts produced by the metalworking industry, which has evolved since the different metal ages in human history [1]. In order to make this type of production feasible, the industry realized that it must improve and optimize its production process. Currently, there are a large number of foundries that employ different production methods. For instance, there are foundries that work with green molding, chemical molding, or shell molding, among others. This type of manufacturing process dates back to ancient metalworking eras. In contrast, investment casting, although not widely adopted, is an industry with very high demand due to it being able to generate very sophisticated parts. As a result, it is a complex and expensive process.

The investment casting process was created thousands of years ago in the Chinese empire. The main characteristic of this process is the possibility of creating very precise castings with difficult geometries to fill. Moreover, it is able to use a wide range of metallic alloys for manufacturing its parts compared with most popular foundry processes. Hence, this process is suitable for high added value and small series of highly demanding parts [2]. The main sectors addressed by this process are the aeronautic, automotive, and weapon-making. These types of industry are final users that require an additional degree of safety of their products [3].

These manufacturing processes, because of their nature, have a common challenge. They are very sensitive to variables related to the ceramic mold building up around the wax pattern, to the melting and pouring conditions, and in some cases, to the final heat treatment. In this way, the main problem is the presence of different defects on the final parts, like shrinkages and pores that require re-fixing of the component or even its final rejection [4]. Another problem is the process itself. The part is only visible at the end of the process, once finishing operations have been carried out. At that point, if problems are discovered, they are converted into significant loses to companies as non-quality costs. The most common strategy to address this problem is to understand the behavior of the process by developing process simulations based on physics concepts like fluid dynamics and heat transfer. These models are focused on forecasting the final performance of produced parts based on variables like the filling speed, heat transfer, and contraction during solidification. They can make predictions in terms of slag formation, shrinkage, or hot cracks, respectively. This kind of task makes the manufactured part more expensive. In addition, castings are affected by a variety of different factors; for example, the metal composition, mold design, and casting conditions, which can influence the final outcome [5].

Currently, the industry is seeking alternatives to avoid part defects [6], providing solutions that can predict the soundness of the parts. Moreover, during the last decade, significant effort was dedicated to improving final product quality, supported by the use of ICT, its integration into manufacturing equipment, and the application of the internet of things.

For example, Dučić et al. [7] reviewed several studies in the literature that make use of artificial intelligence (AI) models to improve parts or processes. Thus, the authors collected information regarding several types of manufacturing processes; for example, sand processes and continuous processes, among others. They also discussed investment casting, describing how ANNs have been used to perform numerical simulations of different mold temperatures [8]. More accurately, they work to manage some aspects such as mold temperature, melting temperature, casting part material, number and location of feeding points, diameter and length of inflow channels, and the angle of the channel with respect to the main sprue axis. Similarly, Pattnaik et al. presented how to optimize the injection process parameters with multiple performance features in the investment casting process using an orthogonal array with gray fuzzy logic. This algorithm identifies an optimal combination of the process parameters [9]. Moreover, recent studies utilize modern techniques such as advanced deep learning models to carry out visual inspections of parts [10]. In this case, the defect has already been produced. This means that this approach does not work proactively, but it shows how AI techniques can be used in various ways to improve the manufacturing process.

The arrival of Industry 4.0 [11] has significantly accelerated efforts to optimize the manufacturing process. Specifically, this kind of work requires digitization of foundry plants, driven by the improved data-gathering capabilities of machinery. Therefore, as a result of ICT advances, different studies have been carried out which use these data as the basis for new systems [12]. For example, ref. [13] presents a data-driven framework based on machine learning techniques for estimating and screening early products in investment casting. Additionally, digital twin technology has significantly contributed to improving manufacturing processes. For instance, Antoniadou et al. focused its research on handling the robots that manage the investment casting molding stages [14]. This kind of tools were also used for checking and detecting defects like deformations [15] and stress [16] in aeronautics parts. Finally, a research paper was presented in the 75th World Foundry Congress (WFC) that presents a digital twin for porosity detection [17], but without checking the best optimization parameters to avoid pores.

Against this background, we try to combine these ICT technologies and ideas for process optimization. We generate a digital twin that is able to observe the manufacturing process, extract the current situation, predict the possible further $t+1$ stationary state, and, when anomalies are detected, provide corrective actions to avoid them. This is similar to Model Predictive Control (MPC) systems [18].

To achieve efficient digitization of an industrial process, several steps were carried out. In this way, this research started from a digital audit evaluating process traceability, frequency, and precision of the controls. Also, digitization analysis of existing data, preprocessing possibilities, and visualization was performed. Later, capture agents were developed to preprocess and store data in a central and ordered database. Moreover, we continued providing access to extracted information and generating different query methods to detect deviations and trends. Next,we built a digital twin, a virtual representation of the process, and we provided it with the tools to identify interconnections between variables and product output characteristics through an advanced data analytics process. Finally, the generation of predictive algorithms to foresee the expected characteristics of the manufactured parts and a recommender system to ensure final results were implemented and included in the final system. For this research, we focused on two defects: (i) mechanical properties and (ii) rejection rate.

The remainder of this paper is organized as follows. Section 2 describes the work and the steps undertaken to achieve the proposed solution. Additionally, this section discusses data generation, the methodology, and the development of the intelligent system. Section 3 presents the results achieved with the proposed approach. Here, we introduce the generated results for several configurations, as well as the final solution created for investment casting. Finally, Section 4 concludes this paper and the research, providing a discussion of the solution and suggesting future work and potential improvements to our proposal.

2. Materials and Methods

Therefore, in an attempt to solve the already defined problem in Section 1, as well as the difficulty of addressing the process as a whole, researchers have proposed the use of the well-known "Divide and Conquer" (*divide et impera*) methodology. More accurately, this methodology tries to divide the general problem into smaller ones. In other words, it tries to transform the original problem into simpler ones that are easier to solve. Thus, once a solution has been found to solve each of them, the combination of all achieved developments solves the general problem. This methodology is widely used to deal with legal challenges [19], mathematical calculations [20], and computational problems (specifically in parallel processing) [21].

Consequently, building on this idea, the steps defined in this work are detailed below (additional information is shown in Figure 1).

1. Identification of the problem and the challenges to overcome: The goal of this initial step is to identify the background and context of the original problem. In essence, we focus on gaining a clear understanding of what we are aiming to solve.
2. Acquisition of knowledge: Collecting high-level knowledge provides the necessary overview to start the research. Nevertheless, later, when we focus on a more specific

aspect of this challenge, this step will be repeated to ensure greater accuracy in the new generation of specific domain solutions.

3. Division of challenges: Starting from the idea of divisions mentioned earlier, we will define the challenges to address and the specific steps for each one. For this research, the following challenges have been identified: (i) digitization and manufacturing process representation, (ii) creation of a proactive system based on predictions, and (iii) retro-feedback for controlling and adjusting the manufacturing parameters. For each of them, the following sub-phases will be performed:
   a Acquisition of specific knowledge: Once the topic is defined, this stage involves expanding the knowledge necessary to address the problem. Frequently, this knowledge acquisition is closely linked to the exploration and understanding of the production process being optimized.
   b Definition of the experiment and the techniques to be used: At this point, the specific research and experiments are outlined for each of the challenges to be addressed.
   c Evaluation: At this stage, the defined experiments are conducted, and results are obtained for the approximation that has been defined.
   d Analysis: Once the previous stage is complete, the collected data from the experiments are analyzed.
   e Interpretation of the results: When each solution has been determined for all identified challenges, we will combine them.

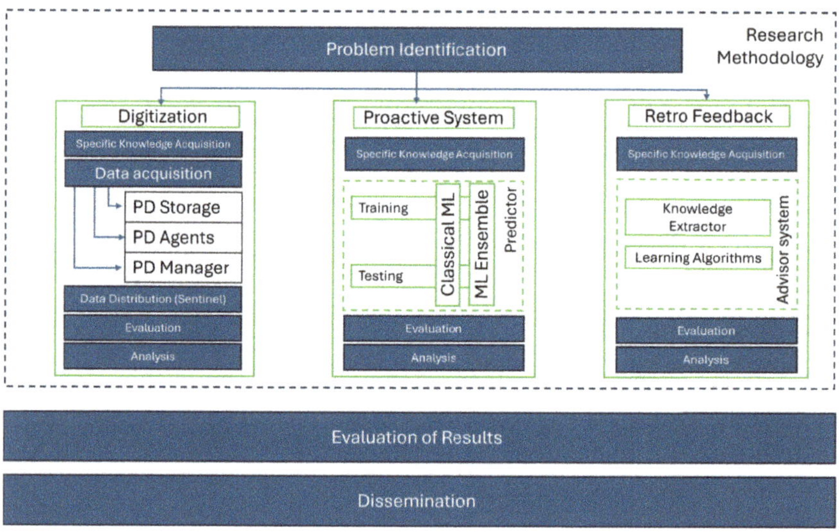

Figure 1. Research methodology and explanation of AI-based digital twin system.

Any type of optimization of the manufacturing process, such as the manufacturing of castings using an investment casting process, involves exhaustive control of all associated operations. The more control there is and the fewer fluctuations that occur, the more reliable the results of the process. In this manner, the optimization and stabilization of the entire manufacturing process must be supported by Information and Communication Technologies (ICT). Thus, according to Boscher et al. [22], the main goals are as follows:

1. Digitization of the process: It is fundamental and necessary to digitally represent the manufacturing process.
2. Expand the amount of digitized information, achieving a representative set that facilitates the understanding and management of the process.
3. Generate a robust IIoT (Industrial Internet of Things) system designed to correctly define the appropriate ICT solution.
4. Provide a solution that, in addition to describing the current behavior, can provide digitally calculated solutions that improve the real system.

Consequently, after applying the aforementioned methodology and the main goals described by Boscher et al., the global proposed solution is defined as a System of Systems (SoS) comprising an agent-based data gathering architecture for creating a complete manufacturing process digital twin. This system focuses on detecting anomalies through predictions and, finally, an advisory system to redirect the process to normality.

2.1. Digitization and Manufacturing Process Representation

As defined in [23], a system is a collection of interconnected elements that, when combined, produce results unattainable by the elements operating independently. These elements can be complex and large in scale, consisting of sub-elements working together to achieve a common objective.

The concept of a system of systems refers to a scenario in which the constituent elements are themselves collaborative systems, each exhibiting the characteristic of operational independence. In particular, each individual system can achieve a functional purpose independently, without relying on its involvement in the broader system of systems. Furthermore, each system maintains managerial autonomy, meaning it is managed and evolves to fulfill its own goals rather than those of the overarching system [24]. As discussed by [25,26], these attributes distinguish a system of systems from large monolithic systems. Fields such as enterprise architecture and service-oriented architecture address systems with these defining features, enabling the development of such solutions.

The architecture of a system is critical to its success in meeting the objectives of its stakeholders [27]. In this case, it is defined as the collection of structures necessary to understand the system, including its components, the relationships between these components, and their properties.

In light of this explanation, the general sub-challenge addressed in this research is to create different individual systems for data collection to build the digital representation of the process. Each system can operate independently and solve the acquisition problem within its own area or domain. Moreover, all of these modules are designed with the necessary communication capabilities to interact and carry out their specific tasks toward achieving the final objective: the optimization of the production process as a whole.

To carry out this data gathering process, the Production Data Manager tool, PDManager, developed by the Azterlan Research Center is used (for more information, please visit https://www.azterlan.es/en/kh/pdmanager, accessed on 20 January 2025). Specifically, PDManager is a real-time production control system designed to guarantee digitization, traceability, and the orderly storage of key parameters in a centralized database for the manufacturing process of cast components.

This system is composed of three root elements:

1. PDStorage: A centralized relational database where all the gathered data are correlated, keeping the production history. In addition to being used for monitoring and recording information in real time, it can be employed for knowledge generation and predictive model creation based on these provided data. This kind of storage system and its capability to centralize data and information is discussed in the literature [28,29].

2. PDAgents: Small software artifacts created as services that focus on the specific task of interacting with third-party entities (i.e., other databases, files, or even machinery), extracting the necessary data from the production process itself. Krivic et al showed in [30] how these developments can create the needed data flowing ecosystem for IoT management. The creation of this type of micro-service is the axis of a more complex software architecture that can also help in other domains like smart agriculture [31].
3. PDManager modules: The PDManager system has different modules (some of which can be seen in Figure 2) that, first, allow the operator to interact with and monitor the area where they are located and, second, provide a tool to perform manual correlation of data when automatic correlation is not possible.

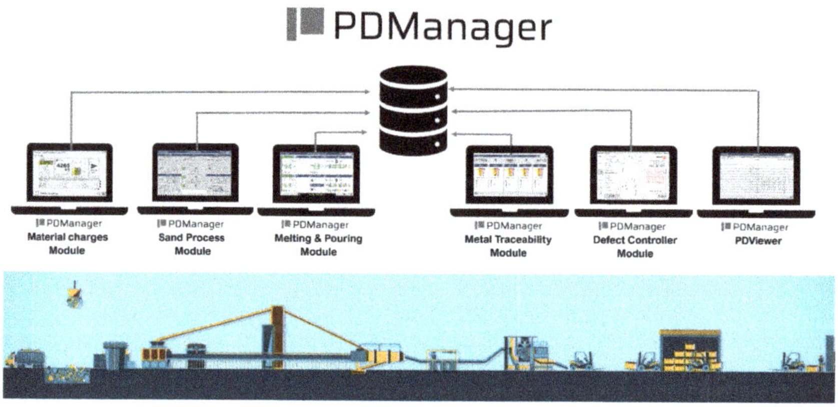

Figure 2. PDManager architecture overview where several specific modules manage each production process step and gather data to correlate and store in a central database.

Regarding the process explanation given in Section 1, to address the aforementioned management process, data must be extracted from the entire manufacturing process. The deployment of PDManager focuses on implementing different modules that manage the following process areas: (i) primary coatings, (ii) secondary coatings, (iii) melting, and (iv) final inspections.

Specifically, the first stage of data aggregation relates to the coating process. In detail, the primary coating is the phase where the first layer of wax is applied to the model. Its primary purpose is to create the model's surface. To achieve this, a liquid suspension, also known as slurry, is used. The slurry consists of a fine ceramic material and a binder with high heat resistance and good adhesion. Subsequently, the secondary coating involves applying additional layers on top of the primary layer. Its main function is to provide mechanical strength and structural stability to the mold. Therefore, coarser sand is used together with a colloidal silica binder.

The addition of each coating, which will eventually be converted into a shell mold, is of great importance. For primary and secondary coatings, the data to be captured are the environmental data for the room, which are obtained from a third-party platform provided by EKIOM™ company from Paris, France (https://www.ekiom.net/, accessed on 20 January 2025). EKIOM™ records temperature and humidity data with different sensors placed in the primary and secondary areas. In addition, slurry data are extracted from the pre-existing Factory Win platform deployed in the foundry. This information is supplied by a *Microsoft™ Excel™* file located in the coatings laboratory. This document compiles data related to slurry analyses carried out periodically through rigorous internal procedures in the foundry. More specifically, the variables include density, temperature, SiO_2 percentage, and others.

These parameters are critical because if the environmental data are not correct, the mold layers will not dry under optimal conditions, causing mold breaks. Furthermore, if the slurry creation is incorrect, it will cause poor adhesion between layers, which may also cause mold breakages.

Then, in the melting area, the controlled data include the chemical composition of the alloy, the temperature of the furnace, and other variables related to the casting. At this stage, the data flow in two different ways. On the one hand, some data are manually digitized through the PDManager Melting and Pouring module. On the other hand, several pieces of data are stored in the Factory Win platform and are automatically detected and extracted from it. Specifically, composition data are measured via spark spectrometry analysis performed in the chemical laboratory, while the rest of the data are generated by various sensors connected to the corresponding equipment.

For the last area, the final inspection, the gathered information pertains to the quality results of the manufactured castings. The data focus on the occurrence of shrinkages and mechanical properties, such as elongation, which are analyzed in this research. For this last data extraction process, information about inclusions is obtained from PDManager, which is connected to Factory Win and continuously updated with results from fluorescent particle tests performed on all created parts. This process is carried out by qualified technicians who determine the number of pores/inclusions in each part. Additionally, elongation data for castings are provided. For this purpose, representative standard specimens from the manufacturing order are machined and later tested to obtain the final mechanical properties, which are then digitized via PDManager.

Once the data are extracted and stored in the appropriate repository, they should be utilized to improve the day-to-day process. Thus, they will be used to represent the production process, delivering the right information to the right people at the right time. The most effective way to achieve the goal of data distribution is by implementing an observer/observable pattern [32], which is based on the subscriber/publisher paradigm [33].

During the past decade, communication schemes have been redesigned and reimplemented with the aim of integrating data from several heterogeneous data sources. Moreover, the introduction of certain standards (for instance, the IEC 61850 standard for substation automation [34]), which defines a data model oriented toward objects and functions, allows for modeling all the devices of a system by categorizing them according to their functionalities. This technology also enables their integration into a high-speed peer-to-peer communication network through standardization. However, further improvements were needed to establish an open and standardized working environment. The solution was the creation of a real-time publisher/subscriber communication model, as demonstrated in [35]. In fact, this type of communication is widely used and well documented in books and research papers such as the following: [33,36–38].

In a effort to combine this communication and data distribution technologies, Azterlan developed Sentinel (for more information about Sentinel, please visit https://www.azterlan.es/en/kh/sentinel-predictive-control, accessed on 20 January 2025). It is an integral system for data distribution and process monitoring, as well as anomaly detection, digital representations of the process, alert communication, and a tool for incorporating and utilizing different Artificial Intelligence (AI) models. Despite all the features available in the Sentinel system (illustrated in Figure 3), at this stage of development, Sentinel is focused solely on distributing, displaying, and presenting the gathered information. Hence, for now, we define Sentinel as a software system for automated and real-time data distribution. Sentinel displays key information and alerts to the people and locations where they are most useful. It allows for the deployment of dashboards or control panels designed according to user needs. These control panels can be implemented as static displays (on-site) or with navigation capabilities across different levels of information depth (e.g., process managers, laboratory, quality department, maintenance, and management, among others).

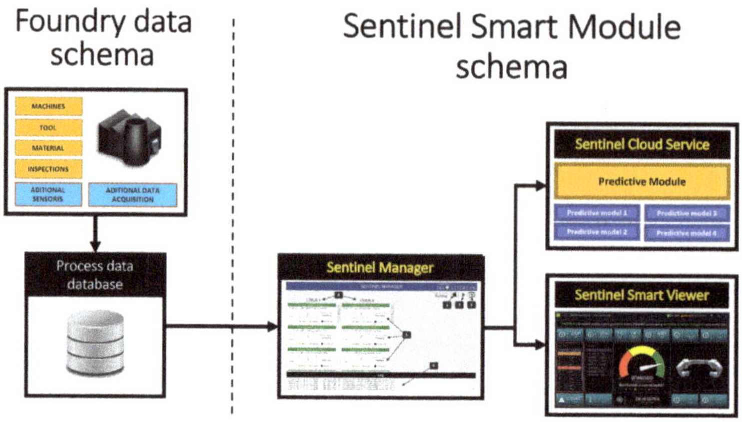

Figure 3. Sentinel architecture overview where the 3 main modules are shown. One is the manager of the system: the place where the business logic is included. Then, the viewer is shown the specific information in the selected manner, and the smart cloud service locates the predictive models and the artificial intelligence modules.

In order to define and design the data distribution, as well as the visualization methods in Sentinel, the following aspects have been analyzed:

1. KPI identification: Firstly, the work team determines the key process indicators that are valuable for the day-to-day work and the management of the process. In this way, the different areas that can be included and the different data that can be employed are studied here.
2. KPI analysis: Once the interests and possibilities were listed, we developed an analysis addressing all key stages of the process. To achieve this, six different variables were compared using the Likert scale [39] and combined in a Star Plot. The variables used are: (i) frequency, (ii) accuracy of the available information, (iii) visualization or its necessity, (iv) capture and storage media, (v) possibility of data access, and (vi) traceability.
3. KPI Priority. After the previously conducted study, a filtering process is developed based on the priority of working on these indicators. This analysis is performed using a scatterplot.
4. Data distribution location. As the final task, the appropriate location for each visualization is determined.

In the end, the management of all input sources was performed, as shown in Figure 4. Four different PDManager capture agents were developed to integrate these data sources. Subsequently, all the information was centralized in a single database, allowing Sentinel to utilize it for data distribution and visualization in this specific use case.

Figure 4. Data gathering: overview scheme of data sources, data capture agents, and centralization of information.

2.2. Creation of a Proactive System Based on Predictions

Thanks to the work defined and described in Section 2.1, we now have all relevant process information available. This information flows in real time through our capture and storage system. Hence, all the described data serve as the raw input necessary to create an intelligent process management system. The collected data enable the digital representation of the process using advanced techniques. In fact, these data allow us to develop a proactive intelligent system that anticipates potential problems in the process. Its creation will be carried out through what is known as a digital twin.

More accurately, the concept of a digital twin [40] refers to the creation of a virtual and intangible representation based on real data. Its objective is to replicate a physical or real situation. In our case, it focuses on representing the investment casting manufacturing process. The main contribution of a digital twin is to decouple the physical world from the virtual one, enabling analysis of how the process operates and subsequently preventing unexpected deviations in both virtual and real representations.

For our use case, the digital twin must facilitate process improvements aimed at defect reduction, energy efficiency, and time-to-market reduction. To achieve these objectives, the digital twin must operate under three clear axioms, as well defined in [41]:

- Proactivity: The system must be able to anticipate adverse situations. In fact, the digital twin makes use of the digital world through simulations and artificial intelligence. Thus, it will be able to determine the possible state of the production process in the near future (i.e., a temporary state $t+1$).
- Adjustment: The management of the virtual environment must always work within a specific configuration. This means that the digital twin must meet the requirements of the manufacturing process. In other words, none of the tests or simulations that are developed will break the rules that govern the physical representation of the process.
- Business intelligence: The twin will even serve as a knowledge management tool. Specifically, it is a repository of business intelligence that encompasses everything needed to manage all the tasks associated with the actual process. By utilizing the digital twin and providing it with this repository, business knowledge will remain within the company, preventing the much-feared knowledge leakage.

For a digital twin to work, it must apply the same methodology that a doctor does. This methodology is called "diagnosis", and its basic steps are as follows [22]:

(i) Observation: The digital twin is based on observation, which serves as the foundation for the digital representation of the real world. Observation focuses on extracting raw data, as previously explained and defined. This observation is essential because it enables the identification of operational patterns, trends, and other aspects that will be used in subsequent tasks. It is important to note that without observation—in other words, without a data capture process—developing this type of technology would not be possible.

(ii) Evaluation: Making use of the knowledge already loaded into the twin, as well as the data that are being produced in real time, our system develops a process known as "evaluation". This process performs different simulations based on the current real situation it receives through "observation". Subsequently, the further operations required to adjust and optimize the process will depend on the evaluations or predictions obtained in this stage.

(iii) Decision making: The previous processes, by themselves, do not add value. That is why a correction or adjustment of the monitored activity is needed. Thus, taking into account the results of the observation and evaluation steps, solver algorithms find the appropriate fit for the purpose of the twin. Afterwards, the system proceeds to communicate the results or actions that must be put into practice [42]. Sometimes, they are sent to humans (M2H–machine to human communication), and other times, they are sent to machines via M2M (machine to machine).

In order to generate a tool capable of representing the reality of the manufacturing process, specifically, the production of molds and parts flowing in the investment casting workflow, it is necessary to be able to represent the flow of these molds in the lost wax casting process and the events that occur in it. In this case, the data obtained from the primary coating, secondary coating, melting, and inspection areas will be transformed into a sequence of enqueued elements that are sequentially characterized in each stage and digitally represented as a FIFO queue.

Hence, our digital twin was formally defined as a queue Q of z discrete molds, where V is the sum of $PC + SC + M + I$ molds (PC for primary coating and previous molds, SC from primary coating to secondary coating, M from secondary coating to melting, and I for final inspections). Some variables will not be informed until the mold arrives at the specific stage where that data are gathered. In the end, the entire representation is defined as $Qx_n, ..., x_2, x_1 \rightarrow Vpc_n, .., pc_2, pc_1, sc_n, .., sc_2, sc_1, m_n, .., m_2, m_1, i_n, .., i_2, i_1$. For our use case, $|V| = 40 \rightarrow |PC| = |SC1| = |M1| = |I1| = 10$, and when the full set of PC molds is ready, they are all moved together to the next step, pushing them forward in the $PC \rightarrow SC \rightarrow M \rightarrow I$ sequence.

In order to reproduce the current situation of the process, the digital twin must be able to model the movements of the molds, as explained before. In this way, it performs event-based management of the system, detecting when a group of molds reaches a new sequential step, represented by each red square in Figure 5. In fact, the digital twin operates under the following events:

- The first event occurs when a set of molds is being generated in the primary coating stage. To detect this, the digital twin is subscribed to the PDManager storage database. During the coating process, the system collects data until the last coating has dried and the robot moves the mold to the next stage. When the full set of molds is completed, the digital twin receives this event from the database and triggers a series of tasks to digitally generate the process state, update the digital twin, perform the associated calculations, and finally, move these molds to the next step.
- The second event is triggered when the secondary coating is applied. The digital twin is again subscribed to the storage, and the event is fired to indicate that some work must be performed. This second event functions similarly to the previous one but pertains to the creation of the final mold. Again, when all molds are created, the

digital representation is updated, and all calculations are executed. Finally, the entire set of molds is promoted to the next stage.

- The last detected event occurs when the casting is finally created. This means that the final event is fired when the metal is poured into the mold. Again, the system operates in batches of molds. The subscription to the PDManager database triggers the management process for this step. At that moment, the digital twin receives the information about the creation of the castings, and all of them are moved to the final steps. These last steps are not monitored in this research, though they could be incorporated in future developments. Nevertheless, after the completion of the castings, the quality of each casting is measured, and these data are gathered for the prediction methods. While this is not a step for the digital twin, it is crucial for anticipating the behavior of each casting concerning mechanical properties and the appearance of porosity.

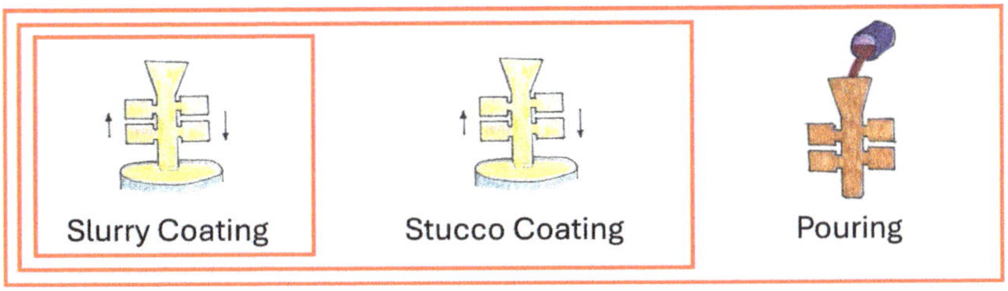

Figure 5. Investment casting process division and grouping for predictions and optimizations. First group, with the slurry coating work (PC). Then, as second group, the combination of both coating stages, slurry, and stucco ($PC + SC$). Finally, the complete group including previous coating stages and the pouring ($PC + SC + M$).

Due to these events and the data gathering process, the digital twin is able to characterize each mold. At this moment, the mold V_j has the set of variables PC_i, SC_i, M_i, I_i that can now be sent to the machine learning models, which will attempt to predict the state the part will reach when the final inspection is carried out. In the same way that the system manages the events, the predictions will also be triggered at every grouping step illustrated in Figure 5.

In order to develop the aforementioned predictions and considering that we have extracted all the manufacturing process results, as well as the recorded results in both prediction objectives, the best approach is the employment of supervised learning. Specifically, this is a type of machine learning where models are trained using labeled data. The labeled data include the corresponding correct output. This learning is performed using statistical classifiers to categorize data based on patterns in the labeled examples. These classifiers learn from the labeled data to make predictions on new and unseen data. The process relies on statistical methods to model the relationship between input features and target labels.

To make future predictions and to properly evaluate the machine learning models for the prediction of both aforementioned objectives, we applied the following methodology.

- Cross validation: In order to obtain a proper representation of the data, we must use as much available information as possible. For this purpose, K-fold cross validation is usually used in machine learning experiments [43]. In our experiments, we performed a K-fold cross validation with $k = 10$. In this approach, our dataset was split into 10 sets of learning (66% of the total dataset) and testing (34% of the total data).
- Teaching the model: For each fold, we performed the learning phase of each algorithm using the corresponding training dataset, applying different parameters or learning algorithms depending on the model. Due to the lack of knowledge about the perfor-

mance of this type of prediction in the investment casting process and considering that this research is in an initial stage, we decided to use classical machine learning models to validate whether the methodology could be useful. More accurately, we used the following models:

- Classical statistical classifiers: This type of classifier has been widely used in machine learning due to its simplicity, interpretability, and effectiveness with relatively small datasets [44]. One of the key advantages of these classifiers is that they are computationally efficient and easy to implement. Although newer machine learning models, such as deep learning approaches, have gained popularity, classical statistical classifiers remain valuable for their reliability and ease of use in many practical applications [45–49]. Specifically, we conducted our research by evaluating the following classical algorithms:
    * Bayesian networks: For Bayesian networks, we used different structural learning algorithms, including K2 [50], hill climber [51], and Tree Augmented Naïve (TAN) [52]. Moreover, we also performed experiments with a naïve Bayes classifier.
    * K-nearest neighbor: For K-nearest neighbor [53], we performed experiments with $k = 1$, $k = 2$, $k = 3$, $k = 4$, $k = 5$, and $k = 6$.
    * Artificial neural networks: We used a three-layer Multilayer Perceptron (MLP) [54] taught using a back-propagation algorithm.
    * Support vector machines: We performed our experiments with a polynomial kernel [55], a normalized polynomial kernel [56], a Pearson VII function-based universal kernel [57], and a radial basis function (RBF)-based kernel [58].
    * Decision trees: We performed experiments with the C4.5 algorithm [59] and random forest [60], an ensemble of randomly constructed decision trees. In particular, we tested the random forest with a variable number of random trees N, from $N = 50$ to $N = 350$ in increments of 50.
    * Voted perceptron: This algorithm, described in [61], is an extension of the basic perceptron algorithm that improves classification performance by combining multiple perceptron models. It was selected because it helps improve accuracy and robustness compared to standard perceptrons.
- Combined machine learning classifiers: Classifiers by themselves are able to obtain good results, but we cannot ensure that a specific classifier is perfectly suitable for the prediction of every objective in the investment casting process. To solve this problem, several studies have combined classifiers [62]. These techniques seek to obtain a better classification decision despite incorporating a higher degree of complexity into the process. From a statistical point of view [63], assuming a labeled dataset Z and n as the number of different classifiers with relatively good performance in making predictions for Z, we can select one of them to solve classification problems. However, there is a risk of not choosing the correct one. Therefore, the safest option is to use all of them and take an average of their outputs. The resulting classifier is not necessarily better but reduces the risk induced by using inappropriate classifiers. From a computational point of view [62], some supervised machine learning algorithms, in their learning phase, generate models based on local maximum solutions. Thus, an aggregation of classifiers is much closer to the optimal classifier than only one of them. Similarly, the casting process itself can be categorized as linear or nonlinear. By using these combination methods, we are capable of designing a collective intelligence system for classification which incorporates both linear and nonlinear

classifiers. The combination methods we used to develop the experiments are detailed below.

* By vote: Using democratic voting to classify elements is one of the oldest strategies for decision making. Extending electoral theory, other methods can allow for combinations of classifiers [64]. Specifically, we tested (i) the majority voting rule, (ii) the product rule, (iii) the average rule, (iv) the max rule, and (v) the min rule.
* Grading: The base classifiers are all the classifiers that we want to combine through the grading method [65], and these were evaluated using k-fold cross validation to ensure that each of the instances was employed for the learning phase of each classifier. Therefore, the classification step is as follows: [65]. First, each base classifier makes a prediction for the instance to be classified. Second, meta-classifiers qualify the result obtained by the base classifiers for the instance being classified. Finally, the classification is derived using only the positive results. Conflicts (i.e., multiple classifiers with different predictions achieving a correct result) can be solved using the vote method or by employing the estimated confidence of the base classifier. For this research, the classifiers used in the grading method are naïve Bayes, a Bayesian network taught with the TAN algorithm and, finally, kNN with k ranging from 1 to 5.
* Stacking: The stacking method [66] is another approach to combining classifiers that aims to improve the ensemble based on the cross-validation method. For the classification process, first, we carry out a query to the classifiers in level 0 (original classifiers). Second, once we obtain the answer from all of them, we apply the transformations of k numbers that produce the input dataset for level 1 (this is the result transformation step). Third, level 1 classifiers derive the solution. Finally, the response is transformed back into the level 0 space to provide the final result. The whole process is known as *stacked generalization* and can be further enhanced by adding multiple stacking levels. Again, and to enable comparisons of this method with grading, the classifiers used are naïve Bayes, a Bayesian network taught with the TAN algorithm and, finally, kNN with k ranging from 1 to 5.
* Multi scheme: This is a meta-classification method implemented by Weka [67] which allows for the combination of classifiers in a simple manner. This method employs a combination rule based on the results obtained via cross validation and the error rate measured as the mean square error from several classifiers.

- Testing the model: For each fold, first, we measured the accuracy of the model; in other words, how well the classifier performs in terms of correctly classified instances. Moreover, we also evaluated the error rate between the predicted value set X and the real value set Y (both having the size of the testing dataset m) with mean absolute error (MAE) (shown in Equation (1)).

$$\mathrm{MAE} = \frac{\sum_{i=1}^{n} |y_i - x_i|}{n} = \frac{\sum_{i=1}^{n} |e_i|}{n}. \quad (1)$$

Similarly, we used Root Mean Square Error (RMSE) (shown in Equation (2)).

$$RMSE = \frac{1}{n} \cdot \sqrt{\sum_{i=1}^{n} (y_i - \hat{y}_i)^2} \quad (2)$$

Finally, we also tested each model measuring the Area Under the ROC Curve (AUC) [68]. This ranges from 0 to 1, where 0.5 indicates random guessing and 1.0 indicates perfect classification. Higher AUC values indicate better model performance.

2.3. Retro-Feedback for Controlling and Adjusting the Manufacturing Parameters

With all the development carried out in this research, we have created an ex ante method to foresee several defects or characteristics in the investment casting manufacturing process. Throughout this research, several topics of discussion have emerged, and we have worked to address them. In particular, by using the classifiers as a stand-alone solution, (i) we cannot be completely sure that the selected classifier is the best one to generalize the manufacturing process, (ii) the learning algorithms employed for creating some of the machine learning classifiers only find a local maximum; hence, the final result is not optimal, and (iii) by using a single classifier, we should generate a classifier close to the process's nature (linear or non-linear). Hence, we solved all these problems by developing and testing several methods to combine heterogeneous classifiers, as explained in Section 2.2. This new approach was safer because we used all the classifiers instead of selecting just one, allowing us to approximate their behavior to the optimal one.

Nevertheless, although we were able to detect the problems using an ex ante method, we were not able to modify the plant parameters to solve them online. In fact, predicting the near-future situation $t + 1$ without the ability to address it will only provide us with the knowledge that we are producing faulty parts before they are evaluated. We will continue to face all the problems associated with these deviations, even though we are aware of their existence. Therefore, as the final part of the digital twin—and also the main component of the system—an advisory system for adjusting the process has been designed to close the loop.

The observation or data extraction process, along with its output tags, has allowed us to work on deriving the knowledge embedded in the data itself. This research has focused on creating an action recommender aimed at maintaining the system within the desired area, defined as standard or normal production. Thus, when the previously explained predictors detect an anomaly, the advisory system will begin working to find a way to redirect the process and prevent the occurrence of that problem.

In this way, to build this system, the knowledge was extracted in two different manners. On the one hand, we extract it from process engineers. This is a manual task that incorporates the gathered expert knowledge into the final system. On the other hand, some patterns were extracted as associative rules using the Tertius [69] algorithm. The module responsible for evaluation and recommendation generation will be aware of the current state of the process (information obtained from the observation of the digital twin), the predicted state the production will reach (predictions or simulations generated by the digital twin), and finally, the set points and limits within which the process must operate (provided by engineers). Once these data have been unified, the process will be automatically redirected to prevent the detected problem or deviation.

Sometimes, the recommendation system will focus on increasing or decreasing the working range of one or more variables. At other times, it will determine that it is better to start producing within new ranges, adjusting the limits of that variable to a new optimal production zone. This system aims to modify control ranges that have become obsolete or to discover new manufacturing trends that optimize the process, reduce scrap, and, consequently, increase productivity.

The generated adjustments in primary and secondary coatings affect the acceptance and control ranges of immersion baths and climatic conditions. Keep in mind that modifications will be made to variables that allow for actionable changes and can be adjusted with small additions. In cases of major modifications, the bath would need to be completely changed, which will not be applied in the current batch but will be considered for the next production. Optimizations in the melting area directly affect changes or adjustments to the chemical composition of the melt to ultimately achieve an optimized metal for casting.

In summary, the recommendation system takes the data for each recorded variable (those defined during the information gathering process detailed earlier) and evaluates them by combining the predictions of the classification models with the working ranges extracted through the learning that the system itself has developed for each variable. In this way, depending on the evolution of the recorded data concerning the output variables (specifically, porosity defects and the mechanical property of elongation), it provides recommendations. These recommendations focus on which variables should be adjusted and the direction of adjustment, whether increasing or decreasing their values. The system is supported by a concise expert system based on process knowledge, which is continuously adapted using the normality ranges detected during process data generation.

3. Results

Once the research work has been developed and the different solutions have been obtained for each of the challenges identified in Section 2, we describe the results achieved in this section. Each identified challenge is summarized in its specific subsection. However, in brief, the solutions to the three defined challenges in our methodology were satisfactory, providing insight into how this approach can assist in managing a production process as complex as investment casting.

3.1. Digitization and Manufacturing Process Representation

The first of the challenges identified through our "divide and conquer" methodology, defined in Section 2, is related to data extraction, digitization, and process representation. Hence, to address this challenge, different tasks were performed, achieving the following results.

Firstly, after the KPI identification—in other words, obtaining a list of areas and possibilities in data extraction tasks—a deep analysis was conducted. Specifically, this analysis focused on comparing and contrasting different manufacturing process areas to determine the feasibility of data capture. To this end, the frequency, accuracy of the data, visualization, capture and storage, access to the data, and their traceability in the different areas of the investment casting process were analyzed. The final results of this analysis are illustrated in Figure 6.

As shown in Figure 6, the lowest scores were observed in the "access to data" and "visualization" categories. The primary reason is that all related data are stored in complex tables, systems, or other sources that are not easily connected. Moreover, there is a lack of visualization tools to effectively distribute this information. Conversely, "frequency" and "accuracy" scored higher due to the rigorous testing procedures already established within the investment casting process for each area. This figure also guided the research team in selecting the areas to be included in this work regarding the measurements. In this way, primary and secondary coating, as well as the melting area and final inspections, were selected.

Secondly, taking into account the vast number of variables that could be extracted in each area, a new analysis was conducted to identify the final list of variables to prioritize. This analysis focused on the expected impact and digitization potential of each selected variable. A summary of these results is shown in Figure 7.

Figure 7 is a dispersion plot where the degree of simplicity in digitization is represented on the y-axis, and the impact of different variables is shown on the x-axis. Furthermore, each selected variable is categorized into stages, with each stage represented by a different color, as described in the legend. The legend refers to stages 1, 2, and 3, which can more accurately be translated as primary coating for stage 1, secondary coating for stage 2, and melting for stage 3.

After conducting this analysis and creating the plot, the variables to be used were selected in the following order. First, the variables that appear in the top-right corner were selected. These variables, from the three areas, are labeled as priority 1 variables and must be gathered in the first iteration of the data gathering work. Second, the variables that appear in the top-left corner, labeled as priority 2 variables, were selected for the second iteration of the process. Third, the variables that appear in the bottom-right corner were selected. Finally, the remaining variables were considered. Hence, this plot was useful for determining the strategy and work plan for data gathering and process representation.

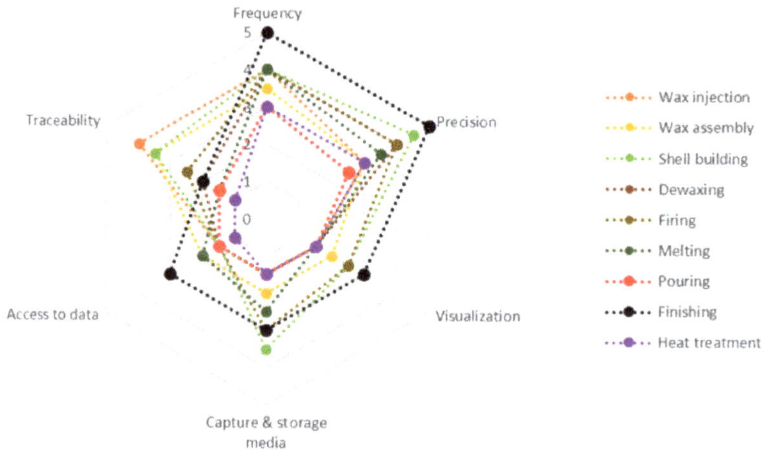

Figure 6. Start plot generated as a summary of results when the different areas were analyzed and evaluated using a Likert scale for 6 different categories such as data traceability, frequency, and precision, among others.

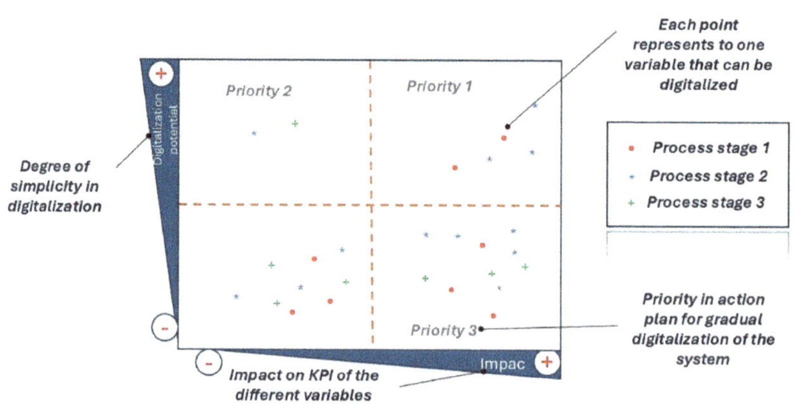

Figure 7. Dispersion plot with the selected area (i.e., primary coating—stage 1, secondary coating—stage 2, and melting—stage 3) correlating the impact, the digitization potential, and the priority of each variable to be added to the system.

Then, once the variables for each area and their priority were defined, the data extraction process was executed. As a result of this work, several visualization screens were created and distributed throughout the plant. These screens were designed in close collaboration with engineers and foundry workers to ensure that the information was displayed in the most effective way and in the correct locations. During this research, 25 screens were developed and distributed across different areas of the process.

The most important developed screens are those related to primary coating and secondary coating, as they handle the most critical variables of the process. With this data distribution and visualization system, anomalies can be detected quickly, facilitating prompt corrective actions. Some screens are shown in Figure 8. Image (a) in the figure displays the specific screen for primary coatings, while image (b) presents data extracted from the melting area. The users can navigate through the screens, and they also have an auto-navigation feature, displaying information in response to triggered events or in a cyclical visualization mode.

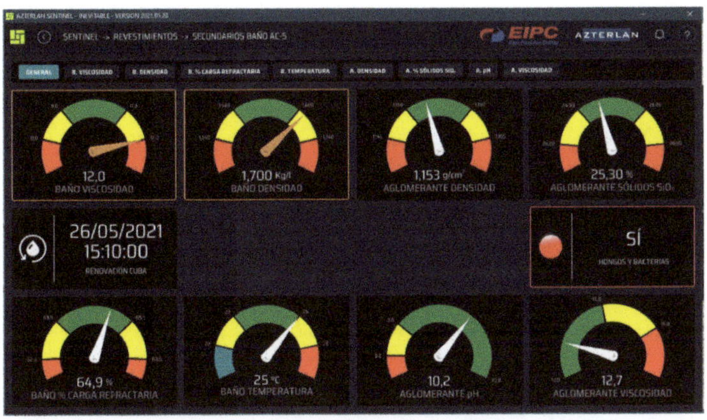

(a)

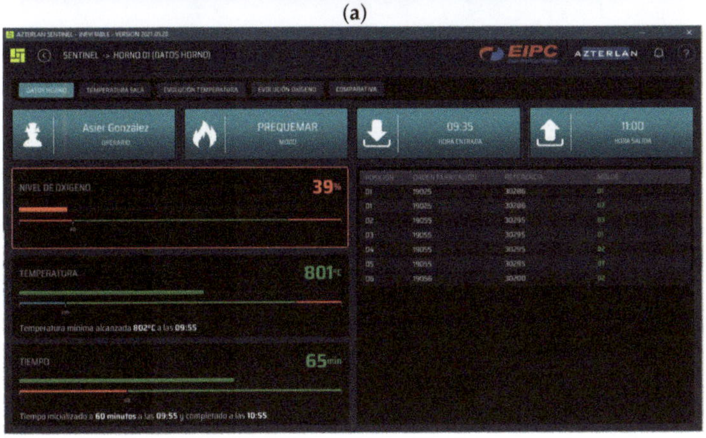

(b)

Figure 8. Generated screens for a Spanish investment casting foundry with Sentinel software v2023.06 to distribute the information over the investment casting plant. (**a**) Primary coating screen with data visualization and data evaluation under predefined limits. (**b**) Melting and furnace information provided by Sentinel in the investment casting process.

Finally, each designed data representation and its corresponding screen was distributed throughout the plant by installing multiple monitors. Figure 9 shows an example of two of these monitors displaying the information identified as critical in the area where the deployment was made.

Figure 9. Examples of Sentinel data distribution deployment over the investment casting plant.

3.2. *Proactive System Based on Predictions*

The second identified challenge focuses on the generation of the prediction system associated with the digital twin. As explained in Section 2.2, machine learning techniques, specifically supervised learning, are used since all gathered evidence is labeled with its corresponding output. Likewise, we worked on the development of predictive models associated with two different objectives: the first focused on predicting the mechanical property of elongation, and the second on predicting the appearance of porosities. Additionally, given that the prediction methodology is applied at three different stages, we trained and tested models that operate in the primary coating area, in the combination of primary and secondary coatings, and finally, in the melting area. Thus, these analyses were conducted first using classical classification models and then using meta-classification models to mitigate potential issues associated with classical models.

This section reports and describes the results that were obtained when the aforementioned predictive models were tested.

3.2.1. Prediction Models Applying Classical Machine Learning Methods

Once we conducted our research using classical machine learning methods, the following results were obtained. To facilitate readability, we have divided the results according to the classification area and then by the selected target.

Primary Coating Area Predictions

Regarding the results achieved by traditional classifiers using primary coating data to predict the elongation of the castings (see Table 1), it can be observed that the highest accuracy value was obtained by applying a kNN classifier with the value of $k = 2$. This classifier was able to achieve a fairly high level of accuracy of approximately 80%. However, the datasets for the learning phase could be enhanced. The rest of the classifiers provided good results, as most of them remain above 75% accuracy. In contrast, surprisingly, one of the SVMs, the one taught with the RBF kernel, did not exceed 60% accuracy. On the other hand, the Bayesian networks performed well, even improving the AUC value, which shows that the management between false positives and false negatives could be better when we use this algorithm.

Table 1. Results predicting the mechanical property elongation when we applied classical machine learning methods using data extracted only from the primary coating area. The best classifier, marked in gray, was the kNN with $k = 2$, with an accuracy level (percentage of correctly classified instances) close to 80%.

Classifier	Accuracy	MAE	RMSE	AUC
Bayes network (K2)	77.48	0.26	0.41	0.81
Bayes network (hill climber)	77.48	0.26	0.41	0.81
Bayes network (TAN)	76.00	0.35	0.43	0.76
Naïve Bayes	76.74	0.27	0.41	0.80
Artificial neural network MLP	71.64	0.34	0.48	0.70
Support vector machines (polynomial kernel)	77.36	0.23	0.43	0.77
Support vector machines (normalized polynomial kernel)	74.05	0.26	0.48	0.74
Support vector machines (Pearson VII)	74.26	0.26	0.47	0.74
Support vector machines (radial basis function)	59.33	0.41	0.63	0.63
Voted perceptron	73.79	0.26	0.47	0.78
K-nearest neighbors (K = 1)	74.55	0.34	0.47	0.71
K-nearest neighbors (K = 2)	79.71	0.32	0.41	0.79
K-nearest neighbors (K = 3)	77.60	0.36	0.43	0.75
K-nearest neighbors (K = 4)	77.74	0.36	0.43	0.75
K-nearest neighbors (K = 5)	76.86	0.36	0.43	0.76
K-nearest neighbors (K = 6)	76.86	0.36	0.43	0.76
C4.5	66.50	0.42	0.48	0.67
Random forest (num. iterations = 50)	75.50	0.34	0.44	0.73
Random forest (num. iterations = 100)	75.31	0.34	0.44	0.74
Random forest (num. iterations = 150)	75.17	0.34	0.44	0.73
Random forest (num. iterations = 200)	75.17	0.34	0.44	0.73
Random forest (num. iterations = 250)	75.50	0.34	0.44	0.73
Random forest (num. iterations = 300)	75.64	0.34	0.44	0.74
Random forest (num. iterations = 350)	75.31	0.34	0.44	0.74

Then, when the same data were used to predict the behavior of castings in terms of pore formation, an accuracy of 76% was achieved using the kNN algorithm. The optimal k value that gave the best results was $k = 1$. It seems that this defect is more difficult to foresee due to the majority of the results not exceeding 70% accuracy. Only one classifier, an artificial neural network, achieved results comparable to the kNN. Perhaps, applying a different type of network and increasing the number of epochs in the learning phase could improve performance. Table 2 summarizes the obtained results, including error rates, to facilitate comparisons between classifiers.

Table 2. Results predicting porosity apparition when we applied classical machine learning methods using data extracted only from the primary coating area. The best classifier, marked in gray, was the kNN with $k = 1$ with an accuracy level (percentage of correctly classified instances) close to 76%.

Classifier	Accuracy	MAE	RMSE	AUC
Bayes network (K2)	62.75	0.39	0.47	0.65
Bayes network (hill climber)	63.62	0.43	0.49	0.47
Bayes network (TAN)	67.07	0.37	0.46	0.68
Naïve Bayes	64.05	0.39	0.46	0.68
Artificial neural network MLP	74.98	0.27	0.41	0.77
Support vector machines (polynomial kernel)	58.46	0.42	0.64	0.44
Support vector machines (normalized polynomial kernel)	65.87	0.34	0.58	0.48
Support vector machines (Pearson VII)	75.43	0.25	0.47	0.64
Support vector machines (radial basis function)	68.75	0.31	0.56	0.50
Voted perceptron	64.04	0.36	0.58	0.61
K-nearest neighbors (K = 1)	75.73	0.32	0.44	0.71
K-nearest neighbors (K = 2)	74.52	0.35	0.45	0.66
K-nearest neighbors (K = 3)	66.09	0.40	0.47	0.56
K-nearest neighbors (K = 4)	67.04	0.40	0.47	0.57
K-nearest neighbors (K = 5)	65.86	0.40	0.46	0.61
K-nearest neighbors (K = 6)	65.62	0.40	0.46	0.64
C4.5	67.79	0.43	0.47	0.49
Random Forest (Num. Iterations = 50)	68.20	0.38	0.47	0.64
Random forest (num. iterations = 100)	69.05	0.38	0.47	0.64
Random forest (num. iterations = 150)	69.59	0.38	0.47	0.64
Random forest (num. iterations = 200)	68.79	0.38	0.47	0.64
Random forest (num. iterations = 250)	69.16	0.38	0.47	0.64
Random forest (num. iterations = 300)	68.62	0.38	0.47	0.65
Random forest (num. iterations = 350)	68.21	0.38	0.47	0.65

Primary and Secondary Coating Area Predictions

The following experiments, illustrated in Table 3, focused on predicting elongation using data from both primary and secondary coatings. The best classifier in this case was the Bayesian network trained with the K2 algorithm. However, when comparing these results with those obtained using only primary coating information, it appears that incorporating secondary coating data introduced noise, leading to a decrease in classifier performance. Again, another classifier that closely approaches the best performance is the MLP artificial neural network with backpropagation. Additionally, the SVM trained with the Pearson VII kernel achieved accuracy values nearly identical to the Bayesian network, differing by only a few decimals. All random forests performed similarly and were very close to the best SVM.

Table 3. Results predicting the mechanical property elongation when we applied classical machine learning methods using data extracted from both primary and secondary coating areas. The best classifier, marked in gray, was the Bayesian network learned taught with the K2 algorithm, with an accuracy level (percentage of correctly classified instances) close to 77%.

Classifier	Accuracy	MAE	RMSE	AUC
Bayes network (K2)	76.95	0.26	0.40	0.84
Bayes network (hill climber)	75.64	0.28	0.42	0.82
Bayes network (TAN)	72.24	0.31	0.43	0.80
Naïve Bayes	74.76	0.27	0.41	0.83

Table 3. *Cont.*

Classifier	Accuracy	MAE	RMSE	AUC
Artificial neural network MLP	75.21	0.27	0.43	0.82
Support vector machines (polynomial kernel)	72.52	0.27	0.49	0.73
Support vector machines (normalized polynomial kernel)	74.48	0.26	0.46	0.75
Support vector machines (Pearson VII)	76.79	0.23	0.44	0.77
Support vector machines (radial basis function)	73.93	0.26	0.47	0.75
Voted perceptron	72.57	0.27	0.48	0.80
K-nearest neighbors (K = 1)	65.79	0.32	0.50	0.74
K-nearest neighbors (K = 2)	66.05	0.33	0.44	0.78
K-nearest neighbors (K = 3)	68.60	0.36	0.43	0.78
K-nearest neighbors (K = 4)	69.50	0.36	0.44	0.78
K-nearest neighbors (K = 5)	69.50	0.36	0.44	0.78
K-nearest neighbors (K = 6)	72.55	0.36	0.43	0.78
C4.5	66.24	0.38	0.48	0.80
Random forest (num. iterations = 50)	74.10	0.34	0.42	0.80
Random forest (num. iterations = 100)	74.24	0.34	0.42	0.80
Random forest (num. iterations = 150)	74.38	0.34	0.42	0.79
Random forest (num. iterations = 200)	74.21	0.34	0.42	0.79
Random forest (num. iterations = 250)	74.36	0.34	0.42	0.79
Random forest (num. iterations = 300)	74.07	0.34	0.42	0.79
Random forest (num. iterations = 350)	74.05	0.34	0.42	0.79

Then, regarding the prediction of porosity formation using primary and secondary coating information, Table 4 summarizes the measured results. In this case, the best-performing classifier was kNN with a value of $k = 6$. Its accuracy was a 71%. As with the elongation prediction, we observe that introducing secondary coating data leads to a decline in results.In this case, there were only two classifiers that reached or exceed 70% accuracy, the aforementioned kNN with $k = 6$ and the voted perceptron.

Table 4. Results predicting porosity apparition when we applied classical machine learning methods using data extracted from both primary and secondary coating areas. The best classifier, marked in gray, was the kNN with $k = 6$ and an accuracy level (percentage of correctly classified instances) close to 71%.

Classifier	Accuracy	MAE	RMSE	AUC
Bayes network (K2)	66.36	0.39	0.45	0.66
Bayes network (hill climber)	63.50	0.44	0.49	0.49
Bayes network (TAN)	68.62	0.41	0.47	0.61
Naïve Bayes	68.80	0.39	0.45	0.68
Artificial neural network MLP	62.02	0.42	0.49	0.59
Support vector machines (polynomial kernel)	66.96	0.33	0.57	0.49
Support vector machines (normalized polynomial Kernel)	66.84	0.33	0.57	0.51
Support vector machines (Pearson VII)	67.93	0.32	0.55	0.56
Support vector machines (radial basis function)	68.75	0.31	0.56	0.50
Voted perceptron	70.09	0.30	0.53	0.66
K-nearest neighbors (K = 1)	69.55	0.39	0.48	0.63
K-nearest neighbors (K = 2)	69.84	0.39	0.48	0.63
K-nearest neighbors (K = 3)	69.84	0.40	0.48	0.62
K-nearest neighbors (K = 4)	69.84	0.41	0.47	0.62

Table 4. *Cont.*

Classifier	Accuracy	MAE	RMSE	AUC
K-nearest neighbors (K = 5)	69.84	0.41	0.47	0.64
K-nearest neighbors (K = 6)	71.48	0.41	0.47	0.65
C4.5	63.91	0.45	0.48	0.46
Random forest (num. iterations = 50)	65.66	0.41	0.47	0.62
Random forest (num. iterations = 100)	66.20	0.41	0.47	0.62
Random forest (num. iterations = 150)	66.48	0.41	0.47	0.62
Random forest (num. iterations = 200)	67.04	0.41	0.47	0.62
Random forest (num. iterations = 250)	67.45	0.41	0.47	0.61
Random forest (num. iterations = 300)	66.91	0.41	0.47	0.61
Random forest (num. iterations = 350)	67.34	0.41	0.47	0.61

Primary, Secondary Coatings and Melting Area Predictions

Finally, using the complete dataset (i.e., data from the three selected areas), the accuracy of the classical machine learning models was tested. First, we extracted the results for elongation prediction, which are shown in Table 5. With the full dataset, the classifiers once again approximated their results to those obtained when only primary coating data were included in the predictive models. In this experiment, we observe that the best classifier, kNN with $k = 6$, is able to match or even outperform the best classifier from the first analysis (another kNN, but in that case with $k = 2$). Comparing the other classifiers, they achieved similar accuracy levels and, in fact, were close to the results obtained when using other subsets of information for their learning phase. Although the best result was obtained with the full dataset (including data from all three areas), it is not certain that the performance of the classifiers improves when using the complete dataset. This leads us to conclude that, in predicting the elongation of a part at a future state $t + 1$, the primary coating stage is the most influential factor affecting the final behavior of this mechanical property.

Table 5. Results predicting the mechanical property elongation when we applied classical machine learning methods using data extracted from both primary and secondary coating areas in addition to melting data. The best classifier, marked in gray, was the kNN with $k = 6$, achieving an accuracy level (percentage of correctly classified instances) close to 80%.

Classifier	Accuracy	MAE	RMSE	AUC
Bayes network (K2)	73.83	0.29	0.40	0.83
Bayes network (hill climber)	73.45	0.33	0.43	0.79
Bayes network (TAN)	76.52	0.30	0.40	0.81
Naïve Bayes	75.93	0.29	0.39	0.83
Artificial neural network MLP	73.98	0.28	0.44	0.79
Support vector machines (polynomial kernel)	71.48	0.29	0.50	0.72
Support vector machines (normalized polynomial kernel)	75.62	0.24	0.44	0.76
Support vector machines (Pearson VII)	72.93	0.27	0.48	0.73
Support vector machines (radial basis function)	60.38	0.40	0.61	0.64
Voted perceptron	72.69	0.27	0.47	0.80
K-nearest neighbors (K = 1)	72.07	0.36	0.50	0.68
K-nearest neighbors (K = 2)	73.93	0.37	0.46	0.75
K-nearest neighbors (K = 3)	78.83	0.36	0.43	0.81

Table 5. *Cont.*

Classifier	Accuracy	MAE	RMSE	AUC
K-nearest neighbors (K = 4)	79.67	0.36	0.42	0.82
K-nearest neighbors (K = 5)	79.24	0.35	0.41	0.83
K-nearest neighbors (K = 6)	80.29	0.35	0.41	0.84
C4.5	65.43	0.41	0.49	0.68
Random forest (num. iterations = 50)	72.62	0.35	0.43	0.81
Random forest (num. iterations = 100)	72.90	0.34	0.43	0.81
Random forest (num. iterations = 150)	72.79	0.34	0.43	0.81
Random forest (num. iterations = 200)	72.33	0.34	0.43	0.81
Random forest (num. iterations = 250)	72.19	0.34	0.43	0.81
Random forest (num. iterations = 300)	72.19	0.35	0.43	0.81
Random forest (num. iterations = 350)	72.19	0.35	0.43	0.81

Second, we tested how well the models performed in predicting the appearance of porosities. Considering all the results achieved using the three different datasets, we can confirm that ex ante detection of this problem is more complex than predicting elongation. Additionally, when analyzing the results in Table 6, we observed once again that data from the secondary coating and melting stages introduced noise and negatively affected classifier performance. In this case, the naïve Bayes classifier achieved the best results, surpassing the kNN with $k = 1$ from the first analysis, which used only primary coating data.

Table 6. Results predicting porosity apparition when we applied classical machine learning methods using data extracted from both primary and secondary coating areas in addition to melting data. The best classifier, marked in gray, was naïve Bayes giving an accuracy level (percentage of correctly classified instances) of close to 70%.

Classifier	Accuracy	MAE	RMSE	AUC
Bayes network (K2)	69.45	0.39	0.45	0.66
Bayes network (hill climber)	66.14	0.44	0.49	0.49
Bayes network (TAN)	65.80	0.41	0.47	0.61
Naïve Bayes	70.55	0.41	0.46	0.62
Artificial neural network MLP	67.32	0.42	0.48	0.56
Support vector machines (polynomial kernel)	68.46	0.32	0.56	0.50
Support vector machines (normalized polynomial kernel)	66.93	0.33	0.57	0.49
Support vector machines (Pearson VII)	64.04	0.36	0.59	0.51
Support vector machines (radial basis function)	68.75	0.31	0.56	0.50
Voted perceptron	66.80	0.33	0.56	0.61
K-nearest neighbors (K = 1)	68.68	0.43	0.48	0.54
K-nearest neighbors (K = 2)	68.68	0.43	0.48	0.54
K-nearest neighbors (K = 3)	68.68	0.43	0.48	0.55
K-nearest neighbors (K = 4)	68.68	0.42	0.47	0.59
K-nearest neighbors (K = 5)	68.68	0.42	0.47	0.59
K-nearest neighbors (K = 6)	68.68	0.42	0.47	0.60
C4.5	66.91	0.44	0.47	0.49
Random forest (num. iterations = 50)	67.04	0.43	0.48	0.55
Random forest (num. iterations = 100)	67.05	0.42	0.48	0.55
Random forest (num. iterations = 150)	67.29	0.42	0.48	0.54
Random forest (num. iterations = 200)	67.04	0.42	0.48	0.54
Random forest (num. iterations = 250)	66.77	0.42	0.48	0.54
Random forest (num. iterations = 300)	67.05	0.42	0.48	0.54
Random forest (num. iterations = 350)	66.64	0.42	0.48	0.54

3.2.2. Prediction Models Applying Meta-Classifiers

After the previous work testing the performance of classical classifiers, we continued our research to analyze and understand the behavior of predictions when using meta-classifiers. In summary, the use of these algorithms aims to mitigate the issues related to testing and selecting classifiers for each target. Although they do not necessarily achieve better results, they stabilize the prediction processes. Next, we describe the measurements conducted in the prediction steps associated with each grouped dataset and both targets, namely elongation and porosity occurrence.

Primary Coating Area Predictions

In the first experiment, focused on predicting elongation, we reproduced the previous experiments using the same dataset from the primary coating area to perform meta-classification-based predictions (see results in Table 7). In this case, we observe that, in general, the process remains fairly stable, with most algorithms achieving an accuracy of around 75%. This corroborates the expected performance of meta-classification algorithms. Specifically, the method that obtained the best results was grading using a C4.5 decision tree, achieving an accuracy of 76%, very close to the best classical classifier, which reached 79%. On the other hand, while grading is a more complex method compared to others, the simpler majority voting approach still achieved a notable accuracy of 75%. In fact, it performed almost as well as the best meta-classification method while offering the advantage of a simpler model combination approach.

Table 7. Results predicting mechanical property elongation when we applied a combination of classical machine learning methods through a meta-classifier using data extracted only from the primary coating area. The best meta-classifier, marked in gray, was the grading method using a C4.5 decision tree for the combination with an accuracy level (percentage of correctly classified instances) of close to 76%.

Classifier	Accuracy	MAE	RMSE	AUC
By vote (minimum probability)	50.02	0.20	0.36	0.68
By vote (maximum probability)	68.40	0.41	0.45	0.77
By vote (average of probabilities)	74.74	0.33	0.42	0.78
By vote (product of probabilities)	50.02	0.20	0.36	0.68
By vote (majority voting)	75.48	0.25	0.46	0.76
Grading (meta: naïve Bayes)	75.74	0.24	0.46	0.76
Grading (Bayes network–TAN)	74.62	0.25	0.47	0.75
Grading (meta: K-nearest neighbors with K = 1)	75.02	0.25	0.47	0.75
Grading (Meta: K-nearest neighbors with K = 2)	75.17	0.25	0.46	0.75
Grading (Meta: K-nearest neighbors with K = 3)	75.02	0.25	0.46	0.75
Grading (Meta: K-nearest neighbors with K = 4)	75.02	0.25	0.46	0.75
Grading (Meta: K-nearest neighbors with K = 5)	75.02	0.25	0.46	0.75
Grading (C4.5)	76.07	0.24	0.45	0.76
Stacking (meta: naïve Bayes)	75.33	0.25	0.46	0.80
Stacking (Bayes network–TAN)	74.67	0.27	0.44	0.77
Stacking (meta: K-nearest neighbors with K = 1)	73.40	0.28	0.48	0.73
Stacking (meta: K-nearest neighbors with K = 2)	70.19	0.31	0.47	0.73
Stacking (meta: K-nearest neighbors with K = 3)	71.17	0.32	0.46	0.75
Stacking (meta: K-nearest neighbors with K = 4)	73.52	0.32	0.44	0.76
Stacking (meta: K-nearest neighbors with K = 5)	73.50	0.33	0.44	0.78
Stacking (C4.5)	72.90	0.31	0.46	0.74
Multi-scheme (Bayes network–TAN)	72.07	0.33	0.48	0.70

Then, using the same dataset, integrating only the primary coating data, we performed the same evaluation to predict the behavior of the manufactured castings in terms of porosity formation. In this experiment (results shown in Table 8), we observed that the best method was multi-scheme, a fairly simple approach that achieved 75% accuracy. This result is comparable to that obtained by the classical unary classifiers analyzed earlier. In any case, when seeking the simplest combination method, classification by majority voting performed very similarly to the best of the combination methods. It should also be noted that the most stable method was grading, as every model achieved close to 75% accuracy. However, in the case of Stacking, we observed fluctuations, with accuracy results ranging between 60% and 73%.

Table 8. Results predicting the porosity apparition when we applied a combination of classical machine learning methods through a meta-classifier using data extracted only from the primary coating area. The best meta-classifier, marked in gray, was the multi-scheme method using a TAN Bayesian network with an accuracy level (percentage of correctly classified instances) of close to 75%.

Classifier	Accuracy	MAE	RMSE	AUC
By vote (minimum probability)	54.62	0.25	0.46	0.58
By vote (maximum probability)	68.75	0.43	0.45	0.67
By vote (average of probabilities)	72.32	0.37	0.44	0.70
By vote (product of probabilities)	54.62	0.25	0.46	0.58
By vote (majority voting)	71.52	0.28	0.52	0.58
Grading (meta: naïve Bayes)	71.50	0.28	0.52	0.59
Grading (Bayes network–TAN)	70.77	0.29	0.52	0.59
Grading (meta: K-nearest neighbors with K = 1)	71.07	0.29	0.52	0.59
Grading (meta: K-nearest neighbors with K = 2)	71.07	0.29	0.52	0.59
Grading (meta: K-nearest neighbors with K = 3)	70.39	0.30	0.53	0.57
Grading (meta: K-nearest neighbors with K = 4)	70.66	0.29	0.53	0.57
Grading (meta: K-nearest neighbors with K = 5)	70.80	0.29	0.53	0.57
Grading (C4.5)	70.84	0.29	0.53	0.57
Stacking (meta: naïve Bayes)	61.87	0.38	0.58	0.71
Stacking (Bayes network–TAN)	69.73	0.40	0.47	0.56
Stacking (meta: K-nearest neighbors with K = 1)	66.12	0.35	0.55	0.61
Stacking (meta: K-nearest neighbors with K = 2)	72.39	0.34	0.49	0.63
Stacking (meta: K-nearest neighbors with K = 3)	69.12	0.35	0.47	0.65
Stacking (meta: K-nearest neighbors with K = 4)	73.82	0.36	0.46	0.64
Stacking (meta: K-nearest neighbors with K = 5)	72.12	0.36	0.45	0.64
Stacking (C4.5)	69.18	0.34	0.49	0.62
Multi-scheme (Bayes network–TAN)	75.62	0.28	0.42	0.76

Primary and Secondary Coating Area Predictions

As the second phase of the experiment for the ex ante predictive system in the investment casting process, following the same approach as with the classical classifiers, we concatenated the information from the primary and secondary coatings to perform elongation prediction. In this new test (shown in Table 9), we achieved accuracy ratios very similar to those obtained with simple classifiers. In fact, the best algorithm was the "by vote" method, which employs the mean of probabilities. Its accuracy was 76.5%, nearly matching the 76.95% achieved with the corresponding Bayesian network. Thus, in search of an even simpler method than the one that produced the best results, the majority voting method again performed comparably to the best meta-classification algorithm. Once again, grading proved to be the most stable method, as indicated by its precision percentages and error rates, all of which followed a consistent performance trend.

Table 9. Results predicting the mechanical property elongation when we applied a combination of classical machine learning methods through a meta-classifier using data extracted from both primary and secondary coating areas. The best meta-classifier, marked in gray, was by vote through the average of probabilities, with an accuracy level (percentage of correctly classified instances) of close to 77%.

Classifier	Accuracy	MAE	RMSE	AUC
By vote (minimum probability)	63.00	0.19	0.35	0.75
By vote (maximum probability)	73.83	0.40	0.43	0.81
By vote (average of probabilities)	76.50	0.31	0.40	0.83
By vote (product of probabilities)	63.00	0.19	0.35	0.75
By vote (majority voting)	74.95	0.25	0.46	0.75
Grading (meta: naïve Bayes)	73.86	0.26	0.47	0.74
Grading (Bayes network–TAN)	74.05	0.26	0.47	0.74
Grading (meta: K-nearest neighbors with K = 1)	74.12	0.26	0.47	0.74
Grading (meta: K-nearest neighbors with K = 2)	72.60	0.27	0.49	0.73
Grading (meta: K-nearest neighbors with K = 3)	73.14	0.27	0.48	0.73
Grading (meta: K-nearest neighbors with K = 4)	73.00	0.27	0.48	0.73
Grading (meta: K-nearest neighbors with K = 5)	73.29	0.27	0.48	0.73
Grading (C4.5)	74.17	0.26	0.47	0.74
Stacking (meta: naïve Bayes)	75.12	0.25	0.46	0.80
Stacking (Bayes network–TAN)	70.05	0.30	0.48	0.77
Stacking (meta: K-nearest neighbors with K = 1)	67.29	0.33	0.53	0.68
Stacking (meta: K-nearest neighbors with K = 2)	66.86	0.33	0.48	0.72
Stacking (meta: K-nearest neighbors with K = 3)	68.90	0.33	0.46	0.74
Stacking (meta: K-nearest neighbors with K = 4)	70.05	0.33	0.45	0.76
Stacking (meta: K-nearest neighbors with K = 5)	72.00	0.33	0.44	0.77
Stacking (C4.5)	66.21	0.36	0.52	0.65
Multi-scheme (Bayes network–TAN)	74.67	0.25	0.44	0.77

Subsequently, performing the same experiment but now focusing on detecting the appearance of shrinkages, we observed that the theoretical basis described in Section 2.2 was correct. The results shown in Table 10 illustrate how the meta-classifiers approximate the performance of the best single classical classifier. The "by vote" method (using the mean of probabilities) achieved almost the same performance as the kNN classifier in the original experiment. Moreover, methods such as majority voting, a simple union model, practically match these results, offering a success rate of 70%. Although it achieved a slightly lower accuracy, grading remained the most stable method. In contrast, stacking did not perform as well as the other methods, suggesting that it is not well suited for this specific case.

Table 10. Results predicting the porosity apparition when we applied a combination of classical machine learning methods through a meta-classifier using data extracted from both primary and secondary coating areas. The best meta-classifier, marked in gray, was by vote through the average of probabilities, with an accuracy level (percentage of correctly classified instances) of close to 71%.

Classifier	Accuracy	MAE	RMSE	AUC
By vote (minimum probability)	59.91	0.28	0.52	0.56
By vote (maximum probability)	68.75	0.42	0.46	0.60
By vote (average of probabilities)	71.27	0.39	0.47	0.63
By vote (product of probabilities)	59.91	0.28	0.52	0.56
By vote (majority voting)	69.80	0.30	0.54	0.58
Grading (meta: naïve Bayes)	70.12	0.30	0.53	0.58
Grading (Bayes network–TAN)	70.84	0.29	0.52	0.59
Grading (meta: K-nearest neighbors with K = 1)	70.27	0.30	0.53	0.59

Table 10. *Cont.*

Classifier	Accuracy	MAE	RMSE	AUC
Grading (meta: K-nearest neighbors with K = 2)	70.27	0.30	0.53	0.59
Grading (meta: K-nearest neighbors with K = 3)	70.27	0.30	0.53	0.59
Grading (meta: K-nearest neighbors with K = 4)	70.27	0.30	0.53	0.59
Grading (meta: K-nearest neighbors with K = 5)	70.27	0.30	0.53	0.59
Grading (C4.5)	69.37	0.31	0.54	0.58
Stacking (meta: naïve Bayes)	50.96	0.49	0.67	0.58
Stacking (Bayes network–TAN)	68.32	0.43	0.47	0.49
Stacking (meta: K-nearest neighbors with K = 1)	62.59	0.40	0.57	0.55
Stacking (meta: K-nearest neighbors with K = 2)	65.55	0.42	0.54	0.54
Stacking (meta: K-nearest neighbors with K = 3)	62.34	0.41	0.51	0.57
Stacking (meta: K-nearest neighbors with K = 4)	65.45	0.41	0.50	0.57
Stacking (meta: K-nearest neighbors with K = 5)	63.25	0.43	0.50	0.56
Stacking (C4.5)	59.12	0.44	0.55	0.52
Multi-scheme (Bayes network–TAN)	62.62	0.41	0.49	0.61

Primary, Secondary Coatings and Melting Area Predictions

Continuing, when we applied data from the three identified stages, we analyzed the prediction of elongation. The obtained results are shown in Table 11. In this experiment, the meta-classification methods were unable to achieve the same performance ratios as the classical ones. In this evaluation, once again, grading proved to be the most stable algorithm, obtaining very similar accuracy values across all tested methods, as well as consistent error-handling measurements. Nevertheless, it is surprising that for this prediction task and dataset, the highest-rated algorithm was one of those created using stacking. It appears to have been better at managing the noise introduced by the addition of new information. Despite this, grading remained close behind. Later, in search of a simpler approach, we re-evaluated the simplest algorithms, such as majority voting. This method performed only three percentage points below the best meta-classification method, which is acceptable given the simplification it provides.

Table 11. Results predicting the mechanical property elongation when we applied a combination of classical machine learning methods through a meta-classifier using data extracted from both primary and secondary coating areas in addition to melting data. The best meta-classifier, marked in gray, was the stacking method using a TAN Bayesian network for combining the results, with an accuracy level (percentage of correctly classified instances) of close to 77%.

Classifier	Accuracy	MAE	RMSE	AUC
By vote (minimum probability)	48.79	0.19	0.34	0.67
By vote (maximum probability)	69.74	0.41	0.45	0.80
By vote (average of probabilities)	73.17	0.33	0.41	0.82
By vote (product of probabilities)	48.79	0.19	0.34	0.67
By vote (majority voting)	73.64	0.26	0.47	0.74
Grading (meta: naïve Bayes)	74.55	0.25	0.46	0.75
Grading (Bayes network–TAN)	74.21	0.26	0.47	0.74
Grading (meta: K-nearest neighbors with K = 1)	74.07	0.26	0.46	0.74
Grading (meta: K-nearest neighbors with K = 2)	73.43	0.27	0.48	0.73
Grading (meta: K-nearest neighbors with K = 3)	73.71	0.26	0.47	0.74
Grading (meta: K-nearest neighbors with K = 4)	74.02	0.26	0.47	0.74
Grading (meta: K-nearest neighbors with K = 5)	74.45	0.26	0.46	0.74
Grading (C4.5)	74.48	0.26	0.46	0.74

Table 11. *Cont.*

Classifier	Accuracy	MAE	RMSE	AUC
Stacking (meta: naïve Bayes)	73.67	0.26	0.47	0.83
Stacking (Bayes network–TAN)	76.83	0.26	0.42	0.80
Stacking (meta: K-nearest neighbors with K = 1)	70.21	0.30	0.50	0.71
Stacking (meta: K-nearest neighbors with K = 2)	71.26	0.31	0.47	0.75
Stacking (meta: K-nearest neighbors with K = 3)	74.24	0.31	0.45	0.76
Stacking (meta: K-nearest neighbors with K = 4)	76.43	0.32	0.44	0.77
Stacking (meta: K-nearest neighbors with K = 5)	75.81	0.32	0.43	0.78
Stacking (C4.5)	70.52	0.33	0.48	0.70
Multi-scheme (Bayes network–TAN)	71.10	0.30	0.46	0.78

Then, the final work focused on meta-classification algorithms using the complete dataset to predict the occurrence of shrinkages. Table 12 summarizes all gathered results. Recalling that the best classical classifier was naïve Bayes with a success rate of 70.55%, in this experiment, we obtained values close to 69% when using the by vote method under the maximum probability algorithm. For this prediction use case, all the algorithms performed very similarly. Thus, both simple and complex algorithms demonstrated their ability to perform the prediction task at comparable levels. In fact, the majority voting method produced results nearly identical to those of the best meta-classification method and even the best-performing classification algorithm. Once again, this experiment reinforces that meta-classification could be a viable option for mitigating the challenges associated with classical machine learning algorithms.

Table 12. Results predicting the porosity apparition when we applied a combination of classical machine learning methods through a meta-classifier using data extracted from both primary and secondary coating areas in addition to melting data. The best meta-classifier, marked in gray, was the by vote under maximum probability method, with an accuracy level (percentage of correctly classified instances) of close to 69%.

Classifier	Accuracy	MAE	RMSE	AUC
By vote (minimum probability)	59.30	0.30	0.54	0.51
By vote (maximum probability)	68.75	0.42	0.46	0.57
By vote (average of probabilities)	65.14	0.41	0.47	0.57
By vote (product of probabilities)	59.30	0.30	0.54	0.51
By vote (majority voting)	68.41	0.32	0.55	0.60
Grading (meta: naïve Bayes)	67.46	0.33	0.56	0.57
Grading (Bayes network–TAN)	65.95	0.34	0.58	0.55
Grading (meta: K-nearest neighbors with K = 1)	67.73	0.32	0.56	0.58
Grading (meta: K-nearest neighbors with K = 2)	67.73	0.32	0.56	0.58
Grading (meta: K-nearest neighbors with K = 3)	68.02	0.32	0.56	0.58
Grading (meta: K-nearest neighbors with K = 4)	68.02	0.32	0.56	0.58
Grading (meta: K-nearest neighbors with K = 5)	68.02	0.32	0.56	0.58
Grading (C4.5)	65.82	0.34	0.58	0.54
Stacking (meta: naïve Bayes)	63.34	0.37	0.57	0.53
Stacking (Bayes network–TAN)	68.59	0.43	0.46	0.50
Stacking (meta: K-nearest neighbors with K = 1)	66.29	0.37	0.53	0.58
Stacking (meta: K-nearest neighbors with K = 2)	67.54	0.38	0.51	0.55
Stacking (meta: K-nearest neighbors with K = 3)	66.62	0.39	0.51	0.54
Stacking (meta: K-nearest neighbors with K = 4)	67.05	0.39	0.50	0.53
Stacking (meta: K-nearest neighbors with K = 5)	68.12	0.39	0.50	0.55
Stacking (C4.5)	63.25	0.42	0.51	0.54
Multi-scheme (Bayes network–TAN)	67.66	0.42	0.47	0.58

Finally, it should be noted that the models used in this study do not require high computational costs. To enhance the readability of this paper, a brief summary is provided below instead of presenting all the detailed tables. For classical classifiers, training times do not exceed 0.09 s per fold (in the case of ANN with MLP), while testing times do not even reach 0.0003 s. In the case of meta-classifiers, learning times are higher, reaching about 3 s per fold in the worst cases (i.e., using grading). However, testing times do not exceed 0.01 s. These results indicate that these predictors could be used in a real-time solution.

3.3. Retro-Feedback for Controlling and Adjusting the Manufacturing Parameters

As presented in Section 2.3, a system responsible for detecting anomalies must complement a system designed to optimize the process by eliminating the detected problems. Thus, the same section explains how this element of our system of systems completes the described digital twin, closing the loop and providing feedback to the plant to implement the proposed corrective actions.

After the study conducted on anomaly detection based on predictions using machine learning models (see the previous section), we observed that detection works best in the primary coating stage. Nevertheless, the system was not modified, and all checks are still being performed. Thus, when any anomaly is detected in the first stage, attempts will be made to resolve it. In some cases, the issue may be corrected, while in others, the problem may persist. In the latter case, the current situation is continuously analyzed in subsequent detection and optimization steps. Otherwise, if no failures are found in that stage and the process advances to the next one, the digital twin will perform the checking operation again, continuing this cycle until all validation checkpoints have been passed.

It should be noted that the importance of this area could change due to modifications in the depth of the learning dataset. Similarly, the recommendations generated could also change depending on the requirements at that time. Even so, the system will need to adapt to new production references and emerging trends. This concludes that the recommendation system must evolve and be adjusted to the changing cycle of a manufacturing process.

The error rates of the production process where this technology has been deployed are low, not exceeding 12% of the produced parts. Considering the original number of faulty castings, the artificial intelligence-based detection system identified 84% of them in the first stage (primary coating). Practically all of these were subsequently resolved by the recommender system. Thus, in the following checks, the parts remained correct and successfully completed the manufacturing process. A small portion, less than 7% of the detections, progressed to the subsequent checkpoints, where some were detected again and corrected. The proposed corrections generated by the recommender system validated that the production limits defined by engineers were appropriate and that adjusting all parameters to those limits was sufficient to address the detected problems. However, in 2% of cases where a change was triggered, it was necessary to adapt the production ranges to optimize the expected manufactured parts. Consequently, for the same reference, different production levels or trends were required depending on the specific production parameters of each part.

In the same way, and in an effort to evaluate the computational cost of the advisor system, we measured that the results are computed in less than 0.001 s. Thus, the combination of predictions with optimization does not exceed 1 second. This fact enables the complete proposed system to be used in a real-time investment casting production process.

In summary, it is a promising system that can be modified in both knowledge and techniques, providing better performance. Nevertheless, the current development has reduced casting rejections to 8%. Moreover, at this moment, aluminum elongation has improved, increasing from 3.5% to 4.5%. Hence, despite the good results obtained, we must point out that since the accuracy of the prediction systems is not as high as desired, some faulty parts remain undetected. However, it is important to consider that the system is still in its early stages and does not yet have large volumes of data for training these learning processes. Improving the detection and prediction systems will directly lead to better early detection and more effective application of the corrective actions generated by our recommender system.

4. Discussion and Conclusions

The investment casting production process generates parts for industries such as aeronautics, where high levels of precision and quality are required. Thus, many research efforts focus on developing tools to mitigate these types of problems. To that end, this research aims to address two of the most critical defects. On the one hand, it focuses on mitigating the appearance of porosities. On the other hand, it works to ensure that elongation values remain within the predefined desired ranges. The contributions made by the research team to achieve the previously described objective are listed below.

First of all, to achieve the aforementioned objectives, the research team worked on improving digitization and reality representation in a digital environment. Specifically, the tasks carried out were guided by a data analysis plan that included: (i) the identification of available data and data that, although initially unavailable, could later be digitized and extracted, (ii) an audit of the status of each area and its variables, (iii) a study of the impact and priority of the areas and their respective variables, and (iv) the creation of a centralized data repository for storing captured data. This last task was accomplished using an agent-based system such as PDManager.

Later, all retrieved data should be exploited. Hence, the first step was to create a low-maturity-level digital twin focused on remote visualization and monitoring. To achieve this, we worked on defining what data should be displayed, when it should be displayed, to whom, and in what manner. This work was translated into the definition of the message communication protocol for information distribution, the design, and the creation of 25 different dashboard screens. Finally, these designed screens were installed in the plant to be useful for workers.

Then, the digital twin was evolved to a higher degree of maturity to operate proactively rather than reactively. The new system integrates simulation and optimization tasks. The simulation, in other words, the predictions, was performed using machine learning. Specifically, supervised learning algorithms were used, as the data gathering process provided labeled output variables for the final prediction. In this research, an extensive analysis was conducted, first evaluating classical unary statistical classifiers and then applying meta-classification algorithms to mitigate the issues associated with traditional classifiers. The results achieved were consistent with the literature. In other words, meta-classifiers performed their predictions as effectively as unary classifiers, achieving accuracy percentages very close to classical methods while avoiding their inherent limitations.

Regarding the optimization process, an advisor system was created using the extracted knowledge of the process. Part of that knowledge was manually gathered from workers and engineers, while the other part was automatically generated from the already collected data. This optimization tool is triggered when the aforementioned predictors detect a critical situation. Once the tool is launched, the calculation process begins to determine the best corrective action if needed, and finally, the recommended actions are communicated to the workers.

Although the results obtained are very promising, we have identified some shortcomings, which are discussed below.

- Amount of data: As the system was developed during this research, the datasets used for the artificial intelligence learning process were small. The ways to address this limitation are: (i) waiting for the dataset to grow as the foundry continues production or (ii) generating synthetic data using techniques such as Monte Carlo simulations [70] or the application of Generative Adversarial Networks (GANs) [71]. Hence, it is expected that when the data quantity increases, the prediction and optimization results will be better. In fact, as is described in [72], as data grow and evolve, a methodology must be implemented to ensure that machine learning models are developed, tested, and deployed in a consistent and reliable manner. Currently, this methodology is not yet defined, making it one of the key areas for future work.
- Accuracy of prediction models: The accuracy achieved by the models was not high. First, the problem may be related to the volume of the datasets. This has already been discussed in the previous point. On the other hand, accuracy may be improved by using newer models, such as deep neural networks [73]. Therefore, future work should focus on identifying better machine learning models capable of representing the manufacturing process more accurately. Moreover, readers must consider that achieving a high accuracy level in machine learning models is subjective. In fact, while accuracy measurements between 70% and 90% may not be ideal, they are realistic, as the current process and workers are not capable of consistently reaching such levels of precision.
- Simple optimization algorithms: Optimization and planning problems are among the most complex in the field of artificial intelligence. For this reason, and given that this research focused on developing an initial prototype, we decided to implement a simple recommendation system based on basic algorithms. However, incorporating new algorithms [74] could enhance the feedback provided to the plant. Additionally, if a computational bottleneck is detected, it may be possible to develop a hybrid system capable of executing quantum optimization algorithms [75] and subsequently processing them using conventional programming techniques.
- Reduced optimization objectives: This work was done to optimize a defect and a mechanical property. However, there are many more defects and many more mechanical properties [5] that should be added in a further research.
- Adaptation to new production trends and changes in manufacturing parameters: Classification systems may become obsolete over time due to changes in manufacturing processes. This is particularly relevant when systems must quickly adapt to different types of data and new castings. The main limitation of traditional classifiers is that they cannot autonomously adjust when receiving new information. To address this challenge, an approach based on continuous learning is proposed, where old models are replaced by new ones, iteratively adapting to changes. A key technique for this process is "sample aging of data" (as a fading factor), which assigns greater weight to new evidence, compensating for the reduced representativeness of older samples. One possible approach is the use of Bayesian compression and Monte Carlo methods to integrate old and new data, enabling the rapid development of new models that achieve higher accuracy. This process facilitates continuous updates and improves state prediction in dynamic systems [76,77]. On the other hand, techniques such as reinforcement learning could provide a solution by adjusting models based on real outcomes observed during the production process [78].

The problems listed and the possible solutions described define the future work to be developed in order to ultimately achieve the most advanced digital twin possible. The desired solution will not only address the issues identified in this research but also many other challenges present in the production process.

Author Contributions: Conceptualization, D.G., J.N. and P.P.R.; methodology, J.N.; software, J.N. and J.A.-P.; validation, D.G., J.N. and P.P.R.; investigation, D.G., J.N., J.A.-P. and F.S.; data curation, D.G. and P.P.R.; writing—original draft preparation, J.N., D.G., J.A.-P. and P.P.R.; writing—review and editing, J.N. and D.G.; project administration, F.S. and P.P.R.; funding acquisition, F.S. and P.P.R. All authors have read and agreed to the published version of the manuscript.

Funding: This research is part of the INEVITABLE project, which has received funding from the European Union's Horizon 2020 research and innovation programme under grant agreement no. 869815.

Institutional Review Board Statement: Not applicable.

Informed Consent Statement: Not applicable.

Data Availability Statement: The dataset has been generated by extracting information from different areas of a manufacturing plant. These data are private and cannot be shared due to the foundry knowledge embedded in it. However, the authors tried to explain the methodology and the tools created to be able to reproduce a similar solution.

Conflicts of Interest: The authors declare no conflicts of interest.

Abbreviations

The following abbreviations are used in this manuscript:

AI	Artificial Intelligence
ML	Machine Learning
DT	Digital Twin
KPI	Key Process Indicator
ICT	Information and Communication Technologies
AI	Artificial Intelligence
IIoT	Industrial Internet of Things
SoS	System of Systems
M2H	Machine to Human
M2M	Machine to Machine
BN	Bayesian Networks
TAN	Tree-Augmented Naïve
kNN	K-Nearest Neighbor
MLP	Multilayer Perceptron
ANN	Artificial Neural Network
SVM	Support Vector Machine
MAE	Mean Absolute Error
RMSE	Root Mean Squared Error
AI	Artificial Intelligence
AUC	Area under the ROC Curve
MPC	Model Predictive Control system
WFC	World Foundry Congress

References

1. Brännvall, M.L.; Bindler, R.; Renberg, I.; Emteryd, O.; Bartnicki, J.; Billström, K. The Medieval metal industry was the cradle of modern large-scale atmospheric lead pollution in northern Europe. *Environ. Sci. Technol.* **1999**, *33*, 4391–4395. [CrossRef]
2. Pattnaik, S.; Karunakar, D.B.; Jha, P.K. Developments in investment casting process—A review. *J. Mater. Process. Technol.* **2012**, *212*, 2332–2348. [CrossRef]
3. Prasad, R. Progress in investment castings. In *Science and Technology of Casting Processes*; IntechOpen: London, UK, 2012.
4. Sabau, A.S. Alloy shrinkage factors for the investment casting process. *Metall. Mater. Trans. B* **2006**, *37*, 131–140. [CrossRef]
5. Beeley, P.R.; Smart, R.F. *Investment Casting*; CRC Press: Boca Raton, FL, USA, 2023.
6. Li, Y.; Li, R. Effect of the casting process variables on microporosity and mechanical properties in an investment cast aluminium alloy. *Sci. Technol. Adv. Mater.* **2001**, *2*, 277. [CrossRef]

7. Dučić, N.; Manasijević, S.; Jovičić, A.; Ćojbašić, Ž.; Radiša, R. Casting Process Improvement by the Application of Artificial Intelligence. *Appl. Sci.* **2022**, *12*, 3264. [CrossRef]
8. Vosniakos, G.C.; Galiotou, V.; Pantelis, D.; Benardos, P.; Pavlou, P. The scope of artificial neural network metamodels for precision casting process planning. *Robot. Comput.-Integr. Manuf.* **2009**, *25*, 909–916. [CrossRef]
9. Pattnaik, S.; Karunakar, D.B.; Jha, P.K. Multi-characteristic optimization of wax patterns in the investment casting process using grey–fuzzy logic. *Int. J. Adv. Manuf. Technol.* **2013**, *67*, 1577–1587. [CrossRef]
10. Yousef, N.; Sata, A. Implementing Deep Learning-Based Intelligent Inspection for Investment Castings. *Arab. J. Sci. Eng.* **2024**, *49*, 2519–2530. [CrossRef]
11. Lasi, H.; Fettke, P.; Kemper, H.G.; Feld, T.; Hoffmann, M. Industry 4.0. *Bus. Inf. Syst. Eng.* **2014**, *6*, 239–242. [CrossRef]
12. Mypati, O.; Mukherjee, A.; Mishra, D.; Pal, S.K.; Chakrabarti, P.P.; Pal, A. A critical review on applications of artificial intelligence in manufacturing. *Artif. Intell. Rev.* **2023**, *56*, 661–768. [CrossRef]
13. Wang, W.; Wang, Y.; Jiang, R.; Cui, K. Machine learning-enabled early prediction of dimensional accuracy for complex products of investment casting (Preprint version). *Int. J. Adv. Manuf. Technol.* **2023**. [CrossRef]
14. Antoniadou, A.; Thunell, A.; Aslanidou, I.; Kyprianidis, K. Application of Digital Twin of Robot Cell in Investment Casting Manufacturing. *Procedia CIRP* **2024**, *130*, 730–735. [CrossRef]
15. Guan, B.; Wang, D.; Ma, H.; Shu, D.; Ding, Z.; Cui, J.; Sun, B. Key Technology and Application of Digital Twin Modeling for Deformation Control of Investment Casting. *Acta Metall. Sin.* **2023**, *60*, 548–558.
16. Mou, S.; Bu, K.; Ren, S.; Liu, J.; Zhao, H.; Li, Z. Digital twin modeling for stress prediction of single-crystal turbine blades based on graph convolutional network. *J. Manuf. Processes* **2024**, *116*, 210–223. [CrossRef]
17. Guan, B.; Wang, D.; Shu, D.; Sun, B. Digital Twin Model of Casting Temperature and Shrinkage Porosity Prediction. In Proceedings of the 75th World Foundry Congress, Deyang, China, 25–30 October 2024.
18. Garcia, C.E.; Prett, D.M.; Morari, M. Model predictive control: Theory and practice—A survey. *Automatica* **1989**, *25*, 335–348. [CrossRef]
19. Posner, E.A.; Spier, K.E.; Vermeule, A. Divide and conquer. *J. Leg. Anal.* **2010**, *2*, 417–471. [CrossRef]
20. Mackey, L.; Jordan, M.; Talwalkar, A. Divide-and-conquer matrix factorization. In Proceedings of the Advances in Neural Information Processing Systems 24 (NIPS 2011), Granada, Spain, 12–17 December 2011; Volume 24.
21. Horowitz, Z. Divide-and-conquer for parallel processing. *IEEE Trans. Comput.* **1983**, *100*, 582–585. [CrossRef]
22. Boschert, S.; Rosen, R. Digital twin—The simulation aspect. In *Mechatronic Futures: Challenges and Solutions for Mechatronic Systems and Their Designers*; Springer: Cham, Switzerland, 2016; pp. 59–74.
23. Cho, J.H.; Wang, Y.; Chen, R.; Chan, K.S.; Swami, A. A survey on modeling and optimizing multi-objective systems. *IEEE Commun. Surv. Tutor.* **2017**, *19*, 1867–1901. [CrossRef]
24. Maier, M.W. Architecting principles for systems-of-systems. *Syst. Eng. J. Int. Counc. Syst. Eng.* **1998**, *1*, 267–284. [CrossRef]
25. Boardman, J.; Sauser, B. System of Systems-the meaning of of. In Proceedings of the 2006 IEEE/SMC International Conference on System of Systems Engineering, Los Angeles, CA, USA, 24–26 April 2006; IEEE: New York, NY, USA, 2006; p. 6.
26. Maier, M.W. Research challenges for systems-of-systems. In Proceedings of the 2005 IEEE International Conference on Systems, Man and Cybernetics, Waikoloa, HI, USA, 12 October 2005; IEEE: New York, NY, USA, 2005; Volume 4, pp. 3149–3154.
27. Bass, L.; Clements, P.; Kazman, R. *Software Architecture in Practice: Software Architect Practice_c3*; Addison-Wesley: Boston, MA, USA, 2012.
28. Kochhar, A. Distributed real time data processing for manufacturing organizations. *IEEE Trans. Eng. Manag.* **1977**, *24* 119–124. [CrossRef]
29. Xiang, F.; Yin, Q.; Wang, Z.; Jiang, G.Z. Systematic method for big manufacturing data integration and sharing. *Int. J. Adv. Manuf. Technol.* **2018**, *94*, 3345–3358. [CrossRef]
30. Krivic, P.; Skocir, P.; Kusek, M.; Jezic, G. Microservices as agents in IoT systems. In Proceedings of the Agent and Multi-Agent Systems: Technology and Applications: 11th KES International Conference, KES-AMSTA 2017 Vilamoura, Algarve, Portugal, 21–23 June 2017; Proceedings 11; Springer: Berlin/Heidelberg, Germany, 2017; pp. 22–31.
31. Kalyani, Y.; Rahman, S.; Collier, R.W. Integration of Hypermedia-Agents, Microservices and Digital Twin for Smart Agriculture. In Proceedings of the PoEM Workshops, London, UK, 23–25 November 2022.
32. Lyon, D.A.; Weiman, C. Observer-conditioned-observable design pattern. *J. Object Technol.* **2007**, *6*, 15–24. [CrossRef]
33. Tarkoma, S. *Publish/Subscribe Systems: Design and Principles*; John Wiley & Sons: Hoboken, NJ, USA, 2012.
34. Baigent, D.; Adamiak, M.; Mackiewicz, R.; Sisco, G. *IEC 61850 Communication Networks and Systems in Substations: An Overview for Users*; SISCO Systems: Sterling Heights, MI, USA, 2004.
35. Ganesan, D.; Lindvall, M.; Ruley, L.; Wiegand, R.; Ly, V.; Tsui, T. Architectural analysis of systems based on the publisher-subscriber style. In Proceedings of the 2010 17th Working Conference on Reverse Engineering, Beverly, MA, USA, 13–16 October 2010; IEEE: New York, NY, USA, 2010; pp. 173–182.

36. Schmidt, D.C.; O'Ryan, C. Patterns and performance of distributed real-time and embedded publisher/subscriber architectures. *J. Syst. Softw.* **2003**, *66*, 213–223. [CrossRef]
37. Rajkumar, R.; Gagliardi, M.; Sha, L. The real-time publisher/subscriber inter-process communication model for distributed real-time systems: Design and implementation. In Proceedings of the Proceedings Real-Time Technology and Applications Symposium, Chicago, IL, USA, 15–17 May 1995; IEEE: New York, NY, USA, 1995; pp. 66–75.
38. Edwards, G.T.; Schmidt, D.C.; Gokhale, A. Integrating publisher/subscriber services in component middleware for distributed real-time and embedded systems. In Proceedings of the 42nd annual Southeast regional conference, Huntsville, AL, USA, 2–3 April 2004; pp. 171–176.
39. Joshi, A.; Kale, S.; Chandel, S.; Pal, D.K. Likert scale: Explored and explained. *Br. J. Appl. Sci. Technol.* **2015**, *7*, 396–403. [CrossRef]
40. Doroshenko, V.; Tokova, O. The Examples of Digitalization of Foundry Production: Virtual Engineering, Digital Twin, Additive Technologies. *Control Syst. Comput.* **2020**, *2889*, 64–69. [CrossRef]
41. Fuller, A.; Fan, Z.; Day, C.; Barlow, C. Digital twin: Enabling technologies, challenges and open research. *IEEE Access* **2020**, *8*, 108952–108971. [CrossRef]
42. Karaadi, A.; Sun, L.; Mkwawa, I.H. Multimedia communications in internet of things QoT or QoE? In Proceedings of the 2017 IEEE International Conference on Internet of Things (iThings) and IEEE Green Computing and Communications (GreenCom) and IEEE Cyber, Physical and Social Computing (CPSCom) and IEEE Smart Data (SmartData), Exeter, UK, 21–23 June 2017; IEEE: New York, NY, USA, 2017; pp. 23–29.
43. Bishop, C.M.; Nasrabadi, N.M. *Pattern Recognition and Machine Learning*; Springer: Berlin/Heidelberg, Germany, 2006; Volume 4.
44. Nasteski, V. An overview of the supervised machine learning methods. *Horizons B* **2017**, *4*, 56. [CrossRef]
45. Jiang, J. A Literature Survey on Domain Adaptation of Statistical Classifiers. 2008. Available online: http://www.mysmu.edu/faculty/jingjiang/papers/da_survey.pdf (accessed on 20 January 2025).
46. Demšar, J. Statistical comparisons of classifiers over multiple data sets. *J. Mach. Learn. Res.* **2006**, *7*, 1–30.
47. Pepe, M.S. *The Statistical Evaluation of Medical Tests for Classification and Prediction*; Oxford University Press: Oxford, UK, 2003.
48. Nieves, J.; Santos, I.; Penya, Y.K.; Brezo, F.; Bringas, P.G. Enhanced foundry production control. In Proceedings of the Database and Expert Systems Applications: 21st International Conference, DEXA 2010, Bilbao, Spain, 30 August–3 September 2010; Proceedings, Part I 21; Springer: Berlin/Heidelberg, Germany, 2010; pp. 213–220.
49. Shetty, R.; Al Majali, A.; Wells, L. Enhanced Classification of Refractory Coatings in Foundries: A VPCA-Based Machine Learning Approach. *Int. J. Met.* **2024**, 1–11. [CrossRef]
50. Cooper, G.F.; Herskovits, E. A Bayesian method for constructing Bayesian belief networks from databases. In *Uncertainty Proceedings 1991*; Elsevier: Amsterdam, The Netherlands, 1991; pp. 86–94.
51. Russell, S.J.; Norvig, P. *Artificial Intelligence: A Modern Approach*; Pearson: London, UK, 2016.
52. Friedman, N.; Geiger, D.; Goldszmidt, M. Bayesian network classifiers. *Mach. Learn.* **1997**, *29*, 131–163. [CrossRef]
53. Guo, G.; Wang, H.; Bell, D.; Bi, Y.; Greer, K. KNN model-based approach in classification. In Proceedings of the On The Move to Meaningful Internet Systems 2003: CoopIS, DOA, and ODBASE: OTM Confederated International Conferences, CoopIS, DOA, and ODBASE 2003, Catania, Italy, 3–7 November 2003; Proceedings; Springer: Berlin/Heidelberg, Germany, 2003; pp. 986–996.
54. Rana, A.; Rawat, A.S.; Bijalwan, A.; Bahuguna, H. Application of multi layer (perceptron) artificial neural network in the diagnosis system: A systematic review. In Proceedings of the 2018 International Conference on Research in Intelligent and Computing in Engineering (RICE), San Salvador, El Salvador, 22–24 August 2018; IEEE: New York, NY, USA, 2018; pp. 1–6.
55. Amari, S.I.; Wu, S. Improving support vector machine classifiers by modifying kernel functions. *Neural Netw.* **1999**, *12*, 783–789. [CrossRef]
56. Maji, S.; Berg, A.C.; Malik, J. Classification using intersection kernel support vector machines is efficient. In Proceedings of the 2008 IEEE Conference on Computer Vision and Pattern Recognition, Anchorage, AK, USA, 23–28 June 2008; IEEE: New York, NY, USA, 2008; pp. 1–8.
57. Üstün, B.; Melssen, W.; Buydens, L. Visualisation and interpretation of support vector regression models. *Anal. Chim. Acta* **2007**, *595*, 299–309. [CrossRef]
58. Cho, B.H.; Yu, H.; Lee, J.; Chee, Y.J.; Kim, I.Y.; Kim, S.I. Nonlinear support vector machine visualization for risk factor analysis using nomograms and localized radial basis function kernels. *IEEE Trans. Inf. Technol. Biomed.* **2008**, *12*, 247–256. [PubMed]
59. Quinlan, J.R. *C4. 5: Programs for Machine Learning*; Elsevier: Amsterdam, The Netherlands, 2014.
60. Cutler, A.; Cutler, D.R.; Stevens, J.R. Random forests. *Ensemble Machine Learning: Methods and Applications*; Springer: New York, NY, USA, 2012; pp. 157–175.
61. Freund, Y.; Schapire, R.E. Large margin classification using the perceptron algorithm. In Proceedings of the Eleventh Annual Conference on Computational Learning Theory, Madisson, WI, USA, 24–26 July 1998; pp. 209–217.
62. Kuncheva, L.I. *Combining Pattern Classifiers: Methods and Algorithms*; John Wiley & Sons: Hoboken, NJ, USA, 2014.

63. Dietterich, T.G. Ensemble methods in machine learning. In Proceedings of the International Workshop on Multiple Classifier Systems, First International Workshop, MCS 2000, Cagliari, Italy, 21–23 June 2000; Springer: Berlin/Heidelberg, Germany, 2000; pp. 1–15.
64. Kittler, J.; Hatef, M.; Duin, R.P.; Matas, J. On combining classifiers. *IEEE Trans. Pattern Anal. Mach. Intell.* **1998**, *20*, 226–239. [CrossRef]
65. Seewald, A.K.; Fürnkranz, J. An evaluation of grading classifiers. In Proceedings of the International Symposium on Intelligent Data Analysis, 4th International Conference, IDA 2001, Cascais, Portugal, 13–15 September 2001; Springer: Berlin/Heidelberg, Germany, 2001; pp. 115–124.
66. Wolpert, D.H. Stacked generalization. *Neural Netw.* **1992**, *5*, 241–259. [CrossRef]
67. Garner, S.R. Weka: The waikato environment for knowledge analysis. In Proceedings of the New Zealand Computer Science Research Students Conference, Citeseer, Wellington, New Zealand, 23–25 August 1995; Volume 1995, pp. 57–64.
68. Hilden, J. The area under the ROC curve and its competitors. *Med. Decis. Mak.* **1991**, *11*, 95–101. [CrossRef]
69. Kaur, J.; Madan, N. Association rule mining: A survey. *Int. J. Hybrid Inf. Technol.* **2015**, *8*, 239–242. [CrossRef]
70. Mooney, C.Z. *Monte Carlo Simulation*; Number 116; Sage: London, UK, 1997.
71. Farahanipad, F.; Rezaei, M.; Nasr, M.S.; Kamangar, F.; Athitsos, V. A survey on GAN-based data augmentation for hand pose estimation problem. *Technologies* **2022**, *10*, 43. [CrossRef]
72. Alla, S.; Adari, S.K.; Alla, S.; Adari, S.K. What is mlops? In *Beginning MLOps with MLFlow: Deploy Models in AWS SageMaker, Google Cloud, and Microsoft Azure*; Apress: New York, NY, USA, 2021; pp. 79–124.
73. Cichy, R.M.; Kaiser, D. Deep neural networks as scientific models. *Trends Cogn. Sci.* **2019**, *23*, 305–317. [CrossRef] [PubMed]
74. Wehrens, R.; Buydens, L.M. Classical and nonclassical optimization methods. In *Encyclopedia of Analytical Chemistry*; John Wiley & Sons: Hoboken, NJ, USA, 2000; pp. 9678–9689.
75. Li, Y.; Tian, M.; Liu, G.; Peng, C.; Jiao, L. Quantum optimization and quantum learning: A survey. *IEEE Access* **2020**, *8*, 23568–23593. [CrossRef]
76. Nieves, J. Salomón: Un Nuevo Enfoque para la Mejora de Procesos de Negocio Mediante la Producción Inteligente Basada en Modelos Predictivos de Control Híbridos y Autoadaptativos. Ph.D. Thesis, Universidad de Deusto, Bilbao, Spain, 2012.
77. Fosci, P.; Nieves, J.; Psaila, G.; Bringas, P.G. Bayesian Generation of Synthetic Data. In Proceedings of the The 19th International Conference on Soft Computing Models in Industrial and Environmental Applications SOCO 2024: Salamanca, Spain, 9–11 October 2024; Proceedings; Springer Nature: Berlin/Heidelberg, Germany, 2024; Volume 1, p. 181.
78. Kaelbling, L.P.; Littman, M.L.; Moore, A.W. Reinforcement learning: A survey. *J. Artif. Intell. Res.* **1996**, *4*, 237–285. [CrossRef]

applied sciences

MDPI

Article

Cybersecurity Requirements for Industrial Machine Control Systems

Leszek Kasprzyczak [1], Anna Manowska [1,*] and Marek Dźwiarek [2]

1 Faculty of Mining, Safety Engineering and Industrial Automation, Silesian University of Technology, 44-100 Gliwice, Poland; leszek.kasprzyczak@polsl.pl

2 Central Institute for Labour Protection—National Research Institute, 00-701 Warszawa, Poland; madzw@poczta.onet.pl

* Correspondence: anna.manowska@polsl.pl

Abstract: The first part of this paper discusses the research context, taking a closer look at the development of Industry 4.0 and the growing importance of the IIoT, which entails new cybersecurity challenges. The issue of cyber threats and the need to increase the level of protection in machine control systems, which are particularly vulnerable to attacks due to their connection to the network, is also presented. The Introduction concludes with a presentation of the article's objective, which is to analyze the requirements of security levels (SLs) and the implementation of relevant international standards. The next section reviews the current research on cybersecurity in machine control systems. This section also points out the research gaps that the article aims to fill. The next section presents the risk assessment used to ensure safety during machine operations based on ISO 12100. The article describes safety functions implemented in machine control systems, including the SIL (safety integrity level) and PL (performance level) specifications. An important part of the article is the creation of a relationship between PL and SL, showing how the safety functions of systems are related to protection against cyber threats. The last part of the article gives a case study in the form of examples of machines and their control systems performing safety functions, which require various SLs depending on the PLs.

Keywords: cybersecurity; machinery control systems; performance levels (PLs); security levels (SLs)

1. Introduction

The effective cybersecurity of industrial systems requires the cooperation of both manufacturers and machine users. Remote access and password monitoring should not be a coincidence, as negligence can result in the appearance of cyber-attacks, for example, by former employees on both the manufacturer's and user's side, as well as other external parties.

Cyber-attacks are primarily associated with attacks via the Internet; however, one should also take into account the unintentional infection of the system by connecting a virus-ridden data carrier, such as a portable memory stick, or deliberate sabotage associated with unrestricted access by an internal company employee to programmable devices on production lines.

Cyber-attacks can cause, among other things, the following:

- Halting production or reducing production;
- Loss of quality of manufactured workpieces, which may not be easy to detect quickly and exposes the company to financial losses;

- Loss of data—encryption by blackmailers demanding ransom;
- Falsification of documentation and the introduction of chaos in various departments of the company;
- Emission of hazardous substances into the environment—contamination of the environment and danger to local residents or the wider area;
- Loss of safety functions in machine control systems, which can directly expose employees to mechanical hazards, hazards associated with the emission of hazardous substances, and many others.

It is therefore important to implement appropriate protections in terms of cybersecurity with expenditures commensurate with the potential consequences caused by cybercrime. A company should have a policy in place related to cybersecurity, which should be constantly improved due to the fact that cyber criminals are constantly looking for opportunities to attack through the vulnerabilities they discover.

Policies related to cybersecurity should address, among other things, the management of passwords for programmable devices, such as the following:

- Rules for creating passwords for newly acquired PLCs/microcontrollers/machine computers;
- How often they should be changed (e.g., due to employee turnover);
- Where they should be stored (on the local computer's disc/on the network on a server, whether in encrypted form; consider that such a computer can also be attacked, resulting in the loss of stored passwords; another solution is to store passwords written on paper);
- Who should have access to stored passwords;
- Rules for supervising compliance with the policy (checking that passwords are not written, for example, with a marker on the controller or on the door of the control cabinet or on electrical diagrams, etc.).

It is also important to deliberately assign permissions and formulate requirements for remote machine operation as follows:

- Encrypted connections required;
- Access only within a certain pool of IP addresses;
- Degree of password complexity;
- Temporary access rather than unlimited time;
- Read-only connection, if sufficient;
- Generation of a post-intervention checksum;
- Recording the date, time, and personal data of the modifier.

Experience shows that as programmable devices are used, vulnerabilities in their software become apparent. This therefore requires the constant monitoring of software updates. This issue is often neglected, giving cyber criminals more freedom of action.

The purpose of this study is to analyze cybersecurity requirements for industrial machine control systems, focusing on their integration with safety levels (SLs) and performance levels (PLs). The study aims to fill the gap in the literature by providing a comprehensive framework for linking safety and security requirements in industrial systems, addressing both hardware and network-level vulnerabilities. The remainder of this article will mainly analyze the aspect concerning the loss of safety functions (SFs) in machine control systems due to a cyber-attack, which can result in hazards to employees. Hazards can result in slight or severe injuries and even the death of a single person caused by a machine. The article does not consider catastrophes (the death of many people as a result of a danger event).

2. Analysis of Cyber Threats in the Industry

With the increasing digitization of industrial processes and the development of IoT and IIoT technologies, the cybersecurity of machine and production line control systems has become a key issue in securing critical infrastructure and industrial automation. Research in this field focuses on analyzing and optimizing measures to protect against cyber-attacks and implementing effective strategies to safeguard against security breaches in control systems. The sources of cyberattacks can be divided into two groups, namely external threats and internal threats. External threats often include cybercriminal organizations or independent hackers who use tools such as phishing, ransomware, and denial-of-service attacks to exploit system vulnerabilities. Internal threats, on the other hand, can result from malicious or negligent actions by employees or others with access to the network [1]. Identifying these sources is crucial to implementing tailored security measures.

Tanveer et al. in [2] describe methods for designing industrial automation applications that are secure against attacks while ensuring the high availability of systems. This work is a key contribution to the issue of security integration in IoT/IIoT applications. Lesi et al. in [3] analyze the issue of distributed security in industrial automation, specifically focusing on IoT vulnerabilities and threats that require multi-layer security in high-risk environments.

Duque Anton et al. in [4] conduct an extensive analysis of the vulnerability of control systems to cyber threats around the world. The findings reveal significant security vulnerabilities that can pose a direct danger to the safety of operators. On the other hand, Buczkowski et al. in [5] introduce the CySec-Tool, which allows for security optimization based on probabilistic attack models. Analysis based on the attack model enables the identification of vulnerabilities in automation and control systems.

Boyes in [6] emphasizes the importance of applying protection standards for industrial networks and the control of industrial systems. This research takes into account the specific principles of designing systems that are resilient to cyber-attacks, which is crucial for managing risk in industrial networks.

An important aspect in cybersecurity research for automation systems is the topic of detecting and defending against malicious activities. A hierarchical approach to managing system complexity and security was discussed by Mesarovic (1970), providing foundational insights into multi-level control systems [7]. Liu et al. in [8] describe scenarios of attacks based on data falsification in power grids, which indicates the need for advanced methods to detect integrity violations. Slay and Miller in [9] detail an incident involving an attack on a water management system, which provides an important case study of the consequences of a lack of cybersecurity in critical infrastructure.

In the context of security certification and compliance assurance, the work of Chen et al. [10] and Gajek et al. [11] take a closer look at the topic of so-called property-based attestation and the TLS (transport layer security) model. These studies bring important aspects to the development of secure communication protocols and protection against attacks.

In the area of key exchange and encryption, the work of Manowska et al. [12] points to new methods of defending against key compromise in key exchange protocols, which provides the foundation for protecting against unauthorized access to machine control systems.

The topic of privacy and security in control systems was addressed by Cutillo et al. in [13]. Their research includes mechanisms for discovering common contacts and protecting user privacy, which can be applied in the context of the remote monitoring of industrial systems.

The article [14] addresses current problems of risk analysis and probabilistic modelling for functional safety management in the life cycle of safety-related systems. Some methodological aspects of the functional safety assessment are outlined that include the modelling of dependent failures or cybersecurity and verifying the safety integrity level (SIL) under uncertainty.

In the article [15], the author identifies typical mistakes of machinery safety-related control systems and mentions the cybersecurity requirements that will be imposed by Machinery Regulation 2023/1230/EU [16] in 2027.

All of the above work underscores the growing need to implement protective measures against cyber threats, but there remains a research gap in the integration of IEC 62443 group of standards on the security for industrial automation and control systems with the safety levels of machine control systems' safety functions. In particular, there is a lack of unambiguous cybersecurity guidelines for machine safety systems within Industry 4.0. This article fills these gaps by proposing the implementation of security standards for machine control systems, taking into account security levels (SLs) and their relationship to the safety functions implemented by machine control systems, providing greater protection against unwanted incidents and increasing the resilience of industrial infrastructure against cyber-attacks.

3. Machine Safety Requirements

3.1. Risk Assessment and Reduction

According to ISO 12100 [17], a risk assessment should be performed as early as at the machine design stage. The risk assessment consists of risk analysis and risk evaluation. The risk analysis consists of the three following steps:

- Defining machine limitations;
- Identifying hazards (e.g., mechanical, electrical, security threats);
- Risk estimation.

For each individual hazard, a risk estimation is performed, which can take several levels, from negligible through low, medium, significant, or high. The higher the risk, the more severe the injury possibly is and/or there is a higher probability of a hazardous event. Thus, the higher the risk, the more reliable and therefore expensive measures must be taken to minimize the risk to an acceptable level.

Also, the Machinery Regulation 2023/1230/EU [16], which will take effect in 2027, requires the use of protections against intrusion with particular attention to the safety functions performed by machine control systems. In the Annex III on Essential Health and Safety Requirements, Section 1.1.9 requires a machine or related product to record the evidence of authorized or unauthorized tampering with respect to that component of hardware when it relates to connecting to or accessing software that is essential to the machine's or related product's compliance.

Thus, depending on the estimated risk that may arise from cyber threats, appropriate measures should be adopted to reduce the risk from that hazard. To estimate the risk from cyber threats, we will use the proposed relationship between PLs and SLs in the next chapters.

3.2. Safety Functions

Risks from certain hazards are minimized with safety-related control systems. A given control system can then implement a single or multiple safety functions.

The requirement specification for safety functions consists of functional requirements and safety integrity. Functional requirements are most often specified as a formulation, such as "Stop the dangerous movement of the machine when the interlocking guard is opened and prevent it from starting until the guard is closed".

The ranking of system state parameters is based on their relative impact on the overall safety and security of the system. Parameters were evaluated using a weighted scoring system, considering criteria such as the frequency of occurrence, severity of potential consequences, and the likelihood of detection. The methodology follows established risk assessment frameworks, including ISO 12100 and ISO 13849-1 [18], which recommend prioritizing parameters based on their contribution to system vulnerability and resilience. This approach ensures that critical parameters are given higher weight in the analysis, reflecting their importance in mitigating cyber and operational risks.

Typically, the safety function is realized with three elements, a sensor that detects the hazard (opening the guard), a logic unit that processes the signals from the sensor, and an actuator connected to the logic unit (e.g., a contactor that shuts down the drive under consideration or a valve that shuts off the operating medium). These elements form an SCS (safety-related control system) according to IEC 62061 [19] or SRP/CS (safety-related part of a control system) according to ISO 13849-1. Due to the greater popularity of ISO 13849 in the industry, we will focus on its requirements in the remainder of this article.

3.2.1. Determination of the Required Level of Safety Integrity

To determine the required performance level (PLr) of a given safety function implemented in the control system, the graph in Figure 1 can be used based on Annex A of ISO 13849-1 [18].

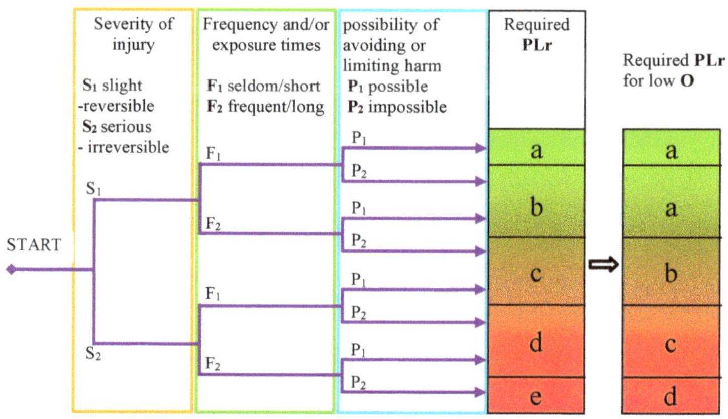

Figure 1. Graph for determining the PLr (own elaboration).

In the graph, path choices are made consisting of the following:

- The severity of the injury (S);
- The frequency of exposure and/or its duration (F);
- The possibility of avoiding or limiting harm (P).

The standard allows for a reduction in one level in the required PLr if the low probability of a hazardous occurrence (O) can be justified.

3.2.2. Achieved PLs and SILs

A given safety function is implemented from safety-related hardware and software elements. The individual subsystems are characterized by the safety parameters required by ISO 13849-1 and/or IEC 62061. On the basis of appropriate formulas or simplified methods, the frequency of dangerous failure per hour PFH_d of the entire safety chain must be determined and on this basis, the achieved PL and/or SIL of the safety function under consideration is obtained—see Table 1. It can be seen from this table that the higher the SIL/PL, the lower the frequency of dangerous failure per hour of the system implementing the safety function in question. In addition, the more elements there are in the safety chain, the greater the sum of their PFH_d will be and therefore, the resulting SIL/PL will be lower, which may result in failure to achieve the target integrity.

Table 1. Determination of SILs and PLs of the system based on PFH_d.

PFHd	SIL	PL
≥10−5 to <10−4	-	a
≥3 × 10−6 to <10−5	1	b
≥10−6 to <3 × 10−6	1	c
≥10−7 to <10−6	2	d
≥10−8 to <10−7	3	e

In case the PL is not known for all subsystems, it is necessary to determine the performance level of such subsystems by itself. The determination of the performance level, PL, for the subsystem is determined based off the following:

- The architecture of the system (categories B, 1, 2, 3, 4);
- The value of the mean time to dangerous failure ($MTTF_d$);
- Diagnostic coverage (DC);
- Common cause failure tolerance (CCF).

We will not discuss all the factors mentioned here, and we refer the interested reader to the analysis of the standard [18] or the publication [20]. In the following, we will focus on explaining the categories of systems related to system architecture, as they are an important part in the subsequent analysis.

3.2.3. System Architecture—Categories

According to [16], there are five safety categories, which are B, 1, 2, 3, and 4. Single-channel systems include categories B, 1, and 2. They differ from each other in that category 1 uses well-tried components (e.g., parts used in the past in similar applications with positive results) and well-tried safety principles (e.g., oversized components), so the probability of failure is lower than in the "weakest" category B. Category 2 additionally includes fault detection in subsystems. Categories 3 and 4 apply to two-channel systems (Figures 2–5). Table 2 compares the different categories.

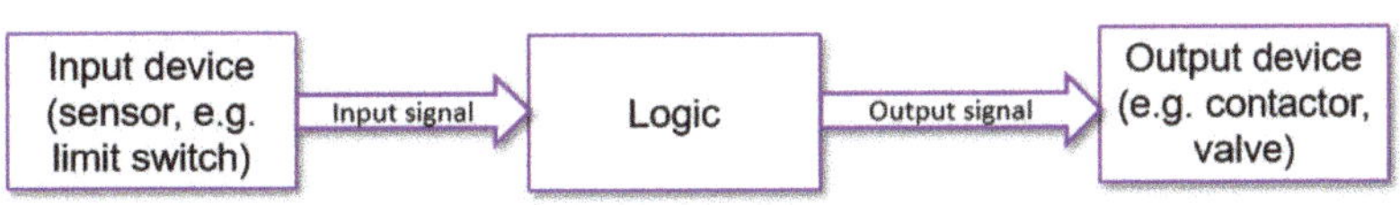

Figure 2. Architecture of the single-channel systems for categories B and 1 (own elaboration).

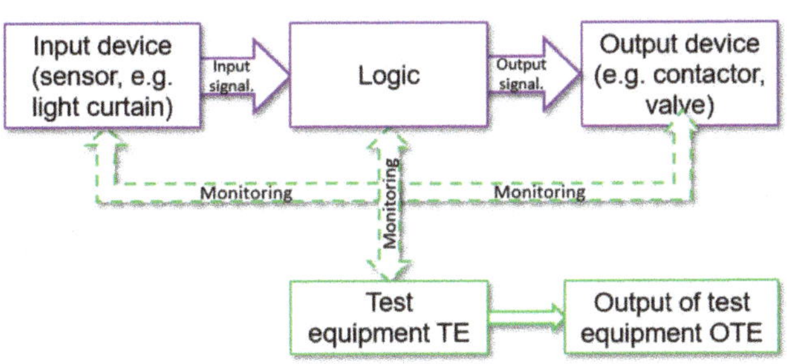

Figure 3. Architecture of systems with monitoring equipment for category 2 (own elaboration).

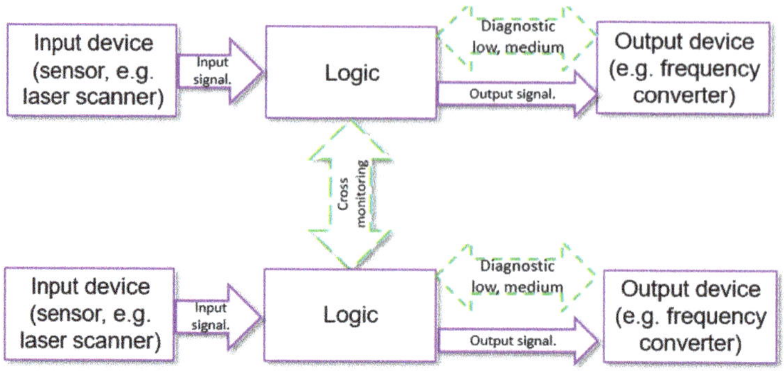

Figure 4. Architecture of redundant systems for category 3 (own elaboration).

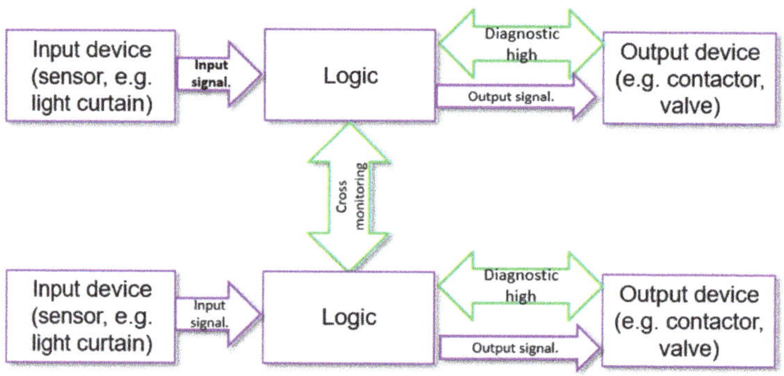

Figure 5. Architecture of redundant systems with the highest diagnostic coverage for category 4 (own elaboration).

Table 2. Comparison of safety categories based on ISO 13849-1.

Category	Features	well-tried safety principles	Failures detection	Redundancy
B	Use of elements that comply with standards and basic safety principles, withstanding expected exposures. Occurrence of failure may result in loss of safety function (single-channel system)			
1	As in B, well-tried components and well-tried safety principles are used. The occurrence of a failure may cause a loss of safety function, but the probability of this is lower than in category B (single-channel system)			
2	As in B, well-tried safety principles are used. The safety function is checked by the control system. The occurrence of a fault may cause the loss of the safety function between checks (single-channel system)			
3	As in B, well-tried safety principles are applied. The two-channel structure is tolerant to a single fault. Low-to-medium diagnostic coverage of 60 to 99%			
4	As in B, well-tried safety principles are applied. The two-channel structure is tolerant of single failure or cumulative failures. High diagnostic coverage ≥99%			

4. Relationship Between Safety Categories and PLs and Security Levels

As mentioned in the Introduction, one of the potential targets of cyber criminals can become the machine's safety systems. A real danger then arises for an operator and maintenance service if they undertake work in machine zones that pose a risk, which should be protected by the control system (e.g., ensuring low speeds to avoid danger;

stopping when a light curtain zone is violated; controlling process parameters such as temperature or liquid level). It is therefore important to link safety-related machine control system requirements with cybersecurity requirements.

However, the stability and cybersecurity of the entire hierarchical infrastructure, which includes interconnected hardware, software, and network components, also plays a crucial role. This hierarchy often comprises multiple layers, from local control systems to enterprise-level networks and cloud-based solutions. Each layer introduces specific vulnerabilities and requires tailored security measures. For example, while the network layer may be prone to denial-of-service attacks, the application layer could be susceptible to data breaches. Analyzing the interdependencies and failure propagation within this hierarchy is essential to ensure not only the safety of individual machines but also the resilience of the entire infrastructure. Future studies should incorporate multi-layered risk assessment frameworks, such as those outlined in IEC 62443 group of standards and ISO/IEC 27001 [21], to address these challenges.

The technical specification IEC TS 62443-1-1 [22] Industrial communication networks—Network and system security—Part 1-1: Terminology, concepts and models recommends at least three SLs (Security Levels 1, 2, 3)—Table 3—while IEC 62443-4-2:2019 [23] Security for industrial automation and control systems—Part 4-2: Technical security requirements for IACS components (industrial automation and control system(s)) gives four SLs (Security Levels 1, 2, 3, 4).

Table 3. Security levels according to IEC TS 62433-1-1 [22].

SL	Qualitative Description
1	Low
2	Medium
3	High

Informative Annex A of IEC 62443-3-2 [24] states that IEC 62443-4-2 [23] defines SLs at four different levels (1, 2, 3, and 4). The higher the SL, the greater the level of security. SL 0 indicates that there are no requirements in this area.

- SL 1—protection against casual or coincidental violation.
- SL 2—protection against intentional violation using simple means with low resources, generic skills, and low motivation.
- SL 3—protection against intentional violation using sophisticated means with moderate resources, IACS-specific skills, and moderate motivation.
- SL 4—protection against intentional violation using sophisticated means with extended resources, IACS-specific skills, and high motivation.

We are considering three levels of machine security because SL4 takes into account sophisticated measures with expanded resources and high motivation, which can be undertaken mainly by highly skilled and equipped special forces teams that are not considered to be involved in attacking industrial machines. SL4 can be considered in the protection of power plants, nuclear power plants, and chemical plants, which if attacked can cause catastrophes.

Moreover, three types of SLs are specified as follows:

- Target, SL-T (required);
- Capability, SL-C;
- Achieved, SL-A.

Type SL-T defines the required effectiveness of countermeasures, devices, and systems that should be implemented to prevent cyber-attacks.

Type SL-A is the actual SL achieved by the actual system. The achieved SL-A level should be greater than or equal to the required SL-T level.

Type SL-C means that the device in question has the ability to provide a given SL when properly configured and integrated.

There is a need to establish a direct relationship between the PL safety level according to ISO 13849-1 and the SL according to IEC TS 62443-1-1 [22]. It can be deduced that the higher the PL is, the higher the risk is reduced by the safety-related control system; therefore, the higher the PL is, the higher the SL should be against cyber-attacks so that the considered safety function is not lost.

The relationship between PL/category and SL can be determined from Figures 6 and 7. Cybersecurity in a four-level system must encompass a wide range of tasks to ensure comprehensive protection and operational efficiency. This includes the following:

- Developing a clear understanding of the system's architecture, vulnerabilities, and potential attack vectors across all levels, from local devices to cloud-based services.
- Implementing synchronized protocols for real-time threat detection and response. This ensures that actions taken at one level (e.g., local control) align with strategies at higher levels (e.g., enterprise management).
- Securing both the physical and virtual components of the system. This includes robust firewalls, encryption methods, and redundancy measures to prevent unauthorized access and ensure data integrity in the network of data exchange.
- Recognizing the human factor in system security, such as errors in judgement, fatigue, or lack of training and mitigating these risks through regular training programmes, ergonomic interfaces, and automated alerts to support decision-making processes.

A fully integrated approach, leveraging group of standards such as IEC 62443 and ISO 27001 [21], is essential to address these diverse tasks. Additionally, advanced tools like AI-driven anomaly detection can enhance the system's ability to identify and counteract threats dynamically.

It is important to note that the analysis presented in this article focuses on specific aspects of cybersecurity, particularly on protection mechanisms at the lower levels of the hierarchy, such as machine control systems and local networks. However, protection at the bottom of the hierarchy does not ensure the cybersecurity of the entire system. A comprehensive approach requires addressing vulnerabilities across all layers, from local control systems to enterprise-level networks and cloud infrastructure. Future research should expand on this work by analyzing the interdependencies and security strategies necessary for ensuring system-wide resilience.

With the assumption that machine control systems are connected to the communications network and may be vulnerable to cyber-attacks, the following guidelines were proposed for the PLr column with the parameter O = 100% (O—the probability of occurrence of a hazardous event):

Category B

Category B allows us to obtain safety levels PLa or PLb. An SF with PLa/b level reduces the risk with a low level (S1, F1, P1/P2; S1, F2, P1).

Category B can be realized as a one-channel electromechanical or programmable system, for example, based on a standard PLC.

In the case of a system built based on electromechanical parts, there is no possibility of a cyber-attack, so SL-T 0 (no protection) is assumed.

In the case of a system built based on programmable components (e.g., a standard PLC), there is a possibility of a cyber-attack, but the risk minimized by the function is low (at the PLa/b level), so SL-T 1 (low level) is assumed.

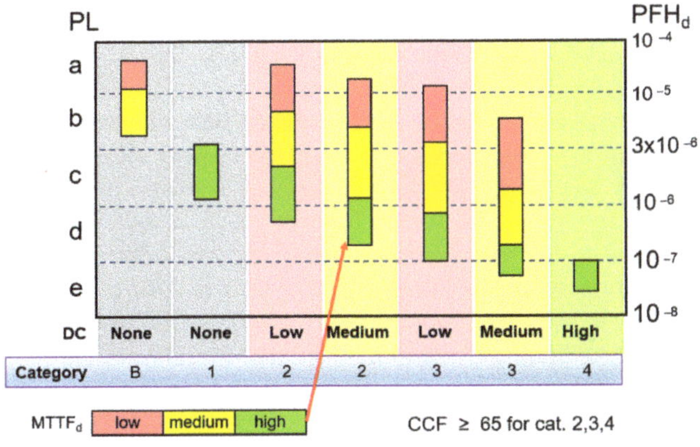

Figure 6. Auxiliary graph for determining the relationship between PL/Cat and SL—determination of the achieved PL, among others, using categories (own elaboration).

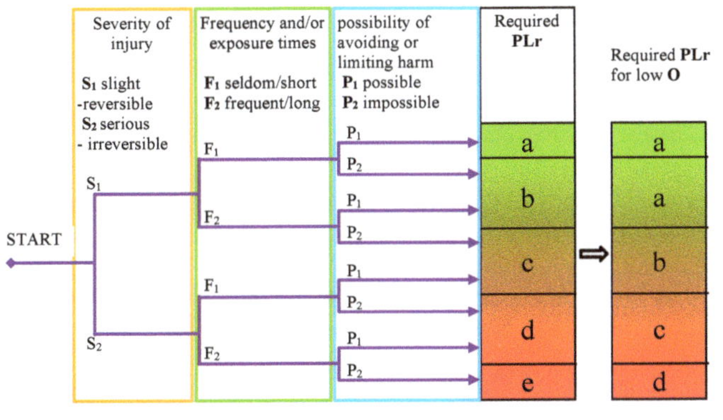

Figure 7. Auxiliary graph for determining the relationship between PL/Cat and SL—parameters S, F, and P for determining the PLr (own elaboration).

Category 1

Category 1 achieves safety levels of PLb or PLc and is mainly applied at the PLc level. An SF with PLc level reduces the risk with a medium level (S1, F2, P2; S2, F1, P1).

Category 1 is implemented as a one-channel system based on well-tried components, which according to ISO 13849-2 [25] includes electromechanical parts. Programmable electronic circuits are not used, as they are not classified as well-tried ones.

In the case of a system built based on well-tried components (electromechanical components), there is no possibility of a cyber-attack, so SL-T 0 (no protection) is assumed.

Category 2

Category 2 achieves safety levels from PLa to PLd, with the most common use for the PLc level, and usage is less common for PLd level. An SF with a PLc level reduces risk with a medium level (S1, F2, P2; S2, F1, P1), while one with a PLd level reduces risk with a higher level (S2, F1, P2; S2, F2, P1).

Category 2 is implemented as a one-channel electronic system with monitoring, so there may be a loss of an SF between testing and the result of not detecting all faults. Category 2 is typically used for safety systems containing a type 2 light curtain according to IEC 61496-1 [26], which is tested by a programmable module.

In the case of a system built with programmable elements, there is the possibility of a cyber-attack. When the minimized risk is low, which corresponds to PLa/b, then SL-T 1 (low level) is assumed. When the minimized risk is medium (at PLc level) and high (at PLd level), SL-T 2 (medium level) and SL-T 3 (high level) are used, respectively.

Category 3

Category 3 allows for safety levels from PLa to PLe, with the most common use for the PLd level. An SF with a PLd level reduces risk with a high level (S2, F1, P2; S2, F2, P1).

Category 3 is implemented as a redundant two-channel system with low- or medium-level diagnostics, so there may be a loss of SF as a result of not detecting all faults. Category 3 is often implemented from two different channels, namely programmable (stopping machine actuators) and electromechanical (cutting off electrical/pneumatic/hydraulic power). However, its typical application is also inverter drives with an STO (safe torque off—see ISO 13850 [27]) stop function, characterized by PLd and category 3.

For systems realizing PLb/c levels and built on the basis of one programmable channel and another electromechanical channel, SL-T 2 (medium level) is adopted. For high-risk minimization (at PLd level), SL-T 3 (high level) is adopted.

Category 4

Category 4 allows for PLe levels of safety. An SF with a PLe level reduces the risk with the highest level (S2, F2, P2).

Category 4 is implemented as a two-channel system with high-level fault detection diagnostics. High diagnostics are provided by programmable electronic systems.

In the case of a system built with programmable components, there is the possibility of a cyber-attack. In this case, the highest risk (at PLe level) is minimized, so SL-T 3 (high level) is adopted.

In the case of using the PLr column with the parameter O << 100%, it is possible to mitigate the security protection requirements with the reasoning outlined above.

5. Case Study—Examples of Determining SLs of Safety Functions Implemented in Machine Safety Systems

In the next section of the paper, examples of machines equipped with safety-related control systems performing specific safety categories according to ISO 13849 are presented. This assumes that control systems containing programmable devices may be connected to a communication network and therefore may be susceptible to cyber-attacks.

5.1. Example 1—Machine Control System: Category B, PLa; Cybersecurity SL-T 0

In many industrial sectors, tank or barrel mixers are used. Such a mixer performs a slow rotary motion, which implies that the hazard can be avoided (parameter P1). No crush and shear zone is created inside a tank of its size. Thus, the potential injury may be light (parameter S1), for example, a bump, abrasion, or cut. The user on average opens the machine several times a day (parameter F1). Taking into account the aforementioned characteristics, the required level is PLr = a.

The safety system is realized with standard parts (not necessarily well tried and tested; see the proximity sensor B1 performing the locking function—Figure 8). Programmable devices and coupling to a communication network are not present.

For a circuit implementing the interlocking function shown in Figure 8, under the assumptions described above, no protection against cyber-attack is required. Thus, SL-T 0 (no protection) is assumed.

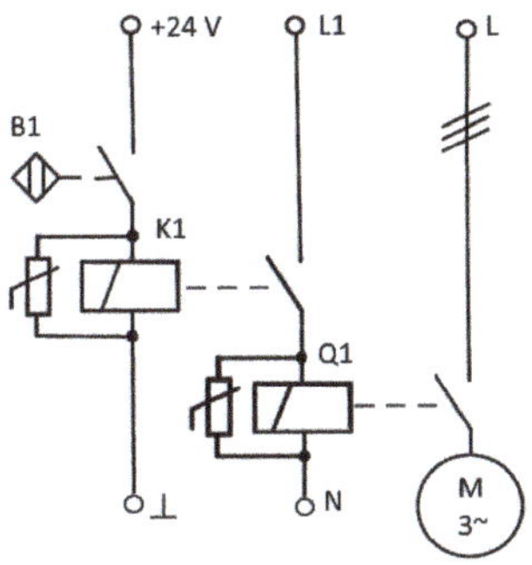

Figure 8. Example of a mixer control system to achieve Pla (own elaboration).

5.2. Example 2—Machine Control System: Category B, PLb; Cybersecurity SL-T 1

Let us consider a bakery machine for kneading dough. Such a machine performs slow rotations (which implies that a hazard can be avoided (parameter P1)) inside a container with smooth walls and dimensions that prevent the formation of crush and shear zones. Thus, it is assumed that potential injuries may be light (parameter S1), such as abrasion. The user has frequent contact with the machine (dough loading/unloading, cleaning) about 20% of the time during the shift (parameter F2). Taking into account the aforementioned characteristics, PLr = b is required.

The safety system is implemented with standard components (not necessarily well tried; see the NO limit switch acting as an interlock and the standard PLC—Figure 9). Basic safety principles are met, i.e., the use of a suppressor on the contactor coil. The machine is equipped with a programmable system that can be coupled to a communication network.

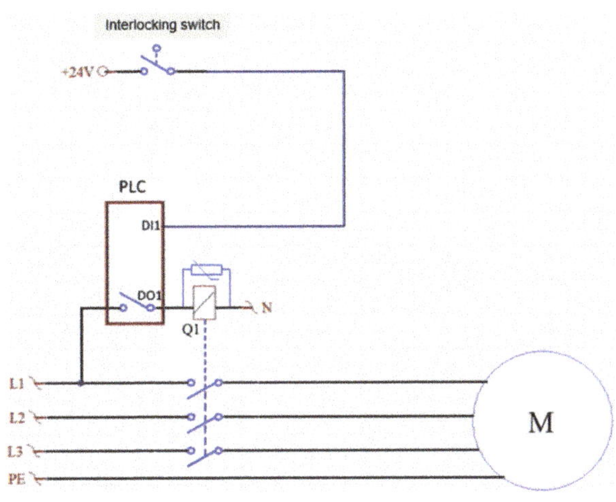

Figure 9. Example of a mixer control system to achieve PLb level (own elaboration).

For the circuit implementing the presented interlocking function in Figure 9 with the assumptions described above, protection against cyber-attack is required. The required protection level is assumed to be SL-T 1 (low level).

5.3. Example 3—Machine Control System: Category 1, PLc; Cybersecurity SL-T 0

Let us consider an SF implementing an emergency stop function, such as a turning machine (conventional lathe). According to ISO 13850 [27], the emergency stop function

(E-Stop) is required to meet at least PLc/Cat. 1. According to ISO 13849-1 [18], category 1 implies the use of well-tried components and well-tried safety principles. According to ISO 13849-2 [25], electromechanical components with a positive opening are considered as well-tried components (see the E-Stop button in Figure 10—the arrow symbol in a circle indicates positive opening). The standard in question also gives a list of well-tried safety principles, including oversizing the contactor's switching current, separating functional circuits from safety circuits. Figure 10 shows separate circuits for the starting and operational stopping of a machine and a separate circuit for the emergency stop. The drawing was simplified by omitting basic safety principles (e.g., the use of surge suppressors on inductive components). The circuit implementing the considered SF does not contain programmable circuits and coupling to the communication network.

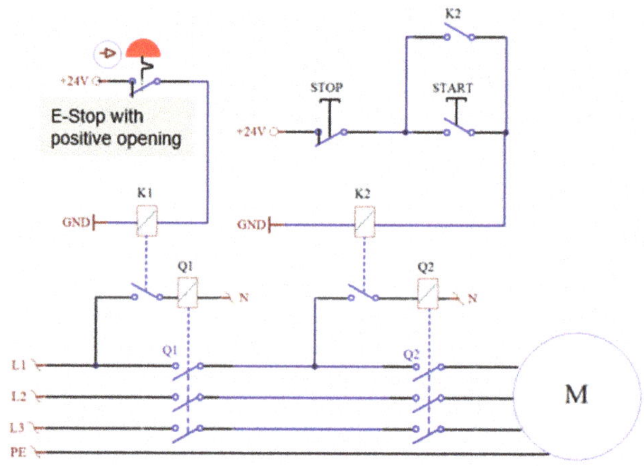

Figure 10. Example of circuits implementing the process operations of the machine and the safety system responsible for the emergency stop to ensure that the PLc level is achieved (own elaboration).

For the circuit implementing the emergency stop function shown in Figure 10, with the assumptions described above, no protection against cyber-attack is required. Thus, SL-T 0 (no protection) is assumed.

5.4. Example 4—Machine Control System: Category 2, PLc; Cybersecurity SL-T 2

Figure 11 shows a turntable protected by a type 2 light curtain according to IEC 61496-1 [26]. The machine makes slow rotary movements (which implies that the danger can be avoided (parameter P1)). The rotary movements create shear points, with the implication that potential injuries could be severe (parameter S2). The user enters the danger zone several times per shift. This implies the F1 parameter is used. Taking into account the aforementioned characteristics, PLr = c is required.

The light curtain is connected to a programmable safety unit (Figure 12) and is cyclically tested by it. However, not all faults can be detected. Therefore, the highest diagnostic DC cannot be achieved. The auxiliary contactor Q1 is included in the feedback loop. The main and auxiliary contacts of the contactor are mechanically connected. When a fault occurs and is detected, the programmable safety relay is able to indicate the fault with a red lamp.

Figure 11. Turntable danger zone protected by type 2 light curtain (own elaboration).

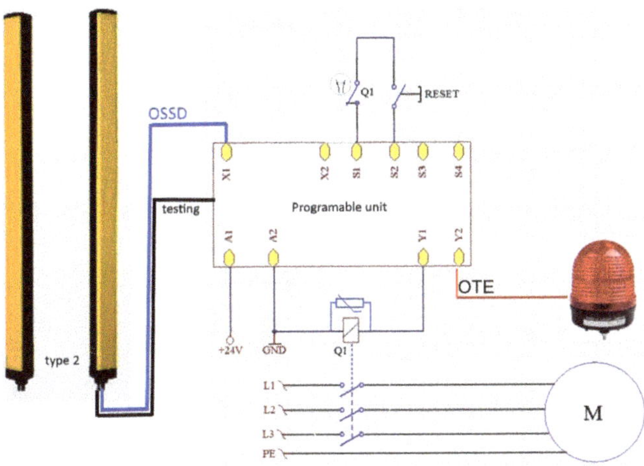

Figure 12. Machine control system to achieve PLc level (own elaboration). OSSD—output signal switching device.

For the circuit implementing the presented function of detecting the violation of the danger zone from Figure 12 with the assumptions described above, protection against cyber-attack is required. The required security level takes SL-T 2 (medium level).

5.5. Example 5—Machine Control System: Category 2, PLd; Cybersecurity SL-T 3

Figure 13 shows a packaging machine. The machine performs rapid rotational movements (which implies that it is unlikely to avoid danger (parameter P2)). Dynamic movements can cause severe impacts or entrapment (suffocation) of a person with the plastic film. Thus, it is assumed that potential injuries may be severe (parameter S2). The user opens the side interlocking guard infrequently, only once or twice per shift during jam removal. This implies the F1 parameter is used. Given the aforementioned characteristics, the required level is PLr = d.

Figure 13. The danger zone of a machine (behind the door) protected by, among other things, an interlocking guard (own elaboration).

The door interlocking sensor is connected to a programmable safety unit (Figure 14). The NC contact of the interlocking sensor is tested, e.g., with test pulses from the programable unit, which makes it possible to detect short circuits to the ground and short circuits to the positive pole of the supply. However, not all types of faults can be detected. Therefore, the highest DC cannot be achieved. The auxiliary contactor contact Q1 is included in the feedback loop. The main and auxiliary contacts of the contactor are mechanically linked. If a fault occurs, the programmable safety unit is able to indicate the fault with a red lamp and disconnect the master contactor Q2 in the master switchgear.

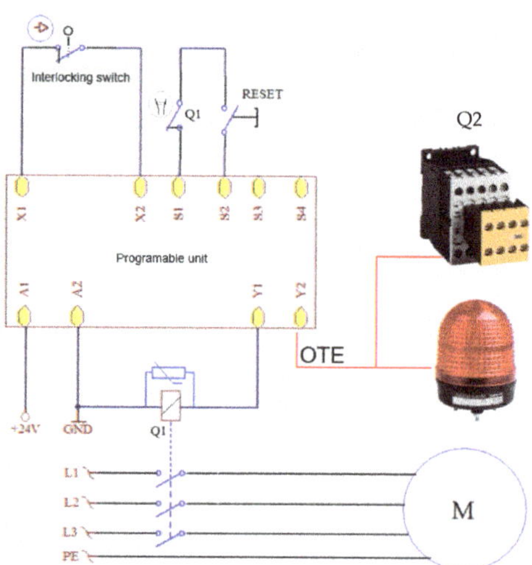

Figure 14. Machine control system to achieve PLd level (own elaboration).

For a circuit implementing the depicted interlocking function of Figure 14 under the assumptions described above, protection against cyber-attack is required. The required security level adopts SL-T 3 (high level).

5.6. Example 6—Machine Control System: Category 3, PLd; Cybersecurity SL-T 3

Figure 15 shows a robotic cell. The robot moves quickly along different trajectories (which implies that the danger (parameter P2) cannot be avoided). Dynamic movements can cause strong impacts to humans, such as to the head, which can lead to death. Thus, it is assumed that potential injuries could be severe (parameter S2). The user enters the cell by violating the protective zone monitored by the laser scanner to pick up the pallet (they do not stay there long). This implies the F1 parameter is used. Based on the graph, the required level is PLr = d. Robotic cells should be designed according to the requirements of ISO 10218-2 [28], which requires the use of the PLr = d level and category 3.

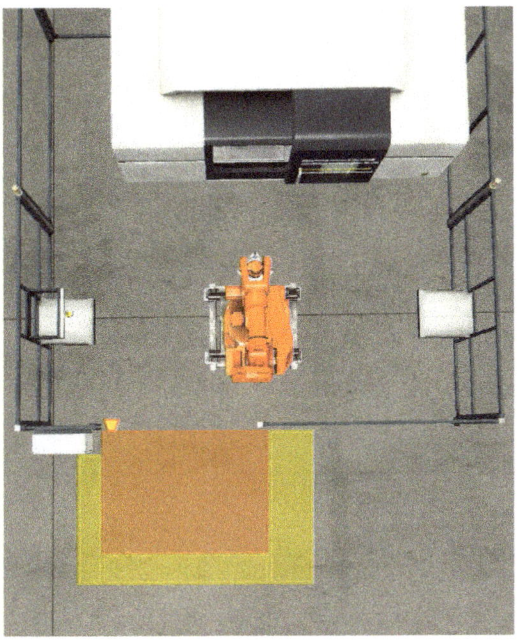

Figure 15. Hazardous zone in a robotic cell protected by a laser scanner (own elaboration).

The laser scanner (typically rated at PLd/Kat.3 level) is connected to a robot controller (typically rated at PLd/Kat.3) equipped with safety functions for stopping the robot drives (Figure 16).

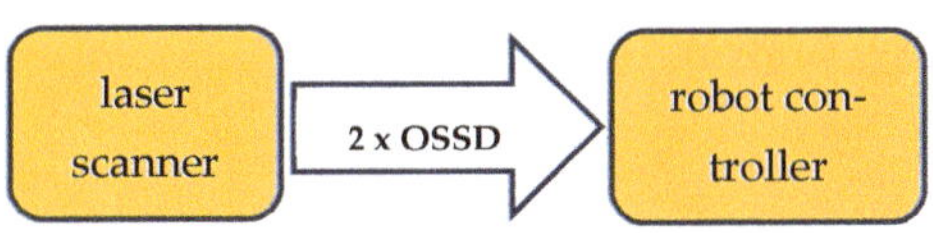

Figure 16. Safety system consisting of laser scanner (PLd/Cat.3) and robot controller (PLd/Cat.3) to achieve PLd/Cat.3 level (own elaboration).

For the circuit implementing the depicted function of detecting the violation of the danger zone of Figure 16 with the assumptions described above, protection against cyber-attack is required. The required protection level is assumed to be SL-T 3 (high level).

5.7. Example 7—Machine Control System: Category 4, PLe; Cybersecurity SL-T 3

Let us consider a hydraulic press. The movement of the press actuator is fast, which implies that danger cannot be avoided (parameter P2). The sliding motion can crush a person or a body part. So, the potential injury is assumed to be severe (parameter S2). The operator inserts and removes the workpiece from the press every few minutes, violating the protective zone monitored by the light curtain type 4 according to IEC 61496-1. This implies parameter F2 is used. Based on the graph, the level PLr = e is required. Hydraulic presses should be designed in accordance with the requirements of ISO 16092-3 [29], which requires a PLr = e level and category 4 for the SF under consideration.

The light curtain (Type 4, PLe/Kat.4) is connected to a programmable safety unit, the outputs of which are connected to redundant electromechanical components with fault monitoring (electrohydraulic valves or contactors) that stop the dangerous movement of the actuator (Figure 17).

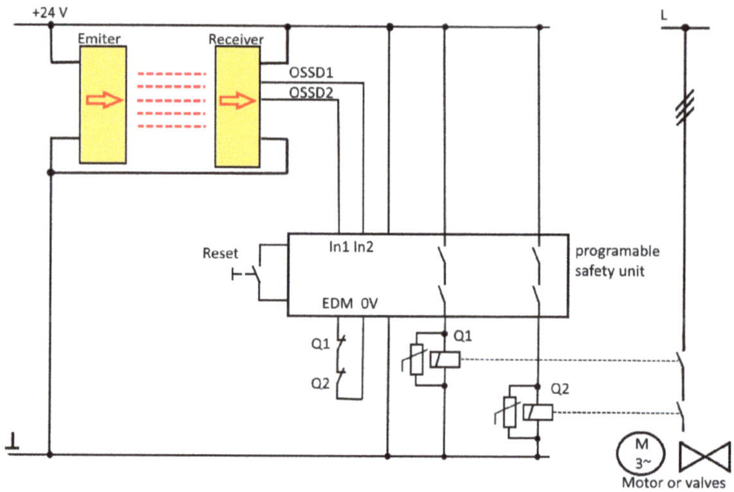

Figure 17. Control system to achieve PLe (own elaboration).

For the circuit implementing the depicted function of detecting the violation of the danger zone from Figure 17 with the assumptions described above, protection against cyber-attack is required. The required protection level is assumed to be SL-T 3 (high level).

6. Summary and Conclusions

This paper presents a proposal for linking PL safety levels of safety functions with SLs. Seven representative examples of various machines and safety functions realized in their control systems were provided. The analysis resulted in the required SL-T cybersecurity levels for each safety function. The next step should be the implementation of appropriate hardware, software, and methods to achieve appropriate SL-A levels based on the required SL-T.

On principle, the cybersecurity objectives should not conflict with safety-related control systems and production efficiency.

Periodic audits related to the effectiveness of the security measures in place are recommended. Countermeasures against cyber-attacks may be audited as needed, and if necessary, controlled cyber-attacks may be conducted to detect existing security vulnerabilities.

Furthermore, the manufacturer should communicate in the form of instructions the requirements for the necessary skills of maintenance services and the necessary training and equipment for ensuring cybersecurity.

The authors suggest further research and recommend implementation of the IEC 62443 series of standards to enhance protection against cyber threats to machine control systems. Currently, the manufacturers provide some technical means, such as configurable industrial security devices that allow for monitoring network traffic and setting certain access rules (e.g., IP pool). These devices can be used to protect certain machines, e.g., robot cells to prevent unauthorized access to the robot controller. Another interesting solution is equipment with RFID keys and a reader that can be used against sabotage directly at the machine. RFID keys give different permissions for different employees to access more or less advanced functions of the machine control system and its ports e.g., USB ports. Thus, collecting new experiences with the implementation of this kind of equipment will be the next activity in cybersecurity research and development.

Author Contributions: "Introduction", L.K. and A.M.; "Analysis of cyber hazards in industry", A.M.; "Safety requirements for machinery", L.K. and M.D.; "Relationship between safety categories and PLs and SLs", M.D. and L.K.; "Case study—examples of determining SLs of safety functions implemented in machine safety systems", L.K. and M.D.; "References", A.M., L.K. and M.D.; supervision, development, and administration of the project, M.D. All authors have read and agreed to the published version of the manuscript.

Funding: This paper is published and based on the results of a research task carried out within the scope of the fifth stage of the National Programme "Improvement of safety and working conditions" supported by the resources of the National Centre for Research and Development, task no. II.PB.18 entitled "Development of a method of risk analysis conducted by machine designers with cybersecurity aspects in view" and the statutory research BK-271/RG1/2024.

Institutional Review Board Statement: Not applicable.

Informed Consent Statement: Not applicable.

Data Availability Statement: The original contributions presented in this study are included in the article. Further inquiries can be directed to the corresponding author.

Conflicts of Interest: The authors declare no conflicts of interest.

References

1. Stallings, W. *Network Security Essentials: Applications and Standards*; Pearson: Boston, MA, USA, 2020.
2. Tanveer, A.; Sinha, R.; MacDonell, S.G.; Leitao, P.; Vyatkin, V. Designing Actively Secure, Highly Available Industrial Automation Applications. *arXiv* **2021**, arXiv:2101.01856.
3. Lesi, V.; Jakovljevic, Z.; Pajic, M. Security Analysis for Distributed IoT-Based Industrial Automation. *arXiv* **2020**, arXiv:2006.00044. Available online: https://arxiv.org/abs/2006.00044 (accessed on 25 September 2024). [CrossRef]
4. Duque Anton, S.D.; Fraunholz, D.; Krohmer, D.; Reti, D.; Schneider, D.; Schotten, H.D. The Global State of Security in Industrial Control Systems: An Empirical Analysis of Vulnerabilities around the World. *arXiv* **2021**, arXiv:2111.13862. Available online: https://arxiv.org/abs/2111.13862 (accessed on 25 September 2024).
5. Buczkowski, P.; Malacaria, P.; Hankin, C.; Fielder, A. Optimal Security Hardening over a Probabilistic Attack Graph: A Case Study of an Industrial Control System using the CySecTool Tool. *arXiv* **2022**, arXiv:2204.11707. Available online: https://arxiv.org/abs/2204.11707 (accessed on 20 September 2024).
6. Boyes, W. *Instrumentation Reference Book*; Butterworth-Heinemann: Oxford, UK, 2010. Available online: https://www.sciencedirect.com/science/article/pii/B9780750683081000577 (accessed on 25 September 2024).
7. Mesarovic, M.D.; Takahara, Y. *Theory of Multi-Level Hierarchical Systems*; Academic Press: New York, NY, USA, 1970.
8. Liu, Y.; Ning, P.; Reiter, M.K. False Data Injection Attacks against State Estimation in Electric Power Grids. *ACM Trans. Inf. Syst. Secur. (TISSEC)* **2011**, *14*, 1–33. [CrossRef]
9. Slay, J.; Miller, M. Lessons Learned from the Maroochy Water Breach. In *International Conference on Critical Infrastructure Protection*; Springer: Boston, MA, USA, 2007; pp. 73–82. [CrossRef]
10. Chen, L.; Löhr, H.; Manulis, M.; Sadeghi, A.R. Property-Based Attestation without a Trusted Third Party. *Inf. Secur. Conf. ISC* **2008**, *5222*, 277–284.
11. Gajek, S.; Manulis, M.; Pereira, O.; Sadeghi, A.R.; Schwenk, J. Universally Composable Security Analysis of TLS. In *Provable Security. ProvSec 2008*; Baek, J., Bao, F., Chen, K., Lai, X., Eds.; Lecture Notes in Computer Science; Springer: Berlin/Heidelberg, Germany, 2008; Volume 5324. [CrossRef]

12. Manowska, A.; Boros, M.; Hassan, M.W.; Bluszcz, A.; Tobór-Osadnik, K. A Modern Approach to Securing Critical Infrastructure in Energy Transmission Networks: Integration of Cryptographic Mechanisms and Biometric Data. *Electronics* **2024**, *13*, 2849. [CrossRef]
13. Cutillo, L.A.; Mark, M.; Thorsten, S. Security and Privacy in Online Social Networks. Handbook of Social Network Technologies. 2010. Available online: https://api.semanticscholar.org/CorpusID:19873542 (accessed on 23 January 2025).
14. Śliwiński, M.; Piesik, E. Designing control and protection systems with regard to integrated functional safety and cybersecurity aspects. *Energies* **2021**, *14*, 2227. [CrossRef]
15. Kasprzyczak, L. Common errors in machine safety-related control systems and methods of their elimination. *J. KONBiN* **2023**, *53*, 141–151. [CrossRef]
16. Regulation (EU) 2023/1230 of the European Parliament and of the Council of 14 June 2023 on machinery and repealing Directive 2006/42/EC of the European Parliament and of the Council and Council Directive 73/361/EEC. Available online: https://eur-lex.europa.eu/eli/reg/2023/1230/oj/eng (accessed on 23 January 2025).
17. *ISO 12100:2010*; Safety of Machinery. General Principles for Design. Risk Assessment and Risk Reduction. ISO: Geneva, Switzerland, 2010.
18. *ISO 13849-1:2023*; Safety of Machinery. Safety-Related Parts of Control Systems—General Principles for Design. ISO: Geneva, Switzerland, 2023.
19. *IEC 62061:2021+A1:2024*; Safety of Machinery. Functional Safety of Safety-Related Control Systems. IEC: Geneva, Switzerland, 2024.
20. Dźwiarek, M.; Hryniewicz, O. Periodical inspection frequency of safety related control systems of machinery—Practical recommendations for the determination. In *Advances in Safety, Reliability and Risk Management*; Grall, B., Soares, G., Eds.; Taylor & Francis Group: London, UK, 2011; pp. 495–502, ISBN 978-0-415-68379-1.
21. *ISO/IEC 27001:2022*; Information security, cybersecurity and privacy protection—Information security management systems—Requirements. ISO: Geneva, Switzerland, 2022.
22. *IEC TS 62443-1-1:2009*; Industrial communication networks - Network and system security—Part 1-1: Terminology, Concepts and Models. IEC: Geneva, Switzerland, 2009.
23. *IEC 62443-4-2:2019*; Industrial Communication Networks—Network and System Security—Part 1-1: Terminology, Concepts and Models. IEC: Geneva, Switzerland, 2019.
24. *IEC 62443-3-2:2020*; Security for Industrial Automation And Control Systems—Part 3-2: Security Risk Assessment for System Design. IEC: Geneva, Switzerland, 2020.
25. *ISO 13849-2:2012*; Safety of Machinery—Safety-Related Parts of Control Systems Part 2: Validation. ISO: Geneva, Switzerland, 2012.
26. *IEC 61496-1:2020*; Safety of Machinery—Electro-Sensitive Protective Equipment—Part 1: General Requirements and Tests. IEC: Geneva, Switzerland, 2020.
27. *ISO 13850:2015*; Safety of Machinery—Emergency Stop Function—Principles for Design. ISO: Geneva, Switzerland, 2015.
28. *ISO 10218-2:2011*; Robots and Robotic Devices—Safety Requirements for Industrial Robots Part 2: Robot Systems and Integration. ISO: Geneva, Switzerland, 2011.
29. *ISO 16092-3:2017*; Machine Tools Safety—Presses Part 3: Safety Requirements for Hydraulic Presses. ISO: Geneva, Switzerland, 2017.

applied sciences

Article

Detection of Pipe Ruptures in Shipboard Firefighting Systems Using Machine Learning and Deep Learning Techniques

Sara Ferreno-Gonzalez [1], Vicente Diaz-Casas [1,*], Marcos Miguez-Gonzalez [1] and Carlos G. San-Gabino [2]

[1] Naval Engineering Department, University of A Coruna, 15403 Ferrol, Spain; sara.ferreno@udc.es (S.F.-G.); marcos.miguez@udc.es (M.M.-G.)
[2] Navantia SA, Ria de Ferrol Shipyard, 15403 Ferrol, Spain; cgarciasg@navantia.es
* Correspondence: vicente.diaz.casas@udc.es

Abstract: In this paper, the application of machine learning and deep learning algorithms for fault and failure detection in maritime systems is examined, specifically focusing on the detection of pipe ruptures in a ship's saltwater firefighting (FiFi) system using pressure sensor data. Neural network models were developed to distinguish between normal operational states and anomalies, as well as to accurately locate pipe faults within the ship. Data were collected using real-world tests with FiFi system sensors, capturing both normal operations and simulated pipe ruptures, and were meticulously labeled to facilitate neural network training. Two neural network models were introduced: one for classifying system states (normal or anomalous) based on time-series pressure data, and another for identifying the location of anomalies related to pipe ruptures. Experimental results demonstrated the efficacy of these models in detecting and localizing pipe faults, with performance evaluated using mean squared error (MSE) across different network configurations. The successful implementation of these machine learning and deep learning algorithms highlights their potential for enhancing maritime safety and operational efficiency.

Keywords: anomaly detection; failure detection; pressure monitoring; FiFi system; machine learning; deep learning; neural network

1. Introduction

Artificial intelligence (AI) serves as a facilitating technology extensively applied in numerous industrial sectors; however, in naval and maritime industries, its development remains nascent.

One of the potential domains where AI can be harnessed aboard ships pertains to fault detection. The introduction of machine- and deep learning-based systems for managing system faults on vessels enables the automatic (or nearly automatic) detection of system faults in real-time through the analysis of data gleaned from sensors embedded in the ship's systems. These AI systems offer a multitude of advantages, including the following:

- Fault Detection: The identification of anomalies or data readings that fall outside the normal range, as captured by sensors distributed across various vessel systems, such as pressure sensors, flow meters, vibration sensors, and temperature sensors, among others.
- False Alarm Identification: Timely decision making is achieved to differentiate genuine system faults from events such as sensor malfunctions or signal loss.
- Precise Fault Localization: By leveraging sensor data comparisons, accurate determination of the fault's location within the system can be achieved.

 https://doi.org/10.3390/app15031181

- Prescription of Action Steps: After the identification and localization of a detected fault, the system can assist in decision making by providing actionable recommendations or even autonomously executing corrective measures. For instance, in the event of a ruptured section of piping, the system may advise the individual in charge of system control to close specific valves.

In this work, the utilization of neural networks for the detection and localization of pipe ruptures within the ship's firefighting system is proposed. This contribution centers on addressing a literature gap by applying AI technologies to the specific domain of fault detection within the maritime industry. Unlike other industrial applications that employ dense sensor networks with broad coverage, this approach utilizes the existing sensor network available, which, in the case of a medium size ship, could be limited to 15–25 pressure transmitters. This limitation presents a significant challenge for fault detection and localization, as the reduced number of sensors could affect the ability to monitor and accurately locate ruptures. However, the proposed methodology is tailored to this limitation using neural networks to process the sensor data, allowing for effective fault detection, including the localization of pipe ruptures.

To provide a comprehensive overview, this paper is organized as follows: The Section 1.1 reviews related work in the field of fault detection in maritime systems. The Section 2 describes the methodology used for data collection and neural network model development. The Section 3 presents the experimental setup and results, including performance evaluation metrics. The Section 4 discusses the implications of the findings and potential applications in maritime safety. Finally, the Section 5 concludes the paper and suggests directions for future research.

1.1. Related Work

1.1.1. Fault Detection in Pipelines

Detecting faults in pipeline systems is a challenge that has been addressed across multiple engineering disciplines for decades. The need for swift identification and localization of ruptures or blockages within pipes has prompted significant advancements in the field.

Techniques for identifying leaks in pipelines range from basic manual inspections conducted by trained technicians to the utilization of advanced satellite imagery. Conventional approaches for detecting issues in pipelines, particularly in water distribution and hydrocarbon systems, are typically grouped into three categories: biological methods, hardware-based methods, and software-based methods [1]. Biological methods focus on visual inspections, while software-based methods incorporate various computational strategies. Hardware-based methods, on the other hand, are classified based on the types of sensors and devices used for fault detection. In their work, Datta and Sarkar [2] offer a comprehensive review of the key methodologies and technologies for detecting pipeline blockages and leaks, as summarized in Table 1.

These technologies are diverse and are used for detecting both blockages and leaks in piping systems, each with specific approaches and methods to address these issues. The choice of the appropriate technology will depend on the specific needs and conditions of the pipeline network being monitored.

Similar classifications can be found in different studies related, above all, to the oil and gas sector. For example, Lu et al. [3] classifies detection techniques into hardware-based and software-based methods (Table 2).

Table 1. Main technologies for pipe blockage/leakage detection.

Blockage Detection Techniques	Leakage Detection Techniques
Vibration analysis: This technique involves monitoring the vibrations in pipes to identify potential blockages. Changes in vibrations can indicate flow issues.	**Negative pressure wave-based leak detection system**: This technique is based on the detection of negative pressure waves generated by leaks in pipes.
Pulse echo methodology leak detection: This technique uses ultrasonic pulses to detect leaks in pipes. The reflection of pulses can reveal the presence of leaks.	**Fiber sensor based**: It uses fiber optic sensors to detect changes in tension or deformation caused by leaks in pipes.
Acoustic reflectometry: It relies on the emission and detection of acoustic waves to locate blockages in pipes. The reflection of waves can indicate obstructions.	**Support vector machine-based pipeline leakage detection**: This technique employs machine learning algorithms like support vector machines to identify patterns related to leaks.
Transient wave blockage interaction and blockage detection: This technique utilizes transient waves to detect blockages in pipes. Changes in wave propagation can signal blockages.	**Piezoelectric acoustic emission sensor**: This sensor detects acoustic emissions caused by leaks in pipes.
Stochastic successive linear estimator: It is based on mathematical and statistical models to estimate the presence of blockages in pipes.	**Filter diagonalization method**: This method utilizes signal processing techniques to identify noise patterns related to leaks.
	Harmonic wavelet analysis: This method focuses on decomposing acoustic signals into harmonic components to detect leaks.
	Genetic algorithm in combination with the inverse transient method: This method combines genetic algorithms with modeling techniques to detect and locate leaks.
	Computational fluid dynamic simulation: This method uses numerical simulations to predict and detect leaks based on fluid flow behavior in pipes.

Table 2. Software and hardware detection methods.

Hardware-Based Method	Software-Based Method
Optical method: This method relies on optical technologies, such as lidar (light detection and ranging), laser diodes, thermal imaging, and spectral imaging. These techniques use light or electromagnetic radiation to detect and analyze objects or phenomena.	**Signal processing-based method**: Signal processing techniques are employed to analyze data collected from sensors placed along the pipeline. Signal processing algorithms, such as filtering, noise reduction, and feature extraction, are used to identify anomalies in the collected data. Deviations from normal operating conditions, such as sudden pressure drops or irregular flow patterns, can trigger alerts for potential pipeline faults.
Acoustic method: Hardware-based acoustic methods involve the use of sound waves, acoustic emissions, ultrasonic waves, and sonar for detection and analysis. They are often used in applications like underwater sonar systems and structural health monitoring.	**Real-time model-based method**: Real-time models of pipeline systems are developed using mathematical and computational techniques. These models simulate the expected behavior of the pipeline under various operating conditions. During pipeline operation, the software continuously compares real-time sensor data with the predictions from the model. Any significant deviation between observed data and model predictions can indicate a fault in the pipeline. For example, a sudden drop in pressure that is not predicted by the model may suggest a leak or blockage.

Table 2. *Cont.*

Hardware-Based Method	Software-Based Method
Distributed optical fiber sensor method: Distributed optical fiber sensors use optical fibers as sensing elements. They can measure various physical parameters like temperature, strain, and vibration along the length of the fiber, making them suitable for structural health monitoring and environmental sensing.	**Neural network method**: Artificial neural networks are trained using historical data from pipeline operations. These networks learn to recognize patterns and correlations within the data. Once trained, neural networks can analyze real-time sensor data and identify abnormal patterns that may indicate pipeline faults. For instance, a neural network can detect changes in flow rates, temperature, or pressure that deviate from expected behavior, suggesting the presence of a fault.
Dynamic pressure transmitter method: This method uses dynamic pressure transmitters to measure pressure changes in real-time. It is commonly employed in industries like oil and gas for monitoring pipelines and wellbore pressures.	**Piezoelectric acoustic emission sensor**: The piezoelectric acoustic emission sensor is a device used for detecting and analyzing acoustic emissions in pipelines. These sensors are sensitive to acoustic signals generated by pipeline defects such as cracks or leaks. When a fault occurs, the sensor converts acoustic waves into electrical signals. These signals can be analyzed to pinpoint the location and severity of the fault. This method is valuable for early fault detection and structural integrity monitoring in pipelines.
Tracer method: Tracer methods involve introducing a substance or marker into a system and tracking its movement to gather information. This is used in various applications, including hydrology, environmental monitoring, and industrial processes.	**Statistical method**: Statistical methods involve the use of statistical analysis to detect anomalies in pipeline data. By establishing statistical norms for various pipeline parameters, such as pressure or flow rates, any data that fall outside these norms can be flagged as a potential fault. Statistical process control charts and outlier detection techniques are often used to identify such anomalies. Unusual data points or trends in the statistics can indicate a pipeline fault.
GPR: GPR uses radar pulses to image the subsurface of the ground. It is commonly used in geophysical and engineering applications for locating objects or anomalies underground.	**Harmonic wavelet analysis**: Harmonic wavelet analysis is employed in pipeline fault detection to extract and analyze harmonic components from sensor data. By identifying specific harmonic patterns in the data, it can reveal irregularities or resonances in the pipeline, often linked to defects. This analysis is particularly useful when investigating faults that result in characteristic harmonic responses.
SmartBall method: The SmartBall method typically involves a free-swimming tool equipped with sensors that can be used for inspecting pipelines. It is used in the oil and gas industry to detect leaks and anomalies.	**Harmonic analysis**: Harmonic analysis is applied in pipeline fault detection to decompose sensor data into harmonic components. It helps identify the fundamental frequencies and harmonics associated with pipeline conditions. When faults cause changes in harmonic patterns, this method can signal abnormalities in pressure, flow, or other parameters. It aids in the recognition of deviations from normal pipeline operation.

The following considerations can be made regarding the analysis performed using the different methods of detecting faults in pipelines:

- Most hardware-based methods focus on the use of sensors and systems, which in some cases involve an additional cost of installation. In addition, thinking about the possible application to the ship's firefighting system, it can be observed that many of these methods are not recommended for use in marine environments due to the problems that can be generated in systems that work with seawater.

- The use of software-based methods has the important advantage that it will require minimal or no investment in additional equipment (including additional sensors or other equipment). However, the use of software-based methods also has some disadvantages, almost always related to the time needed for their development and commissioning, including time required for the development of simulation models that can replicate the system with sufficient reliability and time for data collection in the case of models that are based on real operating data (data-driven models). The following references have been identified in which the use of simulation models for pipe fault detection is analyzed [4–8].
- It has been proven that many of the developments analyzed use pressure measurements for fault detection [9–12].

1.1.2. AI-Based Fault Detection in Pipelines

There are some examples of using AI in pipe fault detection. Laurentys presents the development of an expert system for fault detection [13]. However, everything seems to indicate that the tendency is to take advantage of the benefits that neural networks (NNs) can present for the resolution of problems of this type (analyzing data series, pattern recognition). As examples of what is claimed, both Sukarno and Zhao employ neural networks to detect problems in subsea pipeline systems [14,15]. Table 3 summarizes the information presented by Pérez-Pérez, compiling recent studies related to this field [16].

Table 3. Recent developments in the use of neural networks for detection of pipe faults. Adapted from [16].

Reference	Relevant Information
Leu and Bui [17]	Leu and Bui's study focuses on using Bayesian learning within a neural network to analyze pressure data in a water distribution system. The goal is to detect anomalies or faults in the distribution system.
Zadkarami et al. [18]	This research employs a multi-layer perceptron neural network to analyze pressure and flow data in a simulated crude oil distribution system. The neural network is trained to identify and predict potential issues within the system.
Zadkarami et al. [19]	Zadkarami uses a Dempster–Shafer multi-layer perceptron classifier to analyze pressure and flow data in a simulated crude oil distribution system. This approach aids in the classification and detection of faults.
Gómez-Camperos et al. [20]	In this study, Gómez-Camperos employs a multi-layer perceptron neural network to analyze experimental flow data in a water distribution system. The focus is on the detection of abnormalities within the distribution network.
Jia et al. [21]	Jia et al. use a neural network to analyze pressure data in an experimental water distribution system. While the specific type of neural network is not mentioned, it is used to detect potential issues within the system.
Pulido et al. [22]	Pulido and the team utilize the backpropagation algorithm within a neural network to analyze pressure data in an experimental steam plant system. This aids in identifying and addressing potential faults in the system.
Kang et al. [23]	Kang and colleagues employ a neural network in the space of states to analyze pressure data in an experimental water distribution system. This approach enhances fault detection capabilities within the network.
Zhao et al. [15]	Zhao et al. apply a convolutional network to analyze pressure data in a simulated water distribution system. The neural network is designed to enhance the identification of faults within the simulated environment.
Javadiha et al. [24]	Javadiha employs both convolutional networks and Bayesian reasoning within a neural network framework to analyze pressure data in an experimental water distribution system. This multifaceted approach aids in the detection and classification of faults within the system.

These studies collectively showcase the versatility and effectiveness of neural networks in fault detection within pipe systems, whether in water distribution, crude oil transportation, steam plant operations, or simulated environments. Neural networks prove valuable in enhancing the reliability and safety of these critical infrastructure systems.

Moreover, as can be seen, while there is a significant number of developments employing neural network algorithms to detect problems in pipe systems, no references have been found in which NNs are applied to ship systems. Although there are AI-based developments, particularly those involving agents, these are focused on reconfiguration after fault in piping systems on ships, rather than on detection [25].

1.1.3. Adaptability of Neural Networks for Fault Detection in Shipboard Systems

The application of neural networks (NNs) for fault detection in pipelines has been extensively studied in various domains, including water distribution, crude oil transportation, and steam plant systems [17–24]. These studies demonstrate the effectiveness of NNs in analyzing pressure and flow data, enabling accurate identification of anomalies and faults. Unlike traditional analytical methods, such as Takagi–Sugeno observers, NNs do not rely on explicit mathematical models, making them particularly suitable for complex and variable environments like shipboard firefighting systems.

Ship firefighting systems operate under dynamic and challenging conditions that include the use of seawater, which can corrode or degrade certain hardware-based sensors, which can hinder effective data acquisition and nonlinear interactions among components such as pumps, valves, and piping networks, which are difficult to represent using analytical models.

Methods based on mathematical observers, such as the Takagi–Sugeno descriptor systems, require precise modeling of system dynamics [26,27]. While effective in well-defined systems, these methods face challenges when dealing with unmeasurable premise variables or highly variable operational conditions, such as those encountered in maritime applications.

NNs provide a viable alternative by leveraging historical operational data to identify patterns and correlations. This data-driven approach enables NNs to detect faults robustly, even in the presence of noise or missing data. Additionally, NNs can be adapted to different types of ships with varying system configurations by retraining the models with data specific to each application, thereby enabling both flexibility and scalability.

Although analytical methods and NNs represent different paradigms, they can be integrated to complement each other. Combining the analytical strengths of observer-based methods with the adaptive capabilities of NNs may facilitate the development of hybrid models that enhance fault detection and localization in shipboard systems, offering greater reliability across diverse maritime platforms.

2. Materials and Methods

The development presented is focused on the implementation of an AI-based algorithm that allows, from the readings and analysis of the data obtained from the pressure sensors installed in the ship's FiFi system, the automatic detection of faults, allowing "real" time to achieve the following: (1) Detection of the fault: Identification is achieved by anomalous data readings in pressure sensors, and (2) Identification of the location of the detected fault: By comparing the data from the different sensors for the same event, the location of the fault within the system is identified.

In the development of this work, three differentiated stages can be identified:

- Analysis of the Real System: In the initial phase, an in-depth analysis of the actual system was performed, and a profound understanding of its components, characteristics, and operation was gained.
- Data Acquisition from the Real System: Following this, the acquisition of data from the actual system was carried out, ensuring that enough representative data were obtained.
- Development of the Data-Driven Fault Detection and Localization System: Leveraging the collected and labeled data, the development of a data-driven system was initiated. This system is grounded in neural networks for the detection of anomalous pressure patterns and the pinpointing of fault locations.

When selecting the most suitable technique for fault detection, the no free lunch theorem has been considered [28]. This theorem underscores that there is no universally superior algorithm applicable to all problems. Hence, the decision to employ neural networks for identifying pressure drops in a pressurized water system must be based on the method's appropriateness for the specific problem characteristics.

After the extensive review of related studies, it was decided to use a system based on machine and deep learning compared to other methods, such as the use of a simulation model based on physics, as proposed in [29,30].

Although physics-based models have important advantages [31,32], there are limitations to their application in the proposed case. One of the most important is related to the following. The ship's firefighting system is complex, feeding salt water into various components on the vessel. Some of these components have manual openings that are not monitored by the control system, making it challenging to create a simulation model that ensures all events occurring in the system are simulated.

On the other hand, the use of data-driven models also has important advantages [33,34]. Specifically, in this case, it is intended to differentiate the pressure drop patterns in the case of openings of components that use saltwater from the FiFi system with respect to those that can occur due to rupture of a pipe in the system. The use of neural networks for pattern recognition for anomalies detection is widely [35–37]. In addition, it is proposed that with these same pressure measurements, it is possible to identify the point at which the fault has occurred. In this case, a classification neural network is proposed, a methodology that is also widely tested in other areas [38,39].

The main challenge in the use data-driven models lies in obtaining enough data to cover all the possible scenarios that the ship may face in real life. For this purpose, it is important to note that it seeks to validate the use of a fault detection and location system with the added value that in the future it will continue to learn once implemented on board the ship.

Finally, it should be noted that in numerous literature, it is concluded that important advantages can be achieved using models that combine physics and real data [40–42].

However, in the use case considered, it should be noted that it has been applied to a real ship in operation and, particularly, in a system with a high degree of monitoring of pressure signals, which implies that a significant amount of data can be relatively easily collected. Therefore, significant benefits will not be brought by the use of a combined physical and data-driven system versus a data-driven system. However, its application should be considered in possible developments focused on the use of these systems in other contexts where, for example, the degree of sensorization is not as high, or it is intended to be applied in the early stages of the ship's life cycle.

In conclusion, the choice of machine/deep learning methods, and specifically, neural networks are justified both by their inherent capabilities and the specific requirements of the ship's operational environment, underscoring the no free lunch theorem's principles. References to related studies validate the decision-making process, emphasizing the importance of choosing an algorithm based on the intricacies of the problem at hand.

3. Results

3.1. Use Case Description

The development of the use case has been guided by the methodology described in the preceding section:

(1) The first stage focused on the analysis of the real system.
(2) After that, data acquisition of the real system will be addressed.
(3) Finally, from the real labeled data, the development of the data-driven detection and localization system was carried out.

3.2. Real System Description

The saltwater firefighting system delivers pressurized saltwater to the ship's fire nozzles. It also provides pressurized saltwater to other specialized firefighting services, such as sprinklers and foam stations, along with other shipboard systems and consumers, including the wastewater treatment plant, garbage cooling system, stabilizing fins, propellers, and transversal thrusters, among others.

This firefighting system will be pressurized and supplied with saltwater by four centrifugal pumps designed for continuous operation. Each pump is equipped with a speed regulator and draws water directly from the respective saltwater collectors located within the same chamber. The ship is divided into two main fire zones, with two pumps assigned to each zone.

Furthermore, the FiFi pumps must have adequate capacity to provide the maximum flow required by the firefighting system, even with one pump out of service. The system will be arranged in a vertical ring configuration, subdivided into two main horizontal collectors. The upper collector will be positioned on the main deck, while the lower collector will be located beneath the second deck. Each of the two longitudinal horizontal collectors that form the system can supply the total required flow to the FiFi system under emergency conditions.

3.3. Data Acquisition

Data acquisition tests were conducted on a real ship. For this purpose, a custom datalogger was developed and integrated into the ship's control system network. The historical data gathered under controlled conditions were subsequently utilized for training the neural networks.

It is important to note that the sensor information data used in this study is confidential. The data were collected under strict confidentiality agreements to protect the proprietary information of the ship's systems and ensure the privacy of the operational details. As such, specific details regarding the sensor data cannot be disclosed.

Several tests were performed with the objective of collecting a substantial amount of data, categorized into two types: normal operation and fault behavior.

First, data regarding the normal operation of the system (the FiFi system consuming water) were collected. To collect data corresponding to the normal operation of the system, all relevant consumers were opened, including firefighting nozzles with different flow rates, space sprinklers, and foam stations. Additionally, other shipboard systems were activated, such as bilge ejectors, the wastewater treatment plant, the waste cooling system, stabilizing fins, propellers, and transversal thrusters. These actions allowed for the collection of diverse data on the system's behavior under typical operational conditions. Figure 1 presents two examples of the pressure drop data series collected during the system's normal operation.

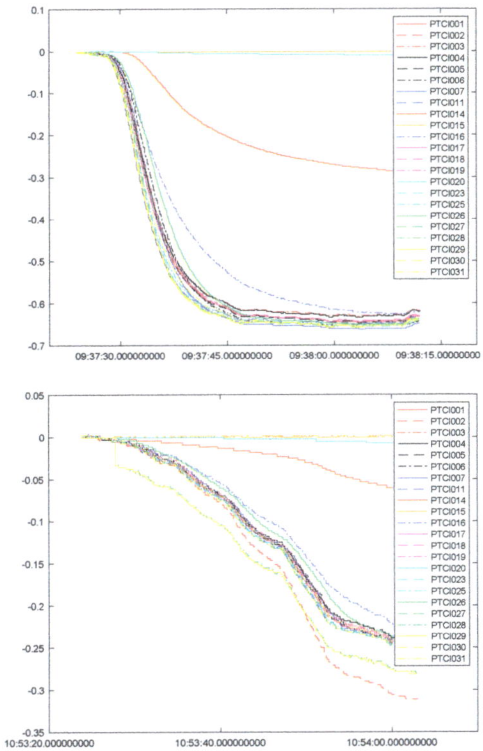

Figure 1. Time series of pressure drop data collected during normal operation (y-axis in bars).

On the other hand, efforts were made to replicate pipeline faults, such as ruptures. For this purpose, quick-opening valves were installed at various points in the system, under the assumption that their behavior would mimic the effects of a pipe section breaking. These quick-opening valves were strategically placed in different locations within the system branches, with varying pipe diameters, to simulate ruptures with different flow rates. Figure 2 illustrates the pressure drops recorded during two pipe break events.

Although this approach aimed to cover a range of rupture scenarios, it is acknowledged that the data collected from these simulated breaks may be insufficient to represent all possible pipe rupture scenarios comprehensively. Nonetheless, the primary goal at this stage of development was to validate the proposed methodology. Future phases will involve extensive neural network training incorporating various fault scenarios, combining real-world data with simulated data. This approach will help address a broader spectrum of pressure drop profiles that may occur under different fault conditions.

It is important to highlight that adjustments to the signal sampling frequency and the precision of pressure measurements (significant digits) were necessary to effectively characterize the pressure drops. These considerations, which may initially appear minor or insignificant, must be carefully addressed when planning data acquisition for digital twin developments. This is because certain functionalities, particularly those leveraging AI or advanced data analysis, may require high-frequency data to detect transient events, whereas routine ship operations do not typically demand high-frequency or high-precision data collection.

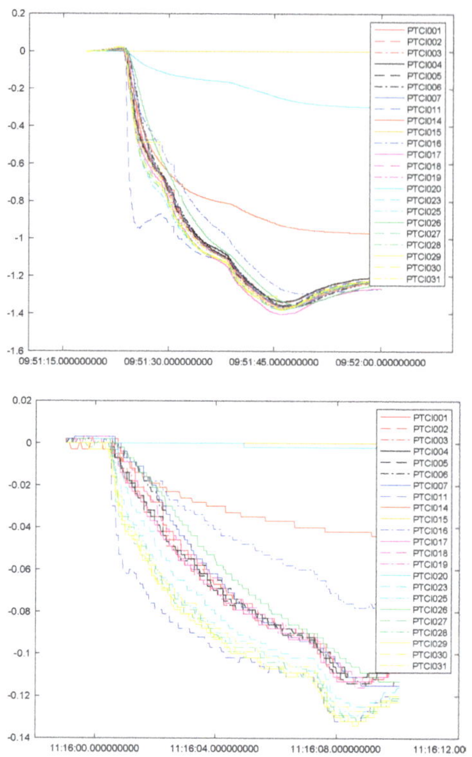

Figure 2. Time series of pressure drop data collected during fault mode (y-axis in bars).

Based on the tests conducted, the following key recommendations and limitations should be considered for the training of neural networks aimed at detecting and localizing faults using real data collected from the ship:

- Data acquisition should be conducted at a frequency of no less than 10 Hz, with a recommended frequency of 20 Hz or higher to achieve optimal system performance. This conclusion is based on the observation that, in cases where data were recorded at lower frequencies, the collected information was insufficient to capture critical events and, therefore, could not be effectively utilized for analysis. Higher sampling frequencies are particularly important for detecting rapid changes in pressure or flow, which are often indicative of faults or anomalies. Insufficient sampling rates may result in data that fail to accurately represent the dynamics of the system, potentially leading to undetected issues or delayed responses.
- For pressurized water systems operating within a range of 8 to 12 bar, it is essential that the pressure signal be recorded with an accuracy of at least one-hundredth of a bar. This conclusion stems from tests conducted with data recorded at a lower precision, specifically with a resolution of one-tenth of a bar, which proved unsuitable for detecting subtle pressure variations.
- The duration of data samples is another critical factor in the detection and diagnosis of faults. Time series shorter than 2 s have been shown to be inadequate for accurately identifying anomalies in system operation, as they do not provide enough information to characterize the behavior or trends in the data. Samples of at least 3 s yield significantly better results, enabling more reliable fault detection. Furthermore, extending the sample duration beyond 3 s enhances the accuracy and robustness of

anomaly identification, as larger datasets allow for a more comprehensive analysis of system behavior. However, it is also important to balance sample size with real-time processing capabilities, as excessively long durations may increase computational demands and affect the responsiveness of the fault detection system.

3.4. AI Development Description

3.4.1. Fault Detection Network

This neural network can identify abnormal operations within the system and can additionally specify the zone of the ship where the anomaly is occurring. Neural networks (NNs) are computational models designed to simulate the functioning of neurons in the human brain, with the objective of solving complex computational problems that are not easily programmable [43]. Therefore, these artificial neural networks are trained to learn from data.

A multi-layer perceptron (MLP) architecture was employed in this study. The MLP is composed of multiple layers of neurons: an input layer, one or more hidden layers, and an output layer. Each neuron in each layer is fully connected to every neuron in the next layer. This configuration allows the network to learn complex patterns and relationships within the dataset, making it suitable for the task of detecting and localizing faults in the ship's firefighting system. The developed algorithm has a general scheme like the following (Figure 3):

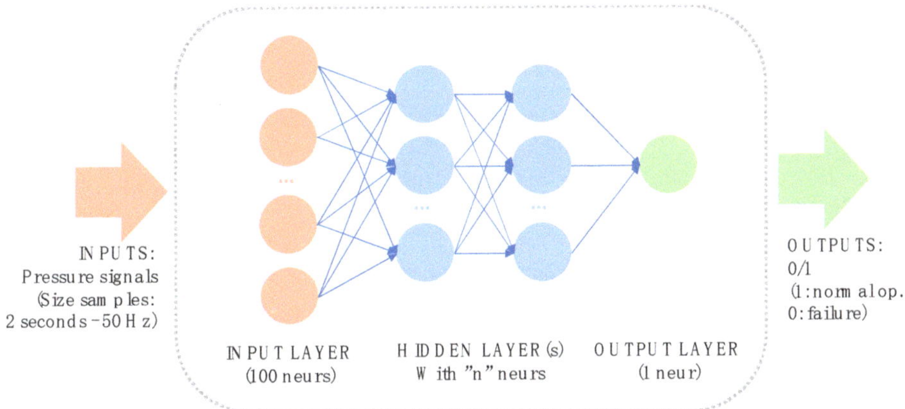

Figure 3. Neural network (fault detection) scheme.

The input data for the neural network consist of a series of pressure measurements from each sensor, capturing both time and pressure values. The output is a binary indicator (0/1) that signifies either a fault or normal operation of the system. In the neural network model, each node functions as a neuron, and the connections between nodes in different layers are represented by arrows. These connections involve multiplying the neuron's output by a weight value, which can either enhance or diminish the activation level of neighboring neurons. Furthermore, at the neuron's output, an activation function or threshold may be applied. This function adjusts the output value or imposes a limit before it propagates to the next neuron, playing a crucial role in the network's learning process.

The architecture chosen for the fault detection was a fitting neural network. In this context, the network is trained on a set of inputs to produce corresponding target outputs. Various configurations of the network, including different numbers of layers and neurons, as well as different sizes of input data samples, were explored to identify the optimal configuration.

A feed-forward, fully connected neural network architecture was selected due to its wide usage and versatility. Error correction learning, specifically a back propagation/gradient descent algorithm, was employed to allow the network to self-adjust its parameters. Bayesian regularization was chosen as the training algorithm to avoid potential overfitting issues. This decision was based on preliminary results obtained using MATLAB's NFTOOL, which allows for straightforward neural network training without programming. The results with Bayesian regularization significantly improved upon those obtained using the Levenberg–Marquardt algorithm.

Since there is no established rule for determining the optimal number of layers or neurons for a neural network, a sensitivity analysis was conducted to identify the optimal structure that minimizes error: a number of layers that varies from 1 to 3 and a number of neurons that varies from 5 to 30.

Manual selection of cases for training, validation, and testing was performed to ensure a correct distribution of real-world cases.

The primary evaluation metric used was the mean squared error (MSE). The network's performance was assessed based on the training, validation, and test errors to ensure the models' generalization capabilities. The performance results were obtained from the three best networks stored by the program for each configuration.

Figure 4 illustrates the algorithm proposed for developing the neural network.

To develop both the detection and localization algorithms, the standard model selection and error estimation procedure was employed [44]. This procedure encompasses a set of techniques utilized in machine learning and statistics for selecting models and estimating generalization error.

The objective of this procedure is to select a model that best fits the available data while avoiding overfitting and underfitting. Overfitting occurs when a model fits the training data too closely, capturing noise and losing its ability to generalize to new data. Conversely, underfitting arises when the model is too simplistic to capture the underlying relationships in the data.

The standard model selection and error estimation procedure generally follows the following steps:

- Data Splitting: The available data are divided into training and test (or validation) sets. The training set is used to fit and train different models, while the test set is used to evaluate the performance of the models and estimate generalization error.
- Model Selection: Different models with different structures or hyperparameters are chosen, which may vary in their complexity. This may involve selecting different neural network architectures, different machine learning algorithms, or different feature sets.
- Training and Cross-Validation: Models are trained on the training set and evaluated on the validation set or through cross-validation. Cross-validation involves dividing the training set into several parts and performing multiple rounds of training and evaluation on different subsets.
- Model Evaluation and Selection: Models are compared and evaluated using performance metrics such as mean squared error, accuracy, F1 score, etc. The model with the best performance on the test set or cross-validation is selected.
- Generalization Error Estimation: Once the final model is selected, the generalization error is estimated by evaluating its performance on the test set, which contains unseen data during the training and selection processes.

The model architecture is grounded in an artificial neural network consisting of one or more hidden layers (defined by 'layers') and a variable number of neurons in each hidden layer (defined by 'neurons'). The flexibility of the network architecture allows for the inclusion of 1 to 3 hidden layers, each featuring a number of neurons ranging from 5 to 50.

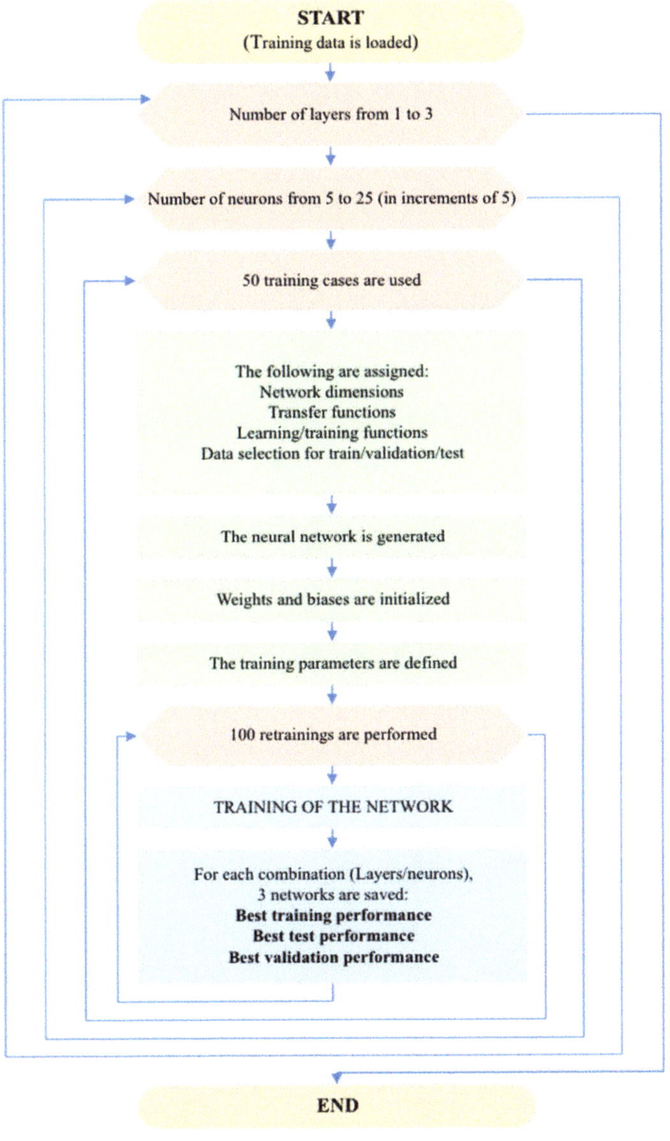

Figure 4. Neural network for fault detection.

The search is constrained for the number of layers within a range of a minimum of one layer to a maximum of three layers. The models considered span from a simple neural network to a deeper network with three hidden layers.

For the numbers of neurons per layer, exploration covers a range from 5 to 50 for each hidden layer. This encompasses models with varying levels of complexity and the capacity to learn sophisticated representations.

Granularity pertains to the number of different values considered for each hyperparameter. In this case, the following parameters are used:

- For the number of layers ('layers'), evaluation encompasses three different values: 1, 2, and 3. This provides a reasonable granularity for exploring models of different depths.
- For the number of neurons per layer ('neurons'), exploration spans 46 different values, ranging from 5 to 50. This search entails a relatively fine granularity, facilitating consideration of a diverse array of neural architectures with differing representation capabilities.

After the training process of the neural network, the regression curves obtained were analyzed, showing the correlation between the targets (x-axis) and the outputs of the system (y-axis). Some examples of regression curves are shown in Figures 5–7.

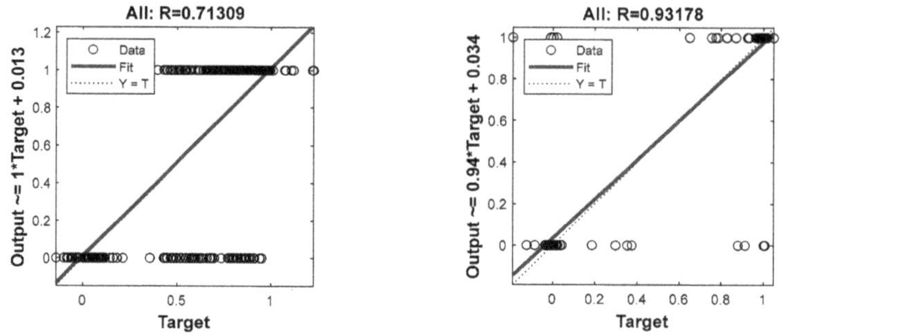

(a) (b)

Figure 5. Regression curves obtained in training: (**a**) 1 layer and 5 neurons; (**b**) 3 layers and 5 neurons. Sample size: 3 s.

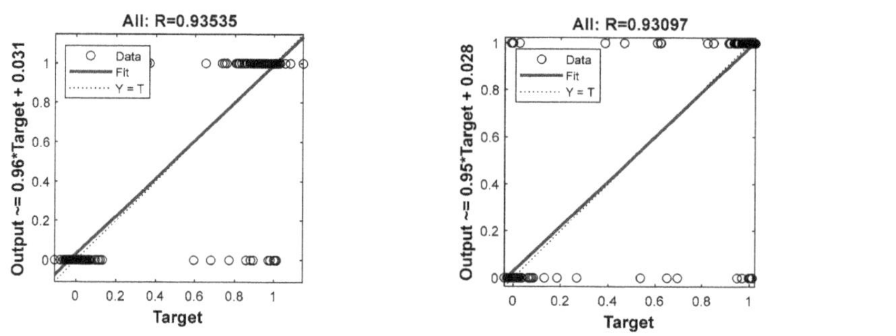

(a) (b)

Figure 6. Regression curves obtained in training: (**a**) 1 layer and 5 neurons; (**b**) 3 layers and 5 neurons. Sample size: 6.5 s.

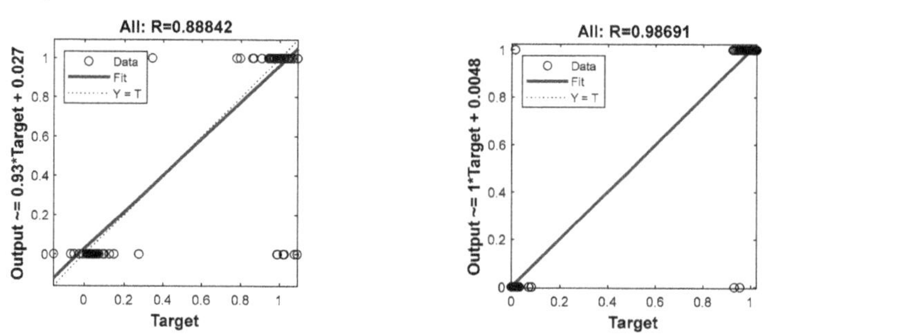

(a) (b)

Figure 7. Regression curves obtained in training: (**a**) 1 layer and 5 neurons; (**b**) 3 layers and 5 neurons. Sample size: 9 s.

- The network training was conducted with a limited number of cases representing normal operation and fault. To achieve better model adjustment, it is necessary to train the neural network over extended periods under real operating conditions and to simulate abnormal scenarios, such as breakages or collapses, to fine-tune the network's performance.
- The optimal sample size for achieving the best network performance was identified as 9 s.
- Networks with 5 to 50 neurons per layer were analyzed. It was observed that using more than 10 neurons per layer did not enhance the network's performance.
- Networks with 1 to 10 layers were evaluated, and generally, better results were obtained with an intermediate number of layers. There was no conclusive evidence that using the minimum or maximum number of layers improved the network's performance.
- For the different sample sizes, there are one or several combinations of the number of layers and neurons that minimize the training error.

3.4.2. Fault Location Network

Using real data collected from the tests, a neural network was tested to approximate the fault location. The network uses pressure measurements from the sensors to determine signal delays. Based on these pressure drop patterns, the network attempts to identify the approximate section of the system where the fault has occurred.

To achieve this, it was necessary to characterize the locations of the sensors and consumers within the system to properly label the positions of elements. This labeling is essential for training the AI-based fault location system. Due to the limitations of the tests conducted, data were collected only from consumers and faults at specific positions on the ship. The ship was divided into nine areas, with the different tests carried out being labeled accordingly (Figure 8). The division into nine zones was determined based on the ship's structure and operational requirements. Specifically, the ship was divided into three vertical zones, corresponding to the ship's three main fire zones. Each of these vertical zones was further subdivided into three horizontal zones. This structured division allows for precise localization of faults and ensures that the neural network can effectively identify and differentiate between different areas of the ship.

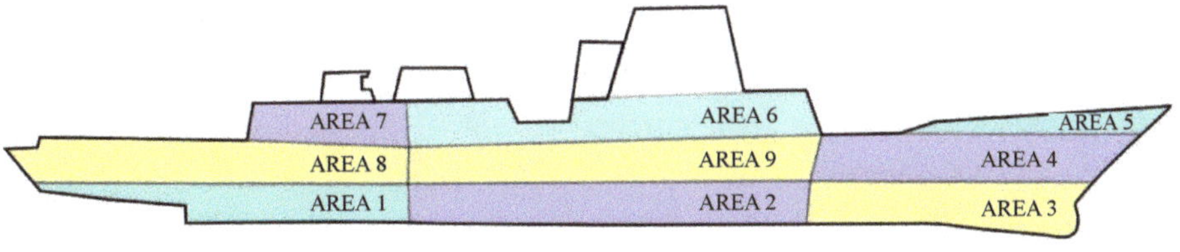

Figure 8. Areas into which the vessel has been divided for fault location.

The architecture selected for the fault detection network was a classification network. Classification networks are a type of feed-forward network designed to classify inputs into target categories.

The input data for the neural network consist of a series of pressure measurements from each sensor, capturing both time and pressure values as shown in Figure 9. The output is a numerical representation of a specific zone on the ship where the anomaly is detected. The same dataset used for fault detection is utilized for the anomaly localization network, but the preprocessing differs for training purposes. In the detection network, raw pressure values from the sensors are employed directly. Conversely, for the localization network, the data are preprocessed to compute the pressure drops per second.

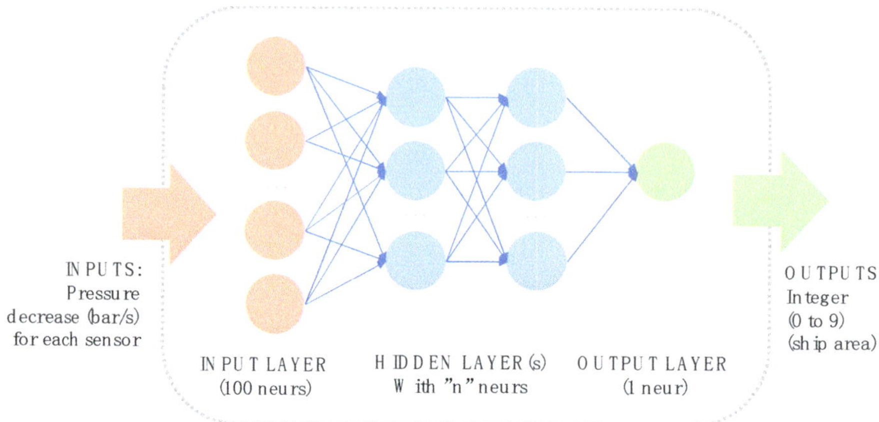

Figure 9. Neural network (fault location) scheme.

Different network configurations, including variations in the number of layers and neurons, as well as the sizes of input data samples, were trained to identify the optimal network performance. Additionally, various training functions were employed, such as the scaled conjugate gradient, Levenberg–Marquardt, and Bayesian regularization. In this particular study, only single-layer networks were used, with the number of neurons reaching up to 50.

Different training functions were employed, including scaled conjugate gradient, Levenberg–Marquardt algorithm, and Bayesian regularization. In this case, only single-layer networks were used, and each configuration was initialized 10 times. For each network initialization, 10 retrainings were performed, retaining the layer with the best performance (minimum MSE).

A schematic of the location algorithm proposed is shown in Figure 10.

The model architecture is based on a single-layer artificial neural network, with the number of neurons specified by the parameter 'neurons'. This design choice reflects a simpler configuration where all processing occurs within a single hidden layer.

The exploration for the number of neurons in this single layer ranges from 5 to 50, providing a spectrum of complexity for the model. The search spans 46 different values, allowing for the consideration of various neural architectures and their respective representation capabilities.

The granularity of the search is defined by the number of different values considered for the 'neurons' parameter, covering 46 values in this case. This fine granularity enables a detailed exploration of the model's performance across a diverse set of neural network configurations.

This approach prioritizes simplicity by employing a single-layer architecture while maintaining flexibility through the exploration of a broad range of neuron values, ensuring a thorough evaluation of the model's capacity to capture patterns and relationships within the data.

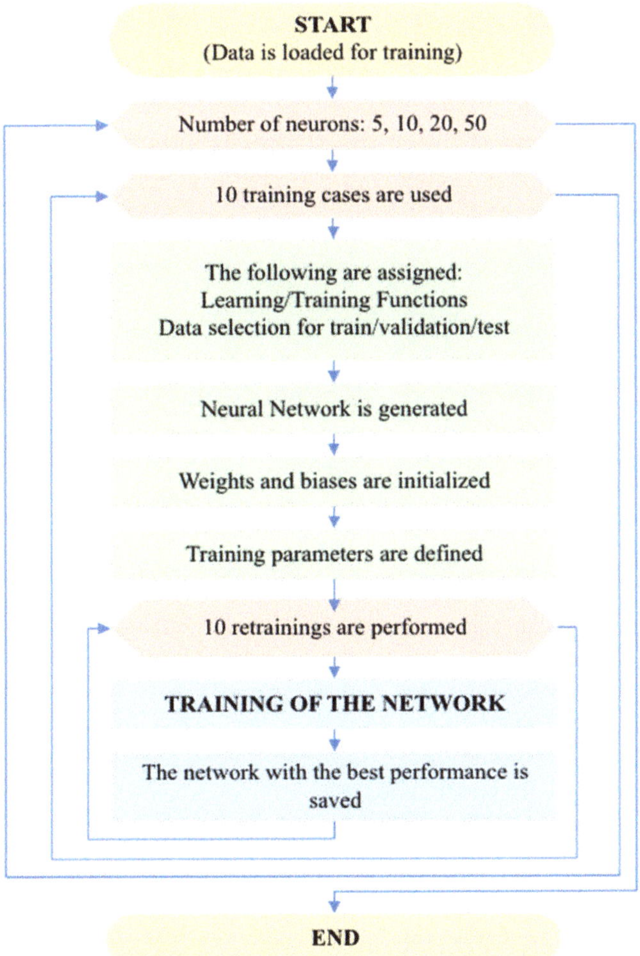

Figure 10. Neural network for fault location.

In this case, we analyzed the receiver operating characteristic (ROC) curves to illustrate the diagnostic ability of the neural network-based fault detection system as its discrimination threshold is varied. The ROC curve is a graphical representation that plots the true positive rate (TPR) against the false positive rate (FPR) at various threshold settings.

- True Positive Rate (TPR): TPR is also known as sensitivity, recall, or probability of detection. TPR measures the proportion of actual positives that are correctly identified by the system. It ranges from 0 to 1 and is plotted on the y-axis.
- False Positive Rate (FPR): FPR is also known as the probability of false alarm. FPR measures the proportion of actual negatives that are incorrectly identified as positives by the system. It ranges from 0 to 1 and is plotted on the x-axis.

The ROC curve provides a comprehensive evaluation of the classifier's performance across different threshold values. A perfect classifier would have a point in the upper left corner of the ROC space (TPR = 1, FPR = 0), indicating 100% sensitivity and 0% false alarms.

Figures 11–13 show the ROC curves obtained from our analysis, demonstrating the effectiveness of the neural network models in distinguishing between normal operation and fault conditions.

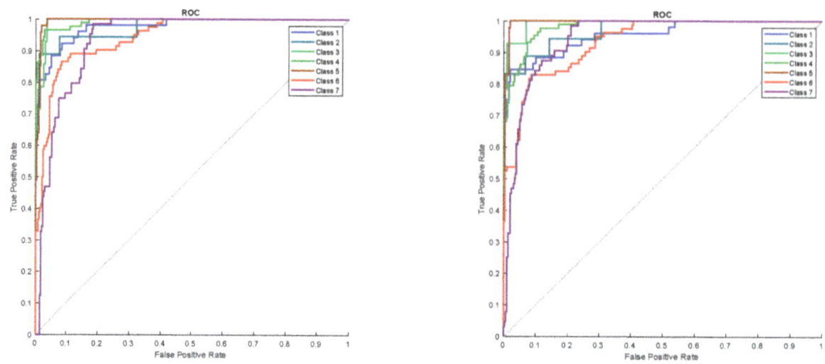

(a) (b)

Figure 11. ROC obtained in training: (**a**) 1 layer and 5 neurons; (**b**) 1 layer and 5 neurons. Training: Scaled conjugate gradient.

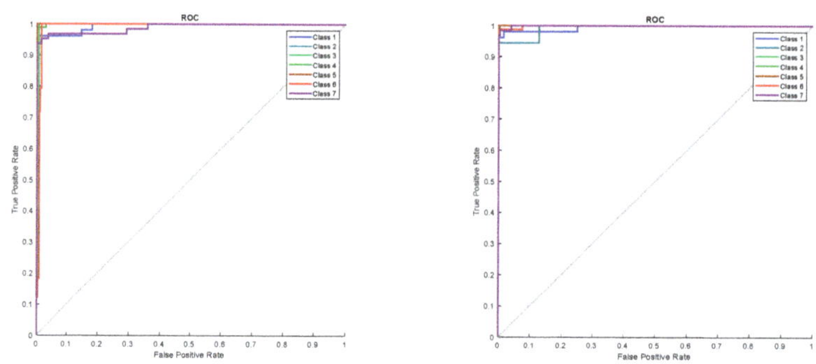

(a) (b)

Figure 12. ROC obtained in training: (**a**) 1 layer and 5 neurons; (**b**) 1 layer and 5 neurons. Training: Levenberg–Marquardt algorithm.

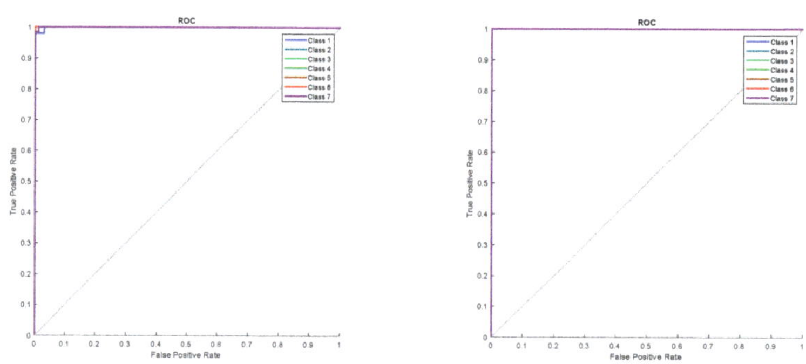

(a) (b)

Figure 13. ROC obtained in training: (**a**) 1 layer and 5 neurons; (**b**) 1 layers and 5 neurons. Training: Bayesian regularization.

- Given the limited amount of available data, the ship was divided into zones, and each consumer opening/pipe break was labeled according to its location within these defined zones. To achieve greater precision in fault detection, it is necessary to acquire a substantial amount of data for training the neural network-based algorithm.

- Several different configurations for the neural network (NN) were defined to determine the best training algorithm and the most effective network structure (number of neurons). The training algorithms used included the scaled conjugate gradient, Levenberg–Marquardt, and Bayesian regularization. Networks with one hidden layer, containing 5, 10, 20, and 50 neurons, were trained.
- The best results were obtained using Bayesian regularization as the training function. The Levenberg–Marquardt algorithm also produced good results, as it did not require a high number of neurons to perform effectively. The poorest results were obtained with the scaled conjugate gradient method.
- It is important to note that the conclusions drawn from these results are based on the premise that the training was conducted with a limited number of training cases, and the identification was performed for relatively large areas of the ship.

4. Discussion

In this work, the development of a method based on the use of neural networks for the detection and location of faults in the FiFi system of a ship has been presented.

This neural network-based system uses the data collected from the sensors of the firefighting system to determine whether the series of pressure data corresponds to normal operation or to the possible rupture of a section of pipe in the system. In addition, the system makes it possible to determine the area of the vessel in which the corresponding breakage has occurred.

To do this, the system has been trained using real data from a ship's FiFi system. Data of normal operation as well as breaks in the pipes of the system have been collected. These data have been labeled for use in training. The results obtained in the training of neural networks for detection and localization of anomalies have been satisfactory.

Data from pressure sensors in the FiFi system must be collected at a higher sampling rate than normally used for system monitoring. However, it has been demonstrated that modifying the sampling rate is feasible. In the case of use considered, with a sampling frequency above 10 Hz, the results obtained were satisfactory, but a sampling rate above 20 Hz is recommended. After analyzing different alternatives in training, it can be affirmed that it is possible to detect and locate the anomaly with a sample size of 10 s.

The data utilized in this study were processed as received from the ship's control system, with modifications made only to the sampling frequency and significant figures. Despite potential challenges, such as noisy data, varying sampling rates, or missing values, the inherent robustness of our neural network models allowed for effective fault detection and localization. It is noteworthy that the noise present in the signals did not pose significant issues during the fault detection and localization processes. This illustrates the practicality of our approach under realistic operational conditions and emphasizes the effectiveness of the methodology even with minimal preprocessing.

Future work will focus on expanding the system by continuously collecting onboard data, enabling the system to learn from new fault scenarios and further improve its fault localization capabilities. Additionally, deploying this system on different ships may require retraining of the neural network to accommodate varying ship configurations and sensor setups, ensuring the model's adaptability to different operational conditions. The integration of hybrid models that combine analytical methods with neural networks will also be explored to enhance fault detection and localization in shipboard systems.

The developed system will be implemented in the ship's digital twin, providing it with intelligence and allowing autonomous detection of faults. Although this methodology has been validated, employing this development on another ship could require retraining of the neural network. This is due to differences in ship configurations and sensor setups that may necessitate the model to adapt to new conditions and ensure accurate fault detection and localization.

5. Conclusions

This work has successfully demonstrated the development of a neural network-based system for detecting and localizing faults in a ship's FiFi system. The use of pressure sensor data collected during both normal operation and pipe break events has shown that neural networks can effectively detect anomalies and pinpoint their location within the vessel.

The results of the study highlight the importance of collecting data at higher sampling frequencies, particularly above 10 Hz, with a recommendation to use rates above 20 Hz for optimal performance. The neural network models have been demonstrated to be robust, effectively handling noisy data and varying sampling rates, and can reliably detect faults with minimal preprocessing.

The methodology presented here holds great promise for real-world applications, especially when integrated into a ship's digital twin for autonomous fault detection. Future work will focus on expanding the system by continuously collecting onboard data, enabling the system to learn from new fault scenarios and further improve its fault localization capabilities.

Furthermore, deploying this system on different ships may require retraining the neural network to accommodate varying ship configurations and sensor setups, ensuring the model's adaptability to different operational conditions.

In conclusion, this study demonstrates the feasibility and potential of using neural networks for fault detection and localization in ship firefighting systems, contributing to improved safety and operational efficiency in maritime operations.

Author Contributions: Conceptualization, S.F.-G., V.D.-C. and M.M.-G.; methodology, S.F.-G., V.D.-C. and M.M.-G.; software, S.F.-G.; validation, S.F.-G.; formal analysis, S.F.-G., V.D.-C. and M.M.-G.; investigation, S.F.-G., V.D.-C. and M.M.-G.; resources, S.F.-G., V.D.-C., M.M.-G. and C.G.S.-G.; data curation, S.F.-G., V.D.-C. and M.M.-G.; writing—original draft preparation, S.F.-G.; writing—review and editing, S.F.-G. and V.D.-C.; visualization, S.F.-G., V.D.-C. and M.M.-G.; supervision, V.D.-C., M.M.-G. and C.G.S.-G.; project administration, V.D.-C. and C.G.S.-G. All authors have read and agreed to the published version of the manuscript.

Funding: This research was funded by Xunta de Galicia and Axencia Galega de Innovacion, grant numbers IN853C2022/01 and ED431C 2022/39.

Institutional Review Board Statement: Not applicable.

Informed Consent Statement: Not applicable.

Data Availability Statement: The data presented in this study are available on request from the corresponding author. The data are not publicly available due to privacy.

Acknowledgments: The results presented in this paper are part of the work developed by the Joint Research Unit formed by Navantia and the University of A Coruna.

Conflicts of Interest: Author Carlos G. San-Gabino was employed by the company Navantia SA. The remaining authors declare that the research was conducted in the absence of any commercial or financial relationships that could be construed as a potential conflict of interest.

References

1. Zhang, J. Designing a Cost-Effective and Reliable Pipeline Leak-Detection System. *Pipes Pipelines Int.* **1997**, *42*, 20–26.
2. Datta, S.; Sarkar, S. A Review on Different Pipeline Fault Detection Methods. *J. Loss Prev. Process Ind.* **2016**, *41*, 97–106. [CrossRef]
3. Lu, H.; Iseley, T.; Behbahani, S.; Fu, L. Leakage Detection Techniques for Oil and Gas Pipelines: State-of-the-Art. *Tunn. Undergr. Space Technol.* **2020**, *98*, 103249. [CrossRef]

4. Bermúdez, J.-R.; López-Estrada, F.-R.; Besançon, G.; Valencia-Palomo, G.; Torres, L.; Hernández, H.-R. Modeling and Simulation of a Hydraulic Network for Leak Diagnosis. *Math. Comput. Appl.* **2018**, *23*, 70. [CrossRef]
5. Meseguer, J.; Mirats-Tur, J.M.; Cembrano, G.; Puig, V. Model-Based Monitoring Techniques for Leakage Localization in Distribution Water Networks. *Procedia Eng.* **2015**, *119*, 1399–1408. [CrossRef]
6. Oyedeko, K.F.K.; Balogun, H.A. Modeling and Simulation of a Leak Detection for Oil and Gas Pipelines via Transient Model: A Case Study of the Niger Delta. *J. Energy Technol. Policy* **2015**, *5*, 16–27.
7. Verde, C.; Molina, L.; Torres, L. Parameterized Transient Model of a Pipeline for Multiple Leaks Location. *J. Loss Prev. Process Ind.* **2014**, *29*, 177–185. [CrossRef]
8. Zhang, T.; Tan, Y.; Zhang, X.; Zhao, J. A Novel Hybrid Technique for Leak Detection and Location in Straight Pipelines. *J. Loss Prev. Process Ind.* **2015**, *35*, 157–168. [CrossRef]
9. Abdulshaheed, A.; Mustapha, F.; Ghavamian, A. A Pressure-Based Method for Monitoring Leaks in a Pipe Distribution System: A Review. *Renew. Sustain. Energy Rev.* **2017**, *69*, 902–911. [CrossRef]
10. Berardi, L.; Laucelli, D.; Ugarelli, R.; Giustolisi, O. Leakage Management: Planning Remote Real Time Controlled Pressure Reduction in Oppegård Municipality. *Procedia Eng.* **2015**, *119*, 72–81. [CrossRef]
11. Giustolisi, O.; Campisano, A.; Ugarelli, R.; Laucelli, D.; Berardi, L. Leakage Management: WDNetXL Pressure Control Module. *Procedia Eng.* **2015**, *119*, 82–90. [CrossRef]
12. Sousa, J.; Ribeiro, L.; Muranho, J.; Sá Marques, A. Locating Leaks in Water Distribution Networks with Simulated Annealing and Graph Theory. *Procedia Eng.* **2015**, *119*, 63–71. [CrossRef]
13. Laurentys, C.A.; Bomfim, C.H.M.; Menezes, B.R.; Caminhas, W.M. Design of a Pipeline Leakage Detection Using Expert System: A Novel Approach. *Appl. Soft Comput. J.* **2011**, *11*, 1057–1066. [CrossRef]
14. Sukarno, P.; Adji Sidarto, K.; Trisnobudi, A.; Setyoadi, D.I.; Rohani, N.; Darmadi, D. Leak Detection Modeling and Simulation for Oil Pipeline with Artificial Intelligence Method. *ITB J. Eng. Sci.* **2007**, *39*, 1–19. [CrossRef]
15. Zhao, X.; Ba, Q.; Zhou, L.; Li, W.; Ou, J. BP Neural Network Recognition Algorithm for Scour Monitoring of Subsea Pipelines Based on Active Thermometry. *Optik* **2014**, *125*, 5426–5431. [CrossRef]
16. Pérez-Pérez, E.J.; López-Estrada, F.R.; Valencia-Palomo, G.; Torres, L.; Puig, V.; Mina-Antonio, J.D. Leak Diagnosis in Pipelines Using a Combined Artificial Neural Network Approach. *Control Eng. Pract.* **2021**, *107*, 104677. [CrossRef]
17. Leu, S.S.; Bui, Q.N. Leak Prediction Model for Water Distribution Networks Created Using a Bayesian Network Learning Approach. *Water Resour. Manag.* **2016**, *30*, 2719–2733. [CrossRef]
18. Zadkarami, M.; Shahbazian, M.; Salahshoor, K. Pipeline Leakage Detection and Isolation: An Integrated Approach of Statistical and Wavelet Feature Extraction with Multi-Layer Perceptron Neural Network (MLPNN). *J. Loss Prev. Process Ind.* **2016**, *43*, 479–487. [CrossRef]
19. Zadkarami, M.; Shahbazian, M.; Salahshoor, K. Pipeline Leak Diagnosis Based on Wavelet and Statistical Features Using Dempster–Shafer Classifier Fusion Technique. *Process Saf. Environ. Prot.* **2017**, *105*, 156–163. [CrossRef]
20. Gómez-Camperos, J.A.; Espinel-Blanco, E.E.; Regino-Ubarnes, F.J. Diagnosis of Horizontal Pipe Leaks Using Neural Networks. *J. Phys. Conf. Ser.* **2019**, *1388*, 012032. [CrossRef]
21. Jia, Z.; Ren, L.; Li, H.; Sun, W. Pipeline Leak Localization Based on FBG Hoop Strain Sensors Combined with BP Neural Network. *Appl. Sci.* **2018**, *8*, 146. [CrossRef]
22. Pulido, B.; Zamarreño, J.M.; Merino, A.; Bregon, A. State Space Neural Networks and Model-Decomposition Methods for Fault Diagnosis of Complex Industrial Systems. *Eng. Appl. Artif. Intell.* **2019**, *79*, 67–86. [CrossRef]
23. Kang, J.; Park, Y.J.; Lee, J.; Wang, S.H.; Eom, D.S. Novel Leakage Detection by Ensemble CNN-SVM and Graph-Based Localization in Water Distribution Systems. *IEEE Trans. Ind. Electron.* **2018**, *65*, 4279–4289. [CrossRef]
24. Javadiha, M.; Blesa, J.; Soldevila, A.; Puig, V. Leak Localization in Water Distribution Networks Using Deep Learning. In Proceedings of the 2019 6th International Conference on Control, Decision and Information Technologies, CoDIT 2019, Paris, France, 23–26 April 2019; pp. 1426–1431. [CrossRef]
25. Janssen, J.A.A.J.; Butler, J.; Worthington, P.; Geertsma, F.D.; den Hartog, M.H. Autonomous, Adaptive, Aware: DINCS. In Proceedings of the 13th International Naval Engineering Conference and Exhibition, INEC 2016, Bristol, UK, 16 April 2016.
26. López-Estrada, F.R.; Theilliol, D.; Astorga-Zaragoza, C.M.; Ponsart, J.C.; Valencia-Palomo, G.; Camas-Anzueto, J. Fault Diagnosis Observer for Descriptor Takagi-Sugeno Systems. *Neurocomputing* **2019**, *331*, 10–17. [CrossRef]
27. Kharrat, D.; Gassara, H.; El Hajjaji, A.; Chaabane, M. Adaptive Observer and Fault Tolerant Control for Takagi-Sugeno Descriptor Nonlinear Systems with Sensor and Actuator Faults. *Int. J. Control Autom. Syst.* **2018**, *16*, 972–982. [CrossRef]
28. Wolpert, D.H. The Lack of a Priori Distinctions between Learning Algorithms. *Neural Comput.* **1996**, *8*, 1341–1390. [CrossRef]
29. Assani, N.; Matić, P.; Katalinić, M. Ship's Digital Twin—A Review of Modelling Challenges and Applications. *Appl. Sci.* **2022**, *12*, 6039. [CrossRef]
30. Glatt, M.; Sinnwell, C.; Yi, L.; Donohoe, S.; Ravani, B.; Aurich, J.C. Modeling and Implementation of a Digital Twin of Material Flows Based on Physics Simulation. *J. Manuf. Syst.* **2020**, *58*, 231–245. [CrossRef]

31. Post, J.; Groen, M.; Klaseboer, G. Physical model based digital twins in manufacturing processes. In Proceedings of the 10th Forming Technology Forum, Enschede, The Netherlands, 12–13 January 2017.
32. Ritto, T.G.; Rochinha, F.A. Digital Twin, Physics-Based Model, and Machine Learning Applied to Damage Detection in Structures. *Mech. Syst. Signal Process* **2021**, *155*, 107614. [CrossRef]
33. Friederich, J.; Francis, D.P.; Lazarova-Molnar, S.; Mohamed, N. A Framework for Data-Driven Digital Twins of Smart Manufacturing Systems. *Comput. Ind.* **2022**, *136*, 103586. [CrossRef]
34. Coraddu, A.; Oneto, L.; Baldi, F.; Cipollini, F.; Atlar, M.; Savio, S. Data-Driven Ship Digital Twin for Estimating the Speed Loss Caused by the Marine Fouling. *Ocean. Eng.* **2019**, *186*, 106063. [CrossRef]
35. Huang, K.-Y. Pattern Recognition to Seismic Exploration. In *Automated Pattern Analysis in Petroleum Exploration*; Springer: New York, NY, USA, 1992; pp. 121–153.
36. Kothari, S.C.; Oh, H. *Neural Networks for Pattern Recognition*; Oxford University Press: Oxford, UK, 1993; pp. 119–166.
37. Audibert, J.; Michiardi, P.; Guyard, F.; Marti, S.; Zuluaga, M.A. Do Deep Neural Networks Contribute to Multivariate Time Series Anomaly Detection? *Pattern Recognit.* **2022**, *132*, 108945. [CrossRef]
38. Esposito, A.; Falanga, M.; Funaro, M.; Marinaro, M.; Scarpetta, S. *Signal Classification Using Neural Networks*; Neural Nets WIRN Vietri-01. Perspectives in Neural Computing; Tagliaferri, R., Marinaro, M., Eds.; Springer: London, UK, 2002; pp. 187–192. [CrossRef]
39. Nishizaki, H.; Makino, K. Signal Classification Using Deep Learning. In Proceedings of the 2019 IEEE International Conference on Sensors and Nanotechnology, Penang, Malaysia, 24–25 July 2019; pp. 1–4.
40. Erge, O.; van Oort, E. *Combining Physics-Based and Data-Driven Modeling for Pressure Prediction in Well Construction*; SciPy: Washington, DC, USA, 2020; pp. 125–131.
41. Kapteyn, M.G.; Knezevic, D.J.; Huynh, D.B.P.; Tran, M.; Willcox, K.E. Data-Driven Physics-Based Digital Twins via a Library of Component-Based Reduced-Order Models. *Int. J. Numer. Methods Eng.* **2020**, *123*, 2986–3003. [CrossRef]
42. Blakseth, S.S.; Rasheed, A.; Kvamsdal, T.; San, O. Combining Physics-Based and Data-Driven Techniques for Reliable Hybrid Analysis and Modeling Using the Corrective Source Term Approach. *Appl. Soft Comput.* **2022**, *128*, 109533. [CrossRef]
43. Serrano-cinca, C. Fundamentos de Las Redes Neuronales Artificiales: Hardware y Software. *Scire Represent. Organ. Conoc.* **1995**, *1*, 103–125.
44. Bartlett, P.L.; Boucheron, S.; Lugosi, G. Model Selection and Error Estimation. *Mach. Learn.* **2002**, *48*, 85–113. [CrossRef]

applied sciences

MDPI

Article

FedSeq: Personalized Federated Learning via Sequential Layer Expansion in Representation Learning

Jae Won Jang and Bong Jun Choi *

Department of Computer Science, Soongsil University, Seoul 06978, Republic of Korea; jwon09@naver.com
* Correspondence: davidchoi@soongsil.ac.kr

Abstract: Federated learning ensures the privacy of clients by conducting distributed training on individual client devices and sharing only the model weights with a central server. However, in real-world scenarios, especially in IoT scenarios where devices have varying capabilities and data heterogeneity exists among IoT clients, appropriate personalization methods are necessary. In this paper, this work aims to address this heterogeneity using a form of parameter decoupling known as representation learning. Representation learning divides deep learning models into 'base' and 'head' components. The base component, capturing common features across all clients, is shared with the server, while the head component, capturing unique features specific to individual clients, remains local. This work proposes a new representation learning-based approach, named FedSeq, that suggests decoupling the entire deep learning model into more densely divided parts with the application of suitable scheduling methods, which can benefit not only data heterogeneity but also class heterogeneity. FedSeq has two different layer scheduling approaches, namely forward (*Vanilla*) and backward (*Anti*), in the context of data and class heterogeneity among clients. Our experimental results show that FedSeq, when compared to existing personalized federated learning algorithms, achieves increased accuracy, especially under challenging conditions, while reducing computation costs. The study introduces a novel personalized federated learning approach that integrates sequential layer expansion and dynamic scheduling methods, demonstrating a 7.31% improvement in classification accuracy on the CIFAR-100 dataset and a 4.1% improvement on the Tiny-ImageNet dataset compared to existing methods, while also reducing computation costs by up to 15%. Furthermore, Anti Scheduling achieves a computational efficiency improvement of 3.91% compared to FedAvg and 3.06% compared to FedBABU, while Vanilla Scheduling achieves a significant efficiency improvement of 63.93% compared to FedAvg and 63.61% compared to FedBABU.

Keywords: federated learning (FL); data heterogeneity; personalized federated learning (PFL); representation learning; meta-learning

1. Introduction

Traditional centralized machine learning collects all raw data and sends them to a central server for training. However, concerns about data privacy have grown among companies and researchers in the era of big data. Moreover, the implementation of stringent legal regulations, such as the General Data Protection Regulation (GDPR) [1] in Europe and the California Consumer Privacy Act (CCPA) [2] in the United States, has underscored the need for new methods of collecting and sharing client data that comply with these laws. In this context, federated learning has emerged as a significant research area, allowing the utilization of diverse data distributed across various devices like smartphones, IoT devices, and wearables while ensuring data privacy.

Federated learning [3], in contrast to centralized machine learning, does not directly share raw client data with a central server. Instead, it trains models on each edge device and shares only the model's weights, aggregating them to update a global model. This training approach ensures privacy, as raw data are not shared with the server, and it offers communication cost advantages when dealing with large data sets. However, in real-world scenarios, local data among clients can be highly heterogeneous, exhibiting varying data distributions. This heterogeneity can lower the performance of the global model during server-side aggregation and may introduce a bias towards specific clients.

Therefore, the need for suitable personalization methodologies arises to capture and optimize each client's unique data characteristics. To address these issues, personalized federated learning (PFL) approaches [4,5] are actively being researched. This study utilizes representation learning, which is one of the PFL approaches. Representation learning divides the layers of a deep learning model into base and head components. In representation learning, the base (or feature extractor)part represents common features for all clients and is shared with the server and all clients. The head (or classifier) part represents unique features for specific clients and remains on the local device, not shared with the server. Typically, the head part uses the last fully connected layer (classification layer). In our experimental setup, this work also designates the head part as the last fully connected layer while setting the remaining layers as the base part. Therefore, the need for suitable personalization methodologies arises to capture and optimize each client's unique data characteristics. To address these issues, personalized federated learning (PFL) approaches [4,5] are actively being researched. This study utilizes representation learning, which is one of the PFL approaches. Representation learning divides the layers of a deep learning model into base and head components. In representation learning, the base (or feature extractor) part represents common features for all clients and is shared with the server and all clients. The head (or classifier) part represents unique features for specific clients and remains on the local device, not shared with the server. Typically, the head part uses the last fully connected layer (classification layer). In our experimental setup, this work also designates the head part as the last fully connected layer while setting the remaining layers as the base part.

The proposed algorithm, FedSeq, subdivides the components of the deep learning model in representation learning more densely than just the base and head. The fine-grained layer expansion is carried out sequentially during multiple iterations of local training and aggregation uniquely characterized by FL architecture. Additionally, the layer scheduling approach of FedSeq was inspired by curriculum learning [6], resulting in the development of both Vanilla and Anti-scheduling. Curriculum learning is a method that, similar to how human learning, gradually progresses from easy examples to more challenging ones. Traditional curriculum learning focuses on determining the difficulty of datasets and utilizes pre-trained expert models on the entire dataset to evaluate the difficulty of each data point. Subsequently, difficulty scores are assigned based on the client's loss using the pre-trained expert model, and training is conducted either by starting with easy examples and progressing to harder ones or vice versa. In the recently researched federated learning environment, curriculum learning [7] also necessitates a well-trained expert model.

However, curriculum learning relies on expert models to assess the difficulty of data points. This dependence can result in significantly reduced performance if the expert models are compromised by malicious attacks or poorly trained. Furthermore, the process of assigning difficulty scores and dividing datasets based on difficulty can complicate operations in a federated learning environment, as highlighted by [7]. In contrast to curriculum learning, our scheduling algorithm does not categorize data based on difficulty levels. Instead, it focuses on decoupling layers according to the principles of representation learning. In typical deep learning models, the initial layers are responsible for extracting low-level features, while the later layers handle the extraction of more complex and abstract features [8]. Building on this insight, this work has concentrated on more densely separating the base layer in representation learning algorithms and sequentially training it, deviating from the traditional curriculum learning approach.

Hence, our algorithm densely divides the base layer, initially freezing the entire layer set and then progressively unfreezing specific layers for training according to a schedule. There are two scheduling methods: *Vanilla* scheduling, which starts by unfreezing layers closest to the input and progresses towards the output, and *Anti* scheduling, which begins by unfreezing layers nearest to the output and works backward. A key advantage of our proposed algorithm is that, during the early rounds, only a portion of the unfrozen base layer is shared with the server rather than the entirety. This approach not only enhances performance but also reduces the communication and computational costs compared to other algorithms.

The remainder of the paper is organized as follows: Section 2 reviews related work on federated learning and personalization techniques, including representation learning. Section 3 introduces the proposed algorithms, Vanilla Scheduling and Anti Scheduling, with detailed explanations of the methodology. Section 4 presents our experimental setup, datasets, and comparative analysis with existing methods. Section 5 discusses the results of the ablation study, examining the impact of different factors on the performance of the model. Finally, Section 6 concludes the paper by summarizing the key findings and suggesting potential directions for future research.

The contributions of this paper are as follows:

- Our algorithm densely divides the base layer to address the heterogeneity of the client's data and class distribution, and it proposes two scheduling methods.
- The implementation of scheduling reduces the need to communicate all base layers in the early stages of training, thereby cutting down on communication and computational costs.
- In scenarios with both data and class heterogeneity, the *Anti* Scheduling approach outperforms other algorithms in terms of accuracy. In contrast, the *Vanilla* Scheduling method significantly reduces computational costs compared to other algorithms.
- This work visually presents the accuracy for each client and mathematically compares the computational costs of each algorithm.

2. Related Work

2.1. Federated Learning

Federated learning is a machine learning technique that enables training while ensuring the privacy of clients' distributed data [3]. However, a significant challenge in real-world federated learning scenarios is the heterogeneity of the data distribution between distributed clients, which requires the application of appropriate personalization techniques.

2.2. Personalized Federated Learning

Personalized federated learning (PFL) has been proposed to address the heterogeneity of client data and can be categorized into several approaches such as clustering, meta-learning, and representation [9]. This section compares four related personalization methods, including representation learning, which are considered similar. Table 1 provides a detailed summary of these personalization methods, highlighting their techniques, descriptions, and limitations.

Table 1. Summary of Personalization Methods in Federated Learning.

Approach	Technique	Description	Limitations/Drawbacks
Meta Learning	MAML [10]	Adapts to new tasks with minimal updates for personalization.	High computational cost and inefficient scaling reduce efficiency in complex environments.
	FOMAML [11]	First-order approximation of MAML to reduce complexity.	Less accurate than second-order differential-based meta-learning performance.
	MetaVers [12]	Enhances robustness across clients with distance-based learning.	High complexity and computational overhead.
Transfer Learning	FedMD [13]	Model distillation for heterogeneous model collaboration.	The model performance is affected by the quality of the public dataset used in the model distillation process.
	FedHealth [14]	Uses pre-trained models for wearable healthcare.	The heterogeneity and noise in wearable data make the model performance unstable.
Multi-Task Learning	Federated MTL [15]	Personalizes models while sharing a global structure.	High communication and computational costs, and the risk of overfitting in some clients can pose challenges.
Representation Learning	FedPer [16]	Adds client-specific layers for personalized learning.	Balancing personalization and model size is challenging.
	LG-FedAvg [17]	Each client learns features tailored to local data while sharing information with the global model to enhance overall performance.	Balancing local and global representations is challenging, with data heterogeneity and high computational and communication costs.
	FedRep [18]	Uses multiple local updates for client-specific classifiers.	Additional personalization processes can increase computational costs, making them inefficient for resource-constrained devices.

Table 1. *Cont.*

Approach	Technique	Description	Limitations/Drawbacks
Representation Learning	FedROD [19]	Improve the global model using Balanced Risk Minimization (BRM) loss function to address class distribution imbalances	High computational and communication costs make it inefficient in resource-constrained environments.
	FedBABU [20]	By updating only the base (feature extractor) and not the head (classifier), it reduces computational costs and achieves efficient personalization.	Enforces a uniform base representation for all clients, which may not be suitable for highly heterogeneous data.
	FedCP [21]	Separates global and personalized features using a Conditional Policy Network, it is trained and prevents the collision of feature information.	Complex implementation and high resources slow the learning process.
	FedCRL [22]	Uses contrastive learning for non-IID data personalization to address label heterogeneity.	High communication and computational overhead, along with sensitivity to incorrect label configurations, can affect the efficiency of contrastive learning-based mechanisms.

2.2.1. Meta Learning

Meta-learning, also referred to as learning to learn, was initially proposed for a few-shot learning. MAML [10] focuses on finding model initialization methods that can rapidly adapt to new and unseen tasks, allowing quick learning of new tasks with limited data. FOMAML [11] employs first-order algorithms, which are computationally less complex compared to other meta-learning algorithms and demonstrate comparable performance without the need for second-order methods. MetaVers [12] uses a combination of distance-based meta-learning and a margin-based loss function to improve the model's robustness across clients.

2.2.2. Transfer Learning

Transfer learning has also been proposed for few-shot learning and is a method to apply knowledge learned in a specific domain to a different domain. It involves adapting a pre-trained backbone from a different domain to a similar but distinct domain using the well-known method of fine-tuning. FedMD [13] solves the heterogeneity problem by transferring and learning knowledge between models with different structures. Additionally, FedHealth [14] proposes a federated transfer learning framework for wearable health data.

2.2.3. Multi-Task Learning

Multi-task learning is a method that can enhance a model's generalization ability by simultaneously learning multiple tasks and sharing knowledge or representations between these tasks. Federated MTL [15] proposes a novel approach that combines federated learning with multi-task learning. This approach improves the performance of each task by addressing multiple related learning tasks simultaneously, enabling efficient learning through the utilization of shared knowledge.

2.2.4. Representaion Learning

The PFL technique this work used is a kind of representation learning, which is a parameter decoupling method to alleviate statistical heterogeneity. Representation learning is a method of training deep learning models by dividing the layers into a base and a head. The base shares common features among clients, while the head layer is kept locally and used for FedPer [16]. LG-FedAvg [17] shows that it generalizes more easily to new devices compared to other learning mechanisms and that fair representations, which obscure protected attributes, are effectively learned through adversarial training. FedRep [18] demonstrates fast convergence in linear regression problems by leveraging distributed computational power among clients to perform many local updates. FedROD [19] shows that there is a discrepancy in the validation methods between general federated learning algorithms and personalized federated learning algorithms. They argue that both local and global model accuracy should be considered and introduce a new loss function to mitigate class imbalance issues. In addition, FedBABU [20] suggests that updating the head in cases where client data is highly heterogeneous can negatively affect personalization. Therefore, during training rounds, a randomly initialized head is used, employing only the body for training and aggregation. Table 1 shows the summary of personalization methods in federated learning.

Table 2 provides a detailed comparison among representation learning methods in federated learning in terms of computational efficiency, head layer utilization, scalability, and flexibility. For computational efficiency, unlike methods such as LG-FedAvg [17] and FedROD [19], which require complex communication protocols or additional loss functions (e.g., BRM in FedROD), FedSeq ensures that only partial layers are progressively updated, minimizing resource consumption. For head layer utilization, FedSeq optimally trains only the base globally and fine-tunes the head locally, ensuring efficient personalization. For scalability, FedSeq uses a split-training approach where only the base layers are trained globally and the head layers are tuned locally. This separation allows for efficient learning while maintaining personalized performance. Finally, for flexibility of personalization,

FedSeq's dynamic updates to sequentially expanded layers provide robust flexibility, distinguishing it from static approaches such as FedBABU [20].

Table 2. Comparison of Representation Learning Methods.

Technique	Computation Efficiency	Head Layer Utilization	Scalability	Flexibility of Personalization
FedPer [16]	✓	Base + Head	Moderate	High
LG-FedAvg [17]	×	Base + Head	Low	Moderate
FedRep [18]	×	Base + Head	Moderate	High
FedROD [19]	×	Base + Head	Low	Moderate
FedBABU [20]	✓	Base Only	High	Moderate
FedCP [21]	×	Base + Head	Moderate	High
FedCRL [22]	×	Base + Head	Low	Moderate
FedSeq (Proposed)	✓	Base Only	High	High

Our work introduces a novel approach to representation learning by employing sequential layer expansion and scheduling methods. Unlike traditional methods that often rely on static or predefined schedules, our Vanilla and Anti Scheduling algorithms strategically decouple and train layers in training rounds. This innovation reduces computational costs and enhances the accuracy of the model, particularly in environments characterized by high data and class heterogeneity. As summarized in Table 2, our proposed FedSeq method addresses key challenges in federated learning, such as computational efficiency, scalability, and flexibility, outperforming existing methods in these critical dimensions.

3. Proposed Algorithm

In this section, this work presents our proposed scheduling algorithms in detail, namely *Vanilla* Scheduling and *Anti* Scheduling. An overview of the proposed algorithm is shown in Figure 1. The proposed algorithm executes the following steps: (1) model distribution; (2) local training via sequential layer expansion (Vanilla or Anti Scheduling); (3) update the server with the refined base parameter $\theta_{i,b}$; (4) aggregate global model θ_G. Then, steps (1)–(4) are repeated up to the predefined condition. Finally, the server fine tunes with base parameter $\theta_{i,b}$ and head parameter $\theta_{i,h}$. As shown in Figure 2, Vanilla Scheduling starts by unfreezing the shallowest layers (closest to the input) and progressively moves towards deeper layers. This method allows the model to capture low-level features early in the training process, which is crucial for building a robust foundational understanding before more high-level features are introduced. Conversely, Anti Scheduling begins with the deepest layers (closest to the output) and progressively unfreezes toward the input. This approach prioritizes the learning of high-level features from the outset, which can be beneficial for complex pattern recognition tasks that depend heavily on such features.

As shown in Figure 2, the structured progression from shallow to deep layers in Vanilla Scheduling, and the reverse in Anti Scheduling, structurally differ from traditional representation learning. In traditional representation learning methods, the base and head of the model are typically trained simultaneously without specific layer prioritization. In our approach, however, each layer's training is specifically timed and prioritized. This strategic scheduling improves the model's ability to adapt to the varying complexities of features throughout the training process.

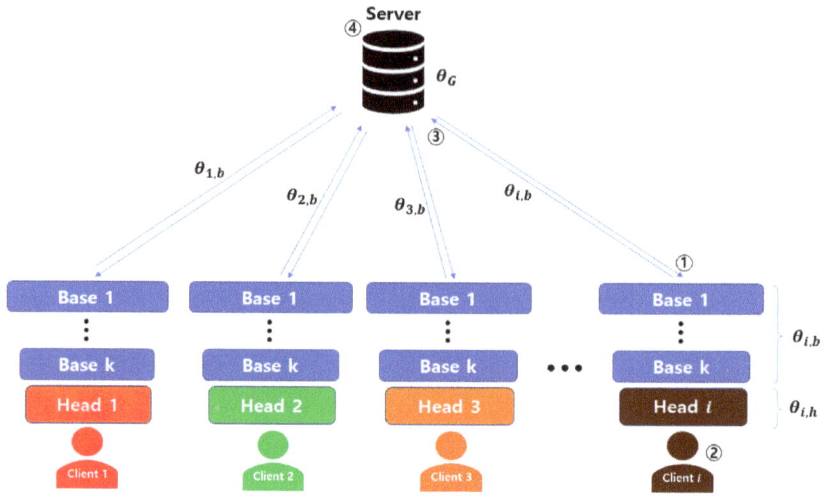

Figure 1. Overview of FedSeq.

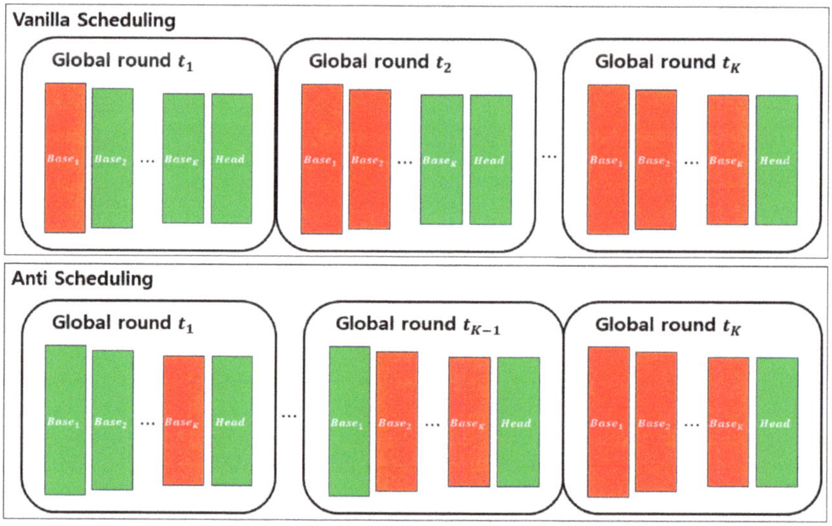

Figure 2. Illustration of the proposed Vanilla and Anti Scheduling algorithms of FedSeq. The **upper** shows Vanilla Scheduling, starting with the shallowest layer and advancing to deeper ones. The **lower** shows Anti Scheduling, which begins with the deepest layer and progresses inversely.

Furthermore, as detailed in Section 5.2, Vanilla Scheduling can achieve comparable accuracy with significantly lower computational costs in environments characterized by high data and class heterogeneity. In contrast, Anti Scheduling excels in achieving the highest accuracy in scenarios where both data and class heterogeneity are pronounced. They both follow the basic federated learning setup and the representation learning as explained below. The list of symbols used in the paper are shown in Table 3.

Table 3. List of Symbols Used.

Symbol	Description
N	Total number of clients
C_i	Client $i \in \{1, 2, \ldots, N\}$
$\lvert D_i \rvert$	Number of data points for client i
$\lvert D \rvert$	Number of data points
T	Number of global rounds
F	Number of fine-tuning rounds
K	Number of base layers
t_k	Unfreeze point (round) of k-th layer
η	Learning rate
$\mathcal{L}$	Loss function
θ_i	Local parameter for client i
θ_G	Global model parameter
$\theta_{i,b}$	Base parameter shared among all clients
$\theta_{i,h}$	Head parameter of client i

As a basic federated learning setup, this work assumes that each client C_i possesses data $D_i = (x_i, y_i) \in R^d$, where $i \in \{1, 2, \ldots, N\}$ represents i-th client out of a total of N clients and d represents the input dimension. Each client i updates its local model parameter θ_i based on its data D_i and the global model parameter θ_G as

$$\theta_i^{(t+1)} = \theta_i^{(t)} - \eta \nabla_{\theta_i} \mathcal{L}(D_i, \theta_i^{(t)}), \tag{1}$$

where η is the learning rate, ∇L is the gradient of the loss function L, and $t = 1, 2, \ldots, T$ denotes the number of rounds. The central server updates the global parameter θ_G based on all clients' local parameter updates as

$$\theta_G^{(t+1)} = \sum_{i=1}^{N} \frac{|D_i|}{|D|} \theta_i^{(t+1)}, \tag{2}$$

where $|D_i|$ is the number of data points for client i, and $|D|$ is the total number of data points.

For representation learning, the model parameters are divided into two components $\theta_i = (\theta_{i,b}, \theta_{i,h})$. Here, $\theta_{i,b}$ represents the base parameter shared among all clients, and $\theta_{i,h}$ represents the head parameter of the i-th client. The model parameters from Equation (1) are modified as follows:

$$\theta_i^{(t+1)} = \theta_i^{(t)} - \eta \nabla_{\theta_i} \mathcal{L}(D_i, \theta_{i,b}^{(t)}, \theta_{i,h}^{(0)}). \tag{3}$$

Excluding FedBABU [20], previous works stop the gradient of the head parameter during training and during the aggregation phase. The global model is updated using both the base and head parameters. However, FedBABU and our scheduling algorithm perform both training and aggregation using only the base without involving the head. Only after training are a few rounds of fine-tuning included using both the base and head.

The aggregation process, which excludes the use of the head, proceeds as follows:

$$\theta_G^{(t+1)} = \sum_{i=1}^{N} \frac{|D_i|}{|D|} \theta_{i,b}^{(t+1)}. \tag{4}$$

Our FedSeq algorithm follows the same training setup as FedBABU [20], wherein the head layer is not trained or aggregated during training; instead, it is fine-tuned for each client after training completion. In FedBABU, the training round sets the learning rate of the head to zero, allowing gradient computation but preventing its application. In contrast, our scheduling algorithm ensures complete decoupling by freezing gradients in both the head and base parts, preventing both computation and application.

3.1. Method 1: Vanilla Scheduling

Vanilla Scheduling is a training method that starts by thoroughly learning the shallowest layers (closest to the input) in the base layer, freezing the rest layers, and then progressively unfreezing them. This enables the model to preferentially learn low-level features and patterns, aiding in better understanding the abstract characteristics and patterns of the data. The training steps of Vanilla Scheduling, which starts with the shallowest layers, can be represented as

$$\begin{aligned}
\theta_i^{(t_1+1)} &= \theta_i^{(t_1)} - \eta \nabla_{\theta_i} \mathcal{L}(D_i, \theta_{i,b_1}^{(t_1)}, \theta_{i,b_2}^{(0)}, \ldots, \theta_{i,b_{K-1}}^{(0)}, \theta_{i,b_K}^{(0)}, \theta_{i,h}^{(0)}), \\
\theta_i^{(t_2+1)} &= \theta_i^{(t_2)} - \eta \nabla_{\theta_i} \mathcal{L}(D_i, \theta_{i,b_1}^{(t_2)}, \theta_{i,b_2}^{(t_2)}, \ldots, \theta_{i,b_{K-1}}^{(0)}, \theta_{i,b_K}^{(0)}, \theta_{i,h}^{(0)}), \\
&\vdots \\
\theta_i^{(t_K+1)} &= \theta_i^{(t_K)} - \eta \nabla_{\theta_i} \mathcal{L}(D_i, \theta_{i,b_1}^{(t_K)}, \theta_{i,b_2}^{(t_K)}, \ldots, \theta_{i,b_{K-1}}^{(t_L)}, \theta_{i,b_K}^{(t_K)}, \theta_{i,h}^{(0)}),
\end{aligned} \tag{5}$$

where $\{t_1, t_2, \ldots, t_K \in T\}$ represent the global rounds where the freeze of each layer is released. Once the first base layer θ_{i,b_1} is sufficiently trained, the freeze on the next base layer θ_{i,b_2} is released for training. This sequential unfreezing and training of base layers up to θ_{i,b_K} defines Vanilla Scheduling. Throughout the training process, the head layer $\theta_{i,h}$ is initialized and kept frozen, only being utilized in the final fine-tuning stage.

3.2. Method 2: Anti Scheduling

Anti Scheduling is a training approach that initiates in the deepest layers (closest to the output) in the base layer, freezing the remaining layers and progressively unfreezing them for sufficient training. This method allows the model to preferentially grasp high-level and various features. The training steps of Anti Scheduling, starting with the deepest layers, can be given as

$$\begin{aligned}
\theta_i^{(t_1+1)} &= \theta_i^{(t_1)} - \eta \nabla_{\theta_i} \mathcal{L}(D_i, \theta_{i,b_1}^{(0)}, \theta_{i,b_2}^{(0)}, \ldots, \theta_{i,b_{K-1}}^{(0)}, \theta_{i,b_K}^{(t_1)}, \theta_{i,h}^{(0)}), \\
\theta_i^{(t_2+1)} &= \theta_i^{(t_2)} - \eta \nabla_{\theta_i} \mathcal{L}(D_i, \theta_{i,b_1}^{(0)}, \theta_{i,b_2}^{(0)}, \ldots, \theta_{i,b_{K-1}}^{(t_2)}, \theta_{i,b_K}^{(t_2)}, \theta_{i,h}^{(0)}), \\
&\vdots \\
\theta_i^{(t_K+1)} &= \theta_i^{(t_K)} - \eta \nabla_{\theta_i} \mathcal{L}(D_i, \theta_{i,b_1}^{(t_K)}, \theta_{i,b_2}^{(t_K)}, \ldots, \theta_{i,b_{K-1}}^{(t_K)}, \theta_{i,b_K}^{(t_K)}, \theta_{i,h}^{(0)}).
\end{aligned} \tag{6}$$

Once the deepest base layer θ_{i,b_K} is sufficiently trained, the freeze on the preceding layer $\theta_{i,b_{K-1}}$ is released for training. Anti Scheduling is thus defined as the sequential unfreezing and training of base layers starting from θ_{i,b_K} and proceeding to the first base layer θ_{i,b_1}. The training progresses in the reverse order of Anti Scheduling, and during this process, the head layer $\theta_{i,h}$ remains frozen and is only utilized in the final fine-tuning phase.

Algorithm 1 outlines the training procedure for both Vanilla and Anti Scheduling. In line 2, a subset of clients is randomly selected. Lines 4–8 describe the Vanilla Scheduling mode operation. When the Vanilla mode is selected, if the current global round t is greater than the layers unfreeze round t_k, as specified in line 5, the algorithm unfreezes the k-th base parameter θ_{i,b_k}. Then, in line 8, the unfrozen base parameters are used to perform a local update.

Lines 9–13 describe the Anti Scheduling mode operations. In Anti mode, as line 10 indicates, if the current global round t exceeds the layer unfreeze round t_k, the algorithm unfreezes the $(K-k+1)$-th base parameter $\theta_{i,b_{K-k+1}}$, which is closer to the head layer. In line 13, the unfrozen base parameters are used for the local update. In lines 15–16, the head is frozen while sending the updated base parameters to the server. In line 18, global aggregation is done after local updates, and fine-tuning is done in lines 20–24, where both base and head parameters are utilized in each client after the global rounds are complete.

Algorithm 1 FedSeq: Layer Decoupling Algorithm with Vanilla and Anti Scheduling

Input: Total global rounds T, Total clients N, join ratio r, Learning rate η, Total base layers K, Fine-tuning rounds F, Scheduling mode $Mode$, Layer unfreeze rounds $t_1, t_2, \ldots, t_K$
Initialize: Global base parameters $\theta^{(0)}_{G,b_1}, \theta^{(0)}_{G,b_2}, \ldots, \theta^{(0)}_{G,b_K}$ and Global Head parameter $\theta^{(0)}_{G,h}$

for $t = 1$ **to** T **do**
  Randomly select $M = \lfloor r \times N \rfloor$ clients
  for Each selected client $i = 1$ **to** M **do**
    if $Mode$ = 'Vanilla' **then**
      if $t \geq t_k$ **then**
        Unfreeze θ_{i,b_k}
      end if
      $\theta_i^{(t+1)} = \theta_i^{(t)} - \eta \nabla_{\theta_i} \mathcal{L}(D_i, \theta^{(t)}_{i,b_1}, \ldots, \theta^{(t)}_{i,b_K}, \theta^{(0)}_{i,h})$
    else if $Mode$ = 'Anti' **then**
      if $t \geq t_k$ **then**
        Unfreeze $\theta_{i,b_{K-k+1}}$
      end if
      $\theta_i^{(t+1)} = \theta_i^{(t)} - \eta \nabla_{\theta_i} \mathcal{L}(D_i, \theta^{(t)}_{i,b_1}, \ldots, \theta^{(t)}_{i,b_K}, \theta^{(0)}_{i,h})$
    end if
    Keep $\theta_{i,h}$ frozen
    Send updated base parameters $\theta^{(t+1)}_{i,b_1}, \ldots, \theta^{(t+1)}_{i,b_K}$
  end for
  Aggregate global model $\theta_G^{(t+1)} = \sum_{i=1}^{N} \frac{|D_i|}{|D|} \theta^{(t+1)}_{i,b}$
end for
for $f = 1$ **to** F **do**
  Unfreeze all layers for each client
  for each client $i = 1$ **to** N **do**
    Update all parameters θ_i for fine tuning
    $\theta_i^{(T+f)} = \theta_i^{(T+f-1)} - \eta \nabla_{\theta_i} \mathcal{L}(D_i, \theta^{(T+f-1)}_{i,b_1}, \ldots, \theta^{(T+f-1)}_{i,b_K}, \theta^{(T+f-1)}_{i,h})$
  end for
end for

4. Experiments

In our experimental setup, the total number of clients N is set to 100, with each round involving a client participation ratio r of 0.1, indicating that 10 clients participate in each training round. The batch size is configured to 10, and the learning rate is set at 0.005. The datasets used in our experiments include MNIST, which consists of 70,000 grayscale images of handwritten digits (0–9) with a resolution of 28 × 28 pixels; CIFAR-10, containing 60,000 color images of size 32 × 32 pixels across 10 classes, such as airplanes, birds, and cars; CIFAR-100[0], which is similar to CIFAR-10 but includes 60,000 images spanning 100 classes, organized into a hierarchy of 20 superclasses; and Tiny-ImageNet, a dataset consisting of 200 classes with 500 training images and 50 validation images per class, each resized to 64 × 64 pixels. To induce heterogeneity among the data distributed to each client, this work sampled from a Dirichlet distribution with a Dirichlet parameter of 0.1, establishing a highly heterogeneous environment. This approach to data distribution is visualized in Figure 3, which illustrates the results of sampling the CIFAR-10 dataset among 10 clients. Despite the high heterogeneity induced by the Dirichlet parameter α of 0.1, MNIST, and CIFAR-10 datasets inherently lack significant class heterogeneity. Therefore, our experiments focus on the CIFAR-100 and Tiny-ImageNet datasets because our approach performs well in environments with substantial data and class heterogeneity. The CIFAR-100 dataset contains 100 different classes, and the Tiny-ImageNet dataset contains 200 classes.

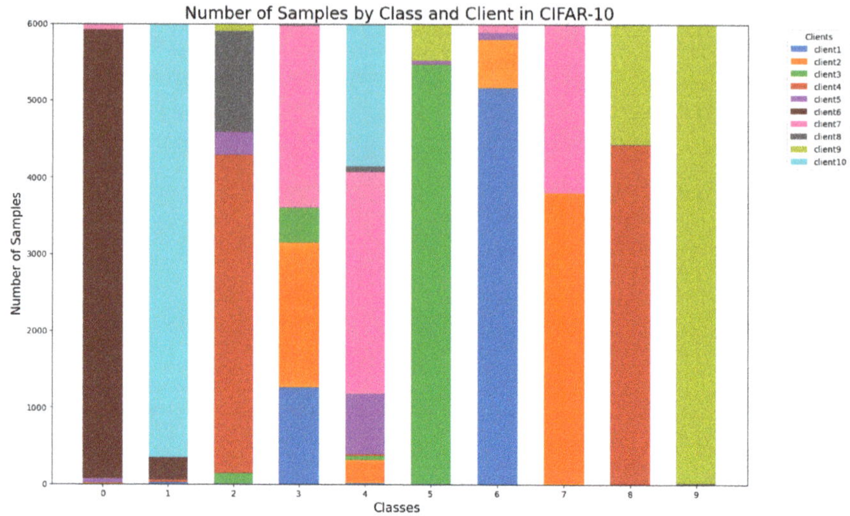

Figure 3. Results of sampling the CIFAR-10 dataset among 10 clients from a Dirichlet distribution. The Dirichlet parameter α is 0.1, generating highly heterogeneous data. However, the nature of the CIFAR-10 dataset does not offer much class heterogeneity.

In our experiments, the proposed algorithm is compared against six baselines, as detailed in the following references: [3,16–20]. The model used is a CNN model comprising two convolutional layers and two fully connected layers. Here, the last fully connected layer is set as the head, and the remaining three layers are designated as the base. The total number of base layers K is set to 3, with t_1 at the 0 (initial) round, t_2 at the 100-th global round, and t_3 at the 200-th global round. Additionally, in FedBABU [20], the learning rate of the head is set to zero during the training rounds, implying that gradients are calculated but not applied. In contrast, our scheduling algorithm achieves complete decoupling by freezing the gradients, thus preventing both computation and application. It will delve into the comparison of computational and communication costs in Section 5.2.

Table 4 presents a comparison of the accuracies achieved by various federated learning algorithms across multiple datasets, including MNIST, CIFAR-10, CIFAR-100, and Tiny-ImageNet. It encompasses representation learning algorithms such as FedAvg [3], FedPer [16], LG-FedAvg [17], FedRep [18], FedROD [19], and FedBABU [20], as well as our proposed Vanilla and Anti Scheduling algorithms. While FedAvg [3] serves as the foundational algorithm in federated learning, it is not a personalized federated learning (PFL) method. Unlike PFL approaches, FedAvg updates both the base and head layers of the model uniformly across clients without personalization. In contrast, the other algorithms explored are PFL methods focused on representation learning. For instance, FedPer [16] retains personalized layers at each client while sharing a global base model. LG-FedAvg [17] decouples global and local updates to improve personalization. FedRep [18] separates model representation from the classifier to facilitate client-specific adjustments. FedROD [19] employs robust optimization to tackle client distribution heterogeneity. A key aspect of both FedBABU and our scheduling algorithms is their approach during the training phases leading up to the final global round, denoted as T. Characteristically, these algorithms exclusively use the base layers and do not employ the head layer during the training rounds, resulting in relatively lower accuracies prior to the final round. To ensure a fair comparison, the accuracy figures for FedBABU and our scheduling algorithms at T represent the performance after fine-tuning. Additionally, it is noteworthy that our scheduling algorithms have achieved high accuracy in environments with significant data and class heterogeneity, demonstrating their effectiveness in processing complex and diverse datasets.

Figure 4 shows the average accuracy of clients on the CIFAR-100 dataset, visualizing the performance of our scheduling algorithms compared to baselines. As can be seen, the earlier round accuracy of our scheduling algorithm is lower than FedAvg and FedBABU, which is attributed to the fact that, in the earlier rounds, not only all base but also head is used, and the training is conducted using only a portion of the unfrozen base layers.

Table 4. Comparison of accuracy.

Algorithm	MNIST		CIFAR-10		CIFAR-100		Tiny-ImageNet	
	Acc. (%)	T	**Acc. (%)**	T	**Acc. (%)**	T	**Acc. (%)**	T
FedAvg [3]	91.48	100	36.87	100	29.04	500	16.97	300
	96.32	200	42.00	200	30.95	1000	14.06	500
	97.48	300	49.36	300	30.34	1500	14.27	1500
FedPer [16]	98.30	100	86.16	100	40.22	500	29.04	300
	98.63	200	87.34	200	41.03	1000	29.24	500
	98.69	300	86.66	300	40.05	1500	29.11	1000
LG-FedAvg [17]	97.95	100	85.75	100	41.06	500	26.46	300
	98.17	200	86.10	200	41.01	1000	26.35	500
	98.13	300	85.91	300	40.80	1500	26.36	1000
FedRep [18]	98.56	100	86.58	100	40.44	500	28.85	300
	98.69	200	88.12	200	41.24	1000	28.54	500
	98.75	300	88.11	300	40.66	1000	28.50	1000
FedROD [19]	98.61	100	86.24	100	49.50	500	37.23	300
	98.95	200	88.01	200	48.70	1000	35.34	500
	99.06	300	88.59	300	50.56	1500	35.35	1000
FedBABU [20]	98.19	100	85.77	100	49.28	500	37.84	300
	98.77	200	86.16	200	52.75	1000	33.78	500
	98.84	300	87.07	300	51.82	1500	32.57	1000
FedSeq (Vanilla Scheduling)	98.21	100	85.82	100	56.86	500	41.86	300
	98.84	200	87.81	200	59.52	1000	39.51	500
	98.99	300	88.58	300	58.49	1500	36.44	1000
FedSeq (Anti Scheduling)	98.34	100	85.73	100	56.17	500	**41.94**	300
	98.81	200	87.67	200	**60.06**	1000	39.67	500
	98.96	300	**88.61**	300	58.58	1500	36.63	1000

Similarly, Figure 5 represents the average accuracy of clients on the Tiny-ImageNet dataset. Our scheduling algorithm's earlier round accuracy is lower than FedAvg and FedBABU, which is consistent with its characteristics. This visualization helps underscore how our scheduling algorithms gradually catch up and potentially surpass other algorithms as the training progresses.

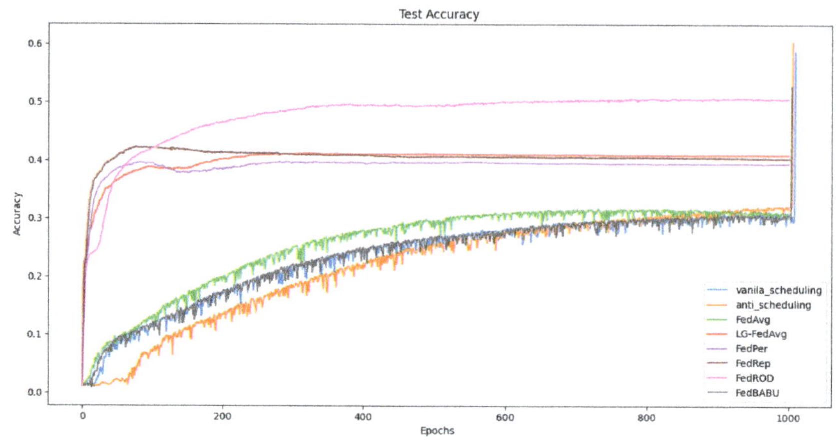

Figure 4. This figure shows the average accuracy of clients on the CIFAR-100 dataset. As can be seen, the earlier round accuracy of our scheduling algorithm is lower than that of FedAvg and FedBABU. This is because, in the earlier rounds, not all base and head were used, and the training was conducted using only a portion of the unfrozen base layers.

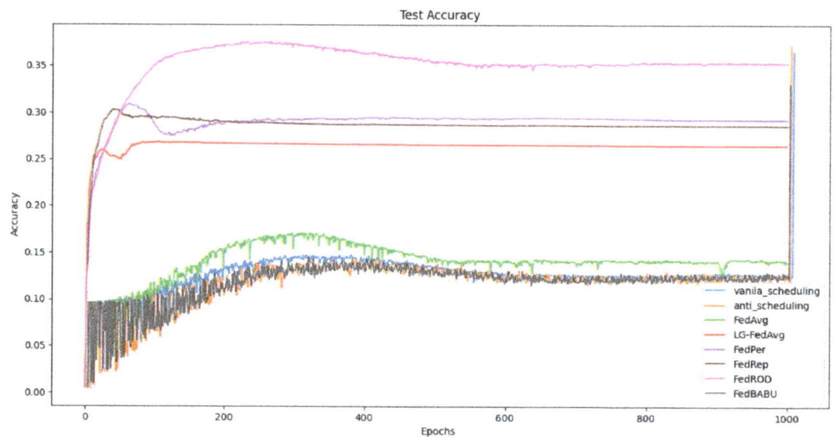

Figure 5. This figure represents the average accuracy of clients on the Tiny-ImageNet dataset, where the initial round accuracy of our scheduling algorithm is lower compared to FedAvg and FedBABU, consistent with its characteristics.

5. Ablation Study

In our ablation study, this work demonstrates the results of varying different parameters. The contents to be covered in the ablation study include:

- Comparison of client-specific accuracy
- Estimation of computational cost for each algorithm
- Effect of layer unfreezing timing on the accuracy
- Application of scheduling to the baseline algorithms

5.1. Comparison of Client-Specific Accuracy

To ensure that accuracy improvements during fine-tuning are not biased or limited to specific clients, This work conducted a comparative analysis of client-specific accuracy between the latest representation learning algorithms and our algorithm. Since the accuracy differences in the MNIST and CIFAR-10 datasets are not significantly pronounced, the comparison was focused on the CIFAR-100 and Tiny-ImageNet datasets. The results demonstrated that the higher average accuracy of our scheduling algorithm was not due to bias towards specific clients but was consistently achieved across all clients.

Figure 6 shows the comparison of client-specific accuracy in the CIFAR-100 dataset. This visualization helps to highlight that our scheduling algorithm achieves consistent accuracy across a spectrum of different clients without favoring any particular group.

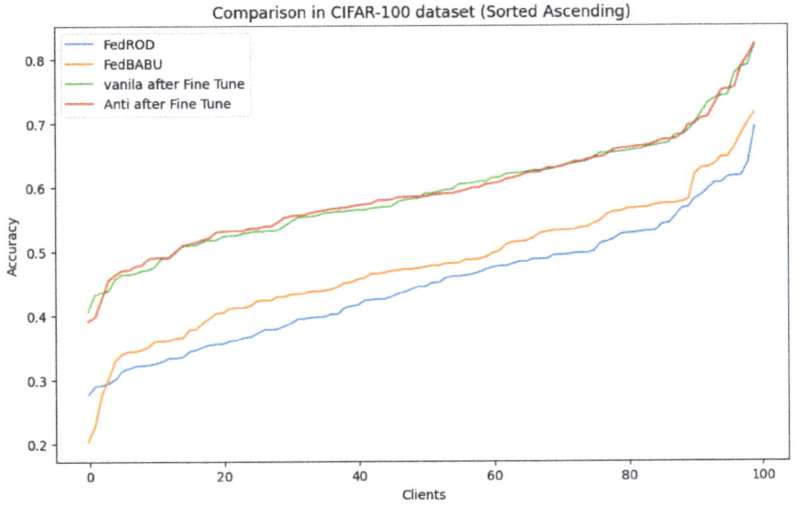

Figure 6. Comparison of client-specific accuracy in the CIFAR-100 dataset. This figure visualizes the accuracy of each client in ascending order.

Similarly, Figure 7 demonstrates the client-specific accuracy in the Tiny-ImageNet dataset. As with CIFAR-100, the visualization confirms that our algorithm manages to maintain high accuracy uniformly across different clients, showcasing its robustness.

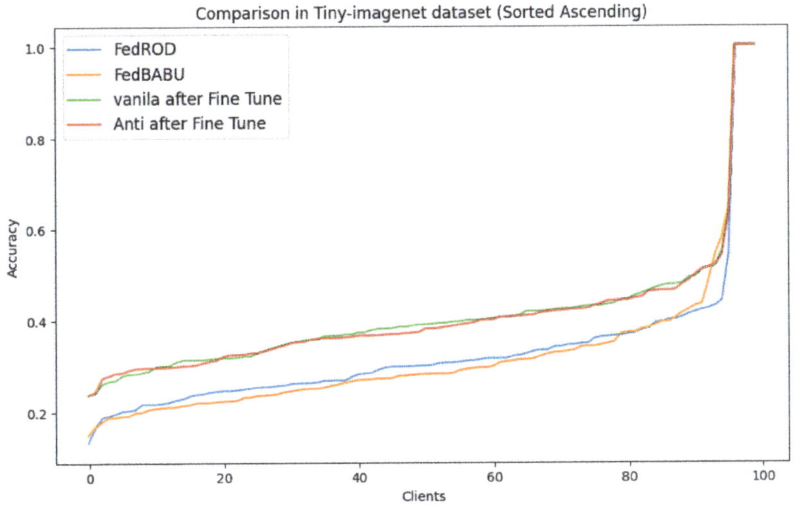

Figure 7. Comparison of client-specific accuracy in the Tiny-ImageNet dataset. This figure visualizes the accuracy of each client in ascending order.

5.2. Estimation of Computational Cost for Each Algorithm

In the actual experimental environment, using non-IID data makes it challenging to estimate computational costs. Therefore, this work estimates the computational costs using the number of FLOPs. The number of parameters in each layer is mentioned in Table 5.

Table 5. Number of parameters per layer.

Layer	Number of Parameters
conv1.weight	800
conv1.bias	32
conv2.weight	51,200
conv2.bias	64
fc1.weight	524,288
fc1.bias	512
fc2.weight	5120
fc2.bias	10
Total	582,026

To compare the computational costs of FedAvg, FedBABU, and our scheduling algorithms, this work considers the data processed by each client in an IID (independent and identically distributed) environment. Costs are measured in FLOPs, and for simplicity, all algorithms are assumed to use datasets with an equal pixel count per image. In datasets like MNIST, CIFAR-10, and CIFAR-100, each with a total of 50,000 training data points and 100 clients, each client processes 500 data points. In the setting of our experiments, a batch size of 10 is used, with each client handling 50 batches per epoch.

For FedAvg, as seen in Table 5, the total model parameters are 582,026, and the computational cost per round is 582,026 $\times$ 50. Thus, the total computational cost for all clients and all rounds is 873.039 billion FLOPs. In the same environment, the computational cost for FedBABU, considering that the head (fc2) layer parameters are not computed during the training rounds, results in 576,896 learning parameters. Hence, the total computational cost for FedBABU is 865.344 billion FLOPs. Using the same method for our scheduling algorithms, the computed parameters result in 314.912 billion FLOPs for Vanilla Scheduling and 838.880 billion FLOPs for Anti Scheduling, as detailed in Table 6.

Figure 8 visually compares the computational costs between FedAvg, FedBABU, and our scheduling algorithms. It illustrates how Vanilla Scheduling significantly reduces computational costs in the earlier rounds by updating only the earlier unfreezed layers. This visualization supports the data presented in Table 6, emphasizing the efficiency of Vanilla Scheduling in managing computational resources.

Table 6. Comparison of Computational Cost.

Algorithm	Number of FLOPs ($\times 10^9$)	T
FedAvg [3]	873.04	300
FedBABU [20]	865.34	300
Vanilla Scheduling	314.91	300
Anti Scheduling	838.88	300

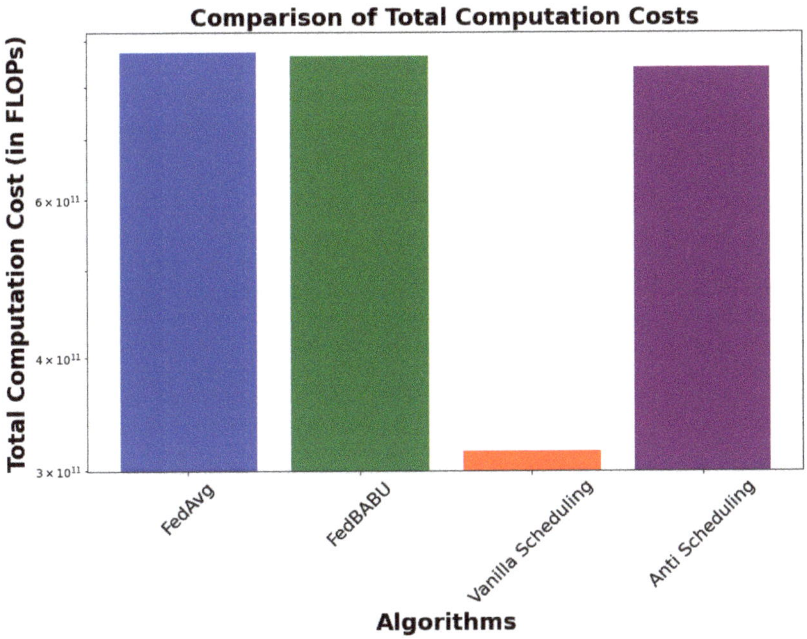

Figure 8. Comparison of computational costs between FedAvg, FedBABU, and FedSeq. Note that FedSeq with Vanilla Scheduling significantly reduces computational costs in the initial rounds by updating only the front-end layers.

5.3. Accuracy Differences Due to Changes in Layer Unfreezing Timing

In our two scheduling algorithms, the number of base layers, t_k, is set to 3, leading to parameter unfreezing occurring across three phases. For instance, in Vanilla Scheduling, training proceeds with the unfreezing of the conv1 layer from round $T = 0$ to 100. Subsequently, from rounds 100 to 200, both conv1 and conv2 layers are unfrozen for training. Finally, from round 200 to the final global round, all base layers, including conv1, conv2, and fc1, are unfrozen and utilized for training. While the unfreezing points in this paper are arbitrarily set for discussing the effectiveness of layer decoupling, an appropriate scheduling method is required accordingly. Therefore, this work compares the differences in outcomes when unfreezing occurs at rounds 50 and 100 instead of 100 and 200.

In the CIFAR-100 dataset, with the global round $T = 1000$ and layer unfreezing round set at $t_1 = 0, t_2 = 100, t_3 = 200$, Vanilla Scheduling achieves an accuracy of 59.52%, while Anti Scheduling achieves 60.06%. However, when the unfreezing round is changed to $t_1 = 0, t_2 = 50, t_3 = 100$, Vanilla Scheduling achieves 58.68%, and Anti Scheduling achieves 59.02% accuracy, slightly lower accuracy. For the Tiny-ImageNet dataset at global round $T = 300$, with $t_1 = 0$, $t_2 = 100$, $t_3 = 200$, Vanilla and Anti Scheduling achieve accuracies of 41.86% and 41.94%, respectively. Changing the unfreezing points to $t_1 = 0$, $t_2 = 50$, $t_3 = 100$ results in accuracies of 41.23% for Vanilla and 41.63% for Anti Scheduling, which are also slightly lower. The insight gained here is that while the timing of layer unfreezing does not significantly affect accuracy, as seen in Section 5.2, it has a substantial impact on computational cost. Therefore, setting larger values for t_k is advantageous where possible.

5.4. Application of Scheduling to Baseline Algorithms

When our scheduling methods were applied to the baseline algorithms, no noticeable improvement was observed in accuracy. This is attributed to the fact that, except for [20], other algorithms update the head during training rounds, which nullifies the effect of freezing base layers. Furthermore, Vanilla Scheduling achieved a performance similar to the non-scheduled approach, while Anti Scheduling, in particular, resulted in significantly lower accuracy. Therefore, naively applying a dense division of the base layer only for scheduling purposes might inadvertently lead to a negative impact on accuracy. Additionally, if the head layer is utilized for local updates during training, the intended effect of freezing the base layers is effectively nullified.

6. Conclusions

This research introduces a layer decoupling technique in representation learning, a domain of personalized federated learning, to address data and class heterogeneity among clients. In traditional representation learning, the model is divided into 'base' and 'head' components, each customized to process the common and unique features of client data, respectively. Our primary contribution focuses on the dense division of the base component in representation learning and the subsequent application of two novel scheduling methodologies, namely Vanilla and Anti Scheduling, to these finely segmented base layers in federated learning architecture. The Vanilla Scheduling approach excels in significantly reducing computational costs without degrading model performance. This aspect is particularly crucial in federated learning environments where resources and computational power are often limited. Conversely, Anti Scheduling demonstrates superior capability in handling scenarios with pronounced data and class heterogeneity. Our experimental analysis, conducted on datasets with high data and class heterogeneity, such as CIFAR-100 and Tiny-ImageNet, shows that these scheduling methods not only contribute to a more efficient training process but also ensure fair improvements in accuracy across all clients. This addresses the challenges of personalized federated learning by ensuring that no single client's data disproportionately influences the global model.

7. Privacy Considerations and Future Work

While federated learning is designed to enhance privacy by keeping raw data on local devices, recent studies such as 'Deep Leakage from Gradients [23]' and 'Inverting Gradients [24]' have revealed that private information can still be reconstructed from shared model gradients, posing potential privacy risks. Our approach may offer an inherent privacy advantage by limiting the number of base layers actively involved in model updates, thus reducing the amount of sensitive information exposed through gradients. However, to further strengthen privacy protection, future work will explore integrating advanced privacy-preserving techniques, such as differential privacy and secure aggregation, into our framework.

Additionally, Future work will involve visualizing the characteristics of each layer at every global round to track changes as training progresses. This approach is expected to facilitate the introduction of more sophisticated scheduling mechanisms that can reflect the unique data characteristics of clients in heterogeneous environments, thereby enhancing learning efficiency. Dynamic scheduling techniques will also be developed to enable rapid adaptation to new data. Additionally, future work will focus on exploring the trade-off between computational cost and learning accuracy by adjusting the layers involved in training. Furthermore, it will extend to how decoupling techniques can be applied to more complex architectures, such as RNN or Transformer models.

Author Contributions: Conceptualization, J.W.J. and B.J.C.; methodology, validation, and formal analysis: J.W.J.; investigation, J.W.J. and B.J.C.; writing, J.W.J.; review and editing, B.J.C.; supervision, B.J.C.; project administration, B.J.C.; funding acquisition, B.J.C. All authors have read and agreed to the published version of the manuscript.

Funding: This research was supported by the MSIT Korea under the NRF Korea (NRF-2022R1A2C4001270) and the Information Technology Research Center (ITRC) support program (IITP-2024-RS-2020-0-01602) supervised by the IITP.

Institutional Review Board Statement: Not applicable.

Informed Consent Statement: Not applicable.

Data Availability Statement: The data presented in this study are openly available in the following: MNIST dataset at https://yann.lecun.com/exdb/mnist/, CIFAR-10 and CIFAR-100 datasets at https://www.cs.toronto.edu/~kriz/cifar.html, and Tiny-ImageNet dataset at http://cs231n.stanford.edu/tiny-imagenet-200.zip (accessed on 11 December 2024).

Conflicts of Interest: The authors declare no conflicts of interest.

References

1. Jacobs, I.; Bean, C. Fine particles, thin films and exchange anisotropy (effects of finite dimensions and interfaces on the basic properties of ferromagnets). *Spin Arrange. Cryst. Struct. Domains Micromagn.* **1963**, *3*, 271–350.
2. Mactaggert, A. The California Privacy Rights and Enforcement Act of 2020. Retrieved October. Available online: https://en.wikipedia.org/wiki/California_Privacy_Rights_Act (accessed on 11 December 2024).
3. McMahan, B.; Moore, E.; Ramage, D.; Hampson, S.; y Arcas, B.A. Communication-efficient learning of deep networks from decentralized data. In *Artificial Intelligence and Statistics*; PMLR; Addison-Wesley Publishing Company: Boston, MA, USA, 2017; pp. 1273–1282.
4. Li, T.; Sahu, A.K.; Zaheer, M.; Sanjabi, M.; Talwalkar, A.; Smith, V. Federated optimization in heterogeneous networks. *Proc. Mach. Learn. Syst.* **2020**, *2*, 429–450.
5. Karimireddy, S.P.; Kale, S.; Mohri, M.; Reddi, S.; Stich, S.; Suresh, A.T. Scaffold: Stochastic controlled averaging for federated learning. In Proceedings of the International Conference on Machine Learning, Virtual, 13–18 July 2020; pp. 5132–5143.
6. Bengio, Y.; Louradour, J.; Collobert, R.; Weston, J. Curriculum learning. In Proceedings of the 26th Annual International Conference on Machine Learning, Montreal, QC, Canada, 14–18 June 2009; pp. 41–48.
7. Vahidian, S.; Kadaveru, S.; Baek, W.; Wang, W.; Kungurtsev, V.; Chen, C.; Shah, M.; Lin, B. When do curricula work in federated learning? In Proceedings of the IEEE/CVF International Conference on Computer Vision, Paris, France, 2–3 October 2023; pp. 5084–5094.
8. Yosinski, J.; Clune, J.; Bengio, Y.; Lipson, H. How transferable are features in deep neural networks? *Adv. Neural Inf. Process. Syst.* **2014**, *27*, 3320–3328.
9. Tan, A.Z.; Yu, H.; Cui, L.; Yang, Q. Towards personalized federated learning. *IEEE Trans. Neural Netw. Learn. Syst.* **2022**, *34*, 9587–9603. [CrossRef] [PubMed]
10. Finn, C.; Abbeel, P.; Levine, S. Model-agnostic meta-learning for fast adaptation of deep networks. In Proceedings of the International Conference on Machine Learning, Sydney, Australia, 6–11 August 2017; pp. 1126–1135.
11. Nichol, A. On first-order meta-learning algorithms. *arXiv* **2018**, arXiv:1803.02999.
12. Lim, J.H.; Ha, S.; Yoon, S.W. MetaVers: Meta-Learned Versatile Representations for Personalized Federated Learning. In Proceedings of the IEEE/CVF Winter Conference on Applications of Computer Vision, Waikoloa, HI, USA, 3–8 January 2024; pp. 2587–2596.
13. Li, D.; Wang, J. Fedmd: Heterogenous federated learning via model distillation. *arXiv* **2019**, arXiv:1910.03581.
14. Chen, Y.; Qin, X.; Wang, J.; Yu, C.; Gao, W. Fedhealth: A federated transfer learning framework for wearable healthcare. *IEEE Intell. Syst.* **2020**, *35*, 83–93. [CrossRef]
15. Smith, V.; Chiang, C.K.; Sanjabi, M.; Talwalkar, A.S. Federated multi-task learning. *Adv. Neural Inf. Process. Syst.* **2017**, *30*, 4424–4434.
16. Arivazhagan, M.G.; Aggarwal, V.; Singh, A.K.; Choudhary, S. Federated learning with personalization layers. *arXiv* **2019**, arXiv:1912.00818.
17. Liang, P.P.; Liu, T.; Ziyin, L.; Allen, N.B.; Auerbach, R.P.; Brent, D.; Salakhutdinov, R.; Morency, L.P. Think locally, act globally: Federated learning with local and global representations. *arXiv* **2020**, arXiv:2001.01523.
18. Collins, L.; Hassani, H.; Mokhtari, A.; Shakkottai, S. Exploiting shared representations for personalized federated learning. In Proceedings of the International Conference on Machine Learning, Virtual, 18–24 July 2021; pp. 2089–2099.
19. Chen, H.Y.; Chao, W.L. On bridging generic and personalized federated learning for image classification. *arXiv* **2021**, arXiv:2107.00778
20. Oh, J.; Kim, S.; Yun, S.Y. Fedbabu: Towards enhanced representation for federated image classification. *arXiv* **2021**, arXiv:2106.06042.
21. Zhang, J.; Hua, Y.; Wang, H.; Song, T.; Xue, Z.; Ma, R.; Guan, H. Fedcp: Separating feature information for personalized federated learning via conditional policy. In Proceedings of the 29th ACM SIGKDD Conference on Knowledge Discovery and Data Mining, Long Beach, CA, USA, 6–10 August 2023; pp. 3249–3261.
22. Huang, C.; Chen, X.; Zhang, Y.; Wang, H. FedCRL: Personalized Federated Learning with Contrastive Shared Representations for Label Heterogeneity in Non-IID Data. *arXiv* **2024**, arXiv:2404.17916.

23. Zhu, L.; Liu, Z.; Han, S. Deep leakage from gradients. *Adv. Neural Inf. Process. Syst.* **2019**, *32*, 14774–14784.
24. Geiping, J.; Bauermeister, H.; Dröge, H.; Moeller, M. Inverting gradients-how easy is it to break privacy in federated learning? *Adv. Neural Inf. Process. Syst.* **2020**, *33*, 16937–16947.

applied sciences

MDPI

Article

A Scalable and User-Friendly Framework Integrating IoT and Digital Twins for Home Energy Management Systems

Myrto Stogia [1], Vasilis Naserentin [2,3], Asimina Dimara [1,4], Orfeas Eleftheriou [2,5], Ioannis Tzitzios [4], Christoforos Papaioannou [6], Mariya Pantusheva [7], Alexios Papaioannou [4,*], George Spaias [2,3], Christos-Nikolaos Anagnostopoulos [1], Anders Logg [2] and Stelios Krinidis [4,6,*]

[1] Intelligent Systems Lab, Department of Cultural Technology and Communication, University of the Aegean, 81100 Mytilene, Greece; mirtw.stog@gmail.com (M.S.); minadimara@gmail.com (A.D.); canag@aegean.gr (C.-N.A.)
[2] Department of Mathematical Sciences, Chalmers University of Technology, 412 96 Göteborg, Sweden; vasilis.naserentin@chalmers.se (V.N.); orfeas@chalmers.se (O.E.); spaias@chalmers.se (G.S.); logg@chalmers.se (A.L.)
[3] Department of Electrical & Computer Engineering, Aristotle University of Thessaloniki, 54124 Thessaloniki, Greece
[4] Management Science and Technology Department, Democritus University of Thrace, 65404 Kavala, Greece; tzijonnis@gmail.com
[5] Code-Flow, 81100 Mytilene, Greece
[6] Management Science and Technology Department, International Hellenic University, 57400 Thessaloniki, Greece; xristofpap@gmail.com
[7] "Big Data for Smart Society" (GATE) Institute, Sofia University "St. Kliment Ohridski", 1164 Sofia, Bulgaria; mariya.pantusheva@gate-ai.eu
* Correspondence: alpapaio@mst.duth.gr (A.P.); krinidis@mst.duth.gr (S.K.)

Abstract: The rise in electricity costs for households over the past year has driven significant changes in energy usage patterns, with many residents adopting smarter energy-efficient practices, such as improved indoor insulation and advanced home energy management systems powered by IoT and Digital Twin technologies. These measures not only mitigate rising bills but also ensure optimized thermal comfort and sustainability in typical residential settings. This paper proposes an innovative framework to facilitate the adoption of energy-efficient practices in households by leveraging the integration of Internet of Things technologies with Digital Twins. It introduces a novel approach that exploits standardized parametric 3D models, enabling the efficient simulation and optimization of home energy systems. This design significantly reduces deployment complexity, enhances scalability, and empowers users with real-time insights into energy consumption, indoor conditions, and actionable strategies for sustainable energy management. The results showcase that the proposed method significantly outperforms traditional approaches, achieving a 94% reduction in deployment time and a 98% decrease in memory usage through the use of standardized parametric models and plug-and-play IoT integration.

Keywords: internet of things; digital twin; home energy management systems; real-time monitoring; IoT architecture

1. Introduction

Approximately 40% of worldwide energy use and 36% of worldwide emissions are generated by buildings and cities, which renders them significant contributors of both global energy consumption and CO_2 emissions [1]. This significant environmental footprint has underscored the need for innovative approaches and cutting-edge technologies in managing and optimizing energy consumption within the residential sector. As a result, various digital technologies like the Internet of Things (IoT) and Digital Twins (DTs) have developed as promising solutions to address the challenges associated with energy management and sustainability while regulating thermal comfort in home environments [2]. These technologies will be more effective when integrated in real-life and real-time scenarios, allowing for immediate data-driven adjustments and optimizations that align with user preferences and environmental goals. Overall, the seamless, real-time integration of IoT and DTs into Home Energy Management Systems (HEMSs) is critical for maximizing energy efficiency, improving user comfort, and supporting the sustainability goals of modern smart cities.

The IoT allows seamless connectivity and real-time data collection from various smart devices, providing granular insights into the energy usage of specific appliances and overall household consumption [3]. Moreover, the continuous data streams generated by IoT networks are pivotal for applications in HEMSs, such as error analysis and prescriptive maintenance [4]. By analyzing these data flows and created patterns within HEMSs, specific applications can predict and address potential system faults or inefficiencies, ensuring uninterrupted operation and reducing energy waste, while extending the lifespan of household devices. In an even broader sense, IoT data can also enhance security within the IoT ecosystem itself through self-healing techniques that autonomously detect and resolve vulnerabilities [5]. This capability to ensure reliable, secure, and efficient operation underlines the critical role of IoT data in modern HEMS applications. Overall, these capabilities make IoT data indispensable for advancing intelligent, resilient, and sustainable HEMSs that adapt dynamically to both user needs and environmental demands.

In parallel, DT technology offers a virtual replica of physical assets while enabling dynamic simulation, predictive analysis, and optimization of systems such as HEMSs. By integrating IoT within these DTs, it is possible to create an advanced, real-time model of the residential environment that can monitor, control, and optimize energy use and other parameters autonomously [6–8]. Visualization of IoT data within DT applications plays a crucial role in enhancing user-centered experiences while providing clear, interactive representations of energy usage and device performance. Such visualizations help users better understand their energy consumption patterns and enable them to make informed decisions about optimizing household energy. Furthermore, visualization tools aid in quickly identifying issues within the IoT network per se, making it easier for users to detect and address problems, such as connectivity issues or device malfunctions, through intuitive graphical insights. This enhanced transparency fosters user engagement and empowers individuals to actively participate in managing their home energy environment more effectively [9].

Nonetheless, one of the primary challenges in integrating IoT with DTs for real-life applications is ensuring that IoT setups are non-intrusive and quick to deploy [10]. Especially in home environments, IoT devices must be easy to install without requiring significant modifications to existing infrastructure, as intrusive setups can discourage adoption and increase complexity while adding inconvenience to the tenants. Furthermore, achieving real-time visualization outcomes from DTs presents scalability and replicability issues [11]. Creating a personalized DT model for each user can be both time-consuming and memory-intensive, as each DT requires dedicated storage and processing resources to maintain an accurate and responsive virtual replica [11]. Moreover, designing and creating these models also demands considerable effort, especially when using custom techniques like 3D scanning to capture unique environments, which further complicates scaling DT applications across many users. This personalized modeling approach can lead to significant resource consumption, particularly when managing high volumes of IoT data, making it a potential bottleneck in effectively scaling DT applications. Additionally, ensuring that DTs are continuously updated in response to real-time IoT data requires efficient data synchronization, which can strain computational resources if not optimized [12]. Addressing these challenges is crucial for making IoT-integrated DT solutions feasible, efficient, and user-friendly in real-world settings.

Overall, HEMSs are increasingly adopting IoT technologies to enable smarter energy management. However, traditional HEMSs face several limitations, including lack of real-time feedback and actionable insights to help users make informed decisions; limited scalability in adapting to diverse residential setups and IoT ecosystems; and challenges in providing predictive capabilities for energy optimization and occupancy trends. These limitations hinder the ability of HEMSs to fully support user engagement, energy efficiency, and sustainability practices. DT technology seems to be a promising solution. While DT technology has shown promise in industrial and commercial applications, its integration with IoT for residential HEMS remains largely unexplored. Existing studies focus predominantly on either DT frameworks for large-scale systems or basic IoT implementations for energy management, without addressing the potential of combining these technologies to enhance scalability, usability, and efficiency in residential settings.

This research aims to fill this gap by proposing a novel DT-enabled HEMS framework that bridges the physical and digital domains, empowering users with real-time insights and predictive analytics for sustainable energy management. The primary scientific goal is to address challenges related to deployment complexity, scalability, and resource efficiency by introducing a standardized parametric model for Digital Twins. This framework emphasizes seamless integration, real-time monitoring, and intuitive visualization to empower users with actionable insights into their energy consumption patterns. By utilizing a pre-defined Digital Twin framework, the solution bypasses the need for extensive customization, such as complex 3D scanning or unique modeling, thereby enabling efficient scalability across multiple users while maintaining resource efficiency. This setup facilitates seamless integration between IoT and Digital Twin systems, allowing users to benefit from the insights and advantages of a Digital Twin without the complexity and effort typically associated with creating and maintaining personalized models. Consequently, this approach makes advanced home energy management more accessible, user-friendly, and effective, even for large-scale deployments. The main novelties of this paper area as follows:

- Non-intrusive, user-friendly plug-and-play IoT setup. The proposed framework simplifies the installation process by leveraging pre-configured IoT devices and standardized interfaces. This approach was empirically validated during the case study implementation, where IoT devices were installed with minimal modifications to existing infrastructure, as detailed in Section 5.
- Pre-designed, scalable Digital Twin model. The proposed standardized DT framework significantly reduces computational demands by avoiding resource-intensive custom modeling. This claim is substantiated by the results in Section 5.4, which demonstrate a 98% reduction in memory usage compared to traditional approaches.
- Enhanced accessibility and usability: The proposed system combines pre-defined DT models with plug-and-play IoT devices, providing users with Digital Twin insights and energy management capabilities through a streamlined setup process requiring minimal maintenance effort.

The remainder of this paper is structured as follows: Section 2 presents a review of related works, highlighting recent advancements in IoT and Digital Twins for home energy management systems. Section 3 defines the proposed Digital Twin framework and its functional objectives within the HEMS context. Section 4 details the IoT integration methodology and middleware framework for real-time data synchronization and device interaction. Section 5 provides a case study demonstrating the practical implementation and validation of the proposed system. Finally, Section 6 concludes the paper by summarizing the findings and discussing future research directions.

2. Literature Review

HEMSs are rapidly evolving as essential technologies for optimizing residential energy use, improving sustainability, and enhancing user comfort. As energy demands grow and renewable sources become more prevalent, integrating IoT technologies and DTs appears to be a promising strategy in advancing these systems. IoT-based HEMSs allow for granular monitoring and control, enabling homeowners to make real-time adjustments, while DTs leverage virtual replicas of physical systems to simulate and optimize energy use. This section reviews recent advancements in IoT and DT architectures within HEMSs, analyzing a range of solutions that highlight both the strengths and challenges of these emerging approaches. Through these technologies, HEMSs are moving closer to achieving smart, self-regulating, and sustainable residential environments.

2.1. IoT for Home Energy Management

IoT-based HEMSs empower homeowners with precise control over energy consumption, fostering smarter and more responsive home environments. This subsection examines current IoT technologies for energy monitoring and device control, highlighting different architectures and approaches in processing, usability, and scalability. Al-Ali et al. [13] and Machorro-Cano et al. [14] introduce IoT-based HEMSs that leverage Big Data collection and analytics. Both collect data from a network of ambient and energy consumption sensors to a centralized server. Al-Ali et al.'s system uses the shelf Business Intelligence software (Hitachi Vantara V2016) for visualization and energy use monitoring, while Machorro-Cano et al. utilizes the J48 classification Machine Learning (ML) algorithm for analyzing consumption and user behaviors to optimize energy efficiency and comfort. In the second case, real-time visualization comes via a mobile app. Gupta et al. [15] propose a Big Data and IoT-driven Energy Management System (EMS) for residential areas that utilizes distributed processing to monitor, visualize, and analyze large-scale energy consumption data for optimizing household and community-level energy use. These approaches enable data-driven insights and predictive analytics but they face challenges with scalability, latency, and security vulnerabilities due to volume, as well as the centralized collection of generated data and high computational demands [16]. Ilieva et al. [17] raise another important question in the context of IoT for HEMSs, which is the connectivity and interoperability of smart home devices. The authors propose a smartFW framework to address the challenges associated with integrating various commonly used communication protocols such as Zigbee, EnOcean, KNX, X10, and Z-Wave.

The challenges that arise from Big Data approaches are partially mitigated with the adoption of cloud-based processing. Condon et al. [18] and P. & S. [19] introduce Cloud-IoT-based HEMSs that use layered architectures for real-time energy monitoring and appliance or socket control. Beyond the sensor network, the communication layer uses the lightweight MQTT protocol while data storage, APIs (middleware layer), analytics, visualization, and user interaction (application layer) are delegated to cloud services. These approaches initially scale easily but can be costly as the number of installations and computational intensity grows. Latency issues and the demand for reliable connection can hinder the real-time aspect of these approaches. Finally, storing sensitive energy consumption data in the cloud raises concerns about data security and user privacy.

The introduction of edge computing with IoT-driven HEMSs utilizes local data processing to enhance real-time decision-making, reduce latency, and improve security. Ferreira et al. [20] propose a low-cost, edge-computing middleware for HEMSs, utilizing microservices to enhance scalability and minimize latency. The middleware is designed with a hybrid approach where basic data collection, processing, and control tasks are handled locally at the edge, while more complex analyses are offloaded to the cloud. Javed et al. [12] propose a resilient, edge-based demand response (DR) optimization system for Smart Energy Systems that uses a local cloud architecture and ML to improve energy efficiency and ensure user comfort. The introduction of additional local cloud nodes allows this scheme to scale to large facilities while keeping data processing local to each node. Iqbal et al. [21] presents an edge-computing-based system that integrates IoT devices with a blockchain to create a secure and decentralized framework for real-time monitoring and prediction of energy usage, using ARIMA for forecasting and smart contracts to facilitate automated transactions for energy trading and DR. Finally, edge computing in IoT-driven HEMSs reduces latency, improves scalability and privacy, and mitigates security risks by limiting data transmission, though it requires managing computational constraints and increased system complexity [22].

2.2. Digital Twins in Residential Energy Management

DTs in residential energy applications represent a transformative approach to energy management, enabling enhanced efficiency and sustainability. These models focus on the complexities of modern systems, extending the integration of IoT schemas for home energy management. The creation of dynamic, virtual replicas of physical assets enables real-time monitoring, predictive maintenance, and data-driven decision-making, leading to optimized energy consumption and improved system efficiency [23]. Recent advancements in Machine Learning (ML) and Artificial Intelligence (AI) further enhance DT capabilities, allowing for intelligent decision-making that adjusts to user behaviors and external factors [24]. This section explores the role of DTs in residential energy management systems, focusing on their potential to create energy-efficient, self-regulating home environments that are aligned with the goals of smart and sustainable living.

Fathy et al. [25] propose a multi-layered DT framework that integrates both household-specific Home Digital Twins (HDTs) and a centralized Energy Digital Twin (EDT) to enhance energy management systems. In this framework, each HDT reflects household energy use patterns and user preferences, enabling local appliance scheduling optimization through edge-deployed reinforcement learning (RL). The EDT, in turn, aggregates energy demand data across households, allowing for dynamic adjustment of dual tariff rates based on real-time demand trends. Complementing this approach, Testasecca et al. [26] introduce a DT framework that leverages Building Information Modeling (BIM), IoT, and ML services to optimize energy usage and sustainability within various case studies, including smart grids, microgrids, and district heating networks. Their findings highlight the benefits and challenges of DT applications in HEMSs, noting key limitations in scalability, data quality, and stakeholder engagement.

De Lope et al. [27] extend the application of AI-driven DTs in HEMSs to optimize hybrid renewable hydrogen systems for self-sufficiency and efficiency. The effectiveness in real-time energy optimization is evident by the implementation in a housing project in Spain but the complexity of the system creates challenges in adaptability and scalability, while the centralized processing and demanding ML algorithms raise concerns regarding security and computational demands on larger scales. Cotti et al. [28] focus on user empowerment by introducing an ML-powered digital twin for smart homes. The system uses an unsupervised machine learning approach to simulate the impact of different appliance modes on energy consumption. Through a user-friendly web-based interface, users can create trigger–action rules and receive recommendations for optimizing energy consumption.

Table 1 presents a detailed comparison of key features and methods across various related works in the domain of IoT-enabled DT systems for energy management. The comparison highlights significant gaps in prior research and underscores the comprehensive capabilities of this paper. The features compared were selected to address the key challenges in deploying IoT-enabled DT systems for HEM. These include scalability, usability, and resource efficiency, critical factors for real-world adoption. 'Non-intrusive IoT Setup' ensures minimal structural modifications for seamless integration in diverse environments, while 'Pre-designed DT Framework' highlights the scalability and efficiency of standardized models, eliminating the need for resource-intensive customizations. The term 'Non-intrusive IoT Setup' focuses on minimizing the impact on existing infrastructure, such as avoiding structural modifications or rewiring, whereas 'Ease of Installation' highlights the simplicity and user-friendliness of the process, such as plug-and-play functionality. While related, these terms address different aspects of deployment. Other features, such as real-time IoT-DT integration and cost-effectiveness, were included to provide a comprehensive comparison with existing solutions. These criteria reflect the essential capabilities needed to advance the usability and accessibility of DT systems. This selection not only benchmarks our framework against current approaches but also underscores its ability to address practical deployment challenges.

Table 1. Comparison of features and methods across related works.

Feature/ Method	Non-Intrusive IoT Setup	Pre-Designed DT Framework	Real-Time IoT-DT Integration	Scalability	Ease of Installation	Cost-Effectiveness	Interoperability
Al-Ali et al. (2017)[13]				✓	✓		
Machorro-Cano et al. (2020) [14]				✓	✓		
Gupta et al. (2020) [15]			✓	✓	✓		✓
Condon et al. (2023) [18]			✓	✓	✓		✓
Ferreira et al. (2022) [20]			✓	✓	✓		
Iqbal et al. (2023) [21]			✓	✓	✓		✓
Testasecca et al. (2024) [26]			✓	✓	✓		✓
This Paper	✓	✓	✓	✓	✓	✓	✓

3. Digital Twin for HEMS

DTs have emerged as a transformative technology for advancing EMSs in residential settings while offering precise, real-time simulations and optimizations. In the context of HEMSs, DTs enable the creation of dynamic virtual replicas of physical homes, integrating spatial and environmental data with IoT-driven insights. This section introduces the DT framework tailored for HEMSs, outlining its key components, functional objectives, and the standardized parametric 3D modeling approach. By bridging physical and digital domains, the proposed DT empowers users with actionable insights and supports sustainable energy practices. The following subsections delve into the development, features, and capabilities of this innovative framework.

3.1. Research Methodology

As discussed, the primary aim of this research is to propose and validate an innovative framework that integrates DT technology into HEMSs. The framework is designed to address key challenges in residential energy management, ensuring the system can adapt to diverse home configurations and varying IoT deployments. Providing intuitive user interfaces with actionable insights for energy optimization. Reducing computational and operational demands through standardized DT models. By bridging the physical and digital domains, the proposed framework enables real-time simulations, predictive analytics, and precise energy monitoring, empowering users to adopt sustainable energy practices while optimizing energy consumption.

To achieve the outlined scientific aim, this study adopts a systematic methodology comprising the following steps:

1. Literature Review: Conducted a comprehensive review of existing HEMS and DT frameworks to identify gaps, establish the novelty of the proposed framework, and define objectives for its development.
2. Framework Design and Development: Developed a DT-enabled HEMS framework, focusing on objectives such as real-time visualization, spatial segmentation, energy tracking, and predictive analytics.
3. Case Study Implementation: Applied the framework to a real-world scenario, simulating a residential building project. The case study incorporates IoT data and spatial modeling to validate the practical functionality of the framework.
4. Simulation and Performance Testing: Conducted simulations to assess the framework's performance in achieving scalability, usability, and resource efficiency. Metrics such as energy consumption patterns, environmental monitoring accuracy, and system responsiveness were evaluated.
5. Validation and Comparison: Benchmarked the results against traditional HEMS approaches to demonstrate the added value of the DT integration in terms of enhanced user experience, energy optimization, and scalability.

This structured methodology ensures a systematic approach to validating the framework's scientific and practical contributions to the field of residential energy management.

3.2. Defining the Digital Twin Framework in HEMSs

A DT serves as a dynamic digital replica of physical systems, offering real-time monitoring, analysis, and control. Within HEMSs, DTs enable the integration of IoT data with spatial and environmental models, bridging the physical and digital domains. This transformation is crucial for optimizing energy management and providing actionable insights into household energy use. The DT framework integrates IoT-driven data collection with virtual modeling to dynamically represent and manage the home environment, enhancing system efficiency and user engagement. Figure 1 depicts the transition from a classical HEMS architecture to an extended system integrating DT capabilities. The classical HEMS structure consists of three primary components:

- Physical Layer: Includes the actual rooms, IoT sensors, and appliances.
- Data Collection and Processing: Handles data streams, middleware communication, and database storage for managing and analyzing energy usage.
- Applications: Offers basic monitoring and control through user-facing applications.

The proposed system builds upon this by introducing a DT Layer, which mirrors the physical environment in a virtual space. This DT Layer enables real-time visualization, advanced simulations, and enhanced interaction. Digital rooms, IoT sensors, and appliances within the DT Layer are synchronized with their physical counterparts, offering users actionable insights and predictive analytics. This architecture bridges the gap between monitoring and actionable control, significantly enhancing the scalability, usability, and efficiency of HEMS.

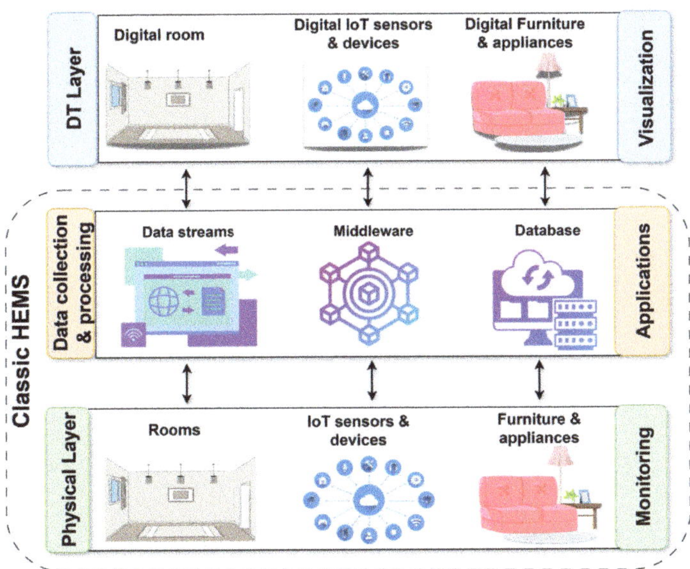

Figure 1. Extended HEMS architecture incorporating DT Layer.

In contrast to traditional HEMS architectures, which rely on static configurations and limited real-time capabilities, the integration of Digital Twins introduces dynamic simulation and predictive analysis. This enables real-time adjustments and optimization based on live IoT data streams, reducing latency and improving user engagement. The proposed DT framework uses standardized models, ensuring scalability and efficient resource usage while allowing for customized interactions with the home environment. By bridging IoT data with spatial models, the system provides granular insights into energy consumption and thermal conditions, leading to enhanced sustainability and user comfort. This research focuses on transforming traditional HEMSs into dynamic, user-centric systems through the integration of IoT and Digital Twins. By enabling real-time simulation, predictive analytics, and enhanced user interactions, this study aims to address scalability and usability challenges in energy management.

Specifically, Figure 2 depicts the transition from a classical HEMS architecture to an extended system with integrated DT capabilities. The diagram compares the two architectures, emphasizing the added value of the DT Layer. A Classical HEMS is limited to the Physical Layer, Data Collection and Processing, and Applications. It primarily focuses on IoT-based data collection and basic user interactions, offering limited insights and lacking predictive capabilities. Meanwhile, in the extended HEMS with DT, the DT Layer transforms the system into a dynamic, interactive platform. This layer provides real-time visualization of household energy use, advanced simulations, and predictive analytics. By mirroring physical rooms, IoT sensors, and appliances in a virtual environment, the DT Layer bridges the gap between monitoring and actionable control, empowering users with enhanced engagement and decision-making tools.

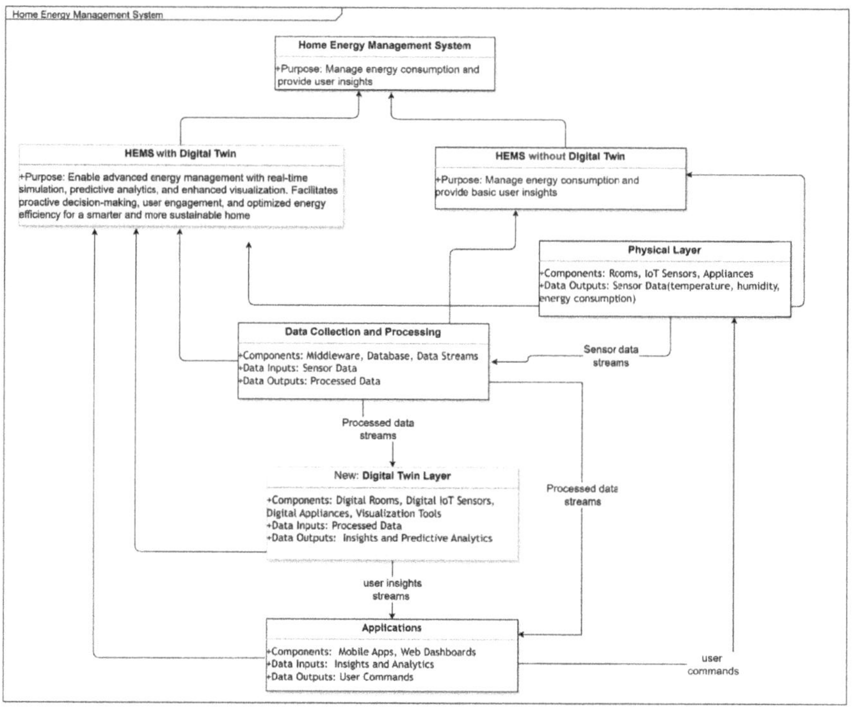

Figure 2. Comparison of HEMS with and without Digital Twin, illustrating system architecture, data flows, and differentiated purposes.

3.3. Functional Objectives and Modeling Priorities

The development of a DT for an HEMS requires a strategic approach to modeling that should emphasize both functionality and precision. This section outlines the primary objectives and priorities guiding the creation of the DT model tailored for HEMS applications. The focus is on enhancing user experience and spatial realism while supporting granular data segmentation, and enabling data analytics. By integrating detailed environmental and energy-related data, the DT model can provide users with an immersive and interactive experience while facilitating real-time insights and energy management. Each objective contributes to the overall aim of achieving a 3D model that is technically robust and adaptable to user needs, environmental conditions, and energy optimization goals within different areas of the home. The functional objectives and modeling priorities (Obj) are listed bellow:

- Obj. 1: Enhance realism and user experience by creating a visually and tactilely accurate 3D model that fosters immersion and ease of navigation within the Digital Twin environment.
- Obj. 2: Support functional segmentation for energy and environmental data by spatially segmenting the 3D model based on material and functional variations, enabling targeted data integration.
- Obj. 3: Capture space-specific energy consumption patterns by enabling the Digital Twin to track and analyze energy use unique to each space (e.g., living room vs. kitchen).
- Obj. 4: Improve environmental monitoring and thermal comfort by using spatial and material segmentation to monitor conditions like temperature and humidity, ensuring each zone meets optimal comfort levels.
- Obj. 5: Facilitate predictive analytics for occupancy and usage patterns, allowing the Digital Twin to predict and adapt to occupancy and behavior trends across different rooms.
- Obj. 6: Enable precision in smart home automation by integrating automation features that adapt to the unique material and spatial characteristics of each room.

3.4. Parametric Standardized 3D Model

DTs have evolved into transformative tools in the Architecture, Engineering, Construction and Operations (AECOs) fields, providing real-time and data-driven digital replicas of physical building structures. These virtual models bridge the gap between physical structures and digital environments, enabling improved monitoring, simulation, and management throughout the overall building's lifecycle. The transition from traditional two-dimensional (2D) design to dynamic Digital Twins represents the evolution of how data from each Digital Twin informs and influences building performance and decision-making. Initially, architectural design was mostly based on 2D drawings, physical or digital, which provided only static representations of structures, detailing spatial layouts, structural elements, and key mechanical systems [29]. The development in three-dimensional (3D) modeling has added a new dimension to architectural design, and the creation of BIM has allowed the creation of parametric models that enclose rich, interconnected data on material properties, spatial relationships, and building systems [30].

As stated in Section 1, this paper aims to minimize the design-processing time and reduce the size of the data associated with each DT model by assembling a standardized, parametric, pre-designed DT framework. This approach eliminates the need for customized per user modeling, therefore facilitating scalability and significantly reducing computational requirements. By standardizing DT fundamentals, the model can be efficiently adapted for different users without extensive customization, ensuring efficient deployment and resource development. The separation and standardization of the design can be categorized according to the basic characteristics of an apartment, which are the number of rooms, the type of common areas (i.e., whether it is a main living and kitchen area or a separate layout of the respective rooms), and the number of toilets. Therefore, the standard design for a studio apartment, a one-room apartment, a two-room apartment, etc., may come up.

To achieve the conversion of this 2D data into a 3D model, architects and engineers use BIM software, which allows the creation of a parametric model that represents both the physical and functional aspects of the building [31]. This process involves first digitizing the spatial layouts and structural elements from the 2D plan, which are then rendered in 3D geometry. Using BIM, engineers can render material properties, simulate structural elements and incorporate electromechanical systems such as Heating, Ventilation, and Air Conditioning (HVAC), plumbing, and electrical infrastructure. This transformation enhances spatial understanding while allowing for the incorporation of feature data, which is essential for the development of the Digital Twin.

Regarding the structural characteristics of each dwelling, there is a clear distinction between the characteristics of the external walls, which define the outline of the dwelling, and the internal walls, which mainly concern the separation of the individual rooms. This differentiation mainly concerns the thickness and composition of the walls and reflects functional and thermal insulation characteristics, as external walls are usually designed to provide necessary insulation, structural stability, and climate resistance. In contrast, internal walls are mainly used for internal layout purposes, which requires a lower density and material composition. This variation in wall specifications is typical and integral to achieving optimal energy efficiency and structural integrity within the compartment, always adapted to best practices in building design. At the same time, a key specification is the provision of natural light and ventilation in each space. It is worth noting that this specification tends to influence the interactions of the DT model with the HEMS and the external environment.

At the same time, by applying different materials to each surface and space, the realistic experience of the user is enhanced during their navigation in the digital environment of the DT. This differentiation of materials not only provides visual and tactile fidelity within the model, but also aids in distinguishing spaces for a more realistic browsing experience. Additionally, the separation of spaces based on material transitions serves as a fundamental preparatory step for transitioning the three-dimensional model into a DT. By aligning specific materials with distinct spatial functions, this approach supports the precise integration of data and functional segmentation, which are critical for DT applications. Each defined area, living room, kitchen, bedrooms, bathroom, hallway, etc. can then be mapped to capture distinct patterns of energy consumption, environmental parameters, and occupancy behaviors, and in this paper's chosen scenario, thermal comfort.

In order to achieve the optimal spatial navigation experience for the user, the 3D model is structured according to a 'dollhouse' concept [32]. These types of views involve creating an open, segmented view of the compartment, enabling users to seamlessly explore the layout and spatial relationships within the model. By presenting internal elements in a clear, unobstructed way, the dollhouse approach enhances spatial understanding and user engagement, making it particularly effective for immersive experiences in Digital Twin applications. Through this systematic design and preparation, the optimal user experience is achieved in terms of navigating the digital space and gathering the desired information provided. Starting from the initial floor plan, continuing with the construction of the 3D model with the applied finishing materials and finally selecting the appropriate perspective, the 3D model fulfills the appropriate prerequisites to be transformed into a digital twin. This step-by-step approach ensures that every layer, from spatial layout to visual fidelity to navigation perspective, helps to create a cohesive and immersive digital environment, aligning the model with the requirements for effective integration of the Digital Twin.

As depicted in Figure 3, the overall workflow consists of six sequential steps designed to develop and integrate a 3D model for DT applications in HEMSs. Each step is closely associated, directly or indirectly, with the Functional Objectives and Modeling Priorities (Obj. 1–6), ensuring that the methodology aligns with key goals such as realism, functional segmentation, energy tracking, environmental monitoring, predictive analytics, and smart home automation. Overall, this methodology is ideal for creating a highly functional and adaptable DT, addressing critical aspects of home energy management with precision and scalability. Each step builds upon the previous one, leading to a robust 3D model that meets the objectives for energy optimization, user comfort, and seamless interaction in a smart home environment.

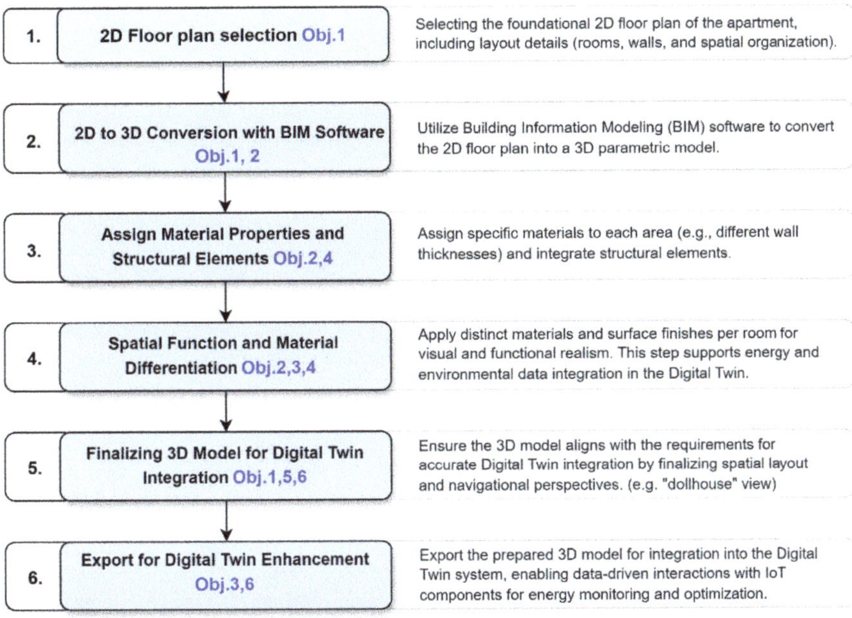

Figure 3. Workflow for 3D model development and DT integration in HEMS.

3.5. Parametric Standardized Digital Twin

Based on the developed comprehensive standardized 3D model within the HEMS framework, a parametric standardized digital twin is created to dynamically simulate the indoor environment and related energy flow. Relevant 3D model data, such as the architectural, structural, and interior building parameters are used as operational parameters also in the DT. There, these are complemented with data about HVAC systems, appliances in the premises (e.g., type, location, power consumption profiles and usage patterns), energy related data (e.g., energy source type, usage patterns and historical data, historical and real-time energy prices), occupancy (e.g., number of occupants and demographics, routines and activities, etc.), and indoor environmental data, such as temperature, humidity, lighting levels, CO_2 levels, air quality, and thermal comfort. Thermal comfort is commonly estimated using the Predicted Mean Vote (PMV) index, a scientifically validated metric that predicts the average thermal sensation of occupants on a scale ranging from cold (-3) to hot (+3) [2]. It refers to state n in which individuals feel satisfied with the indoor conditions and is estimated by temperature, humidity, and personal factors (clothing, activity level) [2]. By leveraging the PMV index, HEMSs dynamically adjust heating, ventilation, and air conditioning while ensuring a balance between comfort and energy efficiency. Outdoor environmental data may also be relevant, as in almost all cases, they affect the inside of the premises as well. In this regard, local climate conditions, air pollution, or external obstacles such as shading from trees or buildings can be reflected and added to the DT.

Once all this data is captured and integrated into a coherent system, it can be used for real-time monitoring. This is not only an informative feature, but also helps in identifying anomalies or deviation from normal patterns. Such data are key for predictive maintenance and addressing potential issues before they escalate, leading to reduced maintenance costs, improved system reliability, and enhanced overall home comfort and safety. Within the digital twin, the aggregated data are cleaned and pre-processed to remove any noise and inconsistencies. More than that, the captured data and their patterns and interactions can be analyzed and optimized. For example, analyzing occupancy patterns can help optimize heating and cooling schedules, while monitoring appliance usage can identify opportunities for energy-efficient alternatives. At the same time, using ML, deep learning, or other artificial intelligence techniques allows DTs to continuously reflect and learn from new changes in the system and thus improve their predictive accuracy over time.

By altering different parameters in the system and running simulations, different what-if scenarios can be simulated virtually, and based on the results, energy-saving strategies can be identified and implemented. Similarly, DTs can be used to predict future energy consumption based on historical data and current conditions. This feature allows for more efficient and proactive energy management. Actions can include, for example, scheduling appliances to work during off-peak hours or adjusting thermostat settings and can be either issued automatically by the system, or prompted by the user. In this regard, the DT can be imported and manipulated by any rendering engine. The model can be further enriched with data and user interactions offered by the capabilities of mainstream game engines. Homeowners can then interact with the DT through a user-friendly interface to monitor room conditions, energy consumption, receive personalized recommendations, and make adjustments as needed. Information relevant to the user is structured and presented in a comprehensive way. The 3D model room visualization is enhanced with prompts and visual clues regarding sensors' status, indoor environmental conditions, and thermal comfort. The latter is only enabled by the IoT integration with the Digital Twin.

4. IoT Integration with Digital Twin

The integration of IoT devices with DTs is a critical step in realizing advanced HEMSs. IoT provides real-time data collection and device control, while DTs leverage these data to create dynamic, virtual representations of home environments. This seamless connectivity allows for real-time monitoring, predictive analytics, and autonomous energy optimizations, bridging the physical and digital realms. This section details the IoT architecture and its integration with the DT framework, including the roles of IoT devices, communication protocols, and middleware for efficient data flow. Emphasis is placed on how IoT facilitates a bi-directional interaction between physical devices and their digital counterparts, enabling intelligent, responsive, and scalable energy management solutions. The described methodology ensures a robust and user-friendly approach to integrating IoT with DTs for effective HEMSs.

4.1. IoT Devices and Data Collection

The Internet of Things Connectivity Node (ICON) is the central entity in an HEMS. The ICON will basically work as a main gateway in a home, coordinating and managing all IoT devices. It may be a personal computer (PC), mini PC, or Raspberry Pi that makes it easy to integrate diverse smart sensors and actuators for smooth connectivity at both local network and cloud-based services. The ICON is an IoT hub that allows devices to communicate with each other and interact effectively, interfacing the immediate environment with larger structures in the network. Such IoT devices are allowed to connect with the ICON through special communication modules and protocols. Additionally, it plays an important role in translating various standards of communication, hence allowing for smooth interaction.

The ICON may be connected with many kinds of IoT devices, which in return provide specific data and functions as detailed in Table 2. These include environmental sensors that track temperature, humidity, and CO_2 levels, wall plugs that monitor the energy consumption of small devices, motion sensors that detect luminance and movement, and heavy-duty smart switches that control high-consumption devices, such as air conditioners (ACs) using an IR AC extender. Additionally, a three-phase energy meter is utilized to monitor energy consumption in households equipped with a three-phase system. In homes without a three-phase setup, one of the existing phases will be used for energy monitoring and management purposes. These IoT devices are designed for low-power operation to extend battery life and reduce the frequency of maintenance. In fact, this is important for devices installed in far-flung areas or those which are intended to run for an extended period, independent of manual interference. It is such protocols that enable continuous communication and energy management, required by both smart home installations and industries.

Table 2. Devices and sensors in an IoT system.

Device Type	Function	Data Collected
ICON	Manages connections	Aggregated sensor data
Communication Module	Facilitates data exchange	Signal communication
Device Management Interface	Configures and controls devices	Device status and configuration
Sensors	Measure various conditions	Temperature, humidity, CO_2, motion, light levels, energy consumption
Appliance Controller	Manages appliance operation	Appliance status
MQTT Broker	Manages data flow	Real-time data handling

The ICON has a mesh network topology, with every device connecting to each other wirelessly in multiple ways. This layout provides the network with better communication reliability as well as increased resilience—data can traverse several paths. Even if one link or device is lost, communication among the rest of the nodes can, by virtue of rerouting them, remain unbroken. Typical of Z-Wave devices in this kind of setup, messages can be passed between devices in a hops manner and thus, the mesh network topology can reach out beyond the communication range of a central controller. In most cases, up to four intermediate nodes are used and this makes communication possible even in distant areas through direct lines. However, a potential drawback of mesh networks is their intricacy; developing a smoothly running system with effective data flow usually requires high-level techniques. Nevertheless, its strength and adaptability are the main factors of the technology that make it most suitable in the fields where communication between the devices is very high. In contrast, a star network topology, employed in solutions like Z-Wave Long Distance (LR), has a central hub that communicates directly to each device without any intermediary nodes. This design has the benefit of clear communication paths and less latency, which is especially beneficial for devices further from the hub. The star topology is simple and it is a good solution in situations where the only requirement is short-distance communication with no delays. In order to ensure an easy process for the users, the ICON interface is designed as a Docker container. This containerized architecture creates an environment where services can run independently, so changes and maintenance can happen without affecting other functions. In addition, users can also easily add, configure, and manage connected sensors on the ICON device. Thanks to the reliability of mesh networks, the operational simplicity provided by Docker makes the ICON communication system remain strong and flexible.

The data collected by these IoT devices is sent, using the MQTT protocol, to a MQTT broker such as Mosquitto. The efficiency of this lightweight messaging system ensures the real-time transfer of data. The sensor information formatted in JSON format has a unique identifier for each sensor. This standardized format ensures easy integration and accurate handling of various types of data, such as temperature, humidity, and energy consumption. For a detailed representation of this data flow and integration process, the data collected might be locally stored or transmitted to a cloud server for further analysis. Edge computing performs preliminary data processing effectively at the source. In general, data analysis on the edge optimizes resources, improves transmission speed, and accelerates decision-making. This approach further supports sophisticated data management with accurate analytics.

The flow of the IoT system, as illustrated in Figure 4, begins with the ICON, which serves as the central controller for connections and interactions throughout the system. From this node, it connects to specific modules for a reliable exchange of information. These modules, sensors, and appliance controllers communicate with each other using low-power protocols designed for energy conservation and scalability. The proposed network has a mesh topology, together with a star network topology. The mesh network allows for improved redundancy because there are more paths that data can travel to ensure that communication is good in case something like a device or a link goes down. The star network simplifies routing by connecting directly with the ICON hub, thereby reducing latency, especially for those devices that are further away. This will ensure robust and efficient communication across the network.

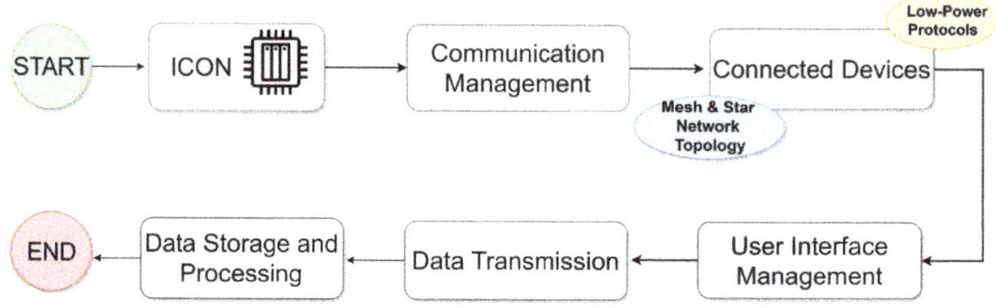

Figure 4. Data flow and integration process of HEMS.

4.2. Middleware Framework

Middleware is an essential software layer that facilitates communication and service integration between operating systems, applications, and DTs, while providing critical services (i.e., communication, authentication, API management, processing). By managing data flow and interaction in real-time, middleware enables seamless coordination between physical devices and their virtual counterparts in DT frameworks. This capability is particularly critical in complex environments such as IoT systems, where reliable and scalable distributed operations are required to maintain an accurate and responsive Digital Twin. Middleware thus supports the development of efficient, scalable applications that continuously synchronize real data with digital replicas, enabling real-time analysis, predictive insights, and system optimization.

As depicted in Figure 5, the MQTT middleware framework in an IoT setup where various constrained devices (e.g., temperature sensors) generate data for applications or other devices is presenteds. MQTT clients act as publishers and subscribers, while managing this data exchange. In distributed IoT systems, middleware manages protocols and data flows and abstracts hardware complexities to provide a unified interface. MQTT, a widely used middleware solution, uses a publish/subscribe model for efficient data distribution [33]. In this architecture, a sensor can publish data to an MQTT broker, which then distributes it to subscribed clients on specific topics (e.g., topics A, B, or C). Compared to protocols like HTTP or CoAP, MQTT's lightweight design optimizes it for IoT applications by minimizing bandwidth and power consumption, making it ideal for low-resource IoT devices [34].

MQTT stands out as an effective protocol for real-time, low-latency communication in IoT systems, providing an efficient publish/subscribe mechanism tailored to devices with limited power and bandwidth resources. Unlike HTTP and CoAP, MQTT's lightweight design is optimized for minimal resource consumption, making it particularly suitable for IoT environments [35]. Middleware frameworks that integrate MQTT also facilitate cross-platform communication, particularly in edge computing environments, by enabling local data processing and reducing reliance on centralized networks. As shown, MQTT brokers deployed on edge devices support continuous data exchange even in offline scenarios, improving the reliability and responsiveness of local IoT systems and ensuring that critical functions function regardless of external network conditions.

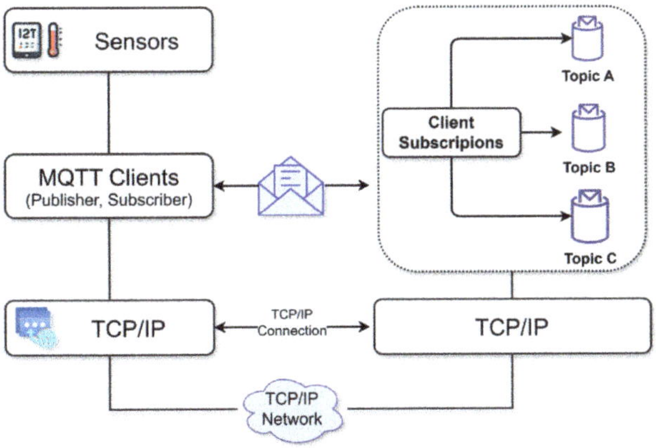

Figure 5. Gateway Middleware Framework.

In Figure 6, an IoT application architecture in which middleware plays a critical role in ensuring seamless data flow between physical devices, applications, and digital twins is represented. In IoT systems integrated with DTs, middleware not only synchronizes real data with virtual models, but also ensures that these digital replicas remain accurate and up-to-date. This allows DTs to simulate, analyze, and predict behaviors in systems such as home energy management, where real-time energy consumption data from sensors can serve as the basis for optimization and control decisions. By connecting various IoT devices and supporting edge processing, middleware improves both scalability and responsiveness, enabling digital twins to operate effectively in real-time and even offline, making them powerful tools for proactive management in complex environments such as Smart Homes and Smart Cities.

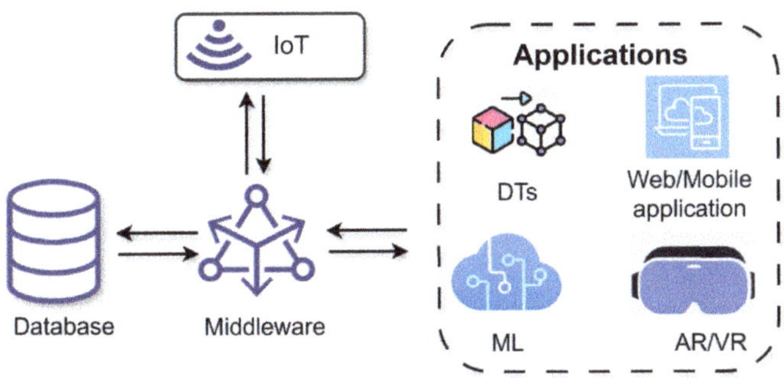

Figure 6. Architecture of IoT-enabled middleware and applications.

5. Case Study: Practical Implementation of DT for HEMS

The case study and simulation presented in this section aim to validate the proposed framework's effectiveness in addressing the primary scientific objectives of this research. Specifically, in this section, the proposed framework is validated by addressing the objectives outlined in Section 3.3 and their corresponding use cases. The following objectives are validated:

- Realism and Immersion (Obj. 1). Use Case: Navigation and Interaction in a Digital Twin Environment. The simulation includes a visually and spatially accurate 3D model, allowing users to navigate and interact with the Digital Twin environment, improving realism and user experience.

- Functional Segmentation and Data Integration (Obj. 2 & 5): Use Case: Zone-Specific Energy Monitoring. The Digital Twin uses spatial segmentation of the 3D model to integrate energy and environmental data for targeted monitoring, improving precision and usability.
- Space-Specific Energy Tracking (Obj. 3):Use Case: Energy Analysis Across Zones. The framework tracks patterns unique to specific spaces (e.g., living room vs. kitchen), providing actionable insights tailored to individual zones.
- Environmental Monitoring and Thermal Comfort (Obj. 4): Use Case: Monitoring and Adjusting Comfort Levels. By leveraging material and spatial segmentation, the simulation monitors temperature and humidity across different zones, ensuring thermal comfort and energy efficiency.
- Precision in Smart Home Automation (Obj. 6): Use Case: Automated Room-Specific Adjustments. Automation features are tailored to the unique material and spatial characteristics of each room, enabling precise control over smart home devices.

Overall, the case study and simulation demonstrate the successful validation of the proposed DT framework in fulfilling the key scientific objectives of this research. These include enhancing realism and user engagement through immersive 3D modeling, enabling precise energy and environmental monitoring with spatial and functional segmentation, and facilitating predictive analytics and automation for efficient and user-centric energy management. These outcomes highlight the framework's ability to bridge physical and digital domains, optimize energy consumption, and support sustainable practices in residential energy systems, thereby addressing the scalability, usability, and efficiency challenges outlined in this study.

5.1. Experiment Setup

The ICON was applied on a Raspberry Pi 5 (Rpi5) (Cambridge, UK) [36]. The Z-Wave was selected as this protocol is reliable and low power; hence, it can offer flawless communication between devices in a smart home. Sensors and devices were connected to a central hub or gateway through the use of a Z-Wave dongle [37], which efficiently enabled integration and management while keeping the communication stable and reliable. These components were utilized to enable communication with various smart home sensors, functioning as the main gateway that interfaced the Raspberry Pi with a network of devices via the Z-Wave protocol. This controller translated between the Z-Wave communication standard and the Raspberry Pi, facilitating interaction with compatible sensors, such as the MCO Home (Tokyo, Japan) Z-Wave CO_2 sensor [38] for air quality monitoring, the Aeotec Heavy Duty Smart Switch Gen5 (Hamburg, Germany) [39] for managing high-power appliances, the Three-phase Energy Meter [40] for real-time energy consumption data, the Smart Plug Fibaro v2 (Wysogotowo, Poland) [41] for remote control of standard appliances, the FIBARO Motion Sensor [42] for motion detection, and the ZXT-600 AC Master (Remotec, Hong Kong, China) [43] for HVAC control. Table 3 below contains a list of all the devices that were used.

Table 3. Devices and sensors in Z-Wave IoT system.

Device Name	Brand	Type / Description
Raspberry Pi 5 [36]	Raspberry	Lightweight desktop computing
Aeotec Z-Stick 7 [37]	Aeotec	Z-Wave controller for home automation
MCO Home - Z-Wave CO_2 [38]	MCO Home	CO_2 Sensor with Z-Wave compatibility
Aeotec Heavy Duty Smart Switch Gen5 [39]	Aeotec	High-power smart switch for appliances (Z-Wave)
3-Phase Smart Meter [40]	Qubino	Energy monitoring for three-phase systems
Smart Plug Fibaro Z-Wave Plus v2 [41]	Fibaro	Smart plug with energy monitoring (Z-Wave Plus)
FIBARO Motion Sensor Z-Wave Plus White [42]	Fibaro	Motion and temperature sensor (Z-Wave Plus)
ZXT-600 AC MASTER [43]	Remotec	Z-Wave-to-IR bridge for air conditioner control

The visualization of IoT integration identifies the interconnected network of devices, data flows, and systems that facilitate the exchange of data across the IoT platform. The following graphic shows the main elements of the IoT architecture such as sensors, interconnectivity protocols, cloud infrastructure, and data analytics modules, which make it possible to form real-time insights. Through visualization, these individual components and their complex interactions become clear and enhance efficiency in the data-based decision-making process.

Figure 7 illustrates the data on an IoT platform, giving real-time information, as well as information about the pattern of events and in-depth information obtained from the data. Therefore, these graphical items helpfully depict the entire project's data flow.

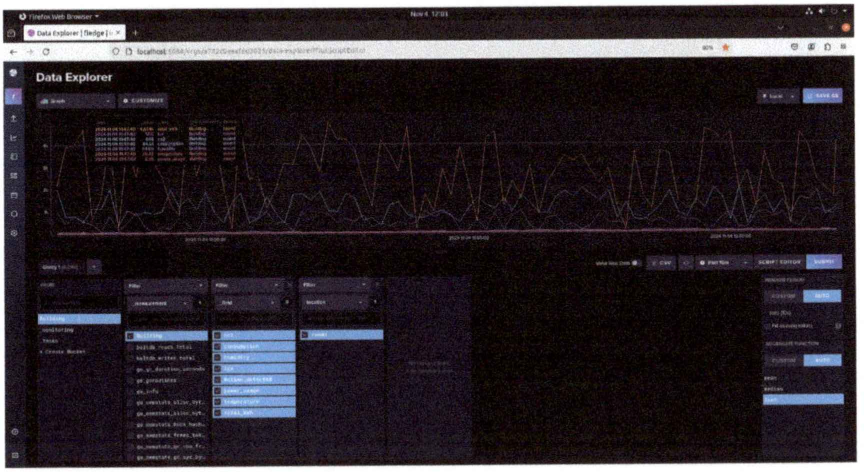

Figure 7. Time series data from sensors.

5.2. Parametric Standardized 3D House Model

For the implementation of the HEMS, a residential apartment design was selected as the basis for the DT model. The two-dimensional floor plan of this apartment includes two bedrooms, an open-plan living and kitchen area, a bathroom, and a central hallway connecting all spaces. The layout also features exterior balcony openings, allowing natural light and ventilation (Figure 8). During the 3D modeling phase, key structural elements were incorporated to closely reflect realistic building characteristics. Exterior walls were constructed with a thickness of 30 cm, integrating both masonry and external thermal insulation to enhance energy efficiency. Interior partition walls, primarily for space delineation, were assigned a thickness of 15 cm. Following the structural setup, openings for external windows, balcony doors, and the main entrance were positioned according to the floor plan, facilitating natural light entry and cross-ventilation. Interior doors were strategically placed to support room connectivity and privacy where needed.

Once the structural layout was completed, materials were applied to the model to reflect a realistic home environment. Wood flooring was implemented throughout the apartment, except in the bathroom, where tiles were used to resist moisture. Additionally, walls in each space were painted with unique colors to visually differentiate rooms, which supports usability and enhances the Digital Twin model's data segmentation for energy management. Bedrooms, the hallway, and the open-plan area all have distinct hues that improve the user's spatial awareness within the Digital Twin interface.

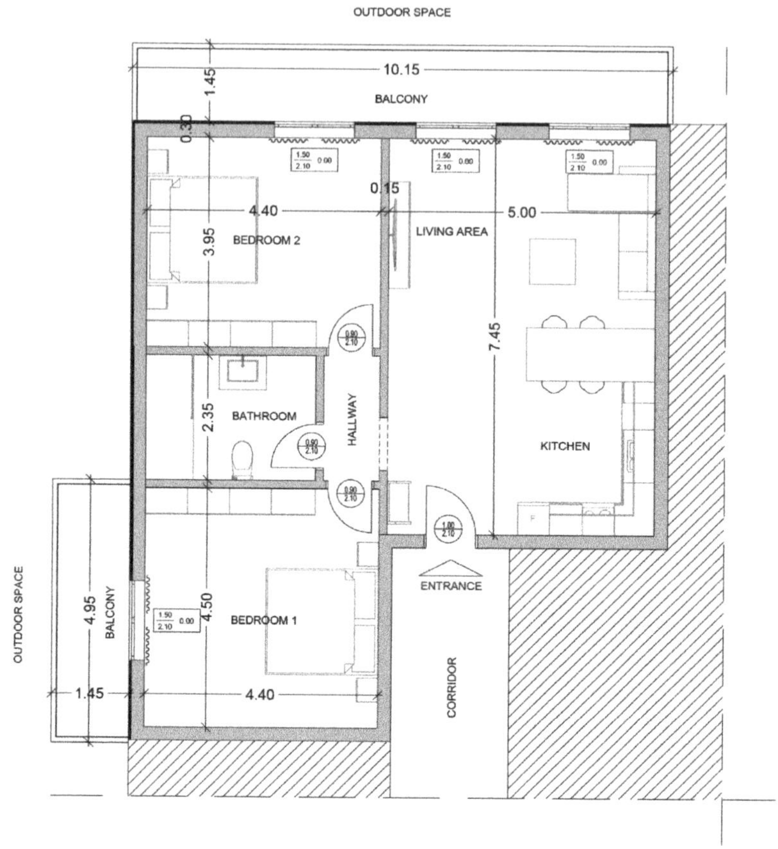

Figure 8. 2D model for HEMS.

To improve immersion, essential furnishings were incorporated. Bedrooms were furnished with beds, wardrobes, and curtains for shading. In the open-plan living and kitchen area, a complete kitchen setup with a dining table and appliances was modeled, alongside a living area with a sofa, coffee table, and TV. The bathroom was equipped with standard sanitary fixtures, including a washbasin, toilet, and shower. Following the application of all materials and furnishings, the model was prepared for transformation into a fully interactive Digital Twin. This model provides users with an immersive experience, mirroring the apartment's layout and aesthetics while allowing for advanced energy management, environmental monitoring, and data-driven insights within the Digital Twin framework. Figure 9 presents the parametric standardized 3D house mode.

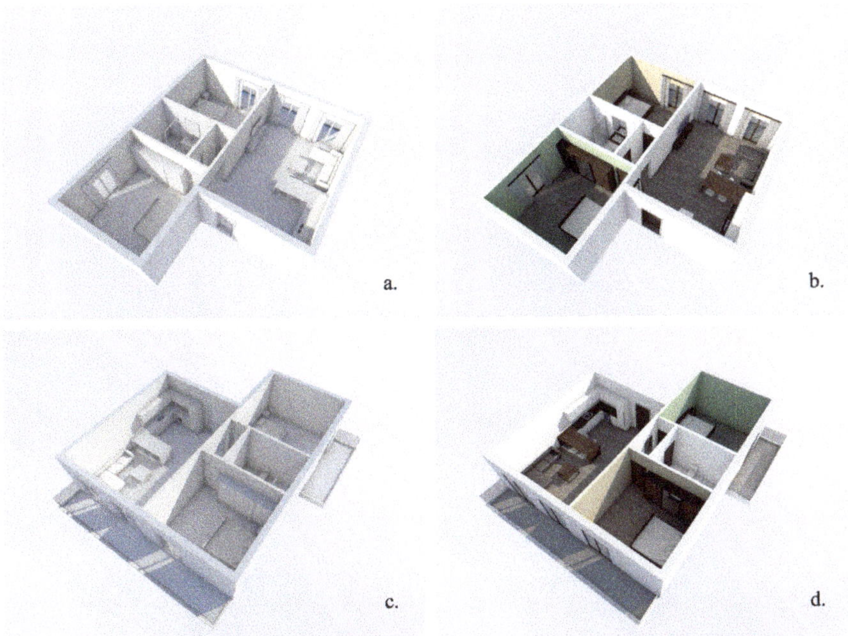

Figure 9. Parametric standardized 3D house model. 3D models illustrating the development stages of a standardized parametric house model for DT integration in an HEMS. (**a**,**c**): Bare 3D structural layouts emphasizing spatial relationships, furnished with essential furniture and appliances, shown from different perspectives. (**b**,**d**): Models enriched with applied materials and distinct room-specific color coding to enhance realism, spatial differentiation, and data segmentation, supporting immersive visualization and energy management within the DT framework.

5.3. Digital Twin for HEMS

This section presents the implementation and functionality of the DT framework for an HEMS, focusing on its real-world application. Initially, it discusses the integration of IoT sensors within the DT environment, enabling real-time operational monitoring and fault detection. Furthermore, the system's capability to track and visualize indoor environmental parameters is explored, such as temperature and humidity, providing users with actionable insights. Finally, it highlights the use of thermal comfort metrics, including the PMV index, to optimize indoor conditions while ensuring energy efficiency. These components collectively validate the DT's role in enhancing energy management, user engagement, and system reliability.

5.3.1. Status of Sensors in DT

One critical aspect of monitoring indoor conditions in an HEMS is ensuring the operational status of all connected sensors. Often, alerts and logs generated by such systems remain unnoticed or unread by end-users, leading to delayed responses to sensor malfunctions. This can undermine the accuracy and reliability of the HEMS, as sensor data are fundamental to maintaining optimal indoor conditions. In this paper, a user-friendly framework is proposed to visualize sensor statuses in real-time within the DT environment. The process begins with each sensor in the IoT network continuously collecting data and transmitting it to the ICON. This transmission includes not only environmental measurement but also the sensor's operational status (i.e., active, non-active). Once the data are received by the ICON, they are processed and stored in the database. The database serves as a reliable repository, where the operational status of each sensor is recorded along with historical and real-time data. This ensures that the system has a robust record of sensor activity, which can be referenced at any time.

Using the generated 3D house model as a basis, virtual sensors corresponding to real ones can be overlaid on top of the model to match the real sensors' positions (Figure 10). The Unreal Engine 5 software used in the DT framework communicates with each sensor via API calls [44]. These API interactions allow the Digital Twin to retrieve the real-time operational status of the sensors and visually update their status within the 3D environment. The retrieved data are visualized within the DT using an intuitive and user-friendly interface. Each sensor is represented in the virtual model with a simple color-coded scheme to indicate its status. Green indicates that the sensor is functioning correctly (i.e., active), while red highlights sensors that are malfunctioning or offline (i.e., non-active). This straightforward visualization enables users to quickly identify and address any issues.

Figure 10. DT visualization of HEMS with virtual sensors: green indicates functional sensors, and red indicates malfunctions.

In addition to visualization, the system is also capable of generating alerts for malfunctioning sensors. These alerts can be sent via email, SMS, or app notifications, ensuring that users are promptly informed of any issues, reducing the likelihood of unnoticed malfunctions. The alerts complement the visual status indicators, making the monitoring process both proactive and accessible. This approach enhances the usability and reliability of the HEMS. By providing immediate feedback through the DT, users can address sensor issues in a timely manner. The integration of IoT devices, centralized data storage, API communication, and real-time visualization ensures that the Digital Twin remains an accurate and interactive representation of the physical system. This proactive monitoring framework improves system performance, enhances user engagement, and ensures optimal energy management and environmental comfort.

5.3.2. Indoor Monitoring in DT

The DT environment is not only designed for monitoring the operational status of sensors but also for taking actionable steps to interact with their physical counterparts. By integrating real-time sensor data into the 3D house model, the DT enables a more comprehensive understanding of indoor conditions such as temperature and humidity as depicted in Figure 11. In the DT, the virtual sensors corresponding to real ones are placed in their physical locations within the house layout. These sensors actively track key parameters (e.g., temperature, humidity). The DT retrieves real-time data from IoT sensors through API calls, ensuring continuous synchronization with the physical environment. For instance, in Figure 11, a green indicator signifies that the corresponding sensor is functioning properly and provides data on the current indoor conditions, such as 28 °C temperature and 75% humidity.

Figure 11. Indoor conditions monitoring in DT.

Beyond monitoring, the DT enables users to take direct actions based on the displayed sensor data. For example, if indoor conditions deviate from optimal comfort levels, users can trigger changes, such as adjusting the thermostat or activating ventilation systems, directly through the DT interface. These actions are communicated back to the physical devices via the IoT network, ensuring that the desired changes are implemented seamlessly. This bidirectional communication and interaction make the DT a powerful tool for proactive indoor environment management. By combining real-time monitoring, intuitive visualization, and actionable controls, the DT enhances user engagement and ensures that indoor conditions are maintained effectively. The figure illustrates this functionality, showing how real-time data and user-triggered actions are visually and operationally integrated into the system.

5.3.3. Thermal Comfort in the DT

The system is designed to seamlessly integrate with other services and applications (Section 4.2), enabling enhanced functionalities such as estimating thermal comfort using the PMV index [45]. The PMV index provides a scientifically validated measure of thermal comfort; this index is estimated in real time based on environmental parameters such as temperature, humidity, and personal factors, and the results are stored in the system's database. Figure 12 showcases the PMV data as calculated in real time. The thermal comfort conditions are visualized for the three different rooms within the house. As seen, the PMV values for the living room and bedrooms exhibit slight variations throughout the day, reflecting different usage patterns and environmental influences. Despite these differences, the overall fluctuations remain within a moderate range, indicating stable comfort levels across the rooms.

To represent thermal comfort visually within the Digital Twin, a color map is implemented based on the PMV scale as shown in Figure 13.

Each wall and room area is dynamically updated to reflect its thermal comfort level, with colors ranging from blue (cooler) to green (neutral) and red (warmer). This visualization allows users to intuitively assess the thermal conditions of their home and make informed adjustments if necessary, such as modifying HVAC settings to maintain optimal comfort Figure 14. The integration of real-time PMV estimation, visualization, and actionable controls within the Digital Twin enhances the user experience and ensures energy-efficient home management while maintaining thermal comfort.

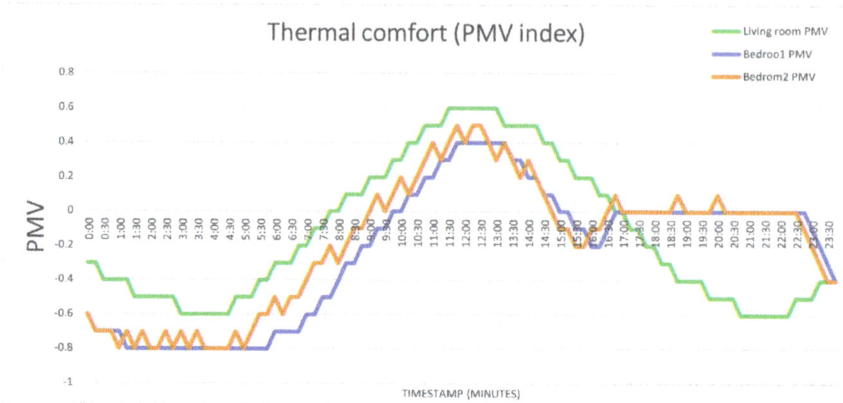

Figure 12. Thermal comfort conditions.

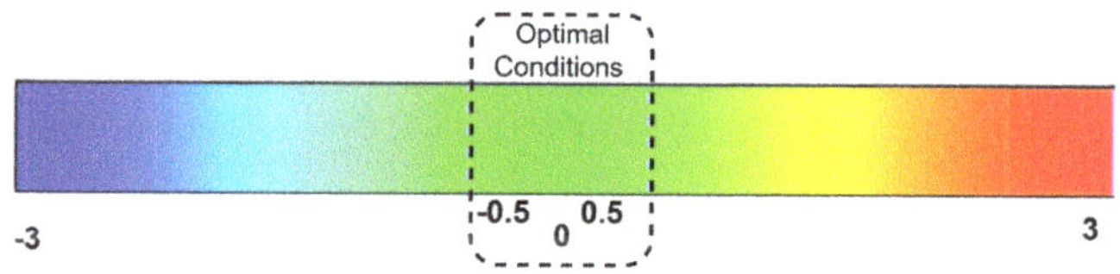

Figure 13. PMV scale color map.

Figure 14. Thermal comfort in DT.

The integration of real-time PMV estimation, visualization, and actionable controls within the Digital Twin enhances the user experience and ensures energy-efficient home management while maintaining thermal comfort. The results of the case study are illustrated on the GitHub repository [46].

5.4. Evaluation of Key Performance Metrics

The scientific aim of this research was validated through a set of carefully defined Key Performance Indicators (KPIs) that measure the framework's effectiveness in achieving its objectives. These KPIs included real-time system performance, predictive accuracy, scalability, usability, and energy efficiency. Specifically, the real-time system performance was assessed by measuring data synchronization latency, ensuring seamless integration of IoT data into the Digital Twin environment. Scalability was demonstrated through system response times under varying loads, maintaining robust performance even with increased IoT device connections. Usability was estimated through user experience based on ease of navigation and actionable insights.

In Table 4, the KPIs for evaluating the suggested framework for IoT-integrated HEMSs are outlined. The table highlights essential aspects such as the setup time required for plug-and-play IoT integration and DT framework installation, emphasizing non-intrusiveness with minimal structural modifications. Real-time monitoring is measured by latency and memory efficiency, ensuring the synchronization of IoT data within the DT environment. Metrics for system performance include the ability to minimize storage requirements by using reusable 3D models and maintaining RAM utilization during high-load operations. Additionally, scalability and seamless integration are evaluated through metrics like data reflection time, model build time, and resource efficiency, ensuring the system's readiness for real-world applications.

Table 4. Key performance metrics for evaluating IoT-integrated DT framework in HEMS.

Metric	Proposed Framework	Traditional IoT Systems ([13–15,47])
Setup Time for IoT Deployment	Average 15 min per user	Average 30–45 min per user
Intrusiveness in Installation	<5% requiring structural modifications	20–30% requiring structural modifications, including rewiring and new fixtures
Time to Build DT for All 50 Households	1 h total (standardized model)	200–300 h total (4–6 h per house for customized modeling)
Overall Time for 50 Users (IoT + DT)	∼13.5 h	∼225–275 h
Setup Time for IoT Deployment	Average 15 min per user	Average 30–45 min per user
Memory Usage for DT	<500 MB (single model for all users)	∼25 GB total (500 MB per model ×50 models)
Scalability	Highly scalable with standardized DT models	Limited scalability due to custom modeling and extensive resource requirements
Interoperability	Seamless integration with diverse IoT protocols (Zigbee, Wi-Fi, Z-Wave)	Often protocol-specific, requiring additional middleware for compatibility
User Experience	Intuitive 3D visualizations, satisfaction score $\geq 4.7/5$	Often lacking in real-time visualization, satisfaction score ∼3.5–4/5

This comprehensive approach ensures the proposed framework not only meets technical and operational standards but also aligns with user expectations for non-intrusiveness and intuitive interaction. The integration of IoT and DT technologies, evaluated through these performance indicators, demonstrates the potential to optimize energy efficiency, enhance real-time monitoring, and provide actionable insights for sustainable energy management in modern households. As such, the study contributes significantly to the advancement of scalable and user-friendly solutions for smart energy management, paving the way for future research and practical implementations in the HEMS domain.

A comparative analysis with traditional HEMS systems highlights the transformative potential of integrating Digital Twin technology. The comparison evaluates improvements in real-time data synchronization, predictive capabilities, and overall system scalability, demonstrating how the proposed framework addresses limitations in conventional systems. This dual approach ensures a comprehensive assessment of the framework's performance and its practical implications for users and HEMS. As a result, the importance of the standardized DT model, where users still enjoy the full benefits of a DT-enabled HEMS, in a scenario involving 50 new users is considered. Comparing the suggested framework to traditional methods of both IoT and DT integration, the results are summarized in Table 5. The proposed framework demonstrates significant efficiency and scalability advantages. By utilizing a single, standardized DT model and plug-and-play IoT devices, the framework reduces the time and resource burdens typically associated with traditional systems.

Table 5. Comparison of proposed IoT-integrated DT framework and traditional IoT systems in deployment time, intrusiveness, and scalability for 50 users.

Metric	Proposed Framework	Traditional IoT Systems ([13–15,17])
Setup Time for IoT Deployment	Average 15 min per user	Average 30–45 min per user
Intrusiveness in Installation	<5% requiring structural modifications	20–30% requiring structural modifications, including rewiring and new fixtures
Time to Build DT for All 50 Households	1 h total (standardized model)	200–300 h total (4–6 h per house for customized modeling)
Overall Time for 50 Users (IoT + DT)	∼13.5 h	∼225–275 h
Memory Usage for DT	<500 MB (single model for all users)	∼25 GB total (500 MB per model × 50 models)
Scalability	Highly scalable with standardized DT models	Limited scalability due to custom modeling and extensive resource requirements
Interoperability	Seamless integration with diverse IoT protocols (Zigbee, Wi-Fi, Z-Wave)	Often protocol-specific, requiring additional middleware for compatibility
User Experience	Intuitive 3D visualizations, satisfaction score 4.7/5	Often lacking in real-time visualization, satisfaction score ∼3.5–4/5
Cost (Approximate)	EUR 180 hardware per household plus negligible setup costs; EUR 1–2 for one model	EUR 300 hardware per household plus EUR 20–30 setup costs plus EUR 40–50 per model (EUR 2000–EUR 2500)

Specifically, based on the results, a 94% reduction in overall deployment time was achieved, minimizing the effort required to set up IoT systems and build the DT. Moreover, the use of a single standardized DT model resulted in a 98% reduction in memory usage compared to the traditional approach, which involves creating individual DT models for each household. With plug-and-play capabilities, the framework reduced IoT setup time per user by 50%, providing a more streamlined and efficient process. The non-intrusive nature of the proposed framework resulted in 75% fewer installations requiring structural modifications, ensuring easier adoption and implementation in diverse home environments. These results clearly demonstrate the superiority of the proposed framework in terms of time, scalability, and user convenience while maintaining the high-quality experience and energy management capabilities enabled by Digital Twin integration. In addition to these operational efficiencies, the cost analysis highlights the economic benefits of the proposed framework. In terms of cost for a 50-household deployment, the proposed framework is significantly more economical, with an estimated total cost of approximately EUR 9050 (EUR 180 hardware per household + negligible setup costs and EUR 1–2 for the standardized model). In contrast, traditional systems require an estimated EUR 15,000–EUR 20,000 (EUR 300–EUR 400 per household due to higher hardware, setup, and custom modeling expenses). This translates to a cost reduction of 40–55% for the proposed framework, making it a highly cost-effective solution for large-scale adoption in smart home technologies.

5.5. Limitations, Challenges, and Extensions

The proposed framework offers significant advancements in enhancing HEMSs through the integration of DT technology. However, certain limitations and challenges remain to be addressed. Scalability is a key consideration, as the framework has been evaluated within specific IoT configurations, and its application across diverse and larger-scale residential setups with more complex IoT ecosystems requires further validation. Additionally, while the framework demonstrates robust predictive capabilities, ensuring consistent accuracy under dynamic and unpredictable user behaviors in real-world environments presents an important area for further exploration. User engagement and usability assessments have primarily been based on predefined use cases. Broader validation across varied demographics and user preferences is essential to refine the framework's design and functionality. Another important consideration is the adaptability and generalizability of the DTs. While effective for specific scenarios, ensuring these models can accommodate diverse home layouts and IoT device capabilities remains a challenge.

In terms of implementation, deploying the framework across heterogeneous residential infrastructures and ensuring seamless compatibility with varying IoT configurations presents practical complexities. Additionally, the lack of standardized DT models tailored for residential environments highlights the need for collaborative efforts to establish universal standards. Data privacy and security also emerge as critical concerns, requiring robust measures to safeguard user information and foster trust. Lastly, integrating advanced technologies such as artificial intelligence, machine learning, and renewable energy systems introduces new opportunities but also challenges in ensuring interoperability and optimizing system performance. Despite these limitations, the framework establishes a strong foundation for advancing residential energy management, providing clear pathways for addressing these challenges and guiding future research.

Moreover, while the current study validates the proposed framework using a two-bedroom residential layout, this choice was intentional to demonstrate the feasibility and benefits of utilizing a predefined framework. Future work could explore adapting this framework to larger and more complex environments, such as multi-storied buildings. Future iterations should also consider incorporating predefined room types and leveraging modular grid-based designs to dynamically construct more complex structures. This enhancement would significantly improve the framework's adaptability and scalability, broadening its applicability while maintaining its inherent advantages.

The proposed framework was designed with scalability and flexibility in mind, allowing for future extensions to address additional factors and scenarios. For instance, the framework can be augmented to include mechanisms for handling network disconnections, sensor failures, and high data loads to improve robustness in real-world applications. Moreover, while the current implementation focuses on thermal comfort using PMV indices, it can be extended to incorporate additional environmental factors such as noise levels and air quality. These enhancements would provide a more holistic approach to home energy management, ensuring a comprehensive understanding of occupant comfort and environmental sustainability. By building on the existing modular and adaptable design, such extensions can be seamlessly integrated without compromising the framework's simplicity and usability.

The most critical achievement of the proposed framework is the seamless integration of IoT devices with the Digital Twin environment, which forms the foundation for various advanced visualizations. By leveraging real-time data collected from IoT sensors, the framework enables a wide range of interactive and informative visual representations, including energy consumption patterns, thermal comfort levels, and occupancy trends. These visualizations can be further tailored to incorporate other environmental factors, such as noise levels, air quality, or even predictive analytics for device performance and energy optimization. The flexibility and modularity of this IoT integration ensure that users can gain actionable insights through intuitive dashboards or immersive 3D interfaces, enhancing their understanding and control over home energy management systems.

6. Conclusions

This study presents an innovative framework for integrating IoT technologies with Digital Twins in Home Energy Management Systems. By leveraging a standardized parametric 3D modeling approach, the proposed solution addresses key challenges such as scalability, deployment complexity, and resource optimization. The framework demonstrates significant advancements over traditional methods, achieving a 94% reduction in deployment time and a 98% decrease in memory usage, while ensuring non-intrusive installation and seamless integration of diverse IoT protocols.

The integration of real-time monitoring, predictive analytics, and user-friendly visualizations empowers households to optimize energy consumption and maintain thermal comfort effectively. Additionally, the incorporation of metrics like the PMV index enhances the precision of environmental adjustments, ensuring a balance between energy efficiency and user comfort. The scalability and interoperability of the framework make it a robust solution for large-scale deployments, contributing to the development of sustainable and intelligent residential environments.

Future research will focus on creating a user-friendly system that enables residents to construct their Digital Twin homes by selecting and customizing pre-designed rooms. Users will be able to adjust parameters such as dimensions, layouts, and furnishings to build a virtual representation closely resembling their actual house. This approach will combine the efficiency of standardized models with the flexibility of user customization, streamlining the adoption process and providing precise energy management tailored to individual household configurations.

Author Contributions: Conceptualization, M.S., A.D. and V.N.; methodology, A.D. and S.K.; software, A.D., A.P., O.E. and G.S.; validation, A.D., M.S., I.T. and A.P.; formal analysis, C.P.; investigation, A.D. and M.P.; resources, I.T. and V.N.; data curation, G.S. and A.P.; writing—original draft preparation, M.S. and O.E.; writing—review and editing, A.L., C.-N.A. and S.K.; visualization, C.P.; supervision, C.-N.A., S.K. and A.L.; project administration, S.K.; funding acquisition, C.-N.A., V.N. and A.L. All authors have read and agreed to the published version of the manuscript.

Funding: This research received no external funding.

Institutional Review Board Statement: Not applicable.

Informed Consent Statement: Not applicable.

Data Availability Statement: The data presented in this study are available on request from the corresponding author. The data are not publicly available due to privacy.

Acknowledgments: This work was partially supported by the FLEdge project F-DUT-2022-0337. The FLEdge project is funded by the General Secretariat of Research & Innovation goals (GSRI) under the Driving Urban Transitions (DUT) Partnership by the Bulgarian National Science Fund (BNSF) under agreement no. KP-06-D002/5 (GATE) and by the European Union. This work was also supported by the SEED4AI project under programme 16880—KE83201 implemented in the framework of the National Recovery and Resilience Plan 'Greece 2.0', with funding from the European Union—NextGenerationEU (Implementing Agency: EL.ID.E.K). Finally, this work was supported by the GATE project funded by the H2020 WIDESPREAD-2018-2020 TEAMING Phase 2 programme under grant agreement no. 857155.

Conflicts of Interest: Author Orfeas Eleftheriou was employed by the company Code-Flow. The remaining authors declare that the research was conducted in the absence of any commercial or financial relationships that could be construed as a potential conflict of interest.

References

1. Energy Performance of Buildings Directive—energy.ec.europa.eu. Available online: https://energy.ec.europa.eu/topics/energy-efficiency/energy-efficient-buildings/energy-performance-buildings-directive_en (accessed on 19 November 2024).
2. Dimara, A.; Timplalexis, C.; Krinidis, S.; Schneider, C.; Bertocchi, M.; Tzovaras, D. Optimal comfort conditions in residential houses. In Proceedings of the 2020 5th International Conference on Smart and Sustainable Technologies (SpliTech), Bol, Croatia, 2–4 July 2020; pp. 1–6.
3. Syamala, M.; Komala, C.; Pramila, P.; Dash, S.; Meenakshi, S.; Boopathi, S. Machine learning-integrated IoT-based smart home energy management system. In *Handbook of Research on Deep Learning Techniques for Cloud-Based Industrial IoT*; IGI Global: Hershey, PA, USA, 2023; pp. 219–235.
4. Papaioannou, A.; Dimara, A.; Krinidis, S.; Anagnostopoulos, C.N.; Ioannidis, D.; Tzovaras, D. Advanced proactive anomaly detection in multi-pattern home appliances for energy optimization. *Internet Things* **2024**, *26*, 101175. [CrossRef]
5. Papaioannou, A.; Dimara, A.; Kouzinopoulos, C.S.; Krinidis, S.; Anagnostopoulos, C.N.; Ioannidis, D.; Tzovaras, D. LP-OPTIMA: A Framework for Prescriptive Maintenance and Optimization of IoT Resources for Low-Power Embedded Systems. *Sensors* **2024**, *24*, 2125. [CrossRef]
6. Lamagna, M.; Groppi, D.; Nezhad, M.M.; Piras, G. A comprehensive review on digital twins for smart energy management system. *Int. J. Energy Prod. Manag.* **2021**, *6*, 323–334. [CrossRef]
7. Donchev, D.; Petrova-Antonova, D.; Hristov, P.O. An efficient hybrid regression model for energy and water consumption in a municipal kindergarten. In Proceedings of the 2022 7th International Conference on Smart and Sustainable Technologies (SpliTech), Split/Bol, Croatia, 5–8 July 2022; pp. 1–6.
8. Mitkov, R.; Petrova-Antonova, D.; Hristov, P.O. Predictive Modeling of Indoor Environmental Parameters for Assessing Comfort Conditions in a Kindergarten Setting. *Toxics* **2023**, *11*, 709. [CrossRef] [PubMed]
9. Ye, X.; Du, J.; Han, Y.; Newman, G.; Retchless, D.; Zou, L.; Ham, Y.; Cai, Z. Developing human-centered urban digital twins for community infrastructure resilience: A research agenda. *J. Plan. Lit.* **2023**, *38*, 187–199. [CrossRef] [PubMed]
10. Malik, I.; Bhardwaj, A.; Bhardwaj, H.; Sakalle, A. IoT-enabled smart homes: Architecture, challenges, and issues. In *Revolutionizing Industrial Automation Through the Convergence of Artificial Intelligence and the Internet of Things*; IGI Global: Hershey, PA, USA, 2023; pp. 160–176.
11. Tahmasebinia, F.; Lin, L.; Wu, S.; Kang, Y.; Sepasgozar, S. Exploring the benefits and limitations of digital twin technology in building energy. *Appl. Sci.* **2023**, *13*, 8814. [CrossRef]
12. Javaid, M.; Haleem, A.; Suman, R. Digital twin applications toward industry 4.0: A review. *Cogn. Robot.* **2023**, *3*, 71–92. [CrossRef]
13. Al-Ali, A.; Zualkernan, I.A.; Rashid, M.; Gupta, R.; Alikarar, M. A smart home energy management system using IoT and big data analytics approach. *IEEE Trans. Consum. Electron.* **2017**, *63*, 426–434. [CrossRef]
14. Machorro-Cano, I.; Alor-Hernández, G.; Paredes-Valverde, M.A.; Rodríguez-Mazahua, L.; Sánchez-Cervantes, J.L.; Olmedo-Aguirre, J.O. HEMS-IoT: A Big Data and Machine Learning-Based Smart Home System for Energy Saving. *Energies* **2020**, *13*, 1097. [CrossRef]
15. Gupta, R.; Al-Ali, A.R.; Zualkernan, I.A.; Das, S.K. Big Data Energy Management, Analytics and Visualization for Residential Areas. *IEEE Access* **2020**, *8*, 156153–156164. [CrossRef]
16. Hossain, E.; Khan, I.; Un-Noor, F.; Sikander, S.S.; Sunny, M.S.H. Application of Big Data and Machine Learning in Smart Grid, and Associated Security Concerns: A Review. *IEEE Access* **2019**, *7*, 13960–13988. [CrossRef]
17. Ilieva, S.; Penchev, A.; Petrova-Antonova, D. Internet of Things Framework for Smart Home Building. In Proceedings of the Digital Transformation and Global Society, St. Petersburg, Russia, 22–24 June 2016; pp. 450–462.
18. Condon, F.; Martínez, J.M.; Eltamaly, A.M.; Kim, Y.C.; Ahmed, M.A. Design and Implementation of a Cloud-IoT-Based Home Energy Management System. *Sensors* **2023**, *23*, 176. [CrossRef]
19. Sundaramoorthi, P.; Albert Alexander, S. Cloud-based mqtt protocol for power monitoring and socket control system. *Int. J. Adv. Signal Image Sci.* **2023**, *9*, 10–19.

20. Ferreira, L.C.B.C.; Borchardt, A.D.R.; Cardoso, G.D.S.; Mendes Lemes, D.A.; Sousa, G.R.D.R.d.; Neto, F.B.; de Lima, E.R.; Fraidenraich, G.; Cardieri, P.; Meloni, L.G.P. Edge Computing and Microservices Middleware for Home Energy Management Systems. *IEEE Access* **2022**, *10*, 109663–109676. [CrossRef]
21. Iqbal, F.; Altaf, A.; Waris, Z.; Aray, D.G.; Flores, M.A.L.; Díez, I.d.l.T.; Ashraf, I. Blockchain-Modeled Edge-Computing-Based Smart Home Monitoring System with Energy Usage Prediction. *Sensors* **2023**, *23*, 5263. [CrossRef]
22. Fazeldehkordi, E.; Grønli, T.M. A Survey of Security Architectures for Edge Computing-Based IoT. *IoT* **2022**, *3*, 332–365. [CrossRef]
23. Arsecularatne, B.; Rodrigo, N.; Chang, R. Digital Twins for Reducing Energy Consumption in Buildings: A Review. *Sustainability* **2024**, *16*, 9275. [CrossRef]
24. Das, H.P.; Lin, Y.W.; Agwan, U.; Spangher, L.; Devonport, A.; Yang, Y.; Drgoňa, J.; Chong, A.; Schiavon, S.; Spanos, C.J. Machine Learning for Smart and Energy-Efficient Buildings. *Environ. Data Sci.* **2024**, *3*, e1. [CrossRef]
25. Fathy, Y.; Jaber, M.; Nadeem, Z. Digital Twin-Driven Decision Making and Planning for Energy Consumption. *J. Sens. Actuator Networks* **2021**, *10*, 37. [CrossRef]
26. Testasecca, T.; Stamatopoulos, S.; Natalini, A.; Lazzaro, M.; Capizzi, C.M.; Sarmas, E.; Arnone, D. Implementing Digital Twins for Enhanced Energy Management in Three Case Studies. In Proceedings of the 2024 IEEE International Workshop on Metrology for Living Environment (MetroLivEnv), Chania, Greece, 12–14 June 2024; pp. 343–348.
27. De Lope, L.R.; Maestre, V.M.; Diez, L.; Ortiz, A.; Agüero, R.; Ortiz, I. Modeling a digital twin for the optimization of a self-supply energy system for residential use. In Proceedings of the 2024 IEEE International Systems Conference (SysCon), Montreal, QC, Canada, 15–18 April 2024; pp. 1–8.
28. Cotti, L.; Guizzardi, D.; Barricelli, B.R.; Fogli, D. Enabling End-User Development in Smart Homes: A Machine Learning-Powered Digital Twin for Energy Efficient Management. *Future Internet* **2024**, *16*, 208. [CrossRef]
29. Wen, T.; Liang, C.; Fu, Y.M.; Xiao, C.X.; Xiang, H.M. Floor plan analysis and vectorization with multimodal information. In Proceedings of the International Conference on Multimedia Modeling, Bergen, Norway, 9–12 January 2023; pp. 282–293.
30. Cline, L.S. *Sketchup for Interior Design: 3D Visualizing, Designing, and Space Planning*; John Wiley & Sons: Hoboken, NJ, USA, 2023.
31. Leony, A.; Latief, Y.; Wardahni, N.I. The Development of Maintenance and Care System for Public Railway Facility Infrastructure Integrated with Building Information Modeling (BIM) Software Based on Work Breakdown Structure (WBS). *Int. Res. J. Eng. IT Sci. Res.* **2024**, *10*, 49–57. [CrossRef]
32. Saint-Amour, P.K. To Detail a Dollhouse. *Mod. Lang. Q.* **2023**, *84*, 261–272. [CrossRef]
33. MQTT-The Standard for IoT Messaging. Available online: https://mqtt.org (accessed on 18 November 2024).
34. Seoane, V.; Garcia-Rubio, C.; Almenares, F.; Campo, C. Performance evaluation of CoAP and MQTT with security support for IoT environments. *Comput. Networks* **2021**, *197*, 108338. [CrossRef]
35. Jang, W.; Choi, J.; Seo, K. Comparative Analysis of IoT Communication Protocols. In Proceedings of the 2018 International Symposium on Networks, Computers and Communications (ISNCC), Rome, Italy, 19–21 June 2018.
36. Raspberry Pi 5. Available online: https://www.raspberrypi.com/products/raspberry-pi-5/ (accessed on 19 November 2024).
37. Aeotec Z-Stick 7. Available online: https://aeotec.com/products/aeotec-z-stick-7/ (accessed on 19 November 2024).
38. MCO Home-Z-Wave CO2 Sensor. Available online: https://www.z-wavelab.com/image/catalog/PDF/20160531160808.pdf (accessed on 19 November 2024).
39. Aeotec Heavy Duty Smart Switch Gen5. Available online: https://aeotec.com/products/aeoteo-heavy-duty-switch/ (accessed on 19 November 2024).
40. Qubino 3-Phase Smart Meter. Available online: https://qubino.com/products/3-phase-smart-meter/ (accessed on 19 November 2024).
41. Smart Plug Fibaro. Available online: https://www.fibaro.com/gr/products/wall-plug/ (accessed on 19 November 2024).
42. FIBARO Motion Sensor. Available online: https://www.fibaro.com/gr/products/motion-sensor/ (accessed on 19 November 2024).
43. ZXT-600 AC MASTER. Available online: http://manuals-backend.z-wave.info/make.php?lang=en&sku=ZXT-600US&cert=ZC10-17055619. (accessed on 19 November 2024).
44. Sun, Y.; Wang, H.; Zhang, Z.; Diels, C.; Asadipour, A. Executing realistic earthquake simulations in unreal engine with material calibration. *Comput. Graph.* **2024**, *124*, 104091. [CrossRef]
45. Tzitziou, G.; Dimara, A.; Papaioannou, A.; Tzouvaras, C.; Krinidis, S.; Anagnostopoulos, C.N.; Ioannidis, D.; Tzovaras, D. Realtime Multi-factor Dynamic Thermal Comfort Estimation for Indoor Environments. In Proceedings of the IFIP International Conference on Artificial Intelligence Applications and Innovations, León, Spain, 14–17 June 2023; pp. 219–230.
46. Stogia, M.; Naserentin, V.; Krinidis, S. Integrating IoT in Digital Twins for Home Energy Management. Available online: https://github.com/iTechLab2024/A-Scalable-and-User-Friendly-Framework-Integrating-IoT-and-Digital-Twins-for-Home-Energy-Management (accessed on 18 November 2024).
47. Verykokou, S.; Ioannidis, C. An overview on image-based and scanner-based 3D modeling technologies. *Sensors* **2023**, *23*, 596. [CrossRef]

applied sciences

MDPI

Review

Review of Monitoring and Control Systems Based on Internet of Things

Dawid Witczak † and Sabina Szymoniak *,†

Department of Computer Science, Częstochowa University of Technology, 42-200 Częstochowa, Poland; dawwit88@wp.pl
* Correspondence: sabina.szymoniak@icis.pcz.pl
† These authors contributed equally to this work.

Abstract: The Internet of Things is currently one of the fastest-growing branches of computer science. The development of 5G wireless networks and modern data transmission protocols offers excellent opportunities for rapid development in this field. The article presents an overview of monitoring and control systems based on the Internet of Things. The authors discuss various aspects of these systems, including their architecture, applications, and challenges. We focus on analyzing the latest achievements in this field, considering technological innovations and practical applications in various sectors. Also, we emphasize the importance of integrating data from multiple sources and developing data analysis algorithms to ensure the effectiveness and precision of IoT-based monitoring and control systems. The article provides a valuable overview of the current state of knowledge in this dynamic area, inspiring further research and technological development. It also includes case studies showing various IoT device applications and energy consumption management.

Keywords: Internet of Things; monitoring systems; control systems

1. Introduction

The Internet of Things (IoT) is a technological revolution and a change in how we perceive and communicate with the world around us. This is a dynamically developing area of IT, which significantly changes everyday life by integrating an increasing number of devices and systems with the global network. They range from simple home devices, such as thermometers or humidity sensors, to advanced monitoring and control systems in industry. The IoT permeates all spheres of life, providing new opportunities and challenges [1]. In recent years, there has been a clear trend of increasing numbers of home devices equipped with IoT functions. The concept of a smart home is becoming increasingly common, where all elements—from lighting and heating to kitchen appliances and security systems—are connected into one coherent network, enabling remote management and monitoring. However, this is only the tip of the iceberg as the potential of the IoT also goes deep into industry [2,3], transport [4], healthcare [5], agriculture, and many other economic sectors [6,7]. Figure 1 summarizes typical IoT solutions.

IoT technologies use various communication protocols, from popular wireless standards such as Wi-Fi [8], Bluetooth [9], or Zigbee [10,11] to wired protocols such as Modbus [12] or CAN [13]. This diversity allows for flexible adaptation to different requirements and environments while opening doors to new possibilities and applications. In addition to the wireless mentioned above and wired standards, IoT technologies also use several other communication protocols that expand the possibilities and scope of their applications. One such important protocol is GSM [14], which enables communication between IoT devices and mobile networks. Thanks to this, devices can be remotely monitored and controlled even in places without access to Wi-Fi or Bluetooth networks. With the development of mobile technologies, the 5G standard [15,16] is also becoming increasingly important. Moreover, 5G, the fifth generation of mobile technologies, offers extremely fast data transmission speeds and low latencies, which makes it an ideal solution for the IoT applications that require high bandwidth and immediate response. Thanks to 5G, new IoT applications, such as advanced real-time monitoring systems and autonomous vehicles, become possible. Another important protocol gaining popularity on the IoT is LoRa [17,18]. LoRa is a wireless communication protocol that enables data transmission over long distances while consuming minimal energy. Thanks to this, LoRa is used in cases where it is necessary to monitor and control devices in large areas, such as when fields and farms are monitored. Figure 2 summarizes the data transmission protocol used by the IoT. This summary covers the layers of the OSI model in which these protocols operate.

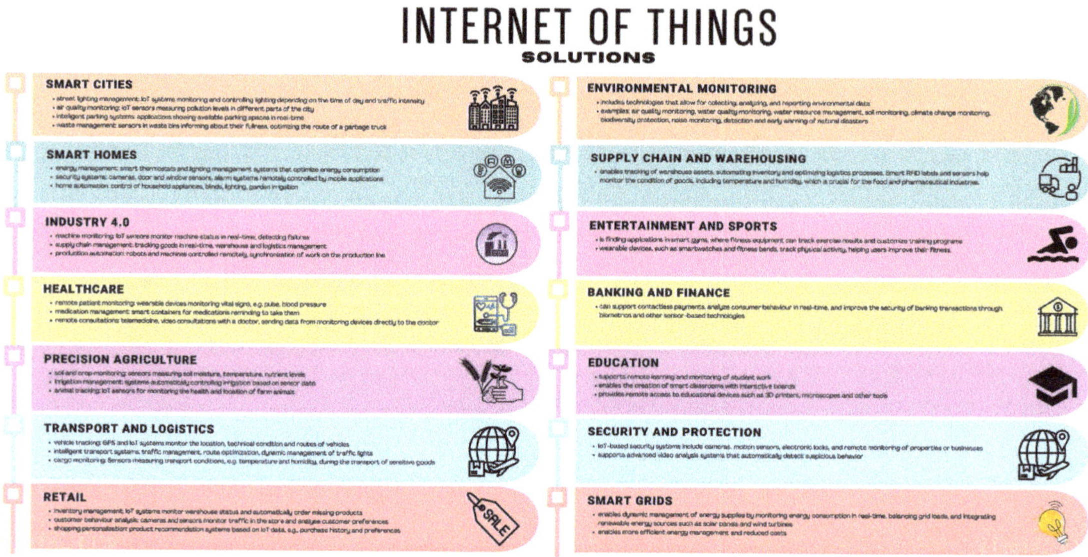

Figure 1. The IoT solutions.

However, with the IoT expansion, new challenges arise, especially in security [19]. Many manufacturers focus on bringing low-cost IoT solutions to market quickly, often at the expense of appropriate security standards. This results in serious vulnerabilities that can be exploited for unauthorized access and data leakage, compromising user privacy and security. Despite these threats, there is enormous potential in developing the IoT. In the era of the dynamic development of the concept of smart cities [20], smart energy [21], and smart agriculture [22], IoT systems are becoming a key tool that enables the optimization of resources, reducing costs, and improving the quality of life.

This article provides an in-depth review of the literature on IoT-based monitoring and control systems. Various solutions were compared to identify their advantages and disadvantages and indicate potential future development directions. The aim is to understand the current state of technology and determine a development path that will enable the maximum use of the IoT's potential for the benefit of society and the environment.

Figure 2. Data transmission protocol used by IoT.

1.1. Motivations and Contributions

Writing an article on IoT-based monitoring and management systems is an exciting challenge and a critical step in understanding and helping to shape the future of technology. The IoT is a dynamically developing field with enormous potential to transform various aspects of our lives, from smart homes and city management to advanced environmental monitoring systems. Through a detailed literature review, we can identify the current state of technology and better understand what solutions are most effective and what challenges we face. This will allow us, as a collective, to consciously shape the future of this technology to benefit society and the environment.

Analyzing the advantages and disadvantages of IoT-based monitoring and management systems is crucial to understanding which technologies are most effective in different contexts and what technical and organizational barriers must be overcome to realize their full potential. We can determine best practices by comparing solutions and indicating areas that require further research and development. Identifying future development directions will help optimize existing systems and identify innovation paths that can lead to more advanced, sustainable, and user-friendly solutions.

This paper focused on IoT-based monitoring and control systems for smart agriculture, predictive Maintenance Systems, healthcare, environmental protection, and smart cities. The article analyzes a variety of IoT-based monitoring and control systems applications, showing their significant impact on improving operational efficiency, thus reducing costs and increasing the quality of services. The purpose of writing this article is not only to document the current state of IoT technology but also to inspire further research and development of new technologies that will fully exploit the potential of the IoT. Indicating future development directions will allow us to concentrate research and investment efforts in the most promising areas, which, in the long run, will benefit not only the technology industry but, above all, the entire society and the natural environment. In this way, the article can become a valuable tool for scientists, engineers, and decision-makers who want to contribute to building a more sustainable and technologically advanced future.

1.2. Methodology

During our research, we collected articles using various search engines (mainly Google Scholar and DBLP). Moreover, we analyzed references from articles found and citations from these papers. Our goal was to compose the most complete and up-to-date review of the security of monitoring and control systems based on the IoT.

1.3. Organization

The rest of this paper is organized as follows. Section 2 presents the related works connected to this manuscript's theme. In Section 3, we provide an overview of the monitoring and control systems based on the IoT. In Section 4, we will summarize and conclude our analysis of the discussed systems. In the Section 5, we will present the conclusions of the entire article, findings from the research, and our plans for the future.

2. Related Works

The area of monitoring and control systems based on the IoT is the subject of intensive research, reflected in numerous scientific publications. The literature contains descriptions of various monitoring and control systems based on the IoT.

Shinde et al. in [23] review IoT-based environmental monitoring systems whose main goal is to provide environmental data from remote locations via the Internet. The presented system uses low-power wireless Internet-connected sensors that transmit their measurements to a central server, enabling remote visualization and data analysis from any Internet-connected device. The developed solution is a comprehensive system covering the physical level (sensors and communication protocol) and data management and storage at the cybernetic level, improving the integration and interoperability of systems and increasing supervision efficiency.

Chakraborty et al. in [24] systematically assesses the recent literature on smart homes and reviews research and development in this field. It presents a detailed picture of the development and features of today's smart home systems, offering deep insight into the latest hardware and trends. The article also discusses important services and their advantages, current and future research trends, and the difficulties and obstacles associated with their implementation.

Yassein et al. in [25] discuss using IoT technologies in various industries, particularly healthcare, where the IoT transforms traditional systems into intelligent healthcare systems. It presents an overview of IoT-based services, software and techniques developed in the health sector, highlighting the benefits of their implementation. The paper's findings are intended to serve as a source of information and reference for medical professionals, researchers, and those interested in smart healthcare.

Tokognon et al. in [26] discuss the importance of the IoT (as a key technology for monitoring systems, resulting from the rapid development of sensor technologies and the convergence of information technologies. It presents a framework for structural health monitoring (SHM) using IoT technologies, considering the technologies used in implementing SHM systems and data routing strategies in the IoT environment. The article also describes big data solutions necessary to manage large and complex data generated by sensors installed on structures.

Bagdadee et al. in [27] discuss the importance of energy management in the context of the growing energy demand for IoT applications and the promotion of green industry. They present a framework for connecting reservations and increasing energy efficiency in IoT-based smart industries, covering solutions for energy generation and low-power device management. The paper also examines case studies, including energy planning in smart factories and wireless energy transfer, while discussing unresolved issues related to IoT-based energy management systems.

Al-Turjman et al. in [28] discuss the growing demand for energy production due to the expansion of population and energy consumers in large cities, highlighting the importance of energy monitoring systems as an effective solution to optimize the growing energy demand and consumption. They review and classify existing energy monitoring approaches and enabling technologies, such as sensors and portable devices, highlighting practical aspects and performance issues. It analyzes key design factors, customization parameters, and real-world use cases while presenting observed patterns and statistics in the field.

Zulkifli et al. in [29] discuss the importance of monitoring water quality in the transition to smart agriculture and the automation of monitoring key components of everyday needs such as water. Reviews the literature on water quality monitoring models, highlighting the need for accurate and complete datasets and precise modeling using sensors to collect water properties during experiments. It analyzes 50 articles from 946 collected papers, focusing on issues of model accuracy, the development of data collection systems and the types of data used, and presents directions for future research in intelligent water quality monitoring.

Jan et al. in [30] discuss the growing problem of safe water shortages caused by population growth, pollution and climate change, highlighting the importance of monitoring water quality, especially in domestic use. Reviews the shortcomings of traditional laboratory water quality testing methods and the weaknesses of wireless sensor network (WSN)-based systems regarding energy management, data security, and communications coverage. The article presents an overview of current IoT-based water quality monitoring systems, focusing on monitoring parameters and smart sensors and design recommendations for more effective systems that can benefit from developments in IoT technologies to improve water quality in-home applications.

Prapti et al. in [31] discusses the emerging field of IoT-based aquaculture, which is part of the 4.0 agriculture era but is lagging in many countries. A review of research published between May and December 2020 examines 30 international scientific papers on water quality monitoring in fish ponds. The article classifies research into five categories—latest research (2011–2020), aquaculture environments, research approaches, the most frequently monitored water quality parameters, and the forms of solutions provided—pointing to the dominance of freshwater aquaculture and the importance of parameters such as temperature and dissolved oxygen and pH in IoT monitoring systems. It also highlights the need for long-term experimental research to identify challenges and propose appropriate solutions. It highlights the importance of real-time monitoring as the most commonly used solution.

Pal et al. in [32] discuss the growing production challenges in the automotive industry and the increase in energy consumption, which lead to increased costs and greenhouse gas emissions, emphasizing the importance of efficient energy use. It presents various methods and mechanisms of energy management in a smart grid using communication technologies and protocols. It proposes the integration of electric vehicles with a smart electrical grid to charge and discharge energy and exchange information effectively. The article also discusses integration strategies, implementation of multi-agent systems to monitor energy flow and maintain grid stability, optimal scheduling of electric vehicle charging, and comparison of standard communication protocols in various scenarios.

Vaidya et al. in [33] present an overview of models of intelligent transport systems (ITS) with advanced traveller information systems (ATIS) and advanced road traffic management systems (ATMS) for intelligent transport. Describes GIS and IoT technologies in ITS, using sensors and detection algorithms worldwide. The ATIS model provides travellers with regional travel information, enabling them to make informed decisions about the best transport mode, route, time and cost. At the same time, ATMS includes real-time data management, vehicle detection and tracking, communications, variable message systems, traffic forecasting and dynamic motion control. The article discusses hardware components such as CCTV cameras, inductive loops, magnetometric, infrared, acoustic, ultrasonic, radar and GPS sensors in ATIS and ATMS systems.

Pandey et al. in [34] discuss the role of technology in agriculture, paying attention to the growing demand for food and the difficulties associated with traditional agricultural methods, such as dependence on human labour, weather variability, and lack of knowledge and technology. It presents an overview of IoT-based solutions that can increase crop productivity, covering soil and plant health monitoring, smart irrigation, and real-time weather forecasting. The article presents the IoT architecture in the smart agriculture model and a schematic model of an automated agricultural system that integrates data from various subsystems using artificial intelligence (AI) algorithms, enabling notifications to be sent to farmers' phones and effective management of fertilizers, pesticides and water, which contributes to increased crops.

Kim et al. in [35] summarizes the application of IoT technology in agricultural automation, analyzing its implementation in various agricultural systems such as management, monitoring, control systems and unmanned machines. IoT-based communication technologies used in agriculture, such as Wi-Fi, LoRaWAN, mobile communication (2G, 3G, 4G), ZigBee and Bluetooth, were also discussed. The article points to the limitations and prospects for the development of the IoT in agriculture, emphasizing that the future development of communication technologies such as 5G will enable a broader and faster use of the IoT in various agricultural processes, which will contribute to the automation of agriculture, improving the quality and efficiency of crops and reducing the labour input.

Hirlekar et al. in [36] highlight the importance of infrastructure, especially bridges, which are key national resources and important for socio-economic development. Draws attention to the need for regular and effective auditing of bridges, which are particularly susceptible to damage and require frequent inspections, to avoid the risk of serious damage that could threaten life and property. The article discusses various techniques used in auditing the health of bridges.

Saini et al. in [37] article presents a systematic review of current knowledge about indoor air quality monitoring systems based on IoT technology. It focuses on design aspects such as types of sensors, microcontrollers, architecture, and connectivity, and it discusses problems related to the implementation of research published in 2015–2020. The review shows that 70% of studies focus on monitoring thermal comfort parameters, 65% on CO_2 levels, and 27.5% on PM levels, while 37.5% and 35% of systems are based on Arduino and Raspberry Pi controllers The article also indicates that only 22.5% of studies used calibration before system implementation, while 72.5% of systems claim energy efficiency.

Lavanya et al. in [38] discuss the problem of traffic jams, which are common in almost every urban area worldwide, and the importance of managing traffic using real-time information. It focuses on traffic control systems based on IoT technology, describing their hardware and software systems and analyzing their operation in an urban context. The study highlights both the advantages and disadvantages of IoT-based traffic control systems, emphasizing that while they have their benefits, they also have certain limitations that must be considered in their design and implementation.

Syed et al. in [39] provides a comprehensive overview of the application of IoT technologies in smart cities, which enable the integration of various devices and technologies, eliminating the need for human intervention. It describes the basic components of the landscape of IoT-based cities and the technologies enabling the operation of these systems, including architectures, network technologies and artificial intelligence algorithms used in smart city systems. The paper also reviews the most commonly used practices and applications in various smart city domains and discusses the challenges of implementing IoT systems in cities while offering countermeasures.

Shah et al. in [40] review existing IoT-based solutions in waste management systems in smart cities, highlighting their role in ensuring sustainable development. It analyzes 16 research articles from the last 5 years to present the state of knowledge about IoT solutions in monitoring waste levels, technologies used and possible solutions. The results indicate that while existing solutions are similar regarding their integration platforms with IoT technologies, they differ in the sensors and communication technologies used, with many previous studies using Arduino Uno. The article supports further research into developing new technologies and improving existing systems.

Laha et al. in [41] present an overview of the impact of IoT technologies on environmental monitoring, covering air quality, water pollution and waste management. Provides an analysis of the development of environmental monitoring systems that have evolved from basic remote monitoring systems to advanced environmental monitoring systems using IoT technology and advanced sensor modules. The study focuses on assessing numerous studies on monitoring air quality, water, waste and general environmental pollution and their impact on the environment, classifying studies by objectives, methods and results, and analyzing the use of sensor technologies, the IoT, and machine learning.

Arjun et al. in [42] present research on using IoT technologies to modernize street lighting systems to reduce energy waste and improve urban lighting management efficiency. Instead of traditional, manual systems that lead to significant energy waste, the article describes how the IoT can automate street lighting, which is crucial to solving the energy crisis. The work discusses various sensors and components used in intelligent lighting systems, which, although often simple, are effective in creating modern, intelligent lighting management systems. The compilation of these articles provides a comprehensive overview of the various applications of the IoT in monitoring and control, showing their importance in various areas of life and industry.

3. Monitoring and Control Systems Based on IoT

In today's dynamic technological environment, the IoT sets new standards for managing and controlling various systems. IoT-based monitoring and control systems are key in smart buildings, industry, and the health sector. This chapter looks at the latest trends and solutions in this field, considering the benefits and challenges of implementing these systems. It also examines the development prospects and what new technologies may shape the future of monitoring and control systems.

3.1. IoT-Based Predictive Maintenance Systems

Nangia et al. in [43] discusses a system for predicting damage in the manufacturing sector designed to minimize downtime and early detection of damage to production machines. This system integrates various IoT-based sensors and uses artificial intelligence to analyze and make decisions about potential failure points. The system consists of a network of sensors placed at strategic points that constantly monitor various operating parameters of machines on the production line, such as temperature, humidity, pressure, current, vibration, air quality, and gas. Additionally, specialized sensors, such as ultrasonic and photoionization, were used. These sensors are connected to a central management system that collects data from many sources and transmits it to the cloud for further processing and analysis. The data cloud uses advanced machine learning algorithms such as the PdM algorithm to identify patterns, forecast trends and generate reports for end users. The described IoT-based environmental monitoring system is an innovative solution that allows for effective monitoring and early detection of machine failures. Its versatile applications and advantages make it a valuable contribution to monitoring and predicting failures using modern technologies.

Elkateb et al. in [44] present an innovative system based on IoT technology, specifically designed for predictive maintenance of circular knitting machines. Machines of this type are crucial for the textile industry, and their unplanned downtimes can generate significant costs and disrupt the production process. The IoT-based system enables real-time monitoring of machines, identification of potential faults, and effective maintenance planning, contributing to increased operational efficiency and cost reduction associated with machine maintenance. The system consists of an advanced printed circuit board (PCB) with an ESP32 microcontroller and various sensors, including speed and machine stop detection. These sensors allow the system to monitor various machine stops such as lycra stop, gate stop, idle stop (caused by human interaction), feeder stop, needle stop, and completed roll. Data collected by the system are stored in a MongoDB database, enabling further analysis and utilization in predictive machine maintenance. The system has been deployed on two different PAILONG circular knitting machines operating at an ambient temperature of 26 degrees Celsius. By utilizing data collected from the sensors, the system provides comprehensive real-time monitoring of the machines, enabling quick detection of potential faults and efficient maintenance planning. The system's main advantage is its ability to provide real-time monitoring of machines and prompt response to any abnormalities in operation. By identifying the cause of machine stoppages, operators can take immediate corrective actions, minimizing downtime and preventing potential breakdowns.

Additionally, IoT technology allows for collecting and analysing large amounts of data, creating increasingly accurate predictive models that can anticipate future machine faults with greater precision. The described IoT system for the predictive maintenance of circular knitting machines represents a significant step forward in the textile industry's industrial maintenance field. Its implementation can significantly increase operational efficiency, reduce machine maintenance costs, and ensure smooth production processes by minimizing unplanned downtimes. It is an excellent example of leveraging modern technologies to improve performance and competitiveness in the industrial sector.

Mourtzis et al. in [45] noticed that the contemporary digitization of manufacturing processes and shifting market demand towards products and services with lower costs have led to the emergence of Product-Service Systems (PSS). The article emphasizes the importance of maintenance, repair, and training within PSS, combined with Augmented Reality (AR). Analyzing large datasets generated by sensors enables quick decision-making. In recent years, energy efficiency issues have become a production priority. Energy consumption significantly impacts costs and production quality. The "cold chain" encompasses equipment and processes that ensure proper conditions for perishable goods from production to consumption. Refrigeration and Cold Storage Systems (RCSS) play a crucial role in preserving the freshness of goods but consume over 50% of supermarket energy. Therefore, monitoring data is essential for optimizing RCSS operation and preventing breakdowns. Existing literature presents various approaches to detecting anomalies in cooling systems. Approaches based on energy analysis, machine learning methods, and fault diagnosis systems have been mentioned.

There are also tools for monitoring energy consumption and detecting refrigerant leaks. Scientific work has proposed monitoring and predictive maintenance systems that leverage IoT technologies and artificial intelligence. The proposed system architecture is based on sensor networks and cloud computing. Components include sensor nodes, a network application, and a user interface. Communication protocols such as HTTP, WebSocket, and TCP are utilized. Deployment involves integrating databases, servers, and software to ensure data flow between them. Sensor nodes have various sensors and communication modules such as Particle Device OS and XBee Wi-Fi. The user interface enables data visualization and the receiving of alerts about failures. The software is developed using

NodeJS, MongoDB, and WebSocket technologies. Implementation includes deploying a sensor network management system that handles communication between sensor nodes and the network application. A prototype device for data acquisition has been developed using microcontrollers and communication modules. This device integrates various sensors, enabling monitoring conditions in refrigeration chambers.

3.2. Monitoring and Control Systems for Smart Agriculture Based on IoT

The development of technology in recent decades has revolutionized many areas of life, including agriculture. Modern agriculture increasingly uses advanced technological solutions that enable production optimization, increased efficiency and cost reduction. One key element of this transformation is monitoring and control systems based on IoT technology. The IoT in agriculture, or precision agriculture, involves using various sensors, devices and analytical systems to collect and analyze data in real time. Introducing IoT systems to agriculture brings many benefits, from monitoring soil and weather conditions through irrigation management to remotely controlling agricultural machines. This makes it possible to increase yields and manage natural resources more sustainably, which is particularly important in the context of climate change and growing requirements for environmental protection.

Rajesh et al. in [46] discuss the transition from manual methods of parameter verification to automated systems using temperature and humidity sensors. They highlighted the development of algorithms programmed into microcontroller-based gateways for effective crop monitoring. Integrating photovoltaic panels for power and a cellular internet interface provides additional functionality to the system. Additionally, advances in wireless networks enable the creation of innovative farming solutions, including remotely controlled GPS-based robots for various tasks such as weeding, spraying, and measuring humidity.

The basic components of the intelligent monitoring system are an Arduino Uno microcontroller board, a GSM modem for communication, a soil moisture sensor, a humidity sensor, a PIR sensor, an LCD, a speaker and ThingSpeak for IoT analysis. These components work together to collect data from the field continuously, compare it to predefined thresholds, and initiate appropriate actions such as turning on fans to regulate temperature or sending alerts to the farmer via SMS or IoT platforms such as ThingSpeak. The system works by continuously collecting data from sensors in the field, including temperature, soil moisture and human presence. When values exceeding predefined thresholds are detected, appropriate actions are initiated, such as turning on fans to regulate the temperature or sending alerts to the farmer via SMS or IoT platforms such as ThingSpeak. The cyclical process ensures real-time monitoring and timely interventions, ultimately leading to the optimization of agricultural practices. A visual representation of the system's work process is presented in a flowchart, illustrating the sequential steps involved in data collection, analysis and action initiation.

Implementing smart agricultural monitoring systems is proving to be very beneficial for farmers. These systems enable them to receive relevant information and data in real time that can be used to make quick decisions. Farmers can receive alerts and monitor field conditions remotely using a GSM modem and Wi-Fi modules, enabling quick interventions and ensuring optimal crop health.

Suma et al. in [47] presents a comprehensive agricultural monitoring system based on IoT technology that uses various sensors such as temperature, humidity, soil moisture and PIR sensors. The data collected by these sensors is transmitted to the microcontroller via the RS232 interface. The control section compares the collected data to the threshold values. If the data exceed the threshold, an audible alarm sounds, and the LED flashes. An alarm is sent as a message to the farmer, after which the power automatically turns off. In manual mode, the user can turn the microcontroller on and off using a button in the Android mobile application, which is carried out using the GSM module. In automatic mode, the microcontroller is turned on and off automatically if the value exceeds the threshold point, and the user automatically receives an alert via SMS. Apart from this, parameters such as temperature, humidity, soil moisture, and PIR sensors show the threshold value. The water level sensor indicates the water level in the tank or water source. The system uses a PIC16F877A microcontroller, a GSM module and various sensors such as a soil moisture sensor, an LM35 temperature sensor and a PIR sensor. The RS232 interface enables communication with a GSM modem to send and receive SMS and telephone calls. The soil moisture sensor uses both analog and digital output, and the LM35 temperature sensor offers a linear output with a range of −55 to +150 degrees Celsius. The PIR sensor detects the movement of people, animals or other objects using infrared radiation. Proteus 8 software was used to simulate the electronic system. The conclusions from the experiment show that the system is a complete solution to field operations and irrigation problems, which can help to improve crop yields and overall agricultural production. In the future, the system can be developed for larger land areas and integrated with soil quality control and plant growth in each soil.

In [48], Mini et al. present a comprehensive IoT system to support agriculture by monitoring environmental conditions and remotely controlling robotic vehicles. The proposed system uses two microcomputers, Arduino Nano and ESP32, which cooperate to collect sensor data and manage vehicle traffic. The Arduino Nano acts as the control unit, managing the vehicle's movement, while the ESP32 acts as the sensor unit, collecting data on temperature, humidity, and soil moisture. These data are then transmitted to the ThingSpeak IoT platform using the built-in ESP32 Wi-Fi module, allowing it to be stored and analyzed in real time. The system also includes DC motors and a motor controller, DHT11 and soil moisture sensors, lithium-ion batteries, a Buck converter that stabilizes the voltage, an HC05 Bluetooth module enabling communication with a mobile application, a buzzer signaling low soil moisture levels, and an OLED display presenting environmental data. Programming is performed using the Arduino IDE, which allows us to write, test and debug code easily. The system collects data via ESP32 and sends it to the cloud, while Arduino Nano controls the vehicle's movement based on commands from the mobile application. When the soil moisture level drops below the threshold, a buzzer signals watering needs. The mobile application allows us to monitor data and remotely control the vehicle in real time. The collected data are analyzed on the ThingSpeak IoT platform, which allows farmers to manage resources effectively. The proposed system offers innovative solutions for agriculture, especially in rural India, where access to advanced technologies is limited, yields are increasing, resource wastage is reduced, and environmental sustainability is improved.

In recent years, the energy sector has been undergoing a significant transformation, driven mainly by the development of modern information and communication technologies. One key element of this evolution is intelligent energy grids, which integrate advanced monitoring and control systems that enable more efficient energy production, distribution and consumption management. The IoT plays a central role in these systems, which allows data to be collected, transmitted, and analyzed in real time from various points of the energy network. Smart energy grids equipped with IoT solutions offer numerous benefits, including improving the reliability of energy supply, optimizing energy consumption and increasing operational efficiency. Thanks to sensors, smart meters and advanced analytical algorithms, it is possible to quickly detect and respond to failures, predict energy consumption patterns, and integrate renewable energy sources more sustainably and efficiently.

Bagdadee et al. in [49] noticed that in the face of complex challenges related to the effective management of electricity, there is a need to develop effective strategies to optimize the location and performance of energy-generating units in distributed systems. This paper presents a multi-objective analysis approach, focusing on power quality and voltage stability issues, to determine the optimal parameters for the location and operation of distributed units. This approach's basis is power quality and voltage stability indicators, effectively combining the effects of increasing real and apparent reactive power. The systematic characterization of these indicators allows for constructing objective functions that consider both power quality and voltage stability issues. The leading equipment used in the proposed system are Arduino-based systems, remote sensors, ultrasonic sensors, and GSM modules. This system allows us to measure power and send the collected data to local offices. Arduino chips form the system's core, providing an interface for receiving and processing sensor data and communicating with the central office via GSM modules.

When analyzing power quality, DMR (DMR meters) meters measure parameters such as power consumption, cable defects, and voltage anomalies, providing a detailed analysis of power quality in a low-voltage system. GSM modules transmit data from DMR meters to the control panel, ensuring a quick response to possible power quality problems. To effectively control power flow and maintain voltage stability, the proposed system uses dynamic power control techniques to ensure smooth operation of the network under various load conditions.

Additionally, this system can monitor and respond to changes in the network in real time, allowing for quick identification and resolution of potential power quality problems. The simulation analysis's conclusions confirm the proposed system's effectiveness in managing electricity in smart energy grids. Thanks to advanced IoT technologies and multi-objective analysis, this system enables optimal location and efficiency of energy-generating units in distributed systems. This translates into increased reliability and efficiency of the entire energy system.

Sulthana et al. in [50] present the design and implementation of an intelligent energy consumption monitoring system that enables automatic reading of the electricity meter and management of electrical devices at home using a dedicated mobile application. The system is based on several key components such as Arduino, a Wi-Fi module, an energy meter, a relay and a transformer. The energy meter used in the system is a clamp-on meter that measures the current voltage, current and power in units of kWh. The Arduino microcontroller reads these parameters and transmits them to the cloud, which allows the user to access current data via the mobile application. Data communication takes place via the Wi-Fi module, which is configured with Arduino. This module allows us to transfer data from the energy meter to the cloud and control electrical devices in our home using a mobile application. The relay controls a home circuit using Arduino, allowing us to turn the circuit on and off using a dedicated mobile app. The transformer converts the mains voltage into a low voltage suitable for the Arduino microcontroller. The system uses the IoT, enabling communication between network devices and remote controls. Expected system results include the real-time monitoring of energy consumption and automatic notification to the user when energy consumption reaches a certain level. The system also allows us to remotely manage electrical devices at home via a dedicated mobile application. The conclusions suggest that an intelligent energy monitoring system provides user convenience by remotely monitoring and managing home energy consumption while reducing the need to manually read energy meters, leading to time and labour savings.

In [51], the authors discuss advanced strategies for monitoring and managing electricity consumption, introducing modern approaches based on IoT technology within intelligent energy grids. Traditional energy transmission systems relied on one-way communication, which hindered the user's ability to generate energy. The solution to these challenges is microgrids and intelligent energy grids that use the latest technologies, such as smart energy meters and the IoT, to enable more efficient, flexible and transparent monitoring and control of energy transactions. Intelligent grids include hybrid power generation, integrating renewable sources such as solar, wind and fuel cells, and using advanced algorithms such as Perturb and Observe for maximum power point tracking (MPPT). The article details the architecture of a power monitoring and control system for solar power generation and how various components, such as Arduino and Raspberry Pi microcontrollers, communicate. Experiments conducted as part of the research confirm the effectiveness of the proposed solutions in monitoring and controlling energy consumption in intelligent energy networks, which contributes to increasing energy efficiency and sustainability.

3.3. IoT-Based Monitoring and Control Systems for Healthcare

Health care is one of the most dynamically developing fields in which technology plays a crucial role in improving the quality of medical care. One of the most promising trends is the integration of IoT technologies into monitoring and control systems, which transforms how patients are diagnosed, treated, and monitored. The IoT in healthcare includes a wide range of devices and applications that enable the collection of medical data in real time, their analysis, and the transfer of information to healthcare systems, allowing for the more precise and effective management of patient's health. The use of the IoT in healthcare brings many benefits, such as remote monitoring of patients, which is especially important for people who are chronically ill, elderly, or living in remote locations. Smart devices such as wearable sensors, smart inhalers, and advanced monitoring systems in hospitals allow for continuous tracking of patients' vital signs, detection of early signs of health deterioration, and immediate medical intervention.

Vasalan et al. in [52] detail the design and implementation of an intelligent patient health tracking system that uses sensors to monitor key health parameters such as body temperature and heart rate and environmental conditions such as humidity and room temperature. These sensors are connected to an Arduino microcontroller that processes the data, displays it on an LCD screen, and transmits it to the cloud via Zigbee wireless technology.

Communication between the sensors and the central server takes place using the Zigbee protocol, which is ideal for applications in sensor networks due to its low energy consumption and the ability to create large mesh networks. Data are transmitted from the local server via WLAN to the medical central server, where it is analyzed and stored. If the patient's previous medical data are missing, the system creates a new identification and starts monitoring. Experimental results, including patient health simulations with various combinations of body temperature and heart rate, confirm that the system effectively diagnoses health conditions such as fever, hypothermia, or the need for immediate medical consultation. The conclusions indicate that the use of IoT technology significantly increases the availability of healthcare, reduces the costs of medical visits and hospitalizations, and enables quick and effective responses to changes in patient's health status, which may be particularly important in crises such as epidemics.

In [53], the authors focus on the role of the IoT in modernizing healthcare systems, emphasizing the importance of remote patient monitoring to improve the availability and quality of medical services. In India, where many people suffer daily from a lack of adequate and timely medical care, developing reliable patient monitoring systems that can be used in hospitals and everyday life becomes crucial. The system described in the article uses the Arduino microcontroller due to its simplicity, ecological characteristics, and low costs. Arduino is the heart of the system, integrating various sensors such as the LM35 temperature sensor, heart rate sensor, pulse oximeter, blood pressure sensor, and ECG sensor. These sensors measure parameters such as body temperature, heart rate, oxygen saturation, and blood pressure, transmitting these data to the microcontroller. Communication in the system occurs via an Ethernet module, which enables an interface with the Arduino microcontroller and connection to the network. This module, which has an IP and MAC address, stores programs and transmits data to the network, allowing authorized users to access information remotely. Data from sensors are sent to the cloud via a wireless network (WSN), which allows them to be accessed from anywhere in the world.

The article also discusses the software for processing data, including scripting languages such as PHP, JSON, and the MySQL database management system. Patient data are stored on a server and published to enable medical staff to monitor it remotely. The experiments confirmed the system's effectiveness in monitoring and diagnosing patients' health conditions. Research conclusions suggest that the IoT in healthcare systems can significantly improve the availability and quality of medical services, especially in rural and hard-to-reach regions. By monitoring patients remotely, doctors can keep up to date with the health of their patients, which can lead to faster responses to changes and better health care.

Bhardwaj et al. in [54] present a comprehensive health monitoring system designed to help diagnose and monitor patients with COVID-19. The system consists of various hardware components, including a microcontroller with a built-in ADC converter, a blood pressure sensor, a non-contact temperature sensor, and an oximeter. The sensors are connected to a Raspberry Pi microcontroller responsible for collecting and transmitting data to the cloud for storage and further analysis. This allows it to automate various systems and cooperate with sensors and external devices. Additionally, the system is scalable, which means it can monitor multiple patients simultaneously, a significant advantage in a medical setting. The system operation process can be divided into three main stages: data collection, data processing, and storage and display of patient parameters. In the first phase, data from the sensors are collected and transferred to the Raspberry Pi microcontroller, where they are processed. The processed data are recorded in the next stage using the I2C interface or other appropriate communication protocols. Finally, the data are stored in the cloud and displayed on a monitor, allowing doctors to quickly and easily monitor patients' condition. While testing the system on various patients, the effectiveness of monitoring health parameters such as heart rate, body temperature, blood pressure, and oxygen level was examined. Comparison test results with commercial sensors showed promising results, with minimal relative errors. The system was also tested for scalability, confirming its ability to monitor multiple patients simultaneously. The research conclusions indicate that the developed health monitoring system based on the IoT can effectively aid in diagnosing and monitoring patients with COVID-19.

3.4. Monitoring and Control Systems for Environmental Protection Based on IoT

In the face of increasing challenges related to climate change, environmental pollution, and the need for sustainable management of natural resources, technology plays an increasingly important role in protecting our planet. One of the most significant achievements in this field is using IoT technology in monitoring and control systems. The IoT enables the collection, analysis, and transmission of environmental data in real time, which allows for better understanding and management of processes occurring in ecosystems. Implementing IoT systems in environmental protection brings numerous benefits such as monitoring air and water quality, waste management, controlling greenhouse gas emissions, and protecting biodiversity. Thanks to a network of sensors, drones, satellites, and advanced analytical systems, it is possible to quickly detect threats such as leaks of hazardous substances, forest fires, or changes in wild animal habitats. This, in turn, allows us to take immediate preventive and protective actions, minimizing the negative impact on the environment.

In [55], the authors describe an advanced environmental monitoring system using mobile robots and IoT technology. Mobile robots have many applications, including monitoring and security, transportation of goods, domestic purposes, and many others. In the work, scientists present a network based on mobile robots designed for remote monitoring and ensuring security via the Internet using the Web IoT platform. Mobile robots remotely controlled via the Internet have been used in various fields such as the manufacturing industry, storage condition assessment, maintenance of nuclear power plants, space exploration, etc. The project used various sensors to monitor the environment, including gas, temperature, and humidity sensors. Data from these sensors are collected by Raspberry Pi and sent to the cloud, where it can be analyzed and used by users using various devices such as notebook computers or smartphones. The system uses Raspberry Pi to communicate with various sensors and control mobile robots. The robots are equipped with Arduino Mega microcontrollers, GPS, compasses, DC motors, and other components necessary for navigation and motion control. All collected data are sent to the IoT platform, which can be analyzed in real time and displayed to users in graphical form. The system has gas, temperature, and humidity sensors for accurate environmental monitoring. Data from these sensors are collected and sent to the cloud, which can be analyzed and displayed to users in a graphical form.

Additionally, the system allows us to control the movement of mobile robots using a mobile application, which allows users to interact with them in real time. The research conclusions indicate that the developed environmental monitoring system using mobile robots and IoT technology can be an effective tool for monitoring and ensuring safety in various fields, including agriculture, air quality monitoring, and weather forecasting. Additionally, this system is scalable and can be adapted to various conditions and user requirements.

Rani et al. in [56] describe an advanced weather monitoring system based on IoT technology, which enables easy access to real-time data on a large scale. This system uses various sensors to monitor many weather parameters such as temperature, humidity, wind speed, light intensity, UV radiation, carbon monoxide levels, soil moisture, rainwater, and precipitation. It includes, among others, DHT11 sensors for measuring temperature and humidity, an anemometer for measuring wind speed, LDR for measuring light intensity, GY8511 for measuring UV radiation, MQ7 for measuring carbon monoxide levels, a hygrometer for measuring soil moisture and rain sensors for detecting precipitation atmospheric. Many features and benefits characterize the system. Its compact design allows for easy rooftop installation and portability to remote locations. Low energy demand enables power supply from solar panels, which reduces costs and enables long-term monitoring in areas where access to power is limited. In addition, the costs of the sensors are lower than in the case of traditional weather monitoring systems, which makes the project more profitable.

Data from the sensors are sent to the website, where they are presented in graphic statistics, enabling access from anywhere in the world and their future use. With fewer moving parts, the system requires less maintenance, which reduces maintenance costs. Additionally, the mobile application sends notifications about sudden weather changes, acting as an effective warning system against unfavorable conditions. The system uses a Raspberry Pi API for more advanced weather forecasts, which analyzes sensor data and predicts accurate results. The system consists of an Arduino Uno microcontroller as the central data processing module, and the sensor data are processed and sent to the database on the website using Node MCU and Ubi dots.

The authors of [57] discuss the growing problem of air pollution, which increasingly affects society due to the rapid development of industrialization and the number of vehicles. Harmful substances in the air, such as terrestrial ozone, nitrogen dioxide, and sulfur dioxide, threaten nature and human health. Chemical pollutants, including suspended particles, carbon monoxide, nitrogen oxides, sulfur oxides, lead aerosols, and volatile organic compounds, contribute to increased disease rates. Advanced research in sensor networks and wireless communication technology has produced several applications of wireless sensor networks in environmental monitoring and pollution control. The paper discusses air pollution monitoring and quality control using sensor nodes in a wireless sensor network. This project aims to create a real-time air pollution monitoring system using IoT technology, enabling the recording of atmospheric pollutant concentrations and establishing action plans for detecting high pollution levels. The system also aims to monitor air quality levels in selected cities with heavy road traffic. Existing monitoring systems are expensive and often use a single sensor, making comprehensive monitoring of air pollutants impossible. In the proposed system, we use many sensors that can detect various types of gases and pollutants present in the air. Data from these sensors are transmitted to the Blynk 2.0 cloud via Wi-Fi connectivity, enabling real-time air quality monitoring via the Blynk smartphone app and the Blynk dashboard in graphs. This design has a low cost and compact size, which makes it portable and easy to maintain. It also has great development potential, enabling additional sensors and integration with smart city initiatives. The project used the ESP32 microcontroller (Node MCU), which reads data from all sensors and then transmits them to the Blynk 2.0 cloud via Wi-Fi. The system also uses the Blynk 2.0 cloud to present data in real time on a mobile application and a web panel.

This way, users can easily monitor air quality and receive notifications when pollutants are detected.

3.5. Monitoring and Control Systems for Smart Cities Based on IoT

With the dynamic development of urbanization and the growing urban population, cities worldwide face numerous challenges related to infrastructure, transport, resource management, and the quality of life of their inhabitants. Advanced technologies, including the IoT, are increasingly used to meet these challenges and make cities more effective, sustainable, and friendly to residents. Smart cities use the IoT to create integrated monitoring and control systems that enable the collection and analysis of data in real time, improving the management of urban infrastructure and services. IoT systems in smart cities are widely used, from road traffic monitoring and public transport management through intelligent street lighting to waste management and air quality monitoring. Thanks to sensors, communication networks, and advanced analytical algorithms, cities can respond more effectively to the needs of residents, optimize energy and resource consumption, and improve the safety and comfort of life.

Sudha et al. in [58] present an innovative approach to street lighting control and monitoring based on IoT technology, representing a breakthrough in urban lighting infrastructure, offering intelligent, more tailored solutions that consider the dynamic needs of modern cities. Using technologies such as NodeMCU microcontrollers, relay modules, light-dependent resistors (LDRs), and motion and environmental sensors, these systems enable dynamic lighting level adjustment depending on traffic, pedestrian activity, and light conditions.

Integrating remote monitoring and management enables city governments to proactively identify problems, optimize performance, and reduce operational costs. Through cause-and-effect analysis, complex control algorithms consider traffic, pedestrian activity, time of day, and weather conditions to optimize lighting levels. It is worth noting that the NodeMCU ESP8266 microcontrollers used constitute the central control units, enabling communication between relays, LDR, and LED sensors. LDRs, strategically placed in urban areas, collect data on light intensity, and relay modules control street lighting.

The system's operation scheme involves using LDR sensors to collect light-intensity data, which is then processed by the NodeMCU ESP8266 microcontroller. Based on these data, the system makes decisions regarding street lighting control, which allows for optimizing energy consumption and minimizing operating costs. The above-mentioned elements and data integration from many sensors and control algorithms constitute a comprehensive system that ensures effective, energy-saving, and intelligent street lighting, which positively affects residents' quality of life and the urban environment.

In [59], the authors present the importance of the problem of environmental pollution by waste and the need to monitor and manage it to protect the environment. Accumulating garbage around streets can be a breeding ground for rats and fleas that carry harmful diseases, leading to epidemics and deaths. Therefore, it is necessary to introduce a waste monitoring system to reduce pollution. The article discusses various IoT-based approaches to waste monitoring, such as intelligent garbage bins using infrared and load sensors, GSM-based alarm systems, and RFID and Zigbee-based systems. In addition, an analysis of municipal waste management in various regions of the world was presented, and the benefits of using intelligent waste monitoring solutions were discussed. As part of the experiments in the article, a waste monitoring system based on the Thingspeak platform was proposed, using ultrasonic sensors and load sensors that collect data on the level and weight of waste in the bin. These data are transmitted in real time to the Thingspeak platform, where it is updated and made publicly available, allowing users to monitor the status of their bin online. Experimental results show that the proposed system effectively monitors the level and weight of waste in the bin, which allows for effective waste collection and disposal management. Additionally, using the Twitter platform to share updates on the status of the bin helps to increase public awareness of waste management and environmental protection. The article's conclusions indicate that intelligent waste monitoring systems can improve city cleanliness, environmental hygiene, and intelligent waste management, which is an important step towards sustainable development and environmental protection.

Priya et al. in [60] noticed that the IoT plays a crucial role in intelligent parking systems. Sensors installed in parking lots collect data on the availability of parking spaces, which are then processed and analyzed to manage parking applications effectively. Traditional parking management systems often need help accurately detect available spaces, especially in large, free parking lots. To overcome them, the paper proposes using infrared sensors to precisely detect parking spaces, eliminating problems related to accuracy, lighting conditions, and weather.

The system architecture includes several phases, including the development of an Android application for parking reservations, identification of vacant spaces using infrared sensors, user authentication using RFID tags, classification of parking spaces based on vehicle size, and navigation to assigned spaces using GPS. In particular, the system is based on Arduino Uno microcontrollers, which are microcontrollers based on the ATmega328P system. They have 14 digital I/O pins, six analog pins, a USB interface, and many other features such as Arduino IDE software programs and interfaces with sensors, Wi-Fi, and RFID modules. Additionally, the system provides visualization tools for parking center owners to monitor reservation details, space availability, and billing information. Implementation details highlight using Arduino microcontrollers, RFID readers, and Wi-Fi modules to enable communication between sensors, mobile applications, and backend systems. The paper also includes experimental results that demonstrate the effectiveness of the proposed system in optimizing parking space utilization and improving user experience.

In summary, the IoT-based smart parking system presented in this paper offers a promising solution for efficient parking management in urban areas. Although the prototype focuses on single-story parking lots, the model can be scaled to multi-story parking facilities, thus contributing to the overall development of innovative city initiatives.

3.6. IoT-Based Monitoring and Control Systems for Transport and Logistics

In the era of globalization and dynamic technological development, the transport and logistics industry faces increasing challenges related to the efficiency, safety, and sustainable management of supply chains. Enterprises increasingly turn to advanced technologies, including the IoT, to meet these challenges. The IoT in transport and logistics enables the collection, analysis, and exchange of data in real time, which allows for more precise monitoring and control of logistics and transport processes. Implementing IoT systems in this industry brings numerous benefits such as route optimization, monitoring transport conditions, vehicle fleet management and real-time shipment tracking. Thanks to sensors, GPS devices, RFID technology and advanced analytical systems, enterprises can increase operational efficiency, reduce costs and improve service quality. In addition, the IoT helps increase transport safety by monitoring the technical condition of vehicles and road conditions.

Salih et al. in [61] proposed an intelligent public communication system based on advanced technology based on a mobile application and the ESP32 microcontroller with a Wi-Fi and GPS module. This microcontroller is installed in each bus, which allows for the real-time monitoring of the vehicle's location and speed. These data are then sent to a cloud server, which is analyzed and made available to users via a mobile application. Within this application, passengers can track the location of buses on Google Maps, find out the estimated arrival time, and calculate the distance to the nearest vehicle. The system operates continuously and automatically: the GPS module in each bus constantly communicates with satellites to obtain current geographical coordinates and speed. These data are then sent via Wi-Fi to the server, processed, and made available in real time to mobile application users. Thanks to this, passengers can quickly and easily obtain the necessary information about the location and arrival time of buses, which allows them to plan their trip better and minimize waiting time at the bus stop. It is worth noting that the proposed system is characterized by ease of use and low costs, making it an attractive solution for public transport users.

Additionally, tests on the streets of Mosul confirmed its effectiveness, which showed high accuracy in determining the location and arrival time of buses. The system will be further developed by adding additional functions to the mobile application, such as passenger counting using sensors and introducing an electronic ticketing system using RFID tags. Thanks to continuous development and improvement, the proposed system has the potential to become an indispensable tool for public transport users, providing them with a fast and comfortable journey.

The authors of [62] propose a bus tracking system using advanced technologies such as RFID, GPS, and GSM to increase the safety of students' travel between home and college. The problem of long waits at bus stops and the increasing number of crimes against students were mentioned, which makes parents concerned. Therefore, the authors proposed a system to monitor students' travel and notify parents about their safety. The system is based on RFID technology, which is used to identify students through unique RFID cards placed in their backpacks. When a student enters, leaves the bus, or exceeds the speed limit, the system automatically sends notifications to parents via SMS and mobile application.

Additionally, the GPS module tracks the bus's location in real time, and the GSM module is used to send notifications. The system consists of three central units: the bus unit, the parent unit, and the college unit. The bus unit has an RFID reader, a GPS module, a GSM module, and a PIC16F877A microcontroller. When a student enters or leaves the bus, the RFID reader records these events, and the GSM module sends notifications to parents. In addition, the system can also detect fires thanks to the use of a fire sensor. The parent unit consists of a mobile application that allows parents to track their students' travels and receive notifications about their safety. However, the college unit uses a web application where the administrator can manage the data related to buses, students, routes, etc. The authors emphasize that this system will increase student travel safety and facilitate the college's bus fleet management. Additionally, they plan to develop the system further by adding parking management and bus communication functions.

4. Discussion

Each of these sectors places different requirements on IoT systems, which leads to the creation of various technological solutions. In agriculture, IoT systems monitor soil and weather conditions and manage irrigation. In health care, the IoT enables the remote monitoring of patients and the management of medical equipment. The IoT tracks shipments, optimizes routes, and manages vehicle fleets in transport and logistics. Smart cities use the IoT to manage urban infrastructure through street lighting, traffic management systems, and air quality monitoring. In environmental protection, the IoT helps monitor and manage natural resources and detect ecological threats. This chapter compares IoT-based monitoring and control systems and considers their specific applications, benefits, and challenges.

After the analysis of existing monitoring and control systems based on the IoT, a summary was made in the form of two tables: Table 1 lists the platforms used in the systems, and Table 2 lists the protocols used for data transmission. We distinguished seven different protocols. The authors of other solutions [43,45,48,50–58,60,61] only marked that they used wireless communication technology. Thus, Table 3 compares the presented system in the scope of chosen parameters.

Table 1. Platforms used in the systems.

Platforms	Systems	Website	Accessed
Arduino	[46,49–51,53,55,60]	www.arduino.cc	1 July 2024
ESP32	[44,48,57,61]	www.espressif.com	2 July 2024
ESP8266	[58]	www.espressif.com	2 July 2024
MCU MT3620	[63]	www.mediatek.com/products/iot-genio/mt3620	5 July 2024
PIC16F877A	[47,62]	www.microchip.com	4 July 2024
Raspberry Pi	[51,54–56]	www.raspberrypi.com	6 July 2024

Table 2. Protocols used for data transmission.

Protocol	Systems
Bluetooth	[43,48]
MQTT	[44]
HTTP	[45]
GSM	[46,47,49,59,62]
Zigbee	[52,60]
Ethernet	[53]
RFID	[59–62]

Table 3. Comparison of presented systems.

Paper	Used Real Prototype	Used Real Data	Practical Using	Data Management	Used AI	Discussed Security	Discussed Architecture	Used LPWAN	Discussed Energy Efficiency
[43]	−	+	+	+	+	−	+	−	−
[44]	+	+	+	+	+	−	+	−	−
[45]	+	+	+	+	−	−	+	−	−
[46]	+	+	+	+	−	−	+	−	−
[47]	+	+	+	+	−	−	+	−	−
[48]	+	+	+	+	−	−	+	−	−
[49]	+	+	+	−	−	−	+	−	−
[50]	+	+	+	−	−	−	+	−	−
[51]	+	+	+	+	−	−	+	−	−
[52]	+	+	+	+	−	−	+	−	−
[53]	+	+	+	+	−	−	+	−	−
[54]	+	+	+	+	+	−	+	−	−
[55]	+	+	+	+	−	−	+	−	−
[56]	+	+	+	+	+	−	+	−	−
[57]	+	+	+	−	−	−	+	−	−
[58]	+	+	+	+	−	−	+	−	−
[59]	+	+	+	+	−	−	+	−	−
[60]	+	+	+	+	+	−	+	−	−
[63]	+	+	+	+	−	−	+	−	−
[61]	+	+	+	+	−	−	+	−	−
[62]	+	+	+	+	−	−	+	−	−

One can see a wealth of choices when considering the microcontrollers used in the examined examples of IoT-based monitoring and control systems. Among them, the three most popular options are Arduino in various variants, ESP32, and Raspberry Pi. Each solution has unique features and capabilities that allow it to adapt to various design needs. Known for its reliability and versatility, Arduino [64] offers a wide range of boards and modules that enable rapid prototyping [65] and easy scaling of projects [66]. ESP32 [67], in turn, is distinguished by advanced communication functions [68], which makes it an excellent choice for projects requiring connection to Wi-Fi and Bluetooth networks [69]. However, Raspberry Pi [70], thanks to its computing power and expansion possibilities [71], is an ideal candidate for more advanced applications where support for the operating system and applications [72] of greater complexity is needed. Thanks to the diversity of these platforms, designers and developers have a wide range of tools to implement their ideas related to the IoT.

When analyzing the protocols or solutions used for data transmission in IoT systems, it is worth noting that one of the most frequently used is undoubtedly Wi-Fi [73] due to its universality, ease of implementation, and high data throughput. Wi-Fi enables fast and stable wireless connections [74], which makes it an ideal choice for projects that require real-time data transmission, such as environmental monitoring or controlling devices from anywhere via the Internet. Apart from Wi-Fi, another frequently used protocol is GSM, which allows communication via a cellular network. This is especially useful in cases where there is no access to a Wi-Fi network or when you need to monitor devices in areas outside the range of your wireless network. Additionally, GSM [75] is used in security systems, vehicle monitoring, and industrial automation, where reliability and wide range [76] are crucial. Both protocols are popular not only because of their technical capabilities but also because of the support from microcontroller manufacturers. There is extensive documentation and a wide selection of modules supporting both Wi-Fi and GSM standards, which significantly facilitates the integration of these solutions into IoT projects. Thanks to this, engineers and creators can quickly and effectively implement communication functions in their projects without spending too much time developing communication solutions.

Low Power Wide Area Network (LPWAN) technology is key in ensuring effective and reliable communication between devices distributed over large areas on the IoT era. LPWAN is a group of network technologies designed for long-distance communication with low power consumption, making it an ideal solution for many IoT applications, including monitoring systems.

The analyzed monitoring and control systems based on IoT technology did not use the LoRa communication protocol. LoRa offers vast opportunities for development and research, thanks to its unique properties that enable devices to communicate in places without GSM network coverage. This is particularly important in IoT applications operating in hard-to-reach areas, such as rural areas, forests, or mountains, where traditional communication methods may fail. Implementing the LoRa protocol brings numerous benefits, including long-distance data transmission with low energy consumption, which is crucial for battery-powered devices. This allows for long-term operation of sensors and other IoT devices without frequently replacing or charging batteries, which is extremely important for keeping operating costs low. One of the main challenges related to implementing LoRa is the need to install gateways that will collect data from end devices and send them to a central server. These gateways act as communication intermediaries, enabling data transfer from distributed sensors to the cloud or local management system. Although installing such gateways may involve some costs and require appropriate infrastructure, it is an investment that can pay off thanks to the opportunities offered by independence from commercial telecommunications networks.

Moreover, LoRa is characterized by a high level of security thanks to advanced data encryption mechanisms, which is crucial in protecting information sent via IoT networks. Introducing this protocol can increase the security and reliability of monitoring and control systems, opening new perspectives for their development and implementation in various sectors such as agriculture, industry, or urban infrastructure management. To sum up, although the LoRa protocol was not used in the analyzed IoT systems, its implementation can significantly increase the functionality and range of these systems. It is, therefore, worth considering for future projects, especially where traditional communication methods fail.

Another LPWAN solution is Sigfox. It is a technology designed to transmit small amounts of data over long distances with minimal energy consumption. It operates in unlicensed frequency bands and uses Ultra Narrow Band modulation, which allows for long ranges and resistance to interference. The advantages of this solution include the operating time of devices that can operate on one battery for many years, even up to 10 years. They have a transmission range of up to 50 km in rural areas and 3–10 km in cities, and the devices used for transmission are not too expensive. The disadvantages, however, are low bandwidth of up to 12 bytes per message and transmission mainly in one direction (from the device to the cloud).

Yet another LPWAN solution is NB-IoT. Narrowband IoT technology was developed within 3GPP standards and operates in licensed frequency bands. It uses narrowband radio channels (200 kHz), which allows for high spectral efficiency and high signal penetration inside buildings. The advantages of this solution include long-range and deep penetration through building walls, the ability to support many devices in a small area, and two-way transmission. The disadvantages of this technology are the need to have a license to use the frequency and slightly higher energy consumption than in the case of LoRa or Sigfox.

LPWAN is the foundation of modern IoT monitoring systems. It offers reliable, long-distance communication with low power consumption, making it ideal for various monitoring applications. Thanks to its unique properties, LPWAN will play a key role in further developing the IoT and creating more intelligent, effective, and sustainable monitoring systems.

Also, based on our findings and thoughts, we identified seven fields of challenges and potential solutions in IoT-based monitoring and control systems. We summarized them in Table 4.

We also identified possible future research directions in IoT-based monitoring and control systems that can help further develop this technology. Future research should focus on creating and developing new system architectures, including hybrid solutions. Developing more flexible and modular architectures will enable easier scaling and integration of new technologies. Such architectures will allow for the dynamic adaptation of IoT systems to changing conditions and requirements. In turn, introducing hybrid architectures that combine the advantages of cloud computing, edge computing, and fog computing can increase the efficiency and flexibility of IoT systems.

The second research direction may concern autonomous IoT systems that can independently monitor, diagnose, and repair their components without human intervention. Such systems can optimize their operations with artificial intelligence and machine learning algorithms. Issues related to autonomous energy and resource management will also be exciting areas for research, as they will allow for the optimization of devices in real time and their adaptation to changing environmental conditions and application requirements.

Another direction of research in the case of monitoring and control systems concerns the use of artificial intelligence and machine learning methods. Here, research can focus on advanced analysis of data generated by IoT devices or making autonomous decisions based on real-time data analysis. Additionally, the methods mentioned above can be used to detect and counteract cyber threats in IoT systems (network monitoring, identifying anomalies, and automatically responding to threats). In addition, essential areas of research that combine the IoT and artificial intelligence are smart cities and smart agriculture. Within smart cities, IoT systems are integrated with urban infrastructure, managing traffic, energy consumption, waste management, and other resources in an automated and optimized way. Developing methods designed for this field will undoubtedly contribute to its evolution in various aspects of urban life. A similar situation occurs in the case of agriculture. These monitoring systems dedicated to agriculture (monitoring soil condition, irrigation, plant growth, or animal health) can lead to more precise and efficient agricultural production methods.

In the context of the IoT-based monitoring and control systems discussed, it is also necessary to mention the security aspects of these environments related to data, users, or the entire network to which devices are connected. As mentioned, the IoT allows for remote monitoring and control of devices over the network, which brings benefits, threats, and challenges related to security.

Many IoT devices are designed with minimal consideration for security. As a result, IoT devices are often the target of Distributed Denial of Service (DDoS) attacks, where hackers take control of many devices and use them to overload the network infrastructure, leading to disruptions in monitoring and control systems. The lack of appropriate authorization and authentication mechanisms in IoT systems can lead to unauthorized access to data or devices. Default access passwords are often used in IoT environments for a long time. In addition, many IoT devices are placed in easily accessible places, which increases the risk of physical manipulation such as disconnecting, modifying, or damaging devices. The need for more standardization and compatibility between different manufacturers can lead to security gaps. This can result in improper encryption of IoT device communications, allowing attackers to intercept sensitive personal, health, and industrial data.

Therefore, each IoT environment should be analyzed in terms of security. The first step is identifying potential threats and estimating the risk of various attack scenarios. Risk analysis helps to understand which system elements are most vulnerable and require additional protection. All data transferred between IoT devices and central systems should be properly encrypted. The SSL/TLS protocol, a widely trusted method, is commonly used to secure data transmission. Additionally, many IoT environments use special security protocols that ensure the security of authentication or the session key agreement process [77,78].

Table 4. Challenges and potential solutions in IoT-based monitoring and control systems.

Challenges	Potential Solutions
Security and privacy	
vulnerability to cyberattacks (malware, Distributed Denial of Service attacks), data interception; limited computing resources make it challenging to implement advanced security mechanisms	development of lightweight encryption protocols that minimize the consumption of computing power and energy; application of blockchain to secure transactions and manage the identity of IoT devices, blockchain offers security against manipulation and unauthorized access; introduction of biometric authentication increases user security
Scalability	
support for dynamic device growth; diversity of generated data; network performance issues in large-scale IoT deployments	moving data processing closer to the source of their generation (edge computing) or local intermediate servers (fog computing) can relieve the central servers and network and increase the scalability of IoT systems; implementing hierarchical architectures, where data are processed at different levels, developing dynamic bandwidth management algorithms that can adjust the network bandwidth to current needs
Interoperability	
use of different communication standards and protocols, which makes their integration in one network difficult; the lack of universal standards can lead to compatibility problems and make it difficult to scale IoT systems	supporting and developing open standards and protocols; creating integrated platforms for managing IoT devices that can support different protocols and standards, enabling easy integration and control
Energy management	
many IoT devices operate on batteries and must be able to function for a long time without replacing them; extending the battery life and reducing the energy consumption of devices are key challenges	development of protocols that minimize energy consumption by shortening transmission time and reducing the number of transmissions; implementation of technologies that convert energy from the environment into electrical energy that powers IoT devices, extending their lifetime without the need to replace batteries; development of energy management algorithms that can dynamically adjust the energy consumption of IoT devices depending on their current needs and battery level
Precise and reliable operation	
IoT systems need to be precise and reliable, especially in critical applications such as healthcare and industry	development of algorithms that can detect and automatically correct errors in real time, increasing the reliability of IoT systems in critical applications; implementation of redundant components and communication paths that can take over the functions of failed elements, ensuring system continuity; application of artificial intelligence and machine learning methods to analyze IoT data, predict failures, optimize device performance, and improve system accuracy and reliability
Throughput and latency in networks	
IoT devices generate huge amounts of data that must be transmitted over the network; low bandwidth or high latency can affect the performance and reliability of systems	5G technology can significantly increase the throughput and reduce latency in IoT networks; the development of advanced compression algorithms that reduce the size of transmitted data without losing its quality allows for more efficient use of the available bandwidth; the implementation of Quality of Service mechanisms that prioritize network traffic according to its importance can ensure the reliability and smooth operation of key IoT applications
Economics and sustainability	
the costs of implementing and maintaining IoT systems, especially at scale, can be high	developing subscription-based business models that allow for the gradual deployment of IoT systems without large upfront investments can make the IoT more accessible; promoting sustainable design of IoT devices that consider ease of recycling and minimize environmental impact can help address waste technology issues; supporting local manufacturing and support for IoT devices can reduce logistics costs and carbon footprints while increasing system availability and reliability

Behavior monitoring and analysis mechanisms should be implemented on the entire administrative side of the environment. Regular monitoring of network traffic and analysis of anomalies can help detect suspicious activities that may indicate attempted attacks. Additionally, separating the IoT network from other networks, such as an office network, can limit the potential scope of an attack. Network segmentation reduces the risk that attackers who have taken control of one device can take control of the entire network. Data collected by IoT devices should be stored securely, with appropriate encryption mechanisms and access policies. It is also worth considering anonymizing data to reduce its value during unauthorized interception.

IoT systems are becoming increasingly complex, and security threats evolve as they develop. This requires continuously adapting security strategies and implementing modern technologies, such as artificial intelligence and machine learning, which can automatically identify and respond to threats in real time.

The urgency of establishing global security standards for IoT devices cannot be overstated. These standards are crucial to ensuring IoT devices' safe and reliable operation, particularly in critical applications such as medicine, transportation, or industrial infrastructure.

Based on other reviews related to the use of the IoT in various areas of life and science and our findings, we can formulate the following remarks and observations:

- IoT-based monitoring and control systems have a positive impact on human life or the environment;
- Advancements in IoT and AI techniques improve the smart agriculture industry through disease identification, smart farm monitoring, and efficient data analysis;
- Combining IoT and AI technologies can enhance crop productivity, reduce costs, and reduce the ecological footprint of conventional farming (also based on [79–82]);
- IoT solutions may reduce hospitalization and overall healthcare spending by reducing readmissions (also based on [83–85]);
- Solutions and technologies used depend on the environment or industry sector in which they operate; we will use different sensors, actuators, or platforms in mining and different ones in agriculture or health care (also based on [44,86–93]);
- Incorporating specially designed IoT devices into smart city infrastructures can be challenging due to city dynamics (also based on [86,94–96]).

Moreover, we noticed that in almost all cited solutions and reviews, the authors highlighted challenges for IoT-based solutions, including technology complexity, privacy and security issues, underdeveloped infrastructure, and some limitations in technology adoption due to underdeveloped policies and mechanisms. So, security, privacy, trust, interoperability, data storage, and ownership and control are very desirable fields of development in IoT-based solutions. Other fields of development are connected with the following:

- Integration with AI methods that can improve convenience, time savings, and better quality of life;
- Wearable technologies that can bring many promising benefits and can significantly impact various aspects of our lives (health monitoring, supporting physical activity, assisting people with disabilities, etc.);
- Solutions to address environmental issues that will improve living in smart cities;
- Data management and edge, fog, and cloud computing platforms to manage data effectively and use it in practice.

As mentioned, the platforms and technologies used depend on the environment or industry sector in which they operate. The most typical platforms mentioned were Phytoprove, Telemetry2u, Sensoterra, Cropx, ONFARM, and Semios. Thus, the most used communication protocols were LoRaWAN, 6LowPAN, LTE, 4G, and ZigBee.

5. Conclusions

IoT technology is revolutionizing how we manage data and processes in various sectors of the economy. The article analyzes a variety of IoT-based monitoring and control systems applications, showing their significant impact on improving operational efficiency, reducing costs, and increasing the quality of services. In agriculture, the IoT allows for precise monitoring of soil and weather conditions, leading to irrigation optimization and increased yields. In healthcare, remote patient monitoring and medical equipment management enable more personalized and effective healthcare. In transport and logistics, the IoT improves shipment tracking, route optimization, and fleet management, which translates into better organization of supply chains. Smart cities use the IoT to manage urban infrastructure, improving residents' quality of life through intelligent traffic management systems, street lighting, and air quality monitoring. In environmental protection, the IoT helps monitor natural resources and detect ecological threats, supporting sustainable development activities. Despite numerous benefits, implementing IoT systems also poses challenges. Data security, system interoperability, and scalability are significant barriers that must be overcome to exploit the potential of the IoT fully.

This article highlighted that although IoT-based monitoring and control systems are widely used, there is still much room for further development and improvement. Further research and innovation in this area will be vital to achieving a more sustainable, efficient, and secure future. The IoT has the potential to become the foundation of intelligent ecosystems, which will support the development of various economic sectors and improve the quality of life around the world.

Despite significant progress, many of these challenges remain open research problems, which require further work on developing new technologies and methods. The proposals for potential solutions presented in the article, such as the use of artificial intelligence, edge computing, or advanced cryptographic techniques, indicate possible directions of development that can help overcome existing barriers.

Future research in the IoT area should focus on further developing autonomous systems, ensuring security in the face of new threats, and on ethical and social aspects related to the widespread implementation of these technologies. Another important direction will be harmonizing standards and regulations, enabling broader integration, and the effective use of the IoT globally.

In summary, the future of IoT technology looks promising. IoT systems have enormous potential to revolutionize various sectors of the economy and everyday life. So, it is necessary to further research and develop technological solutions that will meet today's challenges. However, further research, innovation, and collaboration at various levels are required to fully realize its potential and create intelligent ecosystems that support economic development and improve quality of life worldwide.

Author Contributions: Conceptualization, D.W. and S.S.; methodology, D.W. and S.S.; validation, D.W. and S.S.; investigation, D.W.; resources, D.W. and S.S.; data curation, D.W. and S.S.; writing—original draft preparation, D.W. and S.S.; writing—review and editing, D.W. and S.S.; supervision, S.S. All authors have read and agreed to the published version of the manuscript.

Funding: This research received no external funding.

Institutional Review Board Statement: Not applicable.

Informed Consent Statement: Not applicable.

Data Availability Statement: Not applicable.

Conflicts of Interest: The authors declare no conflicts of interest.

Abbreviations

The following abbreviations are used in this manuscript:

CAN	Controller Area Network
GPS	Global Positioning System
HTTP	Hypertext Transfer Protocol
IoT	Internet of Things
LCD	Liquid-Crystal Display
LoRa	Long Range
MPPT	Maximum Power Point Tracking
PCB	Process Control Block
PSS	Product-Service Systems
RCSS	Refrigeration and Cold Storage Systems
TCP	Transmission Control Protocol
WLAN	Wireless Local Area Network
WSN	Wireless Sensor Network

References

1. Borgia, E. The Internet of Things vision: Key features, applications and open issues. *Comput. Commun.* **2014**, *54*, 1–31. [CrossRef]
2. Aleksic, S. A survey on optical technologies for IoT, smart industry, and smart infrastructures. *J. Sens. Actuator Netw.* **2019**, *8*, 47. [CrossRef]
3. Hu, Y.; Jia, Q.; Yao, Y.; Lee, Y.; Lee, M.; Wang, C.; Zhou, X.; Xie, R.; Yu, F.R. Industrial Internet of Things Intelligence Empowering Smart Manufacturing: A Literature Review. *IEEE Internet Things J.* **2024**, *11*, 19143–19167. [CrossRef]
4. Agarwal, V.; Sharma, S. IoT based smart transport management system. In Proceedings of the International Conference on Advanced Informatics for Computing Research, Gurugram, India, 26–27 December 2020; Springer: Berlin/Heidelberg, Germany, 2020; pp. 207–216.
5. Azzawi, M.A.; Hassan, R.; Bakar, K.A.A. A review on Internet of Things (IoT) in healthcare. *Int. J. Appl. Eng. Res.* **2016**, *11*, 10216–10221.
6. Ioannides, M.G.; Stamelos, A.P.; Papazis, S.A.; Stamataki, E.E.; Stamatakis, M.E. Internet of Things-Based Control of Induction Machines: Specifics of Electric Drives and Wind Energy Conversion Systems. *Energies* **2024**, *17*, 645. [CrossRef]
7. Zeng, F.; Pang, C.; Tang, H. Sensors on Internet of Things Systems for the Sustainable Development of Smart Cities: A Systematic Literature Review. *Sensors* **2024**, *24*, 2074. [CrossRef]
8. Chen, W.; Jeong, S.; Jung, H. WiFi-Based home IoT communication system. *J. Inf. Commun. Converg. Eng.* **2020**, *18*, 8–15.
9. Kalanandhini, G.; Aravind, A.; Vijayalakshmi, G.; Gayathri, J.; Senthilkumar, K. Bluetooth technology on IoT using the architecture of Piconet and Scatternet. *AIP Conf. Proc.* **2022**, *2393*, 020121.
10. Zohourian, A.; Dadkhah, S.; Neto, E.C.P.; Mahdikhani, H.; Danso, P.K.; Molyneaux, H.; Ghorbani, A.A. IoT Zigbee device security: A comprehensive review. *Internet Things* **2023**, *22*, 100791. [CrossRef]
11. Tang, P.; Liang, Q.; Li, H.; Pang, Y. Application of Internet-of-Things Wireless Communication Technology in Agricultural Irrigation Management: A Review. *Sustainability* **2024**, *16*, 3575. [CrossRef]
12. Jaloudi, S. microIoTSCADA: A Tool to Monitor and Control Renewable Energy-Based Systems Using MODBUS. In Proceedings of the 2024 4th Interdisciplinary Conference on Electrics and Computer (INTCEC), Chicago, IL, USA, 11–13 June 2024; pp. 1–6.
13. Khan, M.H.; Javed, A.R.; Iqbal, Z.; Asim, M.; Awad, A.I. DivaCAN: Detecting in-vehicle intrusion attacks on a controller area network using ensemble learning. *Comput. Secur.* **2024**, *139*, 103712. [CrossRef]
14. Santhosh, C.; Kumer, S.A.; Krishna, J.G.; Vaishnavi, M.; Sairam, P.; Kasulu, P. IoT based smart energy meter using GSM. *Mater. Today Proc.* **2021**, *46*, 4122–4124. [CrossRef]
15. Khanh, Q.V.; Hoai, N.V.; Manh, L.D.; Le, A.N.; Jeon, G. Wireless communication technologies for IoT in 5G: Vision, applications, and challenges. *Wirel. Commun. Mob. Comput.* **2022**, *2022*, 3229294. [CrossRef]
16. Saroğlu, H.E.; Shayea, I.; Saoud, B.; Azmi, M.H.; El-Saleh, A.A.; Saad, S.A.; Alnakhli, M. Machine learning, IoT and 5G technologies for breast cancer studies: A review. *Alex. Eng. J.* **2024**, *89*, 210–223. [CrossRef]
17. Li, C.; Cao, Z. Lora networking techniques for large-scale and long-term iot: A down-to-top survey. *ACM Comput. Surv. (CSUR)* **2022**, *55*, 1–36. [CrossRef]
18. Shilpa, B.; Gupta, H.P.; Jha, R.K.; Hashmi, S.S. LoRa interference issues and solution approaches in dense IoT networks: A review. *Telecommun. Syst.* **2024**, *87*, 517–539. [CrossRef]
19. Ammar, M.; Russello, G.; Crispo, B. Internet of Things: A survey on the security of IoT frameworks. *J. Inf. Secur. Appl.* **2018**, *38*, 8–27. [CrossRef]
20. Harmon, R.R.; Castro-Leon, E.G.; Bhide, S. Smart cities and the Internet of Things. In Proceedings of the 2015 Portland International Conference on Management of Engineering and Technology (PICMET), Portland, OR, USA, 2–6 August 2015; pp. 485–494. [CrossRef]
21. Abir, S.M.A.A.; Anwar, A.; Choi, J.; Kayes, A.S.M. IoT-Enabled Smart Energy Grid: Applications and Challenges. *IEEE Access* **2021**, *9*, 50961–50981. [CrossRef]
22. Khan, N.; Ray, R.L.; Sargani, G.R.; Ihtisham, M.; Khayyam, M.; Ismail, S. Current Progress and Future Prospects of Agriculture Technology: Gateway to Sustainable Agriculture. *Sustainability* **2021**, *13*, 4883. [CrossRef]
23. Shinde, S.R.; Karode, A.; Suralkar, S. Review on-IoT based environment monitoring system. *Int. J. Electron. Commun. Eng. Technol.* **2017**, *8*, 103–108.
24. Chakraborty, A.; Islam, M.; Shahriyar, F.; Islam, S.; Zaman, H.U.; Hasan, M. Smart home system: A comprehensive review. *J. Electr. Comput. Eng.* **2023**, *2023*, 7616683. [CrossRef]
25. Yassein, M.B.; Hmeidi, I.; Al-Harbi, M.; Mrayan, L.; Mardini, W.; Khamayseh, Y. IoT-based healthcare systems: A survey. In Proceedings of the Second International Conference on Data Science, E-Learning and Information Systems, Dubai, United Arab Emirates, 2–5 December 2019; pp. 1–9.
26. Tokognon, C.A.; Gao, B.; Tian, G.Y.; Yan, Y. Structural health monitoring framework based on Internet of Things: A survey. *IEEE Internet Things J.* **2017**, *4*, 619–635. [CrossRef]
27. Bagdadee, A.H.; Zhang, L.; Saddam Hossain Remus, M. A brief review of the IoT-based energy management system in the smart industry. In *Artificial Intelligence and Evolutionary Computations in Engineering Systems*; Springer: Singapore, 2020; pp. 443–459.
28. Al-Turjman, F.; Altrjman, C.; Din, S.; Paul, A. Energy monitoring in IoT-based ad hoc networks: An overview. *Comput. Electr. Eng.* **2019**, *76*, 133–142. [CrossRef]

29. Zulkifli, C.Z.; Garfan, S.; Talal, M.; Alamoodi, A.H.; Alamleh, A.; Ahmaro, I.Y.Y.; Sulaiman, S.; Ibrahim, A.B.; Zaidan, B.B.; Ismail, A.R.; et al. IoT-Based Water Monitoring Systems: A Systematic Review. *Water* **2022**, *14*, 3621. [CrossRef]
30. Jan, F.; Min-Allah, N.; Düştegör, D. Iot based smart water quality monitoring: Recent techniques, trends and challenges for domestic applications. *Water* **2021**, *13*, 1729. [CrossRef]
31. Prapti, D.R.; Mohamed Shariff, A.R.; Che Man, H.; Ramli, N.M.; Perumal, T.; Shariff, M. Internet of Things (IoT)-based aquaculture: An overview of IoT application on water quality monitoring. *Rev. Aquac.* **2022**, *14*, 979–992. [CrossRef]
32. Pal, R.; Chavhan, S.; Gupta, D.; Khanna, A.; Padmanaban, S.; Khan, B.; Rodrigues, J.J. A comprehensive review on IoT-based infrastructure for smart grid applications. *IET Renew. Power Gener.* **2021**, *15*, 3761–3776. [CrossRef]
33. Vaidya, R.B.; Kulkarni, S.; Didore, V. Intelligent transportation system using IOT: A Review. *Int. J. Res. Trends Innov.* **2021**, *6*, 80–87.
34. Pandey, A.K.; Mukherjee, A. Review on advances in IoT-based technologies for smart agricultural system. *Internet Things Anal. Agric.* **2022**, *3*, 29–44.
35. Kim, W.S.; Lee, W.S.; Kim, Y.J. A review of the applications of the internet of things (IoT) for agricultural automation. *J. Biosyst. Eng.* **2020**, *45*, 385–400. [CrossRef]
36. Hirlekar, V.; Doshi, P.; Shetty, V.; Tungare, A. Survey on IoT-based bridge health monitoring systems. *Int. J. Res. Eng. Sci. Manag.* **2020**, *3*, 87–91.
37. Saini, J.; Dutta, M.; Marques, G. Indoor Air Quality Monitoring Systems Based on Internet of Things: A Systematic Review. *Int. J. Environ. Res. Public Health* **2020**, *17*, 4942. [CrossRef] [PubMed]
38. Lavanya, N.; Panchami, S. A review on Iot based traffic management system. *Int. J. Eng. Appl. Sci. Technol.* **2020**, *5*, 612–615.
39. Syed, A.S.; Sierra-Sosa, D.; Kumar, A.; Elmaghraby, A. IoT in smart cities: A survey of technologies, practices and challenges. *Smart Cities* **2021**, *4*, 429–475. [CrossRef]
40. Shah, A.; Fauzi, S.; Gining, R.; Razak, T.; Jamaluddin, M.; Maskat, R. A review of IoT-based smart waste level monitoring system for smart cities. *Indones. J. Electr. Eng. Comput. Sci.* **2021**, *21*, 450–456.
41. Laha, S.R.; Pattanayak, B.K.; Pattnaik, S. Advancement of Environmental Monitoring System Using IoT and Sensor: A Comprehensive Analysis. *AIMS Environ. Sci.* **2022**, *9*, 771–800. [CrossRef]
42. Arjun, P.; Stephenraj, S.; Kumar, N.N.; Kumar, K.N. A Study on IoT based smart street light systems. In Proceedings of the 2019 IEEE International Conference on System, Computation, Automation and Networking (ICSCAN), Pondicherry, India, 29–30 March 2019; pp. 1–7.
43. Nangia, S.; Makkar, S.; Hassan, R. IoT based predictive maintenance in manufacturing sector. In Proceedings of the International Conference on Innovative Computing & Communications (ICICC), Delhi, India, 21–23 February 2020.
44. Elkateb, S.; Métwalli, A.; Shendy, A.; Abu-Elanien, A.E. Machine learning and IoT—Based predictive maintenance approach for industrial applications. *Alex. Eng. J.* **2024**, *88*, 298–309. [CrossRef]
45. Mourtzis, D.; Angelopoulos, J.; Panopoulos, N. Design and development of an IoT enabled platform for remote monitoring and predictive maintenance of industrial equipment. *Procedia Manuf.* **2021**, *54*, 166–171. [CrossRef]
46. Rajesh, T.; Thrinayana, Y.; Srinivasulu, D. IoT based smart agriculture monitoring system. *Int. J. Innov. Technol. Explor. Eng.* **2020**, *9*, 325–328.
47. Suma, N.; Samson, S.R.; Saranya, S.; Shanmugapriya, G.; Subhashri, R. IOT based smart agriculture monitoring system. *Int. J. Recent Innov. Trends Comput. Commun.* **2017**, *5*, 177–181.
48. Mini, A.D.; Anuradha, M.A.S.; Asha, G.S.R.; Rekha, J.S.S.; Kamble, S.; Kulkarni, M. IoT based smart agriculture monitoring system. *Int. Res. J. Eng. Technol.* **2023**, *10*, 1442–1448.
49. Bagdadee, A.H.; Hoque, M.Z.; Zhang, L. IoT Based Wireless Sensor Network for Power Quality Control in Smart Grid. *Procedia Comput. Sci.* **2020**, *167*, 1148–1160. [CrossRef]
50. Sulthana, N.; Rashmi, N.; Prakyathi, N.; Bhavana, S.; Kumar, K.S. Smart Energy Meter and Monitoring System using IoT. *Int. J. Eng. Res. Technol.* **2020**, *8*, 50–53.
51. Babu, C.; Kumar, D.D.; Kumar, K.; Reddy, K.J.; Sudha, R. Power monitoring and control system for medium voltage smart grid using IoT. *IOP Conf. Ser. Mater. Sci. Eng.* **2020**, *906*, 012007. [CrossRef]
52. Valsalan, P.; Baomar, T.A.B.; Baabood, A.H.O. IoT based health monitoring system. *J. Crit. Rev.* **2020**, *7*, 739–743.
53. Dinesh, K.; Vijayalakshmi, K.; Nirosha, C.; Krishna, I.S.R. IoT based smart health care monitoring system. *Int. J. Inst. Ind. Res.* **2018**, *3*, 22–24.
54. Bhardwaj, V.; Joshi, R.; Gaur, A.M. IoT-based smart health monitoring system for COVID-19. *SN Comput. Sci.* **2022**, *3*, 137. [CrossRef]
55. Rani, G.J.; Rama, G.S.; Marrikukkala, R.K.; Srikanth, Y.; Reddy, C.V.K. An IOT Based Environmental Monitoring System. *IOP Conf. Ser. Mater. Sci. Eng.* **2020**, *981*, 032025. [CrossRef]
56. Sivakumar, B.; Nanjundaswamy, C. Weather monitoring and forecasting system using IoT. *Glob. J. Eng. Technol. Adv.* **2021**, *8*, 8–16. [CrossRef]
57. Naik, U.U.; Salgaokar, S.R.; Jambhale, S. IOT based air pollution monitoring system. *Int. J. Sci. Res. Eng. Trends* **2023**, *9*, 835–838.
58. Sudha Rani, G.; Naveen Kumar, G.; Anusha, I.; Venkata Jyothi, M.; Niteesh Kumar, P. IoT Based Street Light Controller and Monitoring system. *Int. J. Mod. Trends Sci. Technol.* **2024**, *10*, 274–281.

59. Bhuvaneswari, T.; Hossen, J.; Asyiqinbt, N.; Hamzah, A.; Velrajkumar, P.; Jack, O.H. Internet of things (IoT) based smart garbage monitoring system. *Indones. J. Electr. Eng. Comput. Sci.* **2020**, *20*, 736–743. [CrossRef]
60. Cynthia, J.; Priya, C.B.; Gopinath, P. IOT based smart parking management system. *Int. J. Recent Technol. Eng. (IJRTE)* **2018**, *7*, 374–379.
61. Salih, T.A.; Younis, N.K. Designing an intelligent real-time public trapnsortation monitoring system based on iot. *Open Access Libr. J.* **2021**, *8*, 1–14.
62. Dhanasekar, N.; Valavan, C.; Soundarya, S. IoT based intelligent bus monitoring system. *Int. J. Eng. Res. Technol. (IJERT)* **2019**, *7*, 1–4.
63. Sergi, I.; Montanaro, T.; Benvenuto, F.L.; Patrono, L. A smart and secure logistics system based on IoT and cloud technologies. *Sensors* **2021**, *21*, 2231. [CrossRef]
64. Schmidt, M. *Arduino: A Quick-Start Guide;* The Pragmatic Bookshelf: Dallas, TX, USA, 2015; pp. 1–324.
65. Monk, S.; McCabe, M. *Programming Arduino: Getting Started with Sketches;* McGraw-Hill Education: New York, NY, USA, 2016; Volume 176.
66. Monk, S. *Make: Action: Movement, Light, and Sound with Arduino and Raspberry Pi;* Maker Media, Inc.: Sebastopol, CA, USA, 2016.
67. Babiuch, M.; Foltýnek, P.; Smutný, P. Using the ESP32 microcontroller for data processing. In Proceedings of the 2019 20th International Carpathian Control Conference (ICCC), Turówka, Poland, 26–29 May 2019; pp. 1–6.
68. Kolban, N. *Kolban's Book on ESP32;* Leanpub: Texas City, TX, USA, 2017.
69. Oner, V.O. *Developing IoT Projects with ESP32: Automate Your Home or Business with Inexpensive Wi-Fi Devices;* Packt Publishing Ltd.: Birmingham, UK, 2021.
70. Upton, E.; Halfacree, G. *Raspberry Pi User Guide;* John Wiley & Sons: Hoboken, NJ, USA, 2016.
71. Roberts, K. *Raspberry PI IoT Projects: Prototyping Experiments;* Vermont Ace: New York, NY, USA, 2018.
72. Monk, S. *Raspberry Pi Cookbook;* O'Reilly Media, Inc.: Newton, MA, USA, 2022.
73. Ahammed, M.T.; Boppana, U.M.; Kondapalli, R.; Balaji, P.; Zardar, M.A. Survey on Wireless Fidelity (Wi-Fi) Based Indoor Location Technology for Mobile Devices. In Proceedings of the 2022 Third International Conference on Intelligent Computing Instrumentation and Control Technologies (ICICICT), Kannur, India, 11–12 August 2022; pp. 1465–1470.
74. Kurose, J.; Ross, K. *Computer Networks: A Top Down Approach Featuring the Internet;* Peorsoim Addison Wesley: Boston, MA, USA, 2010.
75. Ghosh, A.; Zhang, J.; Andrews, J.G.; Muhamed, R. *Fundamentals of LTE;* Pearson Education: London, UK, 2010.
76. Glisic, S.G. *Advanced Wireless Communications: 4G Cognitive and Cooperative Broadband Technology;* Wiley: Hoboken, NJ, USA, 2007.
77. Szymoniak, S.; Kesar, S. Key Agreement and Authentication Protocols in the Internet of Things: A Survey. *Appl. Sci.* **2022**, *13*, 404. [CrossRef]
78. Szymoniak, S. Key Distribution and Authentication Protocols in Wireless Sensor Networks: A Survey. *ACM Comput. Surv.* **2024**, *56*, 1–31. [CrossRef]
79. Adli, H.K.; Remli, M.A.; Wan Salihin Wong, K.N.S.; Ismail, N.A.; González-Briones, A.; Corchado, J.M.; Mohamad, M.S. Recent Advancements and Challenges of AIoT Application in Smart Agriculture: A Review. *Sensors* **2023**, *23*, 3752. [CrossRef]
80. Shanthakumari, G.; Vignesh, A.; Harish, R.; Roshan Karthick, R. Advancements in Smart Agriculture: A Comprehensive Review of Machine Learning and IOT Approaches. In Proceedings of the 2024 International Conference on Communication, Computing and Internet of Things (IC3IoT), Chennai, India, 17–18 April 2024; pp. 1–6. [CrossRef]
81. Soussi, A.; Zero, E.; Sacile, R.; Trinchero, D.; Fossa, M. Smart Sensors and Smart Data for Precision Agriculture: A Review. *Sensors* **2024**, *24*, 2647. [CrossRef]
82. Pathmudi, V.R.; Khatri, N.; Kumar, S.; Abdul-Qawy, A.S.H.; Vyas, A.K. A systematic review of IoT technologies and their constituents for smart and sustainable agriculture applications. *Sci. Afr.* **2023**, *19*, e01577. [CrossRef]
83. Rejeb, A.; Rejeb, K.; Treiblmaier, H.; Appolloni, A.; Alghamdi, S.; Alhasawi, Y.; Iranmanesh, M. The Internet of Things (IoT) in healthcare: Taking stock and moving forward. *Internet Things* **2023**, *22*, 100721. [CrossRef]
84. Li, C.; Wang, J.; Wang, S.; Zhang, Y. A review of IoT applications in healthcare. *Neurocomputing* **2024**, *565*, 127017. [CrossRef]
85. Rahman, S.A.; Ibtisum, S.; Podder, P.; Hossain, S.S. Progression and Challenges of IoT in Healthcare: A Short Review. *Int. J. Comput. Appl.* **2023**, *185*, 9–15. [CrossRef]
86. Almalki, F.A.; Alsamhi, S.H.; Sahal, R.; Hassan, J.; Hawbani, A.; Rajput, N.; Saif, A.; Morgan, J.; Breslin, J. Green IoT for eco-friendly and sustainable smart cities: Future directions and opportunities. *Mob. Netw. Appl.* **2023**, *28*, 178–202. [CrossRef]
87. Zhang, H.; Li, B.; Karimi, M.; Saydam, S.; Hassan, M. Recent Advancements in IoT Implementation for Environmental, Safety, and Production Monitoring in Underground Mines. *IEEE Internet Things J.* **2023**, *10*, 14507–14526. [CrossRef]
88. Abatan, A.; Adeyinka, M.A.; Sodiya, E.O.; Jacks, B.S.; Ugwuanyi, E.D.; Daraojimba, O.H.; Lottu, O.A. The role of IT in sustainable environmental management: A global perspective review. *Int. J. Sci. Res. Arch.* **2024**, *11*, 1874–1886. [CrossRef]
89. Zaidi Farouk, M.I.H.; Jamil, Z.; Abdul Latip, M.F. Towards online surface water quality monitoring technology: A review. *Environ. Res.* **2023**, *238*, 117147. [CrossRef]
90. Salman, M.Y.; Hasar, H. Review on environmental aspects in smart city concept: Water, waste, air pollution and transportation smart applications using IoT techniques. *Sustain. Cities Soc.* **2023**, *94*, 104567. [CrossRef]
91. Zhong, D.; Xia, Z.; Zhu, Y.; Duan, J. Overview of predictive maintenance based on digital twin technology. *Heliyon* **2023**, *9*, e14534. [CrossRef]

92. Lu, S.; Lu, J.; An, K.; Wang, X.; He, Q. Edge Computing on IoT for Machine Signal Processing and Fault Diagnosis: A Review. *IEEE Internet Things J.* **2023**, *10*, 11093–11116. [CrossRef]
93. Abouelyazid, M. Advanced Artificial Intelligence Techniques for Real-Time Predictive Maintenance in Industrial IoT Systems: A Comprehensive Analysis and Framework. *J. AI-Assist. Sci. Discov.* **2023**, *3*, 271–313.
94. Hassebo, A.; Tealab, M. Global models of smart cities and potential IoT applications: A review. *IoT* **2023**, *4*, 366–411. [CrossRef]
95. Rafiq, I.; Mahmood, A.; Razzaq, S.; Jafri, S.H.M.; Aziz, I. IoT applications and challenges in smart cities and services. *J. Eng.* **2023**, *2023*, e12262. [CrossRef]
96. Alahi, M.E.E.; Sukkuea, A.; Tina, F.W.; Nag, A.; Kurdthongmee, W.; Suwannarat, K.; Mukhopadhyay, S.C. Integration of IoT-enabled technologies and artificial intelligence (AI) for smart city scenario: Recent advancements and future trends. *Sensors* **2023**, *23*, 5206. [CrossRef]

MDPI AG
Grosspeteranlage 5
4052 Basel
Switzerland
Tel.: +41 61 683 77 34

Applied Sciences Editorial Office
E-mail: applsci@mdpi.com
www.mdpi.com/journal/applsci

www.ingramcontent.com/pod-product-compliance
Lightning Source LLC
Chambersburg PA
CBHW061820210926
51850CB00006B/762
* 9 7 8 3 7 2 5 8 8 1 0 1 7 *